Democracy
and
Ethnography

Published by
State University of New York Press, Albany

© 1998 State University of New York

All rights reserved

Printed in the United States of America

No part of this book may be used or reproduced
in any manner whatsoever without written permission.
No part of this book may be stored in a retrieval system
or transmitted in any form by any means including
electronic, electrostatic, magnetic tape, mechanical,
photocopying, recording, or otherwise without the
prior permission in writing of the publisher.

For information, address the State University of New York Press,
State University Plaza, Albany, NY 12246

Production by E. Moore
Marketing by Fran Keneston

Library of Congress Cataloging-in-Publication Data

Democracy and ethnography : constructing identities in multicultural
  liberal states / Carol J. Greenhouse, editor.
      p. cm. — (SUNY series in national identities)
  Includes bibliographical references and index.
  ISBN 0-7914-3963-1 (hardcover : acid-free paper). — ISBN
0-7914-3964-X (pbk. : acid-free paper)
  1. Multiculturalism—United States. 2. Multiculturalism—Spain.
  3. United States—Ethnic relations. 4. Spain—Ethnic relations.
  5. Democracy—United States—History—20th century. 6. Democracy—
Spain—History—20th century. 7. Ethnology—United States.
  8. Ethnology—Spain. I. Greenhouse, Carol J., 1950–   .
  II. Series.
E184.A1D34 1998
306.2′0973—dc21   97-48473
                                                                 CIP

10 9 8 7 6 5 4 3 2 1

For Janet M. Fitchen
In memory

Contents

Acknowledgments	ix
1. Introduction: The Ethnography of Democracy and Difference *Carol J. Greenhouse and Davydd J. Greenwood*	1

Part I
Diversity and Equality in Liberal Debate — 25

2. Diversity as American Cultural Category *Hervé Varenne*	27
3. The Hypervisible and the Masked: Some Thoughts on the Mutual Embeddedness of "Race" and "Class" in the United States Now *Daniel A. Segal*	50
4. Democracy and Cultural Difference in the Spanish Constitution of 1978 *Jesús Prieto de Pedro*	61
5. Disorderly Differences: Recognition, Accommodation, and American Law *Austin Sarat and Roger Berkowitz*	81

Part II
The Making of Official Discourses of Identity 103

6. American Ethnogenesis and the 1990 Census 105
   Dvora Yanow

7. Difference from the People's Point of View 124
   José Antonio Fernández de Rota Monter

8. Porous Borders: Discourses of Difference in Congressional Hearings on Immigration 143
   Phyllis Pease Chock

9. To Be Basque and to Live in Basque Country: The Inequalities of Difference 163
   Jesús Azcona

10. Acceptable Difference: The Cultural Evolution of the Model Ethnic American Citizen 178
    Bonnie Urciuoli

Part III
Official Discourses and Professional Practice 197

11. The Role of Folklore and Popular Culture in the Construction of Difference in Spain 199
    Honorio M. Velasco

12. Linguistic Constructions of Difference and History in the U.S. Law School Classroom 218
    Elizabeth Mertz

13. From Ethnography to Clinical Practice in the Construction of the Contemporary State 233
    Josep M. Comelles

References 255

About the Authors 287

Index 291

Acknowledgments

For their generous support of the conference that was the original context for the essays collected in this volume, I am grateful to the Institute for European Studies at Cornell University and numerous sponsors at Indiana University-Bloomington: The Multidisciplinary Ventures Fund, the Chancellor's Office, the Office for International Programs, the Office of Research and the University Graduate School, the College of Arts and Sciences, the Honors Division, the School of Journalism, the Law School, the Indiana Center for Global Change and World Peace, the Center for the Study of Law and Society, the Poynter Center, and the Departments of West European Studies, Anthropology, American Studies, Folklore, Middle Eastern Studies, Political Science, and Spanish and Portuguese.

Several colleagues gave us the benefit of their critical readings of an earlier draft of the volume's introduction; our thanks to Stephanie Kane, Phil Parnell, and Chris Peebles in addition to the contributing authors. Fred Aman, Joëlle Bahloul, Peter Bondanella, Julia Lamber, Jane Rhodes, Dan Quilter, David Smith, and Josep Sobrer were discussants at the conference, and we are very grateful to them for ideas that animated the gathering and helped us hone our discussions toward this volume.

The original versions of the essays by Jesús Prieto de Pedro and Honorio M. Velasco were translated from Spanish by Davydd Greenwood and Joanne Van Egan.

Editor's note: This project originated in a collaboration of some eight years' duration before it took its present shape as a book. I am very grateful to Davydd Greenwood for initiating the project, and for productive intellectual exchanges during those years. For most of its history, the volume was also a joint project, but Professor Greenwood withdrew before the work took final form. I continue to think of it as a collaborative work; his name does not appear on the title page by his own request. He was involved in all but the last round of revisions, which included considerable shortening of the manuscript among other things. An earlier version of the volume, including longer versions of several of the essays, is available in Spanish (cited in the bibliography as Greenhouse and Greenwood, *in press*). In that context, special thanks are due to Honorio Velasco and Jesús Prieto de Pedro. Theresa Adams and Roshanak Kheshti provided crucial and collegial assistance in preparing the manuscript for SUNY Press, and I am grateful to the College of Arts and Sciences at Indiana for financially supporting their participation.

    I am grateful to librarians at Indiana University's Main Library and Law Library for assistance with translations, sources, and numerous other details. Keith Buckley, at the Law Library, deserves special note. Warm thanks go to Elizabeth Moore, editor, and Vicki Metcalf, indexer.

    Beyond the demands of production, I owe a great debt of thanks to Roshanak Kheshti, then my research assistant, for lending her anthropological and editorial talents to the task of bringing the volume to completion.

    I dedicate the volume to the memory of Janet M. Fitchen, who was a rare ethnographer and a true democrat.

CAROL J. GREENHOUSE

Chapter 1

Introduction: The Ethnography of Democracy and Difference

Carol J. Greenhouse and Davydd J. Greenwood

To the extent that liberal democracy suffers from tensions between principles of the free market and interventionist social justice, it suffers fundamentally from the flaws in its concept of difference which make diversity and equality antithetical. That contradiction compromises liberal states' efforts to acknowledge and accommodate cultural diversity as a dimension of citizenship. This book is about liberal democracies' involvements in the cultural identification of citizens and the management of difference—that is, the bases of people's identifications with and by others in the public sphere. At the heart of the matter is the fact that official constructions of identity rest uneasily on a basic ambiguity, treating race, culture, ethnicity, sexuality, and other associations as both *natural characteristics of individuals* and *the collective basis of interest groups*. Public debate often breaks down over the definition of terms.

At such moments, it is important to remember that official categories do not monopolize the available terms of understanding—or mobilization—however deeply they may be inscribed in the institutions and preconceptions of modern life. This recognition—which implies a place for an ethnographic project at the heart of democratic change—is this book's starting point. To say that modern liberalism is heir to a concept of diversity that founders on old essentialisms is to refer to a specific history of ideas and administrative improvisations in particular contexts. This collection develops two case studies in tandem, the United States and Spain (the reasons for this choice are explained below). In these countries, official constructions of identity and diversity are the result of both political struggle and partnerships among activists, academic disciplines, politicians, and state administrators.

Modern democratization movements around the world challenge national institutions—and social science—to move past old categories, but those categories remain embedded within institutional organizations, practices, and "common sense"—sometimes to the point where alternatives might seem unthinkable. In this regard, these ethnographic essays show again and again the availability of alternatives within bureaucratic practices themselves, not to speak of the richly varied and flexible imagination for collective life among ordinary people in the society at large. Indeed, our focus on official constructions of identity is only one aspect of the broader question of how people identify with others—though a crucial and largely neglected aspect.

Even before the new social movements and democracies since the late 1970s, some analysts had announced the onset of a critical—even terminal—period in the history of liberalism. In the United States, such assessments (then and now) refer to a social and political fabric strained by the competing pressures for laissez-faire capitalism and welfare state interventions (Lowi, 1979). These exigencies have intensified with the globalization of capital, and other countries, too, grapple with globalization and its local social consequences (Wallerstein, 1995). The relationship between democracy and difference is very much at the core of such confrontations, which extend well beyond economic and political spheres; *multiculturalism* is their key term.[1]

Not coincidentally, the social sciences implicated in the making of the old categories—especially anthropology—are now self-critical in terms similar to the critique of liberalism itself, notably (but not limited to) the "crisis of representation" elaborated by Marcus and Fischer more than a decade ago (Marcus and Fischer, 1986: 7ff). The central thesis of this volume is that liberal democracy and ethnography are related cultural practices, and that an examination of that relationship leads directly to the very heart of the conceptual tensions in the contemporary confrontation of liberalism and multiculturalism—and, one hopes, to an enriched dialogue toward alternative futures. The book defends difference as central to democratic life.

Democracy and ethnography are linked most fundamentally and concretely by the significance of difference in the public sphere. The essays in this collection examine the ways contemporary democratic states make cultural identity into official business, and the consequences and implications for ethnographic practice. The overarching theme is the way national institutions of liberal democracy establish and maintain a problematic conceptual distinction between diversity and inequality, by treating culture and class as largely separate spheres of association. The "classic anthropological model" (to borrow Comelles's phrase, this volume) does the same, taking cultural diversity as its special province.

That distinction is part of a conceptual architecture that rests—today, very uneasily—on an ancient foundational fusion of elements construed as forming natural and social worlds. In that edifice of Western thought, cultural difference is imagined as physical difference, a broad naturalization of difference that subsumes (or potentially subsumes) a range of conceptual categories, such as race, gender, sexuality, and others. These categories and their conceptual arrangements are urgently contested, and even readers who are new to the academic debates will undoubtedly have been exposed to the public controversies. To focus on race for purposes of illustration: many Americans hear "multicultural" as "interracial," missing multiculturalism's critique of the very concept of race. Modern ethnography, too, insists on "race" as a cultural construction, having turned from the biological ground of "phenotypical differences" to the social ground where differences are drawn, defined, and made to matter.

More broadly—and more controversially—the cultural milieu of liberalism's history in the West means that to talk about culture is always already to talk about a history of inequality. This specific a priori is highly problematic, in that official discourses deem otherwise. The cultural history of the liberal state cast its guarantees of equality in terms that presupposed the natural basis of difference, with the result that culture- and class-based demands for equality now compete against each other, and bring into odd proximity some liberal critics of the concept of race and conservative critics of race-based civil rights protections. These are among the tensions that this book addresses, and that account for its focus on the terms of democratic institutions' implication in people's self-identity, and ethnography's involvements in that process—in the hope of opening new lines of discussion.

Some of the essays specifically address questions of ethnographic responsibility in contexts of political struggle; all of them envision ethnography as an active form of democratic participation. The volume opens with an examination of liberalism's tensions and paradoxes with respect to culture and inequality. As already noted, these tensions are the context for each of the chapters and authors' individual reflections on the prospect of using ethnographic knowledge to inform alternative, or fuller, forms of democratic pluralism (see Schön, 1983). While the essays involve different foci and points of view in this regard, their continuity is in their consideration of democracy and ethnography as corollary forms of social knowledge and political agency.

Overall, the book explores that rarely examined terrain between inclusion and exclusion, both within and between democracies. Inclusion and exclusion are never settled questions, anyway, but always only hypotheses continually under experimentation and experiential review. Accordingly, the essays' starting points and the nature of their explorations are shaped by the cultural histories of the democracies in question, including their histories of contest. For this reason, some of the volume's key terms—*democracy, ethnography, culture,* and *difference*—cannot be defined in advance, since our common concern is with how their meanings emerge from specific situations, and might continue to do so in the future.

The essays show that official discourses of difference do not define a fixed architecture of inclusion and exclusion so much as they imply codes for routines and possibilities for political improvisation. In referring to "discourses of difference," we mean the ways self-identity and identification with and by others is inextricably tied to politics. Our use of the word "discourse" for such convergences of terminology, practice, and stakes is influenced by Foucault (1975: xvi–xix). In linking culture to politics, though, we are not suggesting that cultural categories always or only emerge as symbols of opposition.[2] When opposition takes the form of cultural difference, the social processes that produce and maintain that association concretely over time constitute a field of inquiry that is simultaneously political and ethnographic.

In other words, the terms *identity, difference,* and *culture* are always heavily charged with histories of assymmetrical power relations, aspirations, and vulnerabilities. Liberal democracies' commitments to individual liberty and the equality of citizens cannot cancel these histories and encodings; however, it can make them difficult to hear. In this volume, discourses of difference constitute the primary connection we explore between democracy and ethnography, as discourses of difference constitute pluralism and its varied forms. As Chantal Mouffe (1993: 149) has written in this regard, pluralism "cannot be envisaged only in terms of already existing subjects and restricted to their conceptions of the good. What must be addressed is the very process of constitution of the subjects of pluralism." Our attention to the constitution of subjects emphasizes the discursive tensions between race, culture, and class; all of the essays address these tensions directly.

The second connection between democracy and ethnography in these essays is pluralism, as already suggested above. As several essays show vividly (especially those by Sarat and Berkowitz and Comelles), the modern liberal concept of the nation-state maps a place for cultural diversity, but in ways that contain questions of diversity within the state's existing legal and political forms, as if difference is a matter for reconciliation or, even more problematically, for cure. When difference cannot be resolved by law in these ways, it is either relegated to the realm of consumer choice (as in Urciuoli's account in this volume), treated as "unruly" (to borrow Sarat and Berkowitz's term), marginalized as polluting (Chock), or silenced altogether (Fernández de Rota, Yanow). Moreover, they challenge the liberal assumption that culture first and foremost poses problems of organization for society and the state, and they pursue a range of critical directions in relation to this familiar axiom of public debate.

The essays focus on the domains where liberal topographies are made—for example, pedagogy (Mertz), the media (Urciuoli), public administration (Segal and Yanow), law (Prieto de Pedro, Sarat and Berkowitz, and Chock), medicine (Comelles), and the social organization of academic practice (Varenne and Velasco). Some of the essays also examine pressing challenges to liberalism from within the political sphere or at its fringes, for example, by ethnonationalist polemics (Fernández de Rota and Azcona), progressive and revolutionary movements (Comelles), and ultraconservatives (Chock).

The third connection between liberal democracy and ethnography we explore involves exchanges of social knowledge. The contributors to this book have bent their highly varied efforts toward a reflexive ethnographic exploration of the social production of identity at democratic sites: bureaucratic structures and procedures, constitutional texts, academic practices, the media, regulatory regimes and rhetorics, and ethnography itself. They also consider the means, media, and agents of democratic and ethnographic practices in specific situations.

All of the essays examine the ways liberal democratic institutions—notably academia, partisan politics, and federal bureaucracies—nurture and/or curtail social transformation, in the highly selective opportunities they afford for self-identification in the course of their involvements in the production of knowledge about citizens' lives. The contributors are critical of the highly essentialized terms that tend to comprise official discourses of identity, and especially of the specific mythicizations of history, race, and ethnicity that these entail. In pointing out the ways categories are made, the contributors also specify ways they might be remade. In several essays, academic disciplines or professional discourses are explicitly and doubly subject and mode of analysis (Varenne, Segal, Mertz, Velasco, and Comelles). Overall, we hope that the book's reflexive dimension will be read as confirming the relevance of ethnography as a means of identifying spaces for dialogue and innovation where the public scripts for daily life, even within academia, might otherwise tend to foreclose them.

The essays are markedly different in focus, focal length, and overall approach. Our purpose in presenting so self-evidently varied a collection is to emphasize the richness of their common ethnographic ground. Each essay focuses on a different aspect of the terrain where discourses of difference, the public management of inequality, and the allocation of national resources are mutually implicated. As noted above, the book's emphasis is on the sites (offices, classrooms, forms, legislative chambers, etc.) where these discursive and pragmatic arrangements take shape—always provisionally and always among alternatives. Readers should not expect a survey of world democracies or of institutions within any single state. In taking this approach, we hope that the volume will be useful to others who are interested in expanding the mutual relevance of social policy and ethnography. In addition, we hope the volume will encourage and facilitate comparative discussion and research.

DEMOCRACY AND DIFFERENCE AS COMPARATIVE ISSUES

In this book, the democracies and academic disciplines in question are those of the United States and Spain. Our project developed out of a dialogue among scholars working in Spain and the United States (the origins of the project are discussed in a subsequent section). The decision to focus on these two countries was based on a comparison of their particular political and ethnographic experiments with multicultural liberal democracy. It seemed to us that they were, in some ways, already in dialogue, in that each country construed the tensions elaborated in the previous section in similar terms, but then chose different routes. Thus, as we explain briefly here and more fully in a later section, a comparison of Spain and the United States makes an ideal canvas for appreciating the tensions of contemporary liberalism confronted with the multiculturality of its citizens, as well as a starting point for broader ethnographic and comparative discussion, given the transnational sources and consequences of those tensions.

The constitutional traditions of Spain and the United States guarantee cultural diversity, but they do so in inverse terms, from the vantage point of how they design legal spaces for cultural difference. In the United States, it is individual citizenship that provides the template for equality; the cultural rights of groups are highly problematic, as several of the U.S. chapters stress. In Spain, cultural diversity is guaranteed in the idiom of groups' rights, putting the state squarely in the middle of contests over regional nationalisms and ethnicities. Several of the chapters on Spain explore the process of "making" ethnicities in the political sphere, and in some cases their private remaking.

The relationship between ethnography and democracy in the two countries is inevitably political, as anthropologists and other cultural analysts cannot escape taking a position for or against the official paradigms of difference, and in response to their respective national versions of liberal-communitarian debate. In either context, specializing in culture means taking a position on basic issues under current, heated debate. The essays on Spain describe this engagement with particular force, but it is also clear in the substance and tone of the U.S. essays.

A comparative ethnography of the mutual engagements of democracy and ethnography in these two countries has potentially broad relevance, given the new democracies in Europe and elsewhere. As democracies, Spain and the United States have distinctive histories, pluralist logics, and traditions and countertraditions that make them particularly attractive for ethnographic exploration. Moreover, both the United States and Spanish democracies have considerable potential for export, as Habermas and Michnik (Krzeminski, 1994) have noted. They advocate Spain's democracy as a model for Eastern Europe, for its distinctive balancing of community autonomy regionalized within a state structure. U.S. democracy has had a career abroad, too, but in paradigmatically different terms. Where Spanish democracy makes geographic regions the central focus of pluralism, the United States focuses on citizenship and individuals' civil rights, especially in response to demands for equality by groups who are defined (by themselves or others) in terms of race, ethnicity, and/or gender.

The book's attention to ethnography is not limited to anthropology, but several of the essays are about the anthropological profession (Varenne, Segal, Fernández de Rota, Azcona, Velasco, and Comelles). Just as national democracies differ, so do anthropologies. "Anthropology" itself does not constitute a unified field, at home or abroad (wherever these may be). The different anthropologies implicit in Spanish and U.S. democratic experience and explicit in the two countries' academic professions are part of this book's subject; the book is also intended to exemplify the richness of their variety and the vitality of the dialogue across that variety.

In each national context, authors focus on the parallels and tensions between anthropological and public officialized discourses as contexts of social action and theorizing. The essays unfold around three main comparative themes, already elaborated above: first, the influence of state institutions over public discourses of diversity; second, the exchanges between constitutional discourses of diversity and anthropological discourses of difference; and third, the transformation of these structures and exchanges into modes of knowledge, reproduced in academic disciplines and in the professions associated with state practice, especially the legal profession. In all but one essay, authors write about either Spain *or* the United States from the vantage point of one or more of these comparative questions; Comelles's essay, which doubles as the volume's conclusion, is alone in being explicitly comparative, bringing the reader full circle. In the rest of this section, we discuss some of the broader comparative issues that formed the book, and return later to the more specific discussion of the United States and Spain.

The book's comparative themes connect our project to rich veins of recent scholarship within and beyond anthropology. This has been a decade of exciting discovery and debate in legal and political anthropology, gender studies, and cultural studies, as well as new research in the fields of international relations and sociolegal studies. Contemporary debates over essentialism among feminist theorists have provided important terms and issues that now bridge these disciplines (see especially Butler and Scott, 1992 and Schor and Weed, 1994), particularly with respect to the nature of identity of difference. Postcolonial studies have also forged new interdisciplinary dialogues around questions of state power, cultural domination, resistance, and hybridity (see especially Bhabha, 1994 and Chatterjee, 1993). These new trends in scholarship stand in a variety of reflexive and critical positions vis-à-vis rights discourses, positions whose tonalities (e.g., irony) and agendas (e.g., redistributive social and political reform) are perhaps the hallmarks of academic exchange and debate in the 1990s. The contributors to this volume have taken these theorizings, moods, and agendas seriously as warrants for ethnographic research by examining directly how democracy and difference are related in practice.

That the recognition of difference should be so deeply interwoven with regime structures and dynamics suggests both a need and a means for rethinking anthropology's convention of keeping the large-scale social arenas, so active in the constitution of difference, out of sight. European and American anthropology's traditional resistance to studying "at home" remains a lingering example of a classical tradition that placed the state—indeed, any translocal field—outside the ethnographic frame. "Home" is where the classic social science view of the state as merely the distant, neutral containing walls for society and culture is most vividly contradicted by people's everyday encounters with its agencies and its relevance in the organization of experience.

The call for reconsidering the cultural role of large-scale political structures has come primarily from anthropologists and other scholars in cultural studies whose attention has been engaged by the colonial, postcolonial, and subaltern. Their reassessments of the cultural dynamics of colonialism and its historical sequels offer compelling interpretive and comparative issues for our purposes (e.g., Bhabha, 1994; Chatterjee, 1993; Comaroff and Comaroff, 1991; Cooper and Stoler, 1989; Fabian, 1986; Gordon, 1992; and Warren, 1993). Importantly, as these works make clear, British and other colonizing projects overseas also involved rehearsals and constituencies in democracies at home (Comaroff and Comaroff, 1992: ch. 10).

The paradox of there being parallels between colonial domination and democratic processes offers broad scope for comparative research. As the essays indicate in different ways, pursuing this comparative question means more than simply widening ethnography's canvas; it also means finding new ethnographic problems and intellectual frameworks. Some of these call into question mythologies of identity and the nation-state that are deeply embedded in modern democratic practices (on such mythologies and their consequences, see Ferguson, 1994; Herzfeld, 1987; Malkki, 1995; and Wilmsen and McAllister, 1996). Others call into question conventional attributions of agency in large-scale processes of change, conventions charged with racial, class and gendered meaning (see Comaroff and Comaroff, 1991; and Williams, 1996). As these and other works—including the essays here—imply, anthropology is always and inevitably in a highly vulnerable and politicized position vis-à-vis the relationship between cultural difference and those conditions of existence determined by the state.

The history of anthropology in the United States includes many chapters of direct involvement with state administration in colonial and other contexts, for example, the Bureau of Indian Affairs, the immigration quota system, and civil rights and human rights movements. Specifically in reference to the United States and Spain, anthropology's central concern with difference and identity places it at the very point where the affirmative and discriminatory possibilities of the very concept of "culture" meet. As these tectonic forces have moved with the modern retrenchments of the welfare state, anthropology's positions and knowledge are more than ever outside the arena of public discussion and debate in both countries. Similarly, the recursive effects of state practices on self- and collective identities also tends to be rendered invisible, as if these were natural differences (but see Urciuoli, 1996).

The contests between the affirmative and pejorative meanings of diversity in official and other public discourses can be difficult to map, since the opponents sometimes use the same language (e.g., rights, equality, citizenship)—indeed, in some cases, the very language whose ideological and moral mortgagings petitioners resist (in general, see Lazarus-Black and Hirsch, 1994). The claims and contests over democracy's capacity to transform diversity into unity make up the ethnographic terrain on which our contributors have positioned their projects. Exploring such relationships—"the externality at the heart of internality" (Bourdieu, 1990a: 21)—is the traditional province of anthropology (see Latour, 1993: esp. 100–106), a province that now also draws other disciplines into a changing dialogue.[3] This volume's authors come from the fields of anthropology, folklore, law, political science, and public administration in the United States and Spain.[4]

ETHNOGRAPHY: "THE POLITICAL" AND "SOCIETY"

Especially for readers who think of ethnography as limited to village life (or, even moreso, village life far from their own neighborhoods), or of states as working their effects at some remove from something called "social life," the nature of these essays' treatments of large-scale state institutions may be surprising; we offer some words of clarification here.[5]

Some of the essays explore face-to-face interactions, but more of them examine how people model others' reality from the raw material of their own hypotheses about the identities, organization, and the historical processes that (again, in theory) comprise "the nation." Such modelings—evident, for example, in rhetoric, stereotypes, formal categories, and myths—have the power to transform the scale of social relationships, even when they are face-to-face. Face-to-face relationships between bureaucrats and constituents can be rendered "distant" by a variety of rhetorical, gestural, and substantive means.[6] As Comelles emphasizes in his contribution to the volume, the distance between ethnographer and subject is also manipulable, and the history of ethnographic distance intersects with that of the liberal state.

Inserting distance into face-to-face interaction involves registers and rituals with which readers may already be familiar—for example, "official" demands for proofs of identity and status through birth certificates, driver's licenses, and other documents (little rebirths, as it were) or formalities of less tangible kinds—whose cumulative enactments and effects are part of what social scientists mean when they refer to "social structure." These encounters and their effects should not be taken for granted, since they involve reworkings of personal presence that are central to the ways in which bureaucracies lend themselves to the transformation of personal identities and collective purposes (cf. Herzfeld, 1992). And they should not be taken lightly, since such relationships involve potentially high stakes, individually and collectively.

Accordingly, in the essays that follow, "the political" is not some "space," "level," "structure," or "public square" (to borrow current metaphors) that stands outside or above the realms where individuals consider their options and act. Rather, the power of political institutions must be understood as a component of people's agency. Moreover, the essays are not limited to situations in which people are in direct dialogue with state agents; they also illustrate ways in which democratic discourses are implicated in the ways people address each other outside state offices. Indeed, such dynamics make ethnographic study and cultural analysis of political forms and processes relevant and possible. Nation-states cannot be understood as entities apart from, or somehow containing, an internal cultural diversity.[7] State nationalism is inevitably—among other things—a theory linking cultural diversity to the legitimacy of the state itself (cf. Anderson, 1991).

Ethnography dwells on the particulars of human life—the "where" and "how" of eras, trends, and tensions coming to the ground. Given the nature of culture as a discourse of difference, ethnography is also intrinsically comparative (Boon, 1982), and so lends itself to discussions of alternatives not readily apparent from the vantage point of the givens of everyday life. While anthropology is often said (often by anthropologists themselves) to involve the study of "the Other," it is more accurately understood as the study of the "otherwise"—the relationship between the "possible" and the "actual" (to borrow a phrase from François Jacob [Jacob, 1982])—and no less so at home than abroad.

While each of the contributors examines some aspect of the way difference encodes discrimination (on the one hand) and social action (on the other), this does not imply that the authors share a single position on the complex question of whether equality is the means or ends of democracy. The contributors examine equality, inequality, and rights as practices, pursuing somewhat different itineraries as they do so. They also have somewhat different starting points with respect to identity and difference, varying in their attachment (or lack of it) to the idea of an encompassing self-identity as a rubric of solidarity and social action, or as a field for study.

Such debates underscore the tensions between multiculturality conceived in terms of "identities" (social types) and "difference" (self-identification). Both terms operate in the essays, depending on the ethnographic context, but they imply somewhat different histories, contexts and aspirations. "Identities" feature in the essays on official discourses of diversity (e.g., the census form); authors generally refer to "difference" when they are concerned with the ways people identify themselves in some contingent relationship with others. Collective identities conceived in terms of similarity and solidarity are oppositional both as criteria of naming ("us" versus "not us") and as sociological rubrics of competition (see Wagner, 1975 and Dumont, 1977). "Difference," however, is not intrinsically oppositional but insistently plural; "difference" affirms a contingent relationship rather than a bounded set of characteristics. The availability of both terms as alternative social visions has broad implications for a cultural analysis of liberal democracy—as most of the essays show directly.

Let us turn now to the more reflexive dimensions of the volume bearing more directly on anthropological practice in the United States and Spain. As discursive practices, democracy and democratic administration are partially inscribed in the propositional canons of classic social science methodologies. Among the premises that democracy and social science share, for example, are central propositions about individuals as members of communities, communities as elements of social wholes, the role of norms as determinants of social action, collective action as structured and structuring, and equally problematic, the ambiguity between "the norm" (in a purely statistical sense) and "the normal" (in a socially acceptable sense). One way of summarizing the significance of this shared lexicon would be to say that "community," "nation," "law," "society," "power," and "justice" have overlapping meanings in both democratic rhetoric *and* classic social theory.

At the same time, given that politics and social science are mutually implicated at the levels of practice and justifying rationales, one implication of this volume must be to call into question "society," too, as an analytically neutral rubric for ethnography. Several of the essays give particular attention to the construction of "society" as a particular arrangement of organizations, channels of communication, and associations both literal and figurative (Varenne, Segal, Yanow, Fernández de Rota, Chock, and Comelles). Indeed, all contemporary regimes include bureaucratic managers for whom "efficiency" means reductionist, quantitative, scientific measures of costs and benefits, success, or productivity—technologies borrowed from social science. To an important degree, there has also been a reverse traffic, from bureaucracies to the social sciences, as the desire for relevance quietly commits social scientists to others' ideologies and lexicons of bureaucratic management. Several of the essays (Azcona, Fernández de Rota, Urciuoli, Yanow, Velasco, and Comelles) explore this exchange of concepts and agendas directly, as well as their implications for the so-called communities who are supposed to be their beneficiaries. As already noted, the volume also explores the contexts where these arrangements are reproduced, wittingly and unwittingly, as matters for the judiciary, legislatures, and universities (Chock, Mertz, Velasco, Prieto de Pedro, Sarat and Berkowitz, and Comelles).

In offering these reflections, we join the increasing trend in anthropology and sociolegal studies that questions a concept of society as a "whole" reducible to its "parts" (for anthropological interventions, see contributions to Kuper, 1992, especially Strathern, 1992a and Strathern, 1995). Such challenges are significant beyond the academic debates they occasion in anthropology, economics, political science, psychology, and sociology—at least, they ought to be. They are, as implied above, a significant counterdiscourse to a fundamental tenet of bureaucratic-administrative rationality that deems otherwise, and which accounts in part for the persistence of the pragmatic tensions arising from the simultaneous value of diversity and equality—constructed, as they are in contemporary official discourse—as potentially antithetical values.

IDENTITY, DEMOCRACY, AND THE SUBALTERN

Anthropologists are by no means new to the study of law and politics (for a comprehensive historical review, see Vincent, 1990). Conversely, political scientists—to whose province the study of democracy might seem more natural—are no strangers to the idea of culture. Still, sociocultural anthropology was a very late arrival to the full-fledged study of global politics and modern state-level institutions (Vincent puts the date at 1974 [1990: 388 ff.]) And for their part, political scientists have tended to relegate "culture" to some residual category of explanation "a variable, which, if necessary can be controlled for . . . or treated as a form of universal psychology" (Warren, 1993: 10).[8]

The essays imply that in addition to whatever democracy offers as forums for the expression of *interests*, contemporary democratic representation in both the United States and Spain is also predicated on the notion of multiple collective *identities* that must be reconciled to the national society. In Spain, the terms of this accommodation are geographic, in that culture is associated with regional communities. In the United States, the terms of accommodation are (to borrow from Yanow's chapter in this volume) "racethnic." In different ways, all of the articles examine the cultural, political, and legal work entailed in maintaining these associations as features of state legality. Crucially, this means examining the legitimacy of official discourses of identity and difference both as social processes and against fields of alternatives, as these emerge ethnographically.

Given the centrality of communitarianism to official discourses of culture in both the United States and Spain, the tensions surrounding the question of whether and how difference should be understood in communal terms provide a major theme linking the essays on Spain and the United States. In the United States, official discourses of identity emerge from between the competing frameworks of liberalism and communitarianism (these paradigms are examined in detail by Sarat and Berkowitz, this volume). In Spain, official discourses of cultural pluralism entail constitutional guarantees of linguistic pluralism (see especially Prieto de Pedro). In different ways, both systems officialize difference as a matter of individuals' a priori membership in collective groups; Varenne, Segal, Urciuoli, and Mertz (in the U.S.) and Azcona, Comelles and Fernández de Rota (in Spain) are most explicit in confirming the inadequacies of such automatic, a priori ethnicizings of difference. All of the essays address the question of whether official discourses leave scope for self-identification in other terms; all of them find that scope too limited, and all are uneasy with the contemporary appropriations of "culture" by the legal/political sphere. At the same time, they do not define the problems the same way, and they do not share just one vision for remedying them.

In this regard, all of the essays offer studies of various official communitarianisms as viewed from a variety of critical perspectives. In different ways, each of them asks a double question: What is the official discourse about? What does it silence? The recurring refrain across the essays is that official discourses of difference singularize difference (elucidating different "kinds" of difference). In the United States, the official "menu" more readily allows selections of race and ethnicity than it does class (Varenne, Segal, Sarat and Berkowitz, Yanow, and Urciuoli) or gender (Chock and Mertz). In Spain, the official discourses more readily permit selection of singular cultural identities than they do the multiplicity of affiliations and social bonds that people articulate in their own voices—as each of the essays on Spain shows in different ways.

Myths of the nation (e.g., the American melting pot, or regional primordialisms in Spain) valorize particular practices of identification in highly concrete ways (compare Varenne, Chock, and Prieto de Pedro). Such myths— taken up as political charters and academic canons—also preclude public discourses more sensitive to the multiplicity and flexibility of people's everyday associations and self-identifications (see Fernández de Rota, Azcona, Urciuoli, and Yanow). Similarly, academic canons of knowledge share essential features with the language of law and constitutionality, as Comelles, Velasco, Mertz, and Sarat and Berkowitz show most vividly.

However, excavating discourses and silences does not in itself expand democracy's scope. As all of the essays also show, inclusion involves more than adding to the arithmetic of voices. The essays approach the issue of silence as a complex question of recognition and address. One characteristic of those complexities (as the essays also show) is the *dynamic incompleteness* of the connections between everyday forms of association and experience and civil society (i.e., the social extensions of the state's modes of cultural recognition). Gramsci (1971: 52ff.) offers the term "subaltern" for such lapses, together with their context and significance:

> The historical unity of the ruling classes is realized in the State . . . But it would be wrong to think that this unity is simply juridical and political . . . ; the fundamental historical unity, concretely, results from the organic relations between State or political society and "civil society."
>
> The subaltern classes, by definition, are not unified and cannot unite until they are able to become a "State": their history, therefore, is intertwined with that of civil society, and thereby with the history of States. . . . (Gramsci, 1971: 52; notes omitted)

While acknowledging that such "intertwinings" involve issues of consciousness and affective ties, the contributors concentrate more on the question of the rhetorical and discursive locations of such gains and losses within formal processes. These locations turn out to be highly precarious, and—for better or worse—the meanings of identity are never clear in theory or practice. Any discourse of difference is always highly ambivalent, though it does not always make its ambivalences explicit. In the situations explored in this book, official discourses of difference are competitive, given their implied access to entitlements and resources, and ambivalence is potentially costly. It is that zero-sum (i.e., the pressure to choose *an* identity prefigured in official discourse) that constitutes the hegemonic aspect of liberalism of greatest concern to most of the contributors. As already noted, this aspect of the hegemonic order is sustained in part by liberalism itself, given the historical association of diversity with inequality inscribed in contemporary rights debates.

In this context of instability and incompleteness, sustained in part by that hegemonic zero-sum, "subaltern" names what is most relevant about the subject of difference for the transformation of politics. A reference to a group as "subaltern" underscores the comparative and contingent aspects of people's collective status in relation to the workings of politics, markets, civil society and the state—and implies that an examination of these contingencies might bear fruit as an alternative history (Said, 1988: x). The mutual contingencies implicit in "the subaltern" cannot be overstressed, since it is such contingencies—locally acknowledged, unacknowledged, or something in between (Comaroff and Comaroff, 1991: 29–30)—that remind us that anthropologists and other social scientists do not occupy their fields of practice alone. They are practicing in the middle of the field of contemporary politics. In the contexts these essays explore, pretending otherwise can only lead one to the so-called pure categories of ethnonationalist extremism or (as Comelles reminds us) lifeless numbers, or indifference.

IDENTITY, DIFFERENCE, AND RIGHTS

This volume differs from others in the ethnography of law and politics perhaps most vividly in treating "the state" and other institutions not as issues of organization and scale, but as configurations of agents, routines, and improvisational possibilities. We have already suggested some of the ways in which bureaucratic practice can play havoc with the assumed geometries of social distance. In these essays, the relationship between individuals, communities, nations, and cultures is not presented as nested levels of scale or generalizability, but different (and closely related) practices of recognition involving different terms, stakes, and vulnerabilities.

In different ways, the essays explore directly what is ordinarily left to the concealed interstices of political ethnography, that is, the conceptual space "between" political "structures" and the "political imagination," or between the conscious and the unconscious aspects of collective political experience

(Eley, 1994; Moore, 1994: 5–6). In this volume, we take political structures as cultural ideas and approaches that coalesce—chimerically and provisionally, perhaps, but also with great consequence—around particular preoccupations with human differences. Again, as we have already explained, there is no space "between" structure and agency, but only the predictable and unpredictable opportunities and risks individuals face in their efforts to live in dignity and security. The essays focus on ways in which the state's bureaucratic architecture in modern democracies opens, closes, invites, or compromises cultural self-definition and expression.

Particularly in the United States, perhaps, the predominance of the liberal/communitarian debate in public discussions of multiculturalism may make for some unexpected starting points in this volume. Specifically, readers who think of "community" as the natural unit of analysis for social science may find its career in this volume ambiguous and problematic. The essays suggest (some more explicitly than others) that there can be no adequate ethnography of communities until the broader institutional workings of politics beyond community have been understood ethnographically, along with the way ethnographic knowledges are themselves implicated in these institutional operations (cf. Greenhouse, Yngvesson, and Engel, 1994; Mertz, 1994; and Strathern, 1995).

The implications of this volume with respect to community place it in dialogue with classic debates between liberals and communitarians (Sarat and Berkowitz describe these positions and their partial differences). In these debates, individual rights are cast "against" community norms, as it were; however, they presuppose that individuals and communities have an existence prior to, or apart from, the state (e.g., see Sandel 1984: 7). The essays contest this presupposition in a variety of ways. The liberal-communitarian debate construes cultural identity as if it were outside of the national society (whatever that might mean), but the essays show that state institutions are implicated in the character and significance of the very "communities" they regard as if from someplace apart. As feminist theorists Frazer and Lacey (1993: 203) point out, merely affirming "rights of participation" is not sufficient as acknowledgment or inclusion, since histories of discrimination and privilege shape "access to speech and being heard."

With respect to liberal-communitarian debates—and more fundamentally, the idea of "the universalization of liberal democracy" (Mouffe, 1993: 1)—ethnography unfreezes problems of organization to yield their fluid and complex histories, antagonisms, self-identifications, and hoped-for alternatives in practice. How do signs of difference (in the hermeneutic sense) actually circulate as "identities" and "institutions" in public life?[9] What—and who—opens doors or closes them? makes a difference? leaves people indifferent? When is a person an individual? When does he or she become "an

African American" or "a Hispanic" or "a Spaniard" or—for that matter, "a man" or "a woman"? Without some ethnographic and historical grounding in questions such as these, one risks confusing moral schema (behind their masks as "communities") for political mandates, and partisan political debates over recognition for terms of self-identity and consciousness. More problematically still, one forfeits the possibility of conceiving of self-identity apart from the state, since the a priori assumption that all identities are communities makes the state's reach theoretically infinite and all-inclusive.

Such questions underscore the fact that *pluralism*, in this volume, is no mere synonym for *variety*. The authors use the term in a variety of ways, but always as an active term for a dynamic, improvisatory, and high-stakes process by which the state's legal/administrative discourse of difference engages in dialogue with citizens over the terms and conditions of their self-identity. Such projects of cultural management comprise the central social fact of modern states and contemporary political life (Bauman, 1991; Mouffe, 1993). The centrality of the state in structuring "diversity" (through rights, regulation, and policing, e.g.,) involves discourses and practices that are as important to the internal politics of state bureaucracies as they are to the more diffuse hegemonies of the broader society (Greenhouse, 1996: chapters 6 and 7). They unleash forces that can "create" communities or destroy them, recognize "diversity," and limit its expression to acceptable categories. They are powerful, but not all. These are some of the junctures where these essays explore the immanence of "the political," "the social," and "the cultural" in the always-unfinished work of democracy and ethnography.

THE UNITED STATES AND SPAIN

So far, this introduction has focused on the volume's comparative and interpretive frameworks. This section is intended as a guide to help readers anticipate some of the more specific comparative issues as they read back and forth between Spain and the United States.

The key similarity between the democratic discourses of the United States and Spain is that both systems naturalize difference, as if it were beyond question or negotiation. The key difference between them is in the way they acknowledge cultural pluralism. While Americans refer to the "melting pot" and "e pluribus unum," Spain has incorporated "autonomous communities"—conceived as regional cultural communities—into its constitutional structure. And from these discourses flow general political commitments as well as ethnographic trends.

The idea that nations are built one citizen at a time, out of some "natural" common identity, bound together by a social contract mediated through and by the state, is central to everyday and legal concepts of citizenship, community, and civil rights in the United States (Greenhouse, Yngvesson, and Engel, 1994; Sarat and Kearns, 1993; and Yngvesson, 1993). In American ethnographic studies of the United States, anthropologists tend to use language that concedes the "natural" reality of race and gender, the hyphenated boundedness of ethnic groups, and the overall comprehensiveness of standard categories of "identity"—even while acknowledging these as social constructions. Perhaps such elisions are ones in which many Americans are fluent. Indeed, cultural literacy requires knowledge of standard euphemisms and modes of denial that cross and recross race, ethnicity, class, and gender. Such fusions (and the confusions and refusals they imply) both illustrate and compound the entanglements of power, on the one hand, and people's own claims as to who they are and want to be, on the other.

Recent scholarship from anthropology and postcolonial studies (notably Bhabha, 1994) reminds us that these are also *ethnographic* questions: whether or how an individual might be "a minority" or belong to a group (to borrow the conventional verbs and nouns), or the sense in which there *are* groups, are complex ethnographic and historical questions to which very high stakes attach. Belonging and identity are sufficient to affect life chances, attitudes, and even life-or-death choices. At the same time, "choice"—the conventional idiom of self-identification in the United States—is inadequate to the task. "Belonging" is not the same as "choosing," since people may find themselves cast as members of groups or barred from them—and seek alternative solidarities, or be barred from them, as well (cf. Grosz, 1994).

Individuals are—as a matter of course—called on personally to assess and navigate the distance between affirmation and resistance, solidarity and refusal. For ethnographers no less so, it may not be clear how or whether to confront the ready essentialisms of contemporary identity politics without either adopting the same terms—or, alternatively, using a language so alien to the lexicons of public debate as to have no place in it (cf. Comelles, this volume). By the time it is ethnographically relevant to refer to "groups" or "communities," these issues may have been decided, at least to the extent that individual self-identity is already envisioned as collective political mobilization. For readers who are used to the ordinary public terms of "diversity," our approach may seem oddly roundabout; however, our point is that to limit the ethnography of politics to the standard terms of diversity is to make crucial aspects of the research enterprise circular.

These are not just academic questions. They are issues and tensions at the center of the contemporary debates over rights and entitlements, as the recent referenda and ongoing legislative debates over welfare, affirmative action, and immigration restriction in the United States and European countries reveal again and again. The narrowness of the terms of such controversies underscores the urgency of examining and reassessing the taken-for-granted assumptions that limit individuals' social reality and legitimacy to their legal status as members of groups—and limit the salience of group identity to one at a time. Each of the contributors writing on the United States deals with this issue—that is, the agonistic aspects of social categories constructed in these terms.

In Spain and in Europe more generally, the naturalization of social categories is also central to the legitimating discourses of civic life (for analyses, see Greenwood, 1985a, 1985b, 1993; Herzfeld, 1987; Prieto de Pedro, 1992: esp. 183–192; Strathern, 1992b: esp. 128–198). In Spain, the anthropological discourse of difference apparently focuses first on geography, rather than race in the American sense of the term. The "geographized" modality of naturalized difference presupposes a "natural" reality and immutability of ethnic groups, but only insofar as they are geographically localized. The grievances of ethnic groups are addressed to the extent that they form regional geographic communities—a striking continuity with the Hapsburg legacy of regional rule in Spain. Difference and identity become epiphenomena of state forces that always lie just beyond the field of view, supposedly inaccessible to anthropological critique.

Official discourses of difference—including the language of the Spanish Constitution (cf. Prieto de Pedro, 1992)—borrow more directly from ethnographic knowledge in Spain than in the United States.[10] From very early in the Hapsburg system, legal representation through ethnographic portraiture justified special political treatment of regions within the Hapsburg structure. In certain respects, the emergence of the Bourbon system in Spain, through its attempts to suppress the Hapsburg system, created the environment both for liberal revolutions that sought redress of social grievance in class terms and for the maintenance of strong oppositional regional identities. This dynamic resulted in three civil wars and three republics, each trying to seek some accommodation between the idioms of human rights and regional home rule.

In certain respects, the Spanish experience demonstrates most clearly the limits of individual rights as the basis for a liberal state's agenda of delivering social justice to all. The new Spanish constitution recasts the notion of difference within a democratic state to make differences ethnic and to make ethnic differences regional. This converts the issue of difference into issues of home rule rather than into issues of general social justice. Underlying this must be the notion that home rule will result in greater freedom and greater freedom will yield greater social justice.

The resulting social and cultural dynamics are sharply different from those familiar in the United States. To have rights, one must be a member of a regional ethnic group. All regional ethnic groups are oppressed, in the sense that the constitution must return their historical rights to them, and only thus liberating them from the past. To be mistreated as an individual is far less likely to bring redress from the state than to be mistreated as the member of a regional ethnic group. Thus, as Habermas and Michnik also note (op. cit.), Spain is experimenting with something new and volatile: a democratic ethnic welfare state. And while this goes forward, as Velasco, Comelles, and Azcona also emphasize, anthropologists must decide whether to serve as the chroniclers of the regional movements or confront their renderings of identity and difference, a choice having counterparts in the U.S. To step into this arena with comparative and critical perspectives invites serious, even dangerous, reprisals in some places.

THE ESSAYS

The origins of this volume were in the classroom and around a conference table. The class, in 1990, was a summer course for fourteen high school juniors entitled "Difference and Democracy," originally conceived by Davydd Greenwood in response to an invitation from the Telluride Association Summer Program, on the campus of Cornell University. We cotaught the course, and the experience (including a year-long preparation) left us with the strong sense that a constructive sequel might be an extension of the conversation to anthropological and sociolegal colleagues whose writing had influenced our development of its comparative themes, which, like this volume, centered on Spain and the United States.

Accordingly, we continued our collaborative efforts, and co-organized a conference on "Democracy and Difference," which took place over the course of four days in April 1993, on the Bloomington campus of Indiana University. The essays in this volume originated as conference papers on that occasion, each dealing with a different aspect of the question of how democracy and ethnography might be mutually implicated in the United States and Spain.

In its overall structure, the volume relates U.S. and Spanish democratic experiments to the creation and ongoing significance of cultural diversity in both public affairs and academic social science. The essays are grouped into three sections, around three interrelated themes. Each section includes essays about both countries.

The first set emphasizes parallels between constitutional discourses and practices relating to cultural diversity, on the one hand, and anthropological discourses of difference, on the other (Varenne, Segal, Prieto de Pedro, and Sarat and Berkowitz). The second set concentrates on constitutional structures and bureaucratic processes as the contexts that, at least to some extent, structure the forms and meanings of cultural diversity in official public discourses (Yanow, Fernández de Rota, Chock, Azcona, and Urciuoli). The third set focuses on modes of knowledge and self-reproduction in disciplines and professions associated with the public management of diversity—law, anthropology, folklore, and medicine (Mertz, Velasco, and Comelles). Comelles's essay, which is explicitly comparative, also serves as the volume's conclusion. The volume's three sections are introduced further in prologues to each part.

Spain and the United States, and no doubt other democracies as well, foster broad symbolic and material investment in propositions about the nature (literally and figuratively) of cultural identities at home and abroad, geography (origins, borders, and the spatial semantics of cities), tradition, assimilation, and modernity. Some of the essays focus directly on the question of how democracies assert and defend particular constructions of language, geography, and culture as related concepts (see especially Azcona, Fernández de Rota, Urciuoli, and Velasco). The pragmatic consequences of such constructions in the United States and Spain account in part for the fact that discourses of difference travel with relative ease across imagined boundaries between anthropology and politics, or academies and democracies—as well as in the conversations that produced this book. This form of cultural literacy—which is central to any ethnographic study of legal and political culture—is not only a matter of circulating discourses, but also of institutional and legal histories in which anthropologists have been active participants (as the essays on Spain show most directly; for discussion of North American involvements, see Assier-Andrieu, 1993).

In the instance of this volume's particular project, these circumstances compelled and encouraged us to undertake this comparative study. Why should it be that the search for ethnographic problems in democracy's claims to inclusiveness so quickly yields a reflexive consideration of anthropological practices themselves? Contributors to this volume point to provisional answers in the institutional processes that create demands for cultural data and accord it legal relevance, as well as in the extent to which the relevance of anthropology is contingent on those same processes and the contests they involve.

In this sense, this volume can be read as a study of law and politics as cultural practice, that is, of the ways legal institutions project ideas about human potential and desireability onto—and as—everyday life. This wide avenue connects our respective studies of Spain and the United States to current international scholarship in the anthropology of politics and law, and sociolegal studies (see, e.g., Assier-Andrieu, 1996; Chenaut and Sierra, 1995;

Chock, 1991; Comaroff and Comaroff, 1991; Condit and Lucaites, 1993; Domínguez, 1994; Lazarus-Black and Hirsch, 1994; Merry, 1990; Sarat and Kearns, 1993; among others).

As transnationalism and globalization introduce new forms of "tension between cultural homogenization and cultural heterogenization" (Appadurai, 1990: 5), those tensions may be particularly acute for democratic state nationalisms whose symbolic legitimacy rests on their inclusive claims with respect to culturally diverse constituencies. The "crisis of representation" heralded in anthropology by Marcus and Fischer (1986: 7) was equally felt in new challenges—some nationalist, some not—to the cultural legitimacy of states and to ethnography itself. This double meaning of "representation" is particularly vivid in democracies, since the state's legitimacy rests on its claims to represent "the people" both in their individuality and in their chosen associations. The aspect of the crisis of representation that concerns us most in this volume is the legitimation crisis (Habermas, 1976) that gives contemporary questions of ethnographic authority their moral and political stakes.

The crisis of representation in this sense of the term—that is, as a legitimation crisis for both democracy and ethnography occasioned by their increasingly undeniable confrontations with subaltern social movements—is a defining characteristic of postmodernity (e.g., Bauman, 1991; Bhabha, 1994; Bourdieu, 1990b). The volume overall evokes distinct but overlapping scenarios in this regard. In some essays, we learn in detail that the very effort to secure civil rights by marginalized groups reinforces the state's active role in the construction of social identities (see essays by Chock, Sarat and Berkowitz, Segal, and Yanow). At the same time, as other essays show, the entangled discourses of cultural recognition and state control potentially expand the scope for groups' efforts at self-revitalization and mobilization of public resources (Azcona, Fernández de Rota, Prieto de Pedro, Urciuoli, Velasco). In yet other essays, the historical and pragmatic debts of academic disciplines and institutions to social struggles, in other spheres, for multicultural democracy yields a reflexive ethnography that is both critical and engaged (Comelles, Mertz, and Varenne).

Overall, this volume's focus is on the sites—personal, academic, and political—where such junctures and disjunctures are made and felt as both democratic and ethnographic practice. Specifically, we explore some of the contexts where democracy and difference are rendered into a zero-sum arithmetic by democratic institutions themselves, as if unity and difference were somehow inevitably opposites. They are not: the opposite of unity is not difference, but rather the insistence on sameness as a precondition to and confirmation of equality.

The essays find their ethnographic and comparative starting points by focusing directly on the making of such zero-sums. A sequel would be an examination of how this arithmetic operates in the allocation of resources as part of a wider discussion of social movements and change. Another project would investigate personal and collective responses to the officialization of cultural identities, within and beyond the spheres of law. The book's implication is that the "crisis of representation" is not some moment that is likely to pass, given the inherent tensions surrounding official discourses that insist on containing difference. Such crises are multiple and ongoing in both politics and anthropology, and in both, a permanent state of affairs. Far from making either politics or the ethnographic enterprise futile, though, the inevitable disjunctions between description, aspirations, and lived realities can be a source of hope, argument, thoughtful reflection, and experimentation—as they are in the following essays.

NOTES

1. The term "multiculturalism" has many meanings. We use it here to refer simultaneously to social knowledge borne of mutual interest and respect, and positive social change through expanded opportunities for access to collective goods, both tangible and intangible.

2. Similarly, we would not want to be misunderstood as implying that cultural self-identity is not "real," or that it is merely tactical in relation to opportunities for personal or collective advancement. These would be serious misreadings; the selectivity of our own focus on the production of terms and meanings of identity in democratic and academic practice by no means cancels the urgency of understanding how people construe and affirm their own associations. Quite the contrary, our aim is to call into question the monopoly of current official discourses over the terms of inquiry and debate.

3. Mertz (1994: 975) identifies "the examination of the impact of law on collective and individual identity" as "a prime site for the development of [a] new synthetic approach to the study of law and society." The synthesis to which she refers combines attention to "social, economic, and political structures at work in the way people act in and view the world" (975)—superceding "a fairly stale and aged dichotomy in social science analysis" (975, n. 6).

4. Beyond these disciplines, too, we draw on the work of scholars in the fields loosely called ethnic studies, and who are instructively alert to the malleability, dynamism, interestedness, punitiveness, celebratory value, and contradictions of identity questions (e.g., Omi and Winant, 1994; Takaki, 1993; Waters, 1990). As anthropologists move into this arena in partnership with other disciplines, they are inevitably (and constructively) challenged to define the "value added" of an anthropological perspective. We believe the essays collected here demonstrate the value added. In attending to issues ordinarily imagined to be beyond the scope of ethnography, they enhance the possibility of collaboration with other social researchers, legal scholars, and policy makers.

5. The call by anthropologists for ethnographies of large-scale political institutions begins with Nader (1974). As the text below explains, this volume is not conceived as studying "up" as if the state were above or beyond daily life, but rather in terms of some of the contexts in which democratic processes are implicated in self-identity and what Battaglia (1996) terms "self-making." For additional examples and approaches, see especially Appiah and Gates, 1995; Benhabib, 1995; Black Public Sphere Collective, 1995; Fitzpatrick, 1995; Williams, 1996; Wilmsen and McAllister, 1996; and special issues of *American Ethnologist* on "Tensions of Empire" (November 1989) and "Representations of Europe: Transforming State, Society, and Identity" (August 1991).

6. And such "distances" are not always metaphorical. They can also be made literal, as when people lack access to institutions and services. As Harvey (1973) has demonstrated, geography in this sense is a significant dimension of social justice.

7. Yet it is precisely this primordialism that is central to nationalist mythologies of identity. In addition to references cited in note 4, see Anderson, 1991; Azcona, 1984; Balibar and Wallerstein, 1991; Bhabha, 1994; Chock, 1991; Fernández de Rota, 1994; Gellner, 1983; and Herzfeld, 1987. Recent analyses also clarify the tensions—and elisions—between racial and ethnic formulations of nationalism and formulations conceived in terms of class; see especially Rouse, 1995; Urciuoli, 1996; and Woodiwiss, 1993.

8. Notable exceptions include Laitin, 1986; 1992; Scott, 1985; 1990; and Young, 1990.

9. Cf. Comaroff and Comaroff, 1992: 27.

10. In the United States, as we will explain below, it tends to be ethnography that borrows its lexicon from the public domain. For discussion of everyday rubrics of social organization and experience in the United States, see Varenne, 1977 and 1992.

I

Diversity and Equality in Liberal Debate

The essays in this section explore some of the tensions between diversity and equality in the liberal democracies of the United States and Spain. In each country, the state has responded to citizens' recently intensified demands for cultural recognition by enlarging its commitment to equality—but without fully confronting the extent to which the histories and conceptual categories reflected in official discourses of difference tend to make equality and diversity problematic as simultaneous principles—even antithetical from certain public policy perspectives. In this section, official American and Spanish paradigms of difference are juxtaposed, with race and regional culture being central in the two countries' contemporary official discourses of debate. This is an important and complex distinction reflecting different national histories as well as contemporary state practices; however, as we shall see in Parts II and III, the differences of content involve certain similarities of form, arising from the ways the modern state's political and social margins are occasionally, selectively, and provisionally opened to new participants. In both countries, then, the contradiction between equality and diversity arises within democracy itself, at the point where culture and class are constructed in separate terms—terms shaped by the specific histories of the two countries' state formation and democratization movements, contemporary constitutional practice, and other aspects of public culture.

In the opening essay, Varenne reflects on the American "melting pot" as a myth whose effects include powerful public scripts of singularized collective identities that leave individuals highly limited choices in their own public self-identities: one may opt to identify as *a member* of some recognized group, and only with considerably more difficulty with more than one, or in other terms altogether. Varenne critiques this paradoxical requirement of choice as a form of coercion that shapes public dialogue as well as cultural theorizing. Segal considers some of these same conundrums as aspects of bureaucratic routines, exploring the tangles of crossed meanings of race, ethnicity, gender, and class in ordinary encounters.

In Spain, contradiction arises at the point where culture is defined as language communities with origins in the prenational past; Prieto de Pedro's essay reviews the Spanish constitution's treatment of cultural and linguistic pluralism as a feature of federal-regional structure and administration. The section closes with the essay by Sarat and Berkowitz, who define key terms in liberal debates over cultural difference in contemporary American political theory—but with resonances that apply to Spain also—and then draw on them to analyze U.S. Supreme Court cases significant for understanding some of the legal meaning of cultural diversity in the United States today.

All of the authors consider the ethnographic implications of the circumstances and contradictions they explore, in terms of the prospects for ethnography informing and encouraging fresh terms and approaches. As in the rest of the volume, their starting points, substantive arguments and styles are different in ways that also add to the story.

Chapter 2

Diversity as American Cultural Category

Hervé Varenne

Anna Quindlen, an editorialist for the *New York Times,* titled an editorial against xenophobia "Making the Mosaic" (1991). She builds it around "Ms. Miller's third-grade class in Public School 20 in New York City." There, she tells us, "The current student body comes for the Dominican Republic, Cambodia, Bangladesh, Puerto Rico, Columbia, mainland China, Vietnam and El Salvador." There, she continues, "These various faces somehow look the same, upturned and open, as though they were cups waiting for the water to be poured." There, she ends, "new Americans are being minted, [. . .] bits of a mosaic far from complete."

Her point is political. She is resisting any policy aimed at restricting entry into the United States. Her point is also related to an academic dispute that has run in parallel to what is a fundamental issue in the foundation of America: How is the immigration experience to be interpreted? She summarizes this dispute and her solution in the opening sentence to her editorial: "There is some disagreement over which wordsmith first substituted 'mosaic' for 'melting pot' as a way of describing America, but there is no doubt that it is a more apt description."

My goal here is academic more than it is political. I am writing as an anthropologist and I must discipline myself to stay within the confines of academe. In the spirit of the editors of this volume, I am concerned with diversity less as a result of cultural difference and much more *as a cultural process* that produces particular forms of difference within a historical and institutional context. I take it that, whenever human beings move geographically and become intimately intertwined with other human beings, they inevitably enter into a dialogue that produces a particular pattern of institutionalized differences: soon people must act in terms of the identifications their interlocutors have made of them. "Diversity" is never the simple end product of substances living together in some geographical space—as the "mosaic" metaphor suggests. Always, human beings converse with their neighbors and, soon, produce a historical particularity, a "culture" that frames them both. Eventually, the academic, scientific, question is not whether a population is or is not "diverse" but how inevitable diversity is handled locally.

Now, of course, to talk of dialogue and conversation can easily hide issues of power and dominance that have become central to culture theory over the past twenty years. Two persons acting, two groups interacting, are probably never equal in the resources that they bring to the moment of interaction, and there is every reason to believe that such inequalities will get more pronounced as the groups develop a joint history. The diversity that is produced through migration is particularly susceptible to variation related to the historical conditions of the encounters. When European and Africans started their lives together in the Americas, why ever they came, they clearly produced something different in the Caribbean islands with, for example, the development of various creoles, from what they produced on the mainland between the 32nd and the 48th parallels where British English barely evolved into what is now American English. One cannot talk of conversation without talking about the relative "power" of each participant. One should not talk of "voices" without mentioning the choruses that sustain some and drown others. In recent years, this has led to much talk about "hegemony" but the political revulsion against the institutionalization of results based on the relative power of one group over another, has led to an impoverishment of the theoretical conversation. To moralize about hegemony may obscure processes that have more to do with matters of social mass and energy (in a quasi-physical sense) than about sinfulness against liberal democracy.

It is in this context that I look at the evolution of the experience and expression of "diversity" in the United States as framed by an *American* cultural process, that is as a set of symbols, myths, narratives, practices, and institutions that has evolved over 350 years. What we are now made to see as "diversity" in the United States is the product of an elaborate cultural construction. It is a collective endeavor to the elaboration of which many millions have worked. The symbolic and political institutions that make "diversity" real are unavoidable as a constraint and always available as a resource. They frame all who come to the United States in a particular network of interpretations and positions that one must understand *as* American— particularly when our goals are comparative.

In this essay, I weave my own experiences as a migrant and a professional observer with the broader context of the sociological and mythological constructions of experiences such as mine. After twenty-five years in the United States, I remain a legal "alien" who may not directly participate in the public life of the country: I do not have the vote. Thus, I stand in the special position opened by American culture for people such as myself: the position of professional outsider. Concurrently, I refuse the other position that is offered to me within the symbolic space structured by America: the position of the ethnic "French-American." This refusal is made easier since there are no such organized groups in the collective consciousness of the United States. Still, my refusal, like the refusal by a Jewish or Black male of their Jewishness, Blackness (or maleness), is not imperative on any audience. My identification as "French" (or male) can be performed *on* me. It is an external matter constraining, though not determining, on what I can do, or be known as having done, in an American setting. This refusal, however ambiguous, might in fact be taken by someone like Quindlen, and by the sociologists whom she is popularizing, as the proof of my "Frenchness" (an insistence on radical individualism within an externalized contingent social system), and thus the proof of the failure of my years in the United States fully to enculture me, and thus the proof of the failure of the melting pot. My goal here is to trace the lines of this argument as it is summarized in the offering of the image of the "mosaic" as somehow truer than the image of the "melting pot" as a "description of America." Those who follow political discourse in the United States know what is at stake when people fight over "diversity." But this very awareness may mask the concrete logic of the argument. *How* is what is at stake put to the stake? It is my argument here that it is done in a peculiarly American fashion.

The essay starts with an evocation of the kind of experiences in the United States that concern me here. It proceeds through a summary of Sollors's work (1986) on what I will refer to as the great version[1] of the Myth of the Melting Pot. This is expanded into a discussion of the way one might read the Myth as myth rather than as sociological hypothesis. The Myth, in brief, is first about the experience of confronting within one's own locality people who were Others at a safe distance. It is about what one should do with one's reactions to this experience, and what one may expect the ex-Others who may now be Us. It is eventually about the institutions, laws, bureaucratic rules that an American state should evolve, and then legitimately enforce. Most important, the Myth is an instance of the display in text of a peculiar logic in painting a situation and arguing a point.[2] "Melting Pot," "mosaic," "salad bowl," are metaphors stressing one or another aspect of the fundamental myth. They all eventually point to a fundamental American cultural structure that is remaining remarkably stable: the Myth of the determination of the self through His own actions with others whom He has chosen because they are like Him—the Myth of the Individual in Love with His Community.[3] New arrivals find themselves reconstituting, and thus reproducing, the arguments earlier arrivals used against those who were already settled.

PERSONAL EXPERIENCES

My first personal experience with the problem came early in my first field research in the United States (Varenne, 1977). I was being introduced at the beginning of a small party. There was a round of first names that ended with mine. My host's mentioning of the fact that I was a "foreign student" appears to have reminded him that something was missing in this round, and he started around a second time requesting of his friends a nation of origin: "Italian, "Irish/Polish," "Italian, though my father was not." The turn came to a woman who first said that she was "nothing." This would not do and, after a brief series of exchanges, she was identified as "Scottish/English." The round ended and we proceeded to the business of party making.

I knew enough about the United States at that time to recognize that I had just participated in one of those scenes that are most often held up as somehow fundamentally American. This was a social drama, the performative version of textual versions, the version from Quindlen I quoted earlier being but one modern version. Indeed, I had already read many of these versions as I got my intellectual introduction to America during the years preceding my fieldwork. I had read Glazer and Moynihan who taught me first about the "melting pot" by telling me that it had not worked (1963); I had glanced at Novak's *The Rise of the Unmeltable Ethnics* (1971); I had looked at some of the earlier sociological writings that attempted to give a theoretical justification for "melting" aspect of what they could not handle as a metaphor. I had also read Lloyd Warner's account of a parade in Yankee City (1959), and I had heard Milton Singer discuss its relevance to a discussion of ethnicity that would move us away from the essentialism implicit in both versions of the melting metaphor, whether it was the assumption that, after melting, an essential Americanism would establish itself—the nativist hypothesis—, or the assumption that, after generations of interaction, something essentially different persists in the descendants of the immigrants that came over various seas—what was not yet named the "multiculturalist," "mosaic" hypothesis.

My experience, a few miles from Chicago, was, first, a confirmation that these little paragraphs such as Quindlen wrote were not simply a matter of talk or ideational interpretation. They also involved concrete, practical action. Some of this action could be handled as more or less empty, though perhaps prescribed, ritual. But often this ritual was "dramatic" in the sense V. Turner discussed (1986). It often involved the emotions and interests of the participants, and thus became a form of political action that no one can escape who lives in the United States. In a vocabulary that I borrow from ethnomethodology, action marked for ethnicity is a particular kind of accountable practice. In Yankee City, for the tercentenary parade discussed by Warner, as it was again when organizers built the other parades and reenactments discussed by Milton Singer (1986, 1987), the display of what we now call ethnic "diversity" is both prescribed and problematic. At such a time, one cannot simply ignore "the contribution ethnic groups" have made to the development of America. One cannot either let each organizing group do quite what they please. Ethnicity must be represented, but it must represented in a *particular* fashion.

A most striking recent example is the organization of the St. Patrick's Day parade in New York City. Things being on a larger scale in New York than they are in Yankee City, there is not one occasional parade celebrating all ethnic groups, but a parade of parades which, on the yearly calendar dear to structural-functionalist anthropologist, gives a space to emerging ethnic groups to display their particular place in America. The Irish emerged more than 200 hundred years ago but America has been changing over and around what may be their Irish selves and it slowly transforms what is problematical in a display of Irishness. Wearing green and waving banners struck with a golden harp is one thing, displaying Catholicity (as in the bow to the Cardinal as he stands on steps of the Cathedral) is something that comes and goes as more or less scandalous. Forbidding homosexuals from parading under their own banner is something else altogether. The latter is the stuff out of which newspaper editorials are written, and political careers built or broken.

My introduction to the group of friends in Appleton was similarly a moment for doubt and celebration. I was, by all accounts, an outsider. As I came to see it, transforming outsiders into insiders and then back again into outsiders, was the dominant routine practice of these small groups. A proper outsider would not however negotiate his entry into the group in quite the brazen fashion that I was using. I was burning a lot of intermediary steps by simply exercising my right to "drop in any time." I had the excuse of being not only an outsider, but also a foreigner. This turned out to be key. As the introduction proceeded, my unique status was subtly transformed into the status everyone in the room had: I was remade into a French-American. I was now just as different as everyone else, and thus not different at all. In the process, I was made less problematic than the woman who claimed she was "nothing." Foreigners may be "welcomed," "educated," and "counseled." An insider who claims "nothing" is placing himself outside the community with a different kind of difference that is truly dangerous.

AS AMERICAN AS (AMERICAN) DIVERSITY

It is part of the intellectual and political common sense that America is "different" because it was made by immigrants. Japan, it is said, does not have the problems America has "because it is homogeneous." There is, however, no evidence that major population movements into a particular geographical area necessarily produce what has evolved in North America between the 32nd and 48th parallels. The United States has evolved differently from Argentina or Australia and we must be able to analyze the pattern of this difference. This is a general problem as anthropology has come to the relative consensus that no human society is homogeneous in the old sense. Indeed modern readings of philosophers of language and discourse like Bakhtin (1981) all emphasize the many ways through which attempts at centralizing hegemonic interpretations of the world eventually fail as the centrifugal forces of the marketplace tear away at any apparent or temporary homogeneity. All societies, even apparently "homogeneous" ones, are made up by the comings and goings of various groups in various circumstances.[4] All societies are complexes of groups with different interests and local histories relating to other groups in the development of a global history. For all societies, then, dealing with the "other" is a continually renewed problem. Boundaries are never settled. Like the proverbial wall that separated Robert Frost from his neighbor over the hill, they must continually be reconstructed under new conditions.

For those who are interested in America, then, the problem is not the tracing of the coming and settlements of various groups to the continent in general, and the United States in particular. This is a particular kind of social scientific task that only begins to handle a more general problem, that is the ways such movements are handled by the earliest immigrants as they develop the set of institutions, politicolegal and symbolico-interpretive, which later immigrants find and, up to a certain point transform, perhaps in fact by reviving what has always been their strength. Eventually, particular forms of boundary construction became institutionalized in the particular political space where "America" is powerful (dominant? hegemonic?), and those who cross the boundaries of the United States must now deal with them. Ethnicity, in the United States as elsewhere, is less about the history of immigration than about the construction of the person as Other in a particular way. Diversity is a symbol of America, the product of an interpretive evolution. The issue, thereby, is not only one of asserting the extent of the persistent differences, it is also one of understanding how "difference" is reconstructed in the local and not so local practices of people in the country.

What is needed, then, is an anthropology of immigration as told from the point of view of what Margaret Mead once called perceptively the "third" generation. In what is really a brilliant—though perhaps unwitting—structural analysis, she traces the three positions one can occupy in the United States: the position of the new immigrant still rooted in love-hate relationships with the old country (the "first" generation), the position of this immigrant's child typified by a denial of the relevance of the old country (the "second" generation), the position of the immigrant's grandchild typified by a matter-of-fact identification with what is now an "ethnic" group (the "third" generation). Most strikingly, Margaret Mead dared say, "We [Americans] are *all* third generation" (my emphasis; 1965, chapter 3). This was obviously not meant to be taken statistically. It was meant to summarize the peculiarly American interpretation of the encounter with the Other: in a proper America, the Other is not abolished, rather his difference is reconstructed to be made to fit with similar differences made to operate in the same manner. Thus, in the introduction round I talked about earlier, the specific content of "Italian," "Pole," "Scot," "French," was subsumed, just as the content of "Cambodia," "China," "El Salvador," and so on, is subsumed in Quindlen's editorial. At such times there can be no discussion of what the content of any of these categories might be. My Frenchness was not at issue, but rather the equivalence of my difference to that of the other people in the room. What had to be affirmed was that all the categories or groups with which we could be identified were equivalent, and secondary to our fundamental qualities as human beings who were all the same because we were all different.[5] As the constitution affirms: "All men [human beings] are created equal," *not* "all Americans," and even less "all Anglo-Saxons."[6]

The best recent exegesis of the process through which immigration and difference is made into something paradigmatically American is to be found in Werner Sollors's work on the melting pot as metaphor, myth, and performance in American literature and political rhetoric (1986). In his work, the melting pot is treated as something, a symbolic thing obviously, that has served people in the United States, recent immigrants, as well as their great grandchildren, to handle their fate not only descriptively but also prescriptively. In this way, he moves the debate beyond a concern with the "truth" or "efficiency" of the myth (Is it true? Does it work?), to a concern with its contribution to the ongoing history of the United States.

Sollors started with Israel Zangwill's paradigmatic play *The Melting Pot* (1909).[7] He analyzes sensitively its immediate sources in turn-of-the-century New York Jewish socialist circles. He pursues these sources in the various attempts by European writers transplanted on the West Coast of the Atlantic (people like Crèvecoeur, Jefferson, etc.) to explain what appeared to be happening there that they wished to foster. Something new was being done that could not happen in Europe itself: a new man would finally realize politically the Christian rejection of Judaic law. St. Paul met the Indian princess Pocahontas, and in her womb developed something that would encompass the whole of humanity. Sollors does not quite emphasize, as I am doing, that this is a European dream as well as a possible American reality. It may initially have been more of a Protestant European dream but it is clear that, by Zangwill's time, at the turn of the twentieth century, it had become a broader dream, a dream for an institutionalization of universalism that had begun in the United States, but was of course not complete.

Sollors argued that, initially, the melting pot is more a radical political symbol than a conservative sociological theory. It is a discursive practice, a statement within a broader political conversation, a weapon against what was then call "nativism," another tradition in American thinking that continues to strain, and continues to fail, to redefine America according to the tenets of traditional nationalism.[8] In Zangwill's time, and probably throughout the 1920s and 1940s, though in a more hidden manner, the image of the melting pot is a radical image in the struggle between the newer immigrants and the older ones.[9] Even now, when the actual image has lost its power, the other images that are being proposed (rainbows, mosaics, etc.) are to be used in the same manner: they are weapons against those who would close the frontiers in the name of some substantive quality that only native born people encultured near the ideological centers, that is, "Americans," would possess, a soul or spirit that would be so deeply ingrained that "foreigners" (or people encultured in various ghettoes) could not possibly gain access to it. America, in the other image, is the place where these souls cease to make a difference, and this must happen whatever contingent soul Americans themselves might develop over the centuries. America is not British, it is not Anglo-Saxon, it is not Northern European, it is not European, and it will not be African or Asiatic. It will remain "democratic" where the "demos," the people in "we, the people," is continually reconstructed as a plurality of individuals, and not as a community with particular properties. Not that communities, at every level, do not have properties, but that these must not have consequences in those public spheres that America organizes. To paraphrase Sollors (1986: 261), America may not, indeed must not, be American.

The paradox of the melting pot imagery is that it is centrally built around the evidence of difference. There are many tellings of the myth—for it is a myth in the strongest sense of the term—and there are many performances. The actual telling or performance can vary widely. Zangwill's play is one such telling. The famous pageant organized by Henry Ford is a performance with (if Sollors is right) quite a different underlying political message. The casting of many a movie from the glory days of Hollywood is still another.[10] Quindlen recites the myth in the editorial I quoted earlier, and my friends in Appleton improvised on it to deal with a delicate interpersonal situation. There is one prescribed sequence, however, and that is the reciting of a list of exotic peoples. This sequence cannot be more encompassing than the one that appears at the end of Zangwill's play: "Celt and Latin, Slav and Teuton, Greek and Syrian, black and yellow, Jew and Gentile, East and West, and North and South, the palm and the pine, the pole and the equator, the crescent and the cross," (1975 [1909]: 200). This ends with an invocation of God, not the God of our fathers but "the God of our *children*."[11] Without all these people with the many different gods of their fathers, there would be no America, or, rather, there will never be no America (the multiple negatives are essential here), since America is the ideological space where America must never be completed. As I understand it, the myth might be paraphrased as follows:

> In the beginning, peoples from all over the earth came to a new continent. They forgot their earlier attachments and disputes. Together they have been building something new that is a model for the old countries they left behind. Many years later, the flaws of the original building are showing and people from all over the world are joining together in restoring and expanding a work in process that should remain a model for the universe.

THE "MELTING POT" AS MYTH AND SOCIAL SCIENCE

The strength of Sollors's work lies in his taking this myth seriously as myth. I am also aware that to talk of the melting pot as a myth is somewhat dangerous since the word *myth* is commonly used by the critical tradition to refer pejoratively to some groundless tale. A myth in this common sense is a matter of belief that one must abandon when social science has demonstrated that it does not correspond to "reality." This limited understanding of the power of myth must be challenged. Myths are not so much about belief as they are about verisimilitude: they heighten our experience by representing it, that is making it present in a particular salient form. Myths are not to be evaluated for their truth value but rather for their meaningfulness. The "melting pot" is not about the number of melted Americans but rather about the experience of walking down Broadway, hearing its many voices, and trying to make one's own heard.

In myth, authorship is of interest only to academic historians and the aesthetic quality of the telling is of secondary concern. Zangwill may have coined the phrase "melting pot" but he is all but forgotten. Glazer and

Moynihan, like many contemporary critics, like to emphasize that Zangwill's play is "a bad one." They dismiss it as the work of a dissatisfied Jewish socialist immigrant on the way to transforming himself into a Zionist. They even argue that the play is really more about Russia than it is about America, with the Irish and the German thrown in "for comic relief" (1963: 290). This may be so but one might at least entertain the possibility that America is precisely made of dissatisfied immigrants dreaming of a better world in Europe (or, now, Asia). The same argument might be made of the original "pilgrims."[12] Many others came to the United States as a last resort, or even totally against their will, but their experience cannot be dismissed.

In any event, Zangwill as an author who proved a somewhat dissatisfied immigrant is not pertinent. The play, by all accounts, was very successful. The phrase is still with us. Aspects of its plots were reproduced hundreds of times by the myth factories of Hollywood where other immigrants made their case for integration into a particular kind of America through the manipulation of possibly reconstructed traditional arguments about the universality of democracy. What is important about the phrase "Melting Pot" is that it apparently captures something. It was, and it remains theater, allowing one to become spectator to one's own fate, appreciate it aesthetically, and also criticize it. Zangwill's play, in the long run, was appropriated *"sur le mode collectif"* (Lévi-Strauss 1971: 560) and transformed from a statement by an identifiable author into a myth that no one, not even sociologists fifty years later, can ignore. The myth is still alive—in the sense that a language that is spoken, written, and evolving is alive rather than dead. It is particularly alive in the intellectual discussions that take it seriously enough to demonstrate that it is not "fact."

The literature that specifically criticizes "the melting pot" by taking it literally now has a long history. Eventually I want to celebrate it by showing that this critique fully reproduces the myth by expanding an essential ingredient of it, what we might call the "dramatic" moment in the American interpretation of humanity. In the play there is a long episode when "reality" has intruded and tragedy threatens. For a while the hero reintegrates the prejudices of his group; he refuses to accept the possibility that anyone might be transformed, or that there might even be something appropriate to a search for a transformation. The intellectual conversation that moves America also recognizes moments when some group might fall prey to either of two temptations. Zangwill points to situations when, somewhere in the United States, some may take on the mantle of being "the" new American man—which has thereby become old and thus un-American. The same conversation, he notes, points at groups who may be succeeding in closing themselves in a ghetto refusing the transformative process that all who come to America must go through.

The critical literature that concerns me here reads the actual text of Zangwill's play as being an argument for an achieved homogeneity in the population of the United States. Rather than taking the phrase as a description of the streets of New York, they take the phrase as referring eventually to what would come out of the pot, that is a "melted" identity where differences would have been erased. This is indeed the version of the myth that Henry Ford used in the dramatic performances he organized in his factories (Sollors 1986: 89–91). For him perhaps, to celebrate the melting pot was to celebrate one particularity, a limiting form of Americanism that specifically denied the relevance of difference (ethnic or religious—to which we would now add sexual orientation, physical handicap, and so forth). This is the version of the myth that became offensive to generations of ethnic activists, and that has now become the "official" version when the myth is recited as a cautionary tale about what America must *not* become. There is little evidence that it is the version as it originated in the writings of Crèvecoeur and others in the eighteenth century, or in Zangwill's play and many others in the 1920s and 1930s. Conversely, Sollors has no problem ferreting out all the passages where people like Novak harken back to the other version of the myth as they talk about "cauldrons" or "crucibles" to evoke the situation of people in the large urban centers of the United States where ethnicity is most alive. It is thus typical within the genre that Anna Quindlen's editorial against the melting pot should end with a phrase about the "*new* Americans being *minted*" (my emphasis). In such conclusions to attacks on the official myth, as it was in Zangwill's play, the message is one of universalism and freedom, along with a call for the construction or strengthening of institutions and ways of being that foster universalism and freedom. It is also one of individual transformation.

This ideological commitment to America must go through a reaffirmation of the centrality of particular forms of social difference in the United States: there would be no melting pot if there was nothing to melt. It must be possible to demonstrate the continued relevance of the initial condition assumed by the great version of the myth: "In the beginning, and today still, people from all over the world . . ." The myth *requires* an affirmation of difference, and sociologists provided it at the very moment when it may well be the case that the traditional European immigrant groups were becoming undistinguishable from each other. As Glazer and Moynihan wrote in the conclusion to their era-opening *Beyond the Melting Pot*: "The point about the melting pot is that it did not happen" (1963: 290). This closes their analysis of Zangwill's play, which they transformed into a set of hypotheses:

— the children (or grandchildren) of immigrants to the United States, wherever and however they arrived on the continent, will
   a. start interacting with each other in ways impossible in their old country.
   b. stop identifying with the areas of the world their parents came from and the specificities (language, religion, political ideologies) that typified them.

As hypotheses, these statements belong to the realm of verifiability—to the extent at least that one could agree on the operational definitions of, for example, ethnic identification: Does it have to do with living in a different behavioral world? Using the label in some contexts? Remembering where one's grandparents were born? Glazer and Moynihan, having taken on themselves the disciplinary mantle, can then come to the following conclusion:

> It is true that language and culture are very largely lost in the first and second generations, and this makes the dream of "cultural pluralism"—of new Italy or Germany or Ireland in America, a League of Nations established in the New World—as unlikely as the hope of a "melting pot." But as the groups were transformed by influences in American society, stripped of their original attributes, they were recreated as something new, but still as identifiable groups. (Glazer and Moynihan, 1963: 13)

What evidence do they offer, and what evidence do they ignore to arrive at these conclusions? The book is essentially a series of vignettes summarizing the political economy of groups presented "in order of visibility": Blacks, Puerto Ricans, Jews, Italians, and Irish. The logic of the grouping is not discussed. Rather, the reader is referred back to a political common sense that obscures major issues. They do not talk about the rate of intermarriage among identified members of various groups. They do not discuss the implications of the uniformization of the conditions of everyday life as people moved to the suburbs. The list of matters that can be addressed in such a discussion is long indeed. Most important perhaps, the movement of the Irish, and then the Italians, into the center of the political arena, and then their movement into positions of economic privilege is ignored even though it was already well on its way and may be the strongest evidence of integration—if not assimilation. John Kennedy's then recent statement about being American before he was Catholic is not presented as proof of what Zangwill's play had hoped for: that in America, Catholics who had massacred Jews in Europe would now join with them, and with the descendants of slaves, to form the electoral base of one of the two major political parties in the United States. Glazer and Moynihan could not have known that the decade that was starting when they were writing their book would also be the time for a major ideological movement among the children of the people they studied, a movement devoid of reference to ethnic particularisms. There is something fundamentally American in the 1960s symbols of universal love and the search for still another new beginning that would heal humanity through the transformation of each person within it. In the Age of Aquarius, as in the age that Zangwill thought he saw dawning over New York harbor, human particularities will be transcended through the destruction of the hierarchies that support them.

One has but to look at the list of the groups that would not melt in New York City to realize how dated Moynihan's analysis has become: Jews, Italians, and Irish are now "Euro-Americans" or "white ethnics," and any serious attempt at differentiating among them soon becomes contentious. In New York City the Black category has become infinitely more complex than it was in the late 1950s as Carribeans, and now people from various parts of Africa, have been moving in. The Puerto-Rican category has all but disappeared from common parlance as newer immigrants insist on a relationship with Cuba or the Dominican Republic. "Hispanic" may have been designed to deal with these differences and establish a new difference to oppose to Black or White, but the category, and others like "Latino" or "Chicano" that compete with it, does not hide the deep political divisions at play here. A new Moynihan would now probably want to mention various Asian groups, not to mention Middle Eastern ones.

In some ways, of course, this "change" is not quite a change to the extent that *Beyond the Melting Pot* could still be written with an altered cast of characters: New York City, and by extension the United States, is still not a place where ethnic origin makes no difference. One is continually made to group people through the application of criteria such as place or birth, or political activity. Indeed, one is continually *required* to identify oneself in the multitude of administrative forms through which the American State enforces the categories of official relevance.[13]

Conversely, ferreting out actual "differences" between the older ethnic groups—those whose bulk arrived four or five generations ago—become more and more difficult. Ten years after *Beyond the Melting Pot*, Parsons, expanding on an essay by Schneider (1969), already wondered whether the ethnic differences that had been talked about did not belong more to the realm of political symbolism than to the realm of sociological reality (1975). All there would be about the talk of ethnic differences would be precisely the talk about it, the labels, identifications, and the discourses (textual and dramatic) that rely on them and thus reconstitute them.

THE CULTURE OF THE MELTING POT

Such a conclusion, however, stays within a literal reading and fails to catch a more fundamental ideological principle. The peculiarity of the melting pot myth—as social theory rather than as hypothesis about social history—lies in its understanding of human nature, what we might think of as its philosophical anthropology. The myth—and I am talking here of both its popular and critical versions—is founded on a particular view of the constitution of persons within groups. Over the centuries, the vocabulary has changed, and the references to religious salvation may have been transformed into a psychological language. Still, from Crèvecoeur to modern critics, the melting pot myth is fundamentally about identity as socially constituted. It is never so much about the *institutions* to be constructed than about the *person* that will live these institutions and eventually validate them. The model has two aspects, one oriented to fully formed adults that must be placed in a situation where they can express themselves as they really are. The other aspect is more difficult as it concerns persons who are not fully formed, children on the one hand, and newcomers on the other. In either case, whatever is constructed is founded on the principle that American democracy is not quite a natural state that one will necessarily embrace if one is let free to develop away from any constraints. Deliberate ideological activity is necessary to develop the freedom of the persons involved. The dilemma may be best caught by thinking briefly about the place of education in American ideology. Indeed we might write of a Myth of Education that would be the foundation of the Melting Pot. John Dewey, as a person most committed to America, clearly understood that transforming a child into a full participant into a democratic system is by no means a mechanical process (1966 [1916]). Democracy is a particular form of social life, a particular culture we would now say. It is not inscribed in human genes. Conversely, proper human beings must be totally formed to their culture, otherwise their participation is suspect. Thus, the ideological task is clear: a democratic education must deliberately mold an individual in such a way as to reveal the uniqueness of the individual. How to do this will always be a matter of debate given the paradoxical nature of the ideological injunction: Social forces (institutionalized as schools, curriculums, pedagogies, etc.) must exercise themselves in such a way as to deny their own participation in the making of the people on which they are exerted.

One has but to place G. H. Mead alongside John Dewey to grasp the intellectual struggle that moved their colleagues and students at the University of Chicago when they tried to account for the fate of immigrants to the city at the same time that they developed a theory of personhood that was also democratic. To the very extent that pragmatic and symbolic interactional theories of social construction emphasize the fundamental activity of the individual, they must develop a complementary theory of shared meanings: in the proper community all individuals share the same codes, the same understandings, the same orientations, the same values. They are, for all intent and purposes, "alike," if not melted into each other. In the origin myths of this proper community, as told over the centuries by people like Berger and Luckman (1967: 56), already fully selved human beings get together, and internalize each other's habits and their personal responses to these.

A problem however does arise when social psychological theories of society are transformed into theories of human development, socialization, and enculturation. Dewey, Mead, and all their followers more or less matter of factly built over the premise that, through interaction in a community (family), participants, particularly young children, come to adopt or internalize the dominant ways of this community. Through this interaction a child acquires the language, and more important the "culture," of its significant others. When this has been done, in the first few years of life, change is difficult and possibly illegitimate. Schools and other institution must adapt to the culture "*of*" the child. All the ambiguity is in this conjunction of possession. On the one hand, not to respect this culture is to do illegitimate violence to the individual's free constitution. On the other hand, the child is presented as having mechanically become something that has obviously not been chosen.

In research terms, a commitment to interactionist theories of cultural identity must lead to summaries of "American characteristics" and investigations into their relative prevalence. The best of these may be found in the Parsonian work of Kluckhohn and Strodtbeck (1961). A very similar, though perhaps less systematic, approach also characterizes the more recent work of Shweder and his students and colleagues (Shweder and Bourne, 1984): Americanism is a state of the self, a value-orientation, a particular way of conceptualizing the person. More or less wittingly, a social psychology that started as an attempt to take into account the independent activity of individuals ended supporting a slightly modified nativist understanding of America. It is not surprising that, eventually, this would produce a combination of empirical and ideological backlash: not everyone in the United States is "American" by the standard of American social psychology, and this cannot be so on these very same standards. Communal difference is ideologically fundamental and empirically evident, and yet it is made theoretically impossible. There is a problem here.

Most criticisms of the melting pot focus rather narrowly on one type of evidence: there would not be one America, but several. No one has proposed a listing of these various Americas, though one might start with a melting-pot style listing of adjectives identifying people with exotic places over the seas. The listing must be presented as possible though indefinite. A new group may always have to be added. Each of these groups, whatever criteria they may be based on (ethnic, racial, religious, gender, sexual orientation, etc.), theoretically are dealt with in the same way that "America" is dealt with in the nativist approaches: they are all characterized by certain value orientations predominantly shared among the relevant people. Thus "Italian-Americans," "women," or "African-Americans from certain rural counties," are presented as "Americans" are in the other type of work: within their own communities they are all the same (or more alike among themselves than they are with members of other communities—to some level of statistical significance). The fundamental tenets of social psychology with its attendant theories of socialization and enculturation remain standing. The verisimilitude of the original state in the melting pot myth is reaffirmed: in the beginning that is also a continuing present, a multitude of groups come together and struggle peaceably to find institutional, but even more important, personal ways of respecting each other.

AMERICA AS A CULTURE

We are now quite familiar with literary analyses of sociological writing that underline the ideological underpinnings of both theory and practice. Sollors's work, and that of others whom he has brought together in a more recent collection of essays (1989), demonstrates that such analyses can be constructive as well as deconstructive. My intent here is oriented toward building an analysis of America that recognizes the melting pot as one version of even more fundamental myths while attempting to escape the theoretical straitjacket of interactionist approaches to culture. In other words, I am relying on what may be an un-American theory of culture: one that is based on historically evolved constraints, resistance, and cultivation, rather than on internalization or sharing. From this perspective America is not a characteristic of Americans. Rather, it resides in what people who live in the United States cannot escape. Only through such a shift can one understand, and celebrate, the cultured uniqueness of America.

Let us return briefly to the round of introductions I reported on briefly earlier: Was it an occasion to express identities, or was it a prescribed ritual display, in its form, timing, and limitation to the specified setting? It may have been both, particularly if I could agree that my identity was indeed "French," as my host was sure it had to be, and if it was so organized as to represent itself in exactly the manner that the display suggested. If it had not been, or if I had rejected the anthropological discipline of accepting whatever the people I knew constructed for me, then of course I might have had a problem that may have led to my withdrawing or being rejected. Other symbols of identity were in fact more central to participation than was ethnic origin: my friends were quite sure that I could not possibly wish to wear the suit and tie I wore on a Sunday to go to Presbyterian or Methodist services: I had no choice but to wear blue jeans and T-shirts into which I dutifully changed. In either cases, the dress-in-setting was supposed to express "my" self, and to insist on anything else was suspect.[14] Besides dress, alcohol and drug consumption, style of partying, before and after a party behavior, and so forth, all were interpreted as expressions of identity that were also markers of my identity: in secularized puritanism, one knows a person through his symbolic works.

Let us look at another, less local, case. It is well known, though somewhat embarrassing to many Americans (those currently using the interpretive structures provided by America), that color is an all or nothing affair in political identification, whether in terms of interpersonal matters, local politics, or the most public and least local of settings. A person is or is not "Black." There is no room in Congress for a caucus of "half-breeds," "octoroons," and other categories of racial intercourse that were quite developed in earlier Americas. This directly contravenes the understanding of blood descent so well analyzed by Schneider (1968).[15] In a recent issued of *Ebony* (April 1993), Randolph, a journalist for a magazine closely identified with the Black experience in America,[16] frames a feature article about the actress Halle Berry as a tale of adversity confronted, dealt with, and eventually recompensed, first by professional, and then personal success. The key is set in an opening sentence: "Although her memorable roles in a string of hit movies . . . have made her the hottest Black actress in Hollywood, this daughter of a White mother and a Black father would be the first to tell you she has led an uneasy life." This is immediately expanded by a mention of her "identity": "Her internal turmoil started early in life, largely because of the confusion about her racial identity." This is followed by stories of prejudice in a predominantly White high school, and culminates with something that is first treated as coercion, and then transformed into a personal, existential, choice that was the only proper one to the very extent that it was predetermined. This is told in reported speech that emphasizes that we are indeed hearing Halle Berry's voice (rather than that of some journalist):

> My mother cleared it up for me when I was very young. She said when you look in the mirror you are going to see a Black woman.

You're going to be discriminated against as a Black woman so ultimately in this society, that's who you will be. And that's made my life very easy ... I *needed* to make a choice and feel part of this culture. I feel a lot of pride in being a Black woman. (emphasis in the original)

An ironic reading is tempting, particularly if one emphasizes the unacknowledged contradictions in talk about discrimination, a life made easy, and choice. Berry's story could be told as one of possibly tragic, and certainly pathetic, coercion. First a "realist" White mother, then peers in high school, and then a whole society (Hollywood casting agents and directors, editors of *Ebony* looking for a prominent person to sketch who would be considered Black by everyone, etc.), all held Halle Berry to being "Black." In the process, the crowd who produced the tale make culture a matter of self-determination.

My goal here is not to play the irony game. We have no choice but to take seriously actresses and magazine editors who, through whatever personal, political, or commercial processes, did not write Berry's tale on the collective mode.[17] One should recognize the possibility that all the people involved here may, at times, be existentially aware that culture (race, ethnicity) is not a matter of choice. One should also face the fact that they may not easily find the words, and the space to say them, to affirm that one "is" never quite Black or White but that, in America, one inevitably will be *identified* as one or the other. In America, one must even assume this identification personally: One must "feel part" of the assigned culture that must be "one's own" culture. In America, one must *be* American.

AMERICA IN CONVERSATION

Understanding America as the historical remnants of old constructions, that newcomers, children or immigrants, find on their way as they build their own lives is but a first step in understanding the process of a life in the United States. In the brief analyses of the processes of racial identification I conducted, I used the verb of obligation, if not coercion: "must." Theoretically, this *must* is to be understood as "is accountable to."[18] Halle Berry was held accountable by her mother, her peers, and Hollywood, to being Black—she could not *ignore* that all these people were doing to her and with her. She could have *refused* the identification through specific actions that would always have had consequences. She would have had to pay a price since very few persons, and certainly not any person of consequence, would have accepted a self-identification as "White."[19] Similarly, I, in the round of introductions I evoked earlier, could not prevent my hosts from dramatizing the Melting Pot Myth, but I could, as I continue to do, refuse to "pledge allegiance." There is a distinction to be made here. An American in Japan cannot ignore the Emperor; a Japanese in America cannot ignore the skepticism toward any tradition. Neither has to accept the conditions of their everyday life as the right way to be in the world, and they may even work at changing what they find themselves conversing with.

Indeed, when one looks at the history of the United States, and this is true of the history of any society, one never sees simple habitual acceptance and mechanical repetition of old truths. From the earliest, in the seventeenth century already, the smallest communities were racked by dissension about the appropriate means of institutionalizing the messianic space that had opened on the Western shores of the Atlantic Ocean. The War of Independence had many aspects of a civil war. One hundred years later an even more violent war was fought precisely on the grounds of the relationship with possible others who were also coinhabitants, and coparticipants, of the same social space. The slaves were no longer Africans who could be returned to their old country; neither could they be removed to a reserve and given the ambiguous autonomous status that was given to those human beings who used the land before other human beings moved across the Atlantic. Through Reconstruction, the major burst of immigration at the turn of the century, and now through what may be another major burst, things were never settled. People struggled with each other and the traditions that already organized the landscape. But they had no choice but to respond to, and then use, these traditions for their own purposes, whether aggressively (in the first generations of a new migration) or defensively (later on). Immigrants may not melt, but they have no choice except to enter in conversation with everyone else and, in these conversations, to use the only mythical language that is efficacious in an American context: the language of the socially constituted self ("*I am* a so-and-so") with particular rights ("as such *I am* entitled to . . ."). In this conversation, such a call is responded to with a recognition of the call to a self ("indeed *you are* a so-and-so") and then with a reminder of a long list of responsibilities ("You must respect other selves in the manner in which you hope they will respect you"). In America one may have any self one may develop, but the relationship with other selves, in myth and political discourse, is fully regulated.

The Myth of the Melting Pot somewhat hides the principle of its constitution by emphasizing the agency of the individuals caught together on the streets of New York City, and silencing the institutions that organize life there— from the grid pattern that one inherits from eighteenth-century rationalism, to the speeches of journalists and politicians talking about "mosaics." The mosaic metaphor goes further in this process by emphasizing the constituted self (rather than the active one), and de-emphasizing the continual and intimate intercourse of different selves with each other—the strength of the melting pot image. The mosaic metaphor, instead, emphasizes boundaries, and encourages boundary-maintaining activities (uni-ethnic parades, but also block voting, and also perhaps gangs enforcing the purity of one's enclave). The salad bowl metaphor seems a sarcastic one, particularly if one thinks about what happens to salad once it has stayed in a bowl for a few hours. Eventually, however, all these images reconstruct a particular world of universal import—though perhaps not quite the way Thomas Paine intended it when he wrote in the introduction to *Common Sense*, "The cause of America is in a great measure the cause of all mankind" ([1776] 1976: 63). All cultures are of universal import in their very particularity, but only America has found itself at the time and place whence it might diffuse itself around the globe in little more than two centuries.

ACKNOWLEDGMENTS

This essay is the fruit of many experiences and conversations. I am particularly grateful for the understanding and resistance I received from Milton Singer, Phyllis Chock, Carol Greenhouse, René Arcilla, and R. P. McDermott.

NOTES

1. I mean "great version" somewhat like Redfield's talking about Great Traditions. His distinction between "folk society" and "civilization" ([1953] 1962) may be read, in modern jargon as a distinction between "popular" and "hegemonic" cultures (Fiske, 1989)—as long as we keep in mind that the distinction is an analytic one: in the everyday life of people, whether in villages or capital cities, material from both poles are always both resources and constraints.

2. The argument is an expansion of the Chock's work on the "redaction" of ethnicity (1980, 1981, 1989).

3. I am self-consciously using the masculine pronoun here to emphasize the hegemonic aspect of this myth on both men and women. Some have wanted to distinguish the "reality" of individualism to the "reality" of community by seeing the former as "masculine" and the latter as "feminine" (Johnstone, 1990). I see them as mutually constructed within a larger interactional context in which male voices have always been very loud.

4. Indeed, it is only modern conventions about nation-states that makes it commonsensical to deal with Japan as if it were *one* society. There would be much historical reason to think of it, as part of a larger, and quite heterogeneous group, made up (to simplify) of China, Korea, and Japan. Since the Meiji era perhaps, and certainly since the end of World War II, Japan's "society" is a pole within a "world system" in which the United States is a dominant participant.

5. The same line of argument was used when people of different denominations met formally in "community" services. Difference (between Presbyterians, Anglicans, Methodists, Baptists, etc.) was stressed and then encompassed symbolically.

6. From the point of view of a theory of culture as ordered conversation, what is interesting in the famous passage that legislated that slaves in the Southern States be counted as two-thirds persons, is that it was eventually deleted as the stress on the universality of the principle was reaffirmed, with overwhelming force, during the Civil War.

7. For those who would prefer a more recent example from a popular medium, another example might be the film *Mississippi Massala* in which the daughter of an Indian family who escape from massacre in Uganda, falls in love and elopes with the son of a Black family. Like Zangwill's play, *Mississippi Massala* moves from naive love, to the recognition of familial and community opposition, to the recognition of personal prejudice, to the overcoming of first this prejudice, and then the more general one as at least some of the communities recognize the illegitimacy of their attempts to control their children. The last images of the film are of the couple moving into their own future, away from both their old countries.

8. I adopt here Louis Dumont's analysis (1991) of German nationalism as developed in the nineteenth century as prototypical of an ideology that evolved in reaction to the French enlightenment in its universalism.

9. The dramatic fate of W. I. Thomas at the hand of his peers at the University of Chicago (Capetti, 1989) underscores that, whatever one may think of the theories of socialization and enculturation that his sociological tradition developed, one must not see in them nativist theories.

10. In a classic Western movie such as "Shane," both the heroes (Shane as the flawed savior, and the family that temporarily adopts him) and antiheroes (the rancher and his hired hand, the store owner) are unmarked ethnically. The people whom Shane saves, however, are marked through accent, dress, or favorite music.

11. Sollors points out how Erickson dedicated *Childhood and Society* ([1950] 1970) "TO OUR *children's children*" (Erickson's multiple emphases). Margaret Mead, in her little book on the 1960s (1970), celebrated a new kind of third generation that was coming to adulthood at that time: they were "prefigurative" people that who were at work building a radically new world in which their parents were immigrants. The often noted glorification of abstract childhood (and the neglect of actual children) in

American culture would thus seem to be rooted at the deepest ideological level. Parents, that is actual America, will always be "second generation" in relation to the children's "third," and the real America is still to be constructed.

12. W. Penn himself returned to Europe at the end of his life, taking with him a project for the creation of the United States of Europe for which his Pennsylvania was considered to be a precursor. He, too, may have been a dissatisfied immigrant (De Rougemont, 1961: 100–105).

13. The use of the labels can be overinterpreted however. Moynihan himself argued persuasively for the inclusion of a question about self-identification in ethnic terms that is in fact the subject of one of the papers in this collection. As Yanow argues in this collection, the drawing of the choices made available to the people—and the problems raised by people as they answer them—is evidence that the matter is not a simple one of reflecting realities. Most American ethnic realities (children of marriages between people of different groups, people who belong to groups that can legitimately claim two positions—Black and Hispanic, for example, or people who insist on calling themselves "American," etc.) cannot in fact be measured through the questions.

14. What would have been even more suspect, if it had been widely known, was my apparently equally enthusiastic participation in both settings. Which, could I have been asked by a suspicious native, was my "real" self, with whom was I really in community? The serious form of this question centers on the issue of nationality. Eventually, a resident of the United States "must" recognize a new identity, ask for the status of citizen, and pledge allegiance to the flag—freely.

15. As Schneider showed, American kinship is implacably bilateral: one is equally the child of both parents and inherit equally whatever properties are deemed to descend through blood. There is no "choice" possible here. There is no space in this system for a blood characteristic like color to be assigned unilaterally. Thus Judaic theories about the primary role of the mother, and any other unilateral theory of descent, must be suspect. This mechanistic system, however, contravenes democratic principles of choice and transcendence. Schneider begins to deal with this when discussing "love" ("diffuse and enduring solidarity"). One must go must further: blood may be stronger than water, but love (free movement toward another person) transcends them all.

16. See the essay by Urciuoli in this collection for a discussion of a similar magazine identified with the Hispanic experience.

17. The whole episode fits in the "dramatic" moment in the Melting Pot Myth of which I talked earlier: the heroine has taken on "her" group, she is proud of it, and is ready to fight for it. Without an ulterior recognition of the common humanity of members of all groups and their equivalence, this narrative moment would become the pretext to a tragedy, or a way of interpreting an actual tragic occurrence.

18. The reference here is to the work of ethnomethodologists (Atkinson and Heritage, 1984; Garfinkel, 1967).

19. The situation is not so far-fetched given the apparent refusal by some Spanish speaking immigrants from the Caribbean to have anything to do with Blackness, whatever the color of their skins.

Chapter 3

The Hypervisible and the Masked: Some Thoughts on the Mutual Embeddedness of "Race" and "Class" in the United States Now

Daniel A. Segal

> *My purpose has been to attempt to conceive of a deliberative process in which racism does not control all outcomes.*
> —Lani Guanier (1991a: 1154)
>
> *[Race] is both an empty category and one of the most destructive and powerful forms of social organization*
> —Michael Rustin
> *(quoted in Morrison 1993: ix)*

The day after the birth of our first child, I was at home speaking by telephone to my wife, who had remained in the hospital. A form required by the State of California to obtain a birth certificate had been brought to her to sign. Someone at the hospital had filled out most of the required information, including our daughter's *race*. She was "Caucasian." Later when I examined the form, I found that the request had been for either *race or ethnicity*.

For my wife and me, as for many people, the birth of a child was something of a utopian moment. We wanted everything to be right for our daughter. This meant, among other things, that we wanted her to live in a postracial world. And thus, in a fit of unrealistic desire, reflecting a position of white privilege, we decided to cross out "Caucasian" and substitute "human." The hospital staff—we were never sure who made the decision—corrected our error, and returned the form with "Caucasian" typed in once again. I responded with pedagogic tricks borrowed from my experience teaching about racial ideologies. I asked them how they would answer the question for a child with one black parent and one white parent. "Black," I was told. Then I asked whether they believed that such a child was somehow more similar and closer to the black parent than to the white parent, and whether the child was a different race than its white parent. Such arguments had no place in the hospital, where practical affairs (including both genuine medical needs and various bureaucratic exigencies) demanded constant attention. Most likely more frustrated than enlightened, the hospital staff made a call to "Sacramento," that is, to whoever in California's capital city had real authority on these matters. "Race or ethnicity," they were told, is a matter of parental self-reporting. If the parents provided "human" then "human" it was. And so it came to pass that my daughter, Hannah Rebecca, became the first human born in California.[1]

A friend writes: "Recently, our college was hiring a historian. The documents in one finalist's file, and particularly the focus of her research, had established that she was African-American. As a result, information about the candidate was shared with the Black Studies department, which made plans to grant her a secondary appointment, should she be hired for the open position in history. When the candidate arrived for her on-campus interview, however, she was clearly white. The error in prior identification produced confusion and consternation. For instance, one of my African-American colleagues asked a white colleague on the search committee: *'When you talked to her on the phone, did she sound black?'* Hearing of this query provoked another African-American colleague to ask rhetorically: *'How can one respond to such a question?'* "

REPRODUCING/CONTESTING THE OBJECTIVITY OF "RACES"

Most of us who live in the United States today are regularly asked to classify ourselves and others by "race." And as my second ethnographic vignette illustrates, we often do this through inferences based on essentialized notions—for instance, that a person's research topic or their voice reveals that they are or are not a particular race. My concern in this essay is with the problematic of answering such questions, given the established anthropological view that distinct human races do not exist.[2] How can we answer such questions—ordinary requests to identify a person's "race"—in ways that contest and work through, rather than reproduce, our belief in the reality of distinct human races? I want, in short, to look for ways of deploying (or rejecting) terms of racial identity that might fruitfully disrupt and unsettle the entrenched objectification and naturalization of racial distinctions.

In the United States today, many of our encounters with official requests for racial identities are a legacy, most immediately, of the civil rights movements of the 1960s. For the purpose of redressing ongoing discrimination, we note and record the "race" of applicants, voters, citizens, and elected officials. Neoconservative intellectuals have taken much sanctimonious pleasure in deriding this attention to race on behalf of progressive goals, and they have argued that these practices should be replaced with "color-blind" record-keeping and evaluations. This is, in effect, to call for a taboo on acknowledging race, as if an imposed silence will somehow make racism disappear. Such a view is at best painfully naive and, more often than not, cynical and manipulative. While it is true that much of our race-talk does indeed reproduce and reinforce racial distinctions, silence about race has the same effect, since it does nothing to disturb our entrenched, racializing habits of thought and action.

The impotence of silence in the context of a highly racialized social world can be seen by returning to the site of my first ethnographic vignette, the maternity ward. In the United States today, there are significant correlations between infant mortality and racial status: the infant mortality rate *for persons identified* as African-American is more than double that *for persons identified* as whites.[3] This is a substantial, rather than merely a tautological, statistic. It is not that the social practice of the racial identification of persons is based somehow on their "rate of infant mortality." Rather, persons who are identified in racial terms differently are, on this basis, treated differently in U.S. society, and this differential treatment results in the more frequent death of black, brown, and red babies compared to white babies. This painful difference in life chances cannot be challenged or redressed unless it is first something we *represent*. And clearly, this requires that we be noisy, rather than silent, about race. More specifically, it requires that we permit the recording of the "race" of at least a statistical sampling of newborn children. This is, of course, something that I, as a new father, resisted when I crossed out "Caucasian." In general terms, to become silent about race at this historical moment is to be silent about race at a time when racial distinctions remain, to invoke Michael Rustin's formulation, "one of the most powerful forms of social organization" (Rustin quoted in Morrison, 1993: ix). This is not at all the same as being silent about race in a social world free of racial distinctions, and neoconservative calls for silence about race evade this important difference.

We should not, then, regard all race-talk as suspect. Rather, we should focus more specifically on a pervasive feature of our race-talk: the common custom of *abstracting* racial identities from other determinants of life chances in contemporary society, and in particular from "class." To speak and write about race as if it exists on its own—independent of, say, the organization of production—is one of the ways we tell ourselves, over and over again, that race is a natural, rather than a social, property. In short, the habit of abstracting race has the effect of objectifying race.

As an initial example of this, let us return once more to the form required of new parents by the State of California. To see how the form commits an abstraction of race, it is useful to consider what questions went unasked on the form—or, in other words, what silences accompany this public fuss about a baby's "race." Let us note, to begin with, that there was no query about the "class position" of either the child or the parents. Yet surely, just as information about the correlation of rates of infant mortality with racial identities is crucial for understanding U.S. society today, so too is information about the correlation of those rates with class position. We cannot, then, reduce this absence to an instance of "practical reason" or medical "rationality." Rather, we must regard the State of California form for newborn babies as an instrument that effectively disjoins racial identity and class—which is to say it is an instrument that abstracts them from each other.

From this perspective, consider an alternative answer that is much wilder —much "wronger"—than the one my wife and I provided. Imagine that my wife and I had written "bourgeoisie" or "intelligentsia" instead of "human" to report our daughter's "race or ethnicity": How, then, might "Sacramento" have responded? My own guess, as a native informant, is that the bureaucrat who answered the phone in Sacramento would have been less likely to grant us the power of parental "self-reporting" had we responded in this fashion. The awkwardness of identifying a newborn baby as "bourgeoisie" or "intelligentsia" reveals a fundamental disparity between "class" and "identity" as these notions are culturally constituted in the United States today. "Identity" in the United States is not merely that which identifies a person at a particular moment. It is more than an effective indexical, more than a way of pointing at one person among many. Rather, a person's "identity" is something retained from birth (and before) to tombstone (and after). It is this "personal identity" that makes a person at age 70 and at birth "one and the same person," that is, which establishes the *abstract* equalness of the senior and the newborn.[4] Thus, the effect of eliciting information about a newborn's "race or ethnicity" is to discipline possible answers, restricting them, at the very least, to the cultural domain of "identity." This restriction precludes attention to factors outside of the domain of identity. It thereby operates to disconnect or abstract these factors from "race or ethnicity."

The form does, of course, place "race or ethnicity" within a larger set of questions, and thereby supports the possibility of representing statistical relationships between "race or ethnicity" and other variables. For instance, the form also elicited the baby's "sex" and the names of its biological "father" and "mother." But these are also properties of "identity," that is, properties culturally defined as pan-life-cycle constants and not as shifting and contingent aspects of personhood. Moreover, these other properties suggest an important, overall quality of the domain of "identity," for they are epitomizing instances of "the natural," as it is culturally defined (Schneider, 1980 [1968]). At one and the same time, then, the form disjoins "race or ethnicity" from relevant variables (e.g., "class") that are not visibly "natural," while connecting "race or ethnicity" to those that are. Looking at the form as a whole thus suggests that "race or ethnicity" is figured as an element of "nature" and *thereby abstracted from "the social."*

By contrast, let us imagine the rhetorical effects (or in linguistic terms, the *pragmatics*) of a form that did enable the production of statistics showing the relationship between infant mortality and *both* racial identities and class positions. Were such variables systematically brought together in statistical portraits of U.S. society, it might convey the sense that racial identity (figured as comparable and thus analogous to class position) was something other than a natural, objective fact, and that class position (figured as comparable and thus analogous to racial identity) was, contrary to U.S. mythology, a powerful determinant of life-chances. It might, in short, suggest the paradigmatic equivalence of that which is hypervisible and naturalized ("race") and that which is masked and social ("class").

By contrast, in both popular and scholarly portraits of U.S. society, the more frequently encountered pairing of statistics involves "race" and "sex"—which was, of course, a pairing enabled by the State of California's form for newborns. This pairing works rhetorically in a very different way from the one I have imagined above, for both variables are facilely construed as "natural," given their cultural definition in the United States. Let us consider, for instance, popular understandings of the hypervisible correlation between poverty among African-Americans and the poverty among female-headed households. Regrettably, the widespread circulation of this statistical correlation has not resulted in any notable consciousness of the *social* relationships that determine the distribution of wealth. Rather, mass media reports of this correlation suggest and sustain hypernaturalized accounts of the causes of poverty: specifically, accounts that locate the source of poverty in "family structure" and in the clichéd typification of "the black man" as overly masculine, overly sensual, and inadequately socialized—in a word, as *hypernatural*. In this imaginary, the organization of production, not to mention the availability of jobs, simply does not enter the picture.[5]

It is worth noting a general point here: even when they are "true," the statistics that circulate in modern, democratic societies are never simply matter-of-fact, factual matters. Rather they are always motivated, meaningful, and consequential, as is clear when we place them in the context of statistics that are absent.[6]

THE EMBEDDEDNESS OF "RACE" AND "CLASS"

As previously noted, neoconservative voices in the United States increasingly avow a desire to invert the hypervisibility of "race"—that is, to render "race" hypovisible, if not invisible. Consider, for example, the following instance of "public opinion," a broadcasted response to a news story on "environmental racism" that had previously been aired on National Public Radio's "Morning Edition":

> My name is Brad Curley. I live in Dallas, Texas. I was listening to your story this morning on environmental racism. I'm calling because the report was misleading. The story supported the view of some groups of color claiming racism as a reason industrial polluters were located in their neighborhood. But let's be realistic—the reasons industrial facilities are located in areas where people [of color live] are due to zoning and economics, not racism. Unfortunately, only people with lower incomes live in those areas, and many lower-income people are of color. If the story were presented based on economics, people would understand that while the situation was perhaps unfair, it was a fact of life. Thank you. ("Morning Edition," September 15, 1993: 7)

Here the speaker asks us to focus on economics and to discount race. Employing a by now classic move of 1990s neoconservatism, Brad Curley decries the hypervisibility of race and enjoins silence about it. But this inversion fully honors, and reproduces, the separation and mutual abstraction of race and economic status. Moreover, in accounting for residential patterns, Curley deploys a notion of economic status that assumes that existing economic stratification is an inevitable "fact of life." Thus, the attempt to make race invisible does not contest its objectivity; rather, the switch to economics objectifies inequality and thereby supports a fatalistic legitimation of the status quo, inclusive of both race and class stratification.

Ironically, such an abstraction of race from class is characteristic of many of the legal remedies to racism adopted in the aftermath of the Civil Rights movement of the 1960s and now opposed by neoconservatives. A recurring principle of U.S. post–civil rights law is the legal (and cultural) concept of "representation," as in the phrase "underrepresented group." In terms of this legal concept, racism is understood as having produced nonrandom distributions of persons of different "races" in occupations, economic strata, etc. This makes racism a phenomenon that can be measured and known statistically. And in our courts, statistical portraits of under- and over- "representation" are typically used both to argue for, and to structure, affirmative action plans. By these statistical measures, a social order is adequately just once all "races" are proportionately "represented" in all occupations, economic strata, legislative bodies, and so on.

What is problematic about this as a way of modeling and representing racism is that racism does more than produce nonrandom distributions of persons of different races. To define racism in terms of the legal concept of "representation" is quite properly to recognize that racism unfairly situates persons in our social order. Yet at the same time, this construction of racism fails to capture the complex ways racism shapes the social division of labor, the extent of income stratification, and so forth—or to put the matter most concisely, it fails to capture the ways racism shapes "classes." Racism does not only unfairly assign persons to social positions. It also structures the positions themselves: it structures our political economy. We would find a significantly different constellation of class relations (in the United States and throughout the world) were laboring and underemployed persons not divided and disadvantaged by invented racial distinctions (Allen, 1994; Du Bois, 1962 [1935]; Martinez-Alier, 1989; Morgan, 1972; Roediger, 1991; Saxton, 1990; and Segal, 1990). To construe racism as a problem of under- and over- "representation" in existing social positions is, in effect, to treat it not as a structural aspect of our political-economy, but as an independent variable— once again, as an abstraction.[7]

The practice of abstracting "race" that occurs in common legal remedies for racial discrimination can be seen clearly if we compare affirmative action and comparable worth remedies. Today, affirmative action is positioned by neoconservatives as something radical, but we need to recall that throughout the 1970s and early 1980s, U.S. courts generally rejected comparable worth remedies, while finding affirmative action programs acceptable. We should then consider the possibility that comparable worth remedies are a form of redress that, by comparison to affirmative action, represented a more thorough and radical transformation of the established social order, or at least of those elements of the established social order that the courts were concerned to keep in place.

In contrast to affirmative action programs, comparable worth remedies make no direct attempt to alter the distribution of persons of different races in different occupations; rather, comparable worth programs attempt to re-value—which is to say, restructure—different occupations. The underlying assumption is that occupations in which subordinated persons are disproportionately represented have, concomitantly, been undervalued and disempowered. In this view, to cite an often used example, the low pay and status of nursing should be remedied, since as a disproportionately female occupation, nursing has been devalued.

Now because the most often discussed examples of comparable worth remedies involve gender, as does my own example, many progressive social theorists have argued that comparable worth remedies do not respond to racial discrimination. But this criticism of comparable worth rests, I believe, on the prevalent tendency to abstract "race" from its complex embeddedness in social life—in this instance, from patterns of gender discrimination. Commenting more generally on images and narratives of "discrimination" in legal discourse, Kimberlé Crenshaw has written:

> Underlying the legal parameters of racial discrimination are numerous narratives reflecting discrimination as it is experienced by black men, while the underlying imagery of gender discrimination incorporates the experiences of white women . . . The terms of racial and gender discrimination law require that we mold our experience into that of either white women or black men. (1992: 404; see also Hooks, 1991; P. Williams, 1991)

From this perspective, to argue that comparable worth would be a remedy for discrimination on the grounds of gender, but not race, is to ignore the concrete intersection of these categories. And this intersection involves more than the fact some women are persons of color, for it is particularly women of color who are overrepresented in some of the most devalued occupations that are conventionally labeled "female." Perhaps, then, we should say that comparable worth addresses race-gender discrimination in the formation of classes, rather than *abstract* gender discrimination or *abstract* race discrimination (see also Shrage, 1987).

In contrast to comparable worth, affirmative action remedies for racial discrimination are concerned with altering the representation of persons of different race in various positions, but not in revaluing and restructuring those positions. In the short term, this has produced the paradoxical sense that great strides have been made and very little has changed. If we look at certain high-status occupations—particularly, if we look selectively—there are indeed statistically significant increases in the "representation" of persons of color over the last 30 years. Hence, the observation that great changes have taken place, since it is precisely such statistical portraits that are taken as measures of discrimination. Yet because so very few persons of color were in such elite occupations thirty years ago, significant increases in the number of persons of color in these occupations can occur without there being any significant decrease in the percentage of persons of color who work in the lowest paying jobs or live in the miserable conditions of the urban lumpenproletariat. Hence, the observation of stasis (cf. Thelwell, 1992; 88–89).

In theory, continued progress in rates of upward mobility should, in the long term, also alter the overrepresentation of persons of color in the underclass. Yet it seems to me that we have good reason to be skeptical about this liberal dogma that asks us, yet again, to wait for justice. If racism structures our political-economy, then there cannot be a nonracial distribution of persons in occupations, income strata, and so on, *without a substantial transformation of the political economy*—and vice versa, there can be no substantial transformation of the political economy without altering racism.

As an illustration of this point, let us consider again the example of "environmental racism," a phenomena so vehemently denied by Brad Curley. Impoverished persons of color reside where they reside because of both race and class barriers. And some of the barriers that were historically expressed in the idiom of race—for example, laws establishing segregated neighborhoods—now exist as class barriers expressed in the idiom of price. Even if banks and real estate agents were suddenly to end their discriminatory practices, class barriers would make it difficult for the residents of poor neighborhoods to leave both those neighborhoods and their poverty. And since those residents are disproportionately persons of color, risk of exposure to toxic air and water would, as a result, continue to be correlated with race—precisely because, at our historical moment, race is inextricably a matter of class, just as class is inextricably a matter of race. Patterns of racial inequality cannot be addressed purely, or abstractly, as a matter of racism, for they are replicated in ostensibly race-neutral class relations. And vice versa, the constellation of classes in the United States cannot be addressed purely, or abstractly, as a matter of the organization of production, for this constellation of classes is functionally dependent on racism.

Nothing in this argument supports the view that the injuries of "class" are somehow more real or more important than the injuries of "race."[8] And it should be clear that I am certainly not suggesting that talk about racism should be replaced by talk about class oppression. To the contrary, my point is that racial distinctions and class positions are structuring aspects of each other—or better, of a larger constellation of stratification in the contemporary U.S.—and must, therefore be dealt with together. We must refuse, in short, to choose between "race" and "class," as we have so often been asked to do.

NOTES

Acknowledgments: Thanks to the participants in the "Democracy and Difference" conference for their stimulating comments and criticisms following the oral presentation of this essay; thanks especially to Carol Greenhouse and Davydd Greenwood for the invitation to participate in this conference, and to Carol Greenhouse for taking such good editorial care of my manuscript.

1. Domínguez (1986) examines the history of state-controlled racial classification on birth certificates in Louisiana.

2. Works claiming a "scientific" basis for our racial categories have emerged again and again throughout the twentieth century, even though they have—at least since the antiracist work by Boas and DuBois—failed to meet the most basic criteria for scientific publishing. That is, new works of "scientific racism" have failed to present either (1) a new argument, (2) new evidence, or (3) responses that genuinely engage their critics. Were professional standards of scholarship applied in this area, such new works of "scientific racism" would be rejected by editors. Consistent with this history of almost obsessive repetition, the responsorial refutations of these pseudoscientific works inevitably, and quite properly, reproduce the arguments against racial formalism masterfully formulated at the beginning of the twentieth century by Franz Boas and W. E. B. DuBois. For Boas's admirably open-minded exploration of "racial formalism," see the essays collected in Boas (1940: esp. pp. 3–195). Benedict (1934) represents a powerful and historically influential formulation of the "Boasian" refutation of the belief in the objective existence of distinct human races. Stocking (1968: chs. 6 and 8) provides a singularly valuable intellectual history and synthesis of Boas's work on race, as well as its impact on other scholars and beyond. For DuBois's critiques of "scientific racism" and his anticipation of much recent scholarship on the social construction of racial groupings and identities, see in particular DuBois (1968 [1940]: ch. 5). For important work that has initiated a renewed appreciation of DuBois's place in intellectual history as a theorist, see Harrison (1992). On the affinities and divergences between DuBois and Boas, see Baker (1994) and Liss (1998). Barkan (1992) provides a useful history of the scientific debate over "race" in the twentieth century, though I would depart from even the limited sense of closure on scientific racism implied by his narrative.

3. The National Center for Chronic Disease Prevention and Health Promotion (1995) reports that in 1991, the infant mortality rate among "whites" was 7 per 1,000 live births, whereas for "blacks" it was 18 per 1,000 live births.

4. For a comparison with a conception of personhood that heightens discontinuity through a lifetime, see Geertz's masterful analysis of personhood in Bali (1973).

5. The classic source for linking African-American poverty to "family structure" is the so-called Moynihan Report, actually entitled *The Negro Family, The Case*

for National Action (1967). For a powerful critique of this view, see R. T. Smith (1996: chs. 4, 6, 9, 11; and n.d.).

      6. For related work on popular knowledge and understanding of statistics about "ethnic" groupings, see Segal (1993a, 1993b).

      7. Guanier (1991b) makes related criticisms of the emphasis on "representation" in the implementation of the Voting Rights Act. She argues that these have produced an increase in "minority representation," without an increase in response to "minority interests" (1458). In effect, then, Guanier argues that the remedies that have been developed from the Voting Rights Act have succeeded in abstracting "minorities" from their "interests," for in her view the former are represented in the absence of the latter.

Moreover, Guanier criticizes available legal remedies under the Voting Rights Act for being concerned with race alone. In their stead, she seeks remedies that would ensure the representation of the "self-identified interests" of minorities (1458), and she explicitly acknowledges that her remedies are likely to replace primarily racial voting patterns, with the formation of voting coalitions that are not neatly or solely racial, but that are fluid and shifting. Quite obviously, there is no legitimate basis for her vilification as "Clinton's quota Queen," though perhaps the success of this misrepresentation indicates how intensely threatening the possibility of nonracial voting is to neoconservatives.

      8. Much in this final paragraph has appeared, in a somewhat different form, in Segal and Handler (1995); neither essay really "precedes" the other, since their authoring overlapped. For a related discussion, see Sacks (1989).

Chapter 4

Democracy and Cultural Difference in the Spanish Constitution of 1978

Jesús Prieto de Pedro

It is a difficult challenge for a jurist to speak to anthropological experts about their own subject matter—culture—as an object of legal regulation, but the stimulus to contribute to an interdisciplinary dialogue makes this challenge an attractive one.

I will analyze the treatment of cultural difference in the present Spanish Constitution (1978). We will consider the linguistic evolution of the constitutional text; such texts are condensed juridical language, something like a scale model of the juridical organization of a country. But first, to facilitate our dialogue, I want to clarify my lexical-semantic approach to the subject, and make some general observations about public sector actions in relation to culture, as well as other issues surrounding the models used in taking those actions.

THE CONSTITUTIONAL THEME OF CULTURE

As a starting point, it is worth noting that the term *culture*, derived from the Latin term *colere*, originally meant "to cultivate the earth." Its present metaphorical meaning, cultivation of the spirit (*cultivo del espíritu*), was developed in the eighteenth century. This is confirmed by German and French dictionaries from that period, and especially by the first *Diccionario de la Real Academia Española de la Lengua*, called el *Diccionario de Autoridades*, published in the year 1726.[1] Thus, the character of the word's usage is relatively recent, but this does not take away from its power. "Culture"—along with the terms *industry, democracy, classes,* and *art*—expresses the social and intellectual transformations of the nineteenth century, and remains one of the most important words in the shared scientific and political vocabularies of our time (Williams, 1963: 16).

Strange as it may seem to us today, given the present importance of the term, *culture* did not appear in constitutional language until the end of the first quarter of the twentieth century. Together with all of its linguistic derivations—"cultura" in Spanish, Italian, and Portuguese; "culture" in French; "Kultur" in German—the same is true of European constitutions, as well as others. The following analysis applies to primarily, but not exclusively, to European constitutions.

Notwithstanding the fact that the constitutions of the nineteenth century regulated particular institutions and affairs of cultural relevance (education and the press, among others), they did not refer explicitly to *culture* except in very restricted and less formal contexts, for example, selected preambles and expositions of aims. For example, the Girondine constitutions of France, from 1791, include the word *culture* in the article recognizing the right to freedom at work, but did so still using the original agrarian meaning of the word: "*Nul genre de travail, de commerce, de culture ne le peut être interdit*" ("No type of work, commerce, or culture, shall be prohibited").

The 1917 Mexican Constitution is the first important constitution to use the term *culture*,[2] which subsequently appears in the German Weimar Constitution of 1919, the Peruvian Constitution of 1920, and the Polish Constitution of 1921. Nevertheless, the Spanish Constitution of the First Republic in 1931 is one of the first in which usage became more consistent, in that it uses *culture* as a title to one of the chapters detailing citizens' fundamental rights and duties: "Family, economy, and culture." From this moment on, though used only moderately, the presence of this term in constitutional texts increases, and after World War II, becomes universal: the French Constitutions of 1946 and the current constitution of 1958; the Fundamental Law of Bonn of 1947; and the Italian Constitution of 1948 (see Prieto, 1993: chapter 1).

It is only later, in the decade of the seventies, that there has been a clear acceleration in the use of this term in constitutional texts: in the Greek Constitutions of 1975, the Portuguese of 1976, the USSR Constitution of 1977 (now gone), and the Spanish Constitution of 1978. And it is in the current Spanish Constitution where—following Wittgenstein's expression—the "language game" relative to culture is particularly broad and prolix: it speaks of "culture" and of "things cultural" on numerous occasions, and uses a copious lexicon related to that family of terms: languages, art, science, literature, research, museums, libraries, archives, and music conservatories.[3]

Beyond these observations on frequencies of use, we can see two innovations in the Spanish Constitution of 1978 with respect to culture: the more precise and explicit character of the constitutional regulation of this subject, and the new status of cultural themes.

The new regulatory precision arises from the fact that the constitution registers a double notion of culture: one general and the other ethnic (or subjective). This double use is evident from the outset in the Preamble—the part of the Constitution that contains a synthesis of the whole text. There we find reference to the will of the Spanish Nation "to protect all Spaniards and the peoples of Spain in their exercise of human rights, cultures and traditions, languages and institutions . . ." (the ethnic concept of culture) and "to promote the progress of culture and the economy to assure to all a respectable quality of life . . ." (the general concept of culture). Which concept is used at any particular point depends on the exigencies of the context.

The sequence of words "political, economic, social, and cultural life," repeated completely or partially at various points in the constitutional text[4] well reflects the worldview of today's constitutional legislator—a worldview formed by the four great concepts of *the political, the social, the economic*, and the *cultural*. This is a lexical fact evident in all the constitutions ratified during the 1970s. As we compare them, it is as if we were dealing with the strata of an archeological site, in that we can see the order in which the constitutions' thematic concerns emerged.

The European liberal constitutions of the nineteenth century were political constitutions, and their consecrated rights were civil and political rights. The constitutions of the first third of the twentieth century (and in a special way the German Weimar Constitution of 1919) were devoted to economic and social issues: this creates the clause on the "Social State" and gives birth to so-called economic-social rights. Now, another stage is evidenced in the decade of the 1970s in the eruption of cultural concerns: this generates lexical forms and doctrinal categories such as "cultural rights." The term *cultural rights* is now universally used. Other terms that are in more limited, but growing, use include *cultural constitution* and the *cultural state*. The *cultural constitution* refers to a constitution that makes the principles, rules, and choices with regard to cultural materials a theoretical object, and a significant and coherent constitutional focus. The *cultural state* refers to a new stage in the evolution of the democratic state, in which the free existence of culture, cultural pluralism, and the access of citizens to culture are guaranteed in intensified forms.

THE REACH OF POLITICAL POWER

Expressions such as "cultural rights," "cultural state," or "cultural constitution" are consolidations—in legal language—of a new status of culture. They also represent a specific model of legal intervention.

The expression "cultural rights" is one now in extended use in all European legal systems, though this should not be taken to imply agreement on their definition. Even so, one finds it in constitutional law monographs in Germany, Italy, and Spain—whereas such expressions as "cultural constitution" and "cultural state" might strike the British or North Americans as unusual in the contexts with which they are most familiar.

Exactly what are these differences in language about? The core of the matter is that two models of regulation or public policy with respect to culture coexist outside of socialist countries: the English system, which is more closely tied to the classical postulates of the liberal state, and the continental European system, whose paradigm is France, a country that has known a vast development of the cultural functions of public authorities. Without doubt, this difference in approach to cultural regulation is, in and of itself, a reflection of deep cultural differences among the respective countries.

In the English model, the first thing that calls our attention is that the word "state" hardly exists in the juridical-political vocabulary. When defining the object of an intervention, they refer to the "arts" rather than "culture." England is a clear example of the survival (although updated) of a liberal ideology regarding the role of public authorities in relation to culture (Ridley, 1982). In fact, before World War II, public authorities were limited to managing some cultural institutions created as the result of private initiatives, for example, large private donations (such as the National Gallery). But these services and cultural institutions did not rely on a bureaucratic administrative organization responsible for creating unity and coherence in public policy, by means of coordinated actions—as in France.

World War II opened up this process to a greater involvement by public authorities, though without arriving at a substantive modification of the traditional bases of that relationship. During the difficult years of the war, the need to raise the fallen spirits of English society through the promotion of artistic concerts and fortify national feelings led a number of people to create, in 1940, the Council for the Encouragement of Music and the Arts (CEMA) as a private corporation supported with funds from the Parliament. The success of this organization resulted in the creation, in 1945, of the Arts Council, currently the centerpiece of an administrative organization that is only weakly coordinated by a Minister of Arts. Since this ministry does not form part of the government, it wields little political power. The Arts Council illustrates the principal of working at "arm's length" that is characteristic of the role of public power in English cultural administration. This principle was greatly eroded during the 1980s under the regime of Mrs. Thatcher, who removed some members of the boards of directors of the Council for political reasons, and cut the arts budget.

The French model is characterized by strong, organized public action on culture supported by a broad and complex administrative organization specializing in cultural services. Since 1959, this organization has its apex in a Ministry of Culture; General De Gaulle recruited the writer André Malraux to be the first occupant of that ministerial position. Under French law, cultural freedom consists not only in guaranteeing autonomy to culture but also in making that right, its promotion, and promulgation into a responsibility of the public authorities. Notwithstanding the fact that some critics classify this as the promotion of a new religion, that of the "cultural State" (Fumaroli, 1991), the French case is without doubt a highly influential paradigm for European countries.

LAW AND CULTURAL DIFFERENCE

Cultural diversity is typically manifested in one of two ways in contemporary Western societies: ethnic multiculturalism and territorial pluralism. Ethnic multiculturalism is a process that begins in immigration, by which different cultural groups coexist in the national territory. Territorial pluralism divides the state territory among diverse historical communities who are the bearers of different cultural systems. Although these two manifestations are often found together, balanced in different ways, we note that the United States and Spain are the two paradigmatic examples of each these models— ethnic multiculturalism in the United States and territorial pluralism in Spain.

Although the "objective" cultural differences between a Texan and a Californian might not be less than, for example, that between a Basque citizen and an Andalusian in Spain, it is certain that cultural difference in the United States is based, above all, on the difficult integration of the various ethnic communities that arrived in the floods of immigration that formed the United States as a nation. In Spain, too, there is also a real, increasingly vital problem of coexistence among the diverse scattered ethnic groups within its territory (e.g., the Gypsy community or the immigrants from the Magreb). Still, there is no denying that the overwhelming focal issue at the time of the writing of the Constitution of 1978 was the arbitration of a formula for political decentralization that would integrate the different cultural and linguistic realities that historically have comprised Spain.

Contemporary European states were created as diverse cultural communities under the rule *cuius regio, eius religio*.[5] In this process, culture was not a recognized element of political definition until later. The construction of the state initiated a process of reduction of diversity; cultural and linguistic homogenization responded to the need for a widely distributed culture that favored the social mobility industrial society required. It has been said that the states of the industrial era sought "the monopoly of legitimate culture, almost as much as of legitimate violence, if not more" (Gellner, 1988).

Legally, in the democratic state, solutions to this conflict have been either cultural assimilation or cultural autonomy. Cultural assimilation, undoubtedly the more frequent response, has been supported legally through majority rule (*refertur ad universes quod publica fit maiorem partem*),[6] whose effects are the progressive dissolution of the minority cultures within the cultural project supported by the numerical majority or by those who hold a dominant political position in the state.

The other solution has been the concept of so-called cultural autonomy. This term refers to formulations consisting of intensive measures of structural protection in which "not only is the intention to compensate for the minority situation, but also to abolish it partially, by endowing the ethnic group with a locus for self-determination and, above all, with organized power that makes it possible for the group to fill that self-determined space through planned programs of action" (de Witte, 1983).

Cultural autonomy can be built on a personal base or on a territorial base. Personally based cultural autonomy aims to guarantee all members of the ethnic group, regardless of their location in a territory, the development of their cultural singularity. It is an approach which, due to its intrinsic complexity, is rarely applied.[7]

Territorially based cultural autonomy designates a form of state organization (composite states including typically federal and regional states) in which the cultural dimension is given a very considerable weight separate from other factors. The configuration of the territorial division of the State (including the space given to differentiated cultural communities) and the allocation of tasks between the central authorities and the autonomous entities (of which culture is the core) are principal means by which cultural autonomy acquires a territorial aspect.

THE RECOGNITION AND PROTECTION OF CULTURAL DIFFERENCE IN THE SPANISH CONSTITUTION

In Spain, the roots of cultural diversity arose in a very early period. Undoubtedly, the singular geographical situation of this country is one basis of those origins: lying in the extreme south of Europe, bridging the European and African continents—recently separated geologically but still almost touching, with huge lateral balconies facing the Mediterranean and the Atlantic. The Iberian peoples, Phoenicians, Carthaginians, and Greeks, all arrived during the millennium prior to the Christian era. Rome achieved dominance over the lion's share of the Iberian peninsula in 133 B.C., excepting some groups in the north (Asturians and Cantabrians). At the beginning of the fifth century A.D. the waves of tribal people (Suevi, Alani, and Vandals) interrupted the profound romanization of the area, though it should not be forgotten that principal invaders, the Visigoths, were the most romanized of the Atlantic tribes.

This dense history of movement of tribal peoples also includes successive waves Germanic peoples. In the seventh century, the Arab invasion would have a decisive influence on the configuration of the cultural personality of Spain ever after, since these predominantly African peoples remained physically in the peninsula for eight centuries, until 1492 when the Catholic Kings conquered the last Moslem redoubt, the Kingdom of Granada.

This brief synthesis permits us to understand the historical bases of the cultural complexity of Spain. This diversity is not at odds with the fact that Spain is one of the most ancient sovereign Europe states. The bases of its sovereignty were created with the marriage of the Catholic Kings in 1469, a marriage that made possible the dynastic union of the Kingdoms of Castille and of Aragon. Nor should that union be taken as implying the dissolution of the cultural political personality of the various kingdoms of Spain (Aragon, Castille, Leon, Navarre, Granada) during the reign of the Habsburg house (from the beginning of the reign of Carlos I in 1516, until the arrival of the House of Bourbon in 1700).

Nevertheless, it would be wrong to deduce from this that there existed a climate of political support for cultural diversity during that time. The record of religious and racial intolerance with the sad episode of the Inquisition focused on processes of "purity of blood." With the arrival of the House of Bourbon (Felipe V, in 1700), changes took place that deepened the process of political and administrative centralization process already begun by the House of Austria. These changes continued the construction of the centralizing state, a process that included the abolition—even by the use of force—of the *fueros* (traditional regional rights) of Aragon, Catalonia, and Valencia.

With the decline of Spain, a deep internal political and economic crisis developed by the nineteenth century. With the final loss of the American colonies in 1898, the national discussion of these old cultural historical realities—in particular those of Catalonia and of the Basque Country—was reborn. This discussion eventually resulted in the democratic Constitution of the Second

Republic of 1931, in whose writing some of the great intellectuals of the era participated—such as Ortega y Gasset, Madariaga, and Unamuno. That constitution opened channels to self-government for the pluricultural reality of Spain.

But the Civil War (1936) and the dictatorial regime that stemmed from it, guided by General Franco, immediately truncated this project and began a nearly half-century period of strong political and cultural repression.

With Franco's death in 1975, the recovery of democratic freedoms necessitated addressing what was called the "national issue"—now associated with the existence of a linguistic and cultural diversity repressed by the Francoist dictatorship. It is important here to be more precise. Francoism did not repress cultural diversity per se, but culture as a whole. All the cultural wealth of Spain, its common culture, and the regional cultures, were submerged in a coarse mystification of Spanish culture composed of various folkloric Castilian-Andalusian elements.

In putting an end to the Francoist regime on December 27, 1978, the Spanish Parliament approved a Constitution that re-establishes democratic public freedoms and gives a new base for the territorial organization of the state, a base that now is plural. Abandoning the preceding centrist model, the new territorial model of the Spanish state is that of a "composite state" (known popularly as "state of the autonomies") that is organized around the following territorial levels: the state, the Autonomous Communities, the provinces, and the municipalities.

Spain, like France (with its more than 36,000 municipalities), is permitted to retain its municipal minifundism and retains somewhat more than 8,000 municipalities. These municipalities are quite unequal, with some bringing together a few score neighbors and others (e.g., the municipalities of the large metropolitan areas, such as Madrid and Barcelona) having more than four million inhabitants. The provincial organization, also taken from France and implanted in Spain in 1833, includes fifty provinces. And the final piece in this territorial puzzle is the Autonomous Communities, which number seventeen.

This state form is atypical because it is neither a federal state nor a regional state. It has come to be characterized as a "federal-regional state." In fact, in the Spanish Constitution, there is no recognition of the pre-existing states that, through a *pactum foederis*, relinquish part of their sovereignty to constitute a higher political union (as in the United States). Moreover, the autonomy of the units is not awarded by the central state (as in the regional state of Italy), rather, the creation of the autonomous entities is configured as a "right" governed by the principle of voluntarism.

The Constitution neither specified the autonomous entities nor did it draw up their territorial map. It limited itself to the recognition, in the abstract, of the existence of "nationalities" and of "regions," and their part in forming a common nation, the "Spanish nation."[8] It then fixes a procedure by which they can exercise their rights and be constituted as Autonomous Communities. The Autonomous Communities are decentralized territorial political entities (in a way similar to each of the fifty American states) that act out the self-government of the different "nationalities" and "regions" of Spain.

In the development of such constitutional provisions between 1979 and 1983, seventeen Autonomous Communities were created with their respective Autonomy Statutes. The Autonomy Statute is the fundamental law that regulates the organization of the broadest institutions of the Autonomous Community: a parliament elected by universal suffrage with wide legislative powers, a Governing Council and a Superior Court.

Guaranteeing cultural diversity is, without doubt, one of the principal purposes of this model of territorial organization for the Spanish State. In fact, culture is one of the features named explicitly by the Constitution in the concepts of "nationality" and of "region," as it defines these as territorial communities with "common historical, economic, and cultural characteristics."[9]

This reference to culture in relation to such communities no doubt has something like an anthropological meaning, since it is no more than their reflection of the notion of the "peoples of Spain"—whose cultures, traditions, languages, and institutions the Spanish Nation is committed to protect by the Preamble of the Constitution. The Preamble reads in part: "The Spanish Nation . . . proclaims its will to protect to all the Spaniards and peoples of Spain in the exercise of the human rights, their cultures and traditions, languages and institutions."

It is necessary to indicate the debt that the Spanish Constitution has to the language of the anthropology, since the phrase "peoples of Spain" is a term used by anthropological authors (notably Caro Baroja) to name the different historical and cultural communities of Spain. Similarly, anthropological language appears in the Constitution with the words "cultures, traditions, languages and institutions" with which the notion of the peoples of Spain are summarized.

In any case, it can be said that the inclusion of anthropology was fortuitous. During other parts of the discussion that accompanied the elaboration of the Constitution, other terms in the "language game" of cultural pluralism in the were strongly debated—especially the term *nationalities*, which gave rise to harsh polemics that brought the constitutive agreements needed to develop the Constitution to the verge of breakdown. The expression "peoples of Spain" was, on the contrary, peacefully accepted.

THE COMMON CULTURE

In a less direct way, the Spanish Constitution takes into account the coexistence of a common culture among all Spaniards; its promotion and dissemination is guaranteed primarily, though not exclusively, by the central state. At least implicitly, this is the treatment of the Spanish Nation as a cultural nation that predates the Consitutition. In fact, Article 2 says that it is based on the Spanish Nation, not that the Spanish Nation is based on it. Thus a common culture is specifically recognized, since that was the will of the proponents of the precept during the writing of the constitutional text; for example, reference is made to culture as a "duty and essential attribution of the State."[10] The Constitution also sanctions a language, Castilian, as the common language of all the Spaniards.[11]

THE LABYRINTH OF IDENTITIES IN SPAIN

However, the Constitution is not limited to recognizing two disconnected cultural orders, located in independent spheres. Without denying the characteristic economy of the constitutional texts, we can say that the Spanish Constitution offers both explicit and implicit answers to the complex question of the nature of that common culture. The intense and difficult historical discussion about the cultural identity of Spain, its general culture, and its particular cultures (discussion led by Ortega, Madariaga, and Sanchez Albornoz, among others) undoubtedly lurks in the quoted precepts and in the various democratic conceptions that are put forward.[12]

In effect, the Constitution contains a subtle conceptual filigree whose purpose is to provide an integrative vision of the plurality of cultures in Spain. That vision is manifested throughout the text in two different ways: one static and conceptual and the other, dynamic or processual.

From a conceptual standpoint, we can see a constant effort in the constitutional texts to break semantically with the exclusionary use of the terms *Spain* and *Spanish* and instead to refer to the national common culture with the term *Spanish culture* and to the common language with *Spanish*. In the same way, since originally the Latin etymology of *Spain* caused it to be used frequently in the plural, *Hispaniae*, the Constitution now grants an integrative and plural sense to this term, frequently repeating the "peoples of Spain" and the "languages of Spain."

This is also shown in the fact that for naming the common language, there has been a preference for the term *Castilian*, rather than the term *Span-*

ish. This decision was the focus of lively polemics, and it has provoked some critiques originating from the field of the philology, since lexically the term *Spanish* is more suitable than *Castilian* as the name of the current language. But *Castilian* was preferred because, though less frequently used, it emphasizes the historical dimension of the language. In addition, this usage makes it possible for other languages spoken in Spain to be classified as "Spanish languages."[13]

The Constitution is not limited to integrating Spanish cultural diversity conceptually. It is also occupied with fixing the normative channels processually, so that this cultural integration is not broken in the future, especially in relation to the role of the democratic public authorities who express this diversity of cultures. That is the meaning of the last paragraph of Article 149.2 of the Constitution, which imposes on the state the task of facilitating "cultural communication between the Autonomous Communities, in agreement with them."

In the face of entropy, and building on the common cultural group that is general to Spain and that might derive from the separate development of the particular cultures of the peoples of Spain, Article 149 postulates the need for dialogue and cultural exchange between the cultures that form part of that complex system. Thus, in this clause on interculturality there lies a factor of democratic nucleation toward a future common culture with respect to the operation of public authorities. It is integrative in that the base of the unit is the interactive encounter ("communication" is the operative word) of that aggregate of cultures recognized and guaranteed by the Constitution.

Without doubt, from that reciprocal influence many new possibilities for the future development of the common culture arise as an extension and affirmation of the cultures of the parts. And it is also democratic because cultural communication is not a duty imposed by the State, but a matter that is open freely to all the cultures and, through its mediation, to the Autonomous Communities. Because of this, the article states that this duty must be promoted by the State but "in agreement with them [the Autonomous Communities]."

This is the structure of a formulation that carries with it a degree of optimism—and it is not exempt from a dose of naïveté—in clashing with the exclusivist affirmations of deeply rooted nationalist sentiment. Such sentiment is to be found at the center as well as in the periphery, in some sectors of the Spanish population, especially those for whom the horizon is independence rather than integration. But that formula also expresses an idealistic and generous faith in the Spanish people's ability to build their own future while living together.

THE DISTRIBUTION OF COMPETENCIES AMONG TERRITORIAL ENTITIES

The recognition of the double dimension of culture—as a general culture common to all Spanish people and the cultures of the "peoples of Spain"— is directly reflected in the system for the constitutional allotment of tasks between the central institutions of the State and those of the Autonomous Communities. The system turns out to be complex—excessively so—since its overarching rule calls for the full concurrence of competencies of the state and of the autonomous communities. Some matters (health care, transportation, trade, agriculture, etc.) are subject to a distribution of competencies governed by the logical proposition of *inclusius unius, exclusius alterius*—which is to say, what is attributed to one entity cannot also be attributed to another at the same time. In contrast, culture is ordered by the rule of *duality* or the *parallelism* rule. Thus, while the Autonomous Communities have received competencies in the "promotion of culture," this does not mean that the state is freed from having competencies for the "service to the culture" ("promotion" and "service" are equivalent expressions according to scientific doctrine).

This rule is very clearly stated by the Spanish Constitutional Court, but it is not yet absolute since there are also exceptions:

> There is, in the end, a state competence and an autonomous community competence in the sense that, rather than a vertical allotment of competencies, what is produced is a concurrence aimed at the preservation and stimulation of the unique cultural values of the society when appropriate public claims are made.[14]

There are cultural or related matters with respect to which the Constitution has followed a normal allotment system, in as much as it reserves to the state or to the autonomous communities certain functions or aspects. This is particularly clear in issues involving cultural patrimony, the cultural repositories (museums, files, and libraries), music conservatories, and the communication media.

JUSTIFICATION OF THE DISTRIBUTION OF COMPETENCIES

Legal doctrine generally warns of the intrinsic difficulties in all allotment systems involving cultural matters, particularly when the culture concept is understood in its intangible (evanescent) anthropological sense. It has been said that culture consists of "values" and that, therefore, it cannot be fragmented or divided. It has also been claimed that the cultural unit is softer (more "douce") than other unitary competencies of the central authorities, and less necessary since the state does not lack for central competencies.

Thus, in contrast with other culturally decentralized states, such as Germany, where the general and exclusive competence for culture falls to the *Länder*,[15] the Spanish Constitution consecrates a double general competence over culture. This is consistent with the Spanish Constitution's recognition of the existence of two collective cultural orders.

In democratic countries with the tradition of taking on broad tasks in relationship to culture, an additional justification for this formulation would be the convenience of creating a multiplicity of public situations—within the same territorial space—which can neutralize the "directivist pressure" that might otherwise derive from entrusting cultural tasks exclusively to only one territorial collectivity. In any event, the natural rule—and this is what Constitutional Court also said—would be that all collective cultural expressions must be attended by the respective representative powers:

> a reflection on cultural life takes us to the conclusion that culture is both an institutional competence of the state and of the autonomous communities, and we even could add other communities, since also where a community lives, there are cultural dimensions toward which representative public structures can have competencies. (STC 49/1984)

The justification for the broad cultural competencies that local entities (municipalities and provinces) are traditionally recognized to have is found in the above quoted passage.

THE FUNCTIONALITY OF THE SYSTEM

The existence of two active public powers (the state and the autonomous communities), each simultaneously taking broad measures in favor of the promotion and development of culture, frequently gives rise to operational difficulties. And this is more serious if we also take into account the fact that municipalities and provinces, the last levels of the territorial organization of the state, tend to develop broad cultural activities that were traditionally present in the law.

Nevertheless, those difficulties express themselves in an orderly fashion through a modest level of legal conflict between the state and some autonomous communities (mainly the Autonomous Community of Catalonia) over the development of its respective competencies to legislate and administer cultural matters. The Constitutional Court, the guarantor and interpreter of the Constitution, has ruled on roughly twelve complaints—mainly referring to the film industry—with uneven juridical quality, but undoubtedly illuminating important aspects of the issues.

In effect, as has been noted by other authors and in the jurisprudence of the Constitutional Court, the composite Spanish state model places cooperation and loyalty among its essential principles. These acquire very high relief in the area of culture. Collaboration is formalized through organizational techniques (such as the creation of mixed advisory boards or management groups composed of state and Autonomous Community representatives, reserving posts for representatives of the Autonomous Communities in the associated units of the state, etc.) or through functional techniques (agreements between the state and the autonomous communities).

Cultural agreements (for the conservation of cultural patrimony, the management by the autonomous communities of museums, archives, and state-owned libraries, the construction of and restoration of cultural infrastructures, etc.) quickly experienced great development. In general, the autonomous communities have agreed to participate in them, since they have largely been channels for transferring funds from the State. In addition, the state's creation of collaborative organizations at the second level (i.e., compound organizations including those responsible for particular cultural sectors and high-level functionaries) has been a significant element in the state's cultural efforts. This has taken place through legal regulation over the past few years (e.g., in the Law of Spanish Historical Patrimony of June 16, 1985).

However, the balance is not so positive in fact as it might appear in principle, since collaboration also involves distortions and insufficiencies. In effect, the signed agreements are bilateral agreements, not general ones, between the state and each one of the autonomous communities separately. Inevitably, these favor an unequal policy as well as behind-the-scenes agreements. And while organizational collaboration is being accomplished at the technical level of cultural public service, it as yet shows little development at the higher political level. In fact, as opposed to other sectors, in those which were constituted immediately and which have been operating in a regular way, the sectoral conference established by the national government's Minister of Culture and the counselors corresponding to the Autonomous Communities took almost ten years to be constituted (in November of 1992). Up to the moment of this writing, it has not shown many signs of life. These sectoral conferences are the higher organizations for collaboration and political coordination between the state and the autonomous communities. Their agreements should be adopted unanimously, even though they are composed by the supreme political representatives of the State and of the Autonomous Communities in the sector.

OTHER CULTURAL DIFFERENCES

In contrast with the energy and detail the Constitution dedicates to the recognition and support of autochthonous cultural minorities and their articulation with the general Spanish culture, the constitutional construction of the "other" cultural differences remains quite diffuse.

For example, the Constitution contains some references to particular groups and social sectors to which it confers the status of groups with specific cultural needs; this occurs in relation to prisoners, youth, and the elderly.[16] But it maintains silence about other differentiated cultural groups, for example, the Gypsy community and immigrants. It limits itself to anticipating in generic terms that foreigners should enjoy fundamental rights in Spain as fixed in law and in treaties (art. 13.1). The Constitution also deals with the possibility of dual nationality with Ibero-American countries or with other countries that may have had a particular link with Spain (art. 11.3).

The foregoing means that the protection of the other cultural groups is entrusted to the general guarantees derived from the principle of nondiscrimination that covers all Spaniards.[17] Consequently, the protection of cultural difference in this case is channeled through the guarantees to the individual, as groups are not the object of these protections; in a negative mode, this also applies to formal equality. In fact, jurisprudence has used this principle to reject discriminatory actions of a xenophobic or racist character; thus, in an important judgment, the Constitutional Court recently said:

> In the conjunction of both constitutional values, the dignity and equality of all the persons, it is obligatory to assert that neither the exercise of ideological freedom nor the freedom of expression can permit demonstrations or expressions intended to devalue or to generate feelings of hostility against given ethnic groups, foreigners, or religious or social immigrants, since in a state like the Spanish state, in law a social and democratic entity, the members of those collectivities have the right to live together peacefully and to be respected by the other members of the social community.

That guarantee of the equality could be manifest in a "positive affirmation," as we have learned in Europe from the Supreme Court of the United States, in the so-called transformation clause taken from article 9.2:

[It] corresponds to the public powers to promote the conditions so that the freedom and equality of the individual and of the groups in which they are members will be real and effective; to remove the obstacles that hinder or prevent their fulfillment and to facilitate the participation of all citizens in political, economic, social and cultural life.

THE CONSTITUTIONAL SYSTEM OF LINGUISTIC PLURALISM

Linguistic pluralism is a particular dimension of the system of cultural pluralism. From the sociolinguistic point of view, Spain is one of the European countries with the greatest internal linguistic diversity, together with Switzerland and behind Russia. From the fragmentation of low Latin that took place in the Middle Ages there emerged, after the tenth century, a variety of romance languages. Among those that have survived as living languages are Castilian or Spanish, Catalan, and Galician. To them we add, as a fourth Hispanic language with a unique origin, Basque. And there also exist linguistic and dialect varieties of lesser prevalence (the Bable, a dying language that is spoken in Asturias; Aranés, a Gascon language whose survival is maintained in a small area in the valley of Arán; Panocho in the farmlands of Murcia, etc.).

Castilian is spoken by practically the whole the population of Spain (37 million persons) and it is the mother tongue of somewhat more than 30 million of inhabitants. Roughly seven million inhabitants have another language as a mother tongue: Catalan, spoken by half of the population of Catalonia; Mallorquín, a variety of Catalan spoken by 65% of the population of the Balearic Islands; Galician, spoken by 55% of the population of Galicia; Valenciano, spoken by 40% of the population of the Valencian Community; and Basque, spoken by 20% of the population of the Basque Country and 9% of the population of the Foral Community of Navarrre.[18]

Article 3 of the Spanish Constitution of 1978 recognizes this linguistic plurality in the following terms:

1. Castilian is the official language of the State. All the Spanish have the duty to know it and the right to use it.
2. The other Spanish languages also will be official in their respective Autonomous Communities according to their Statutes.
3. The wealth of the different linguistic modalities in Spain is a cultural patrimony that it will be object of special respect and protection.

This is a unique model for linguistic pluralism. Article 3 corresponds to neither the classical territorial formula (in which an exclusive space is reserved to each language and in which it is the only official language) nor the so-called personality model or principle (according to which citizens can be heard in the official national languages in any part of the state territory in which they find themselves).

Thus, we are dealing with a formulation with integrative intent, as was explained above, and that aims at equity, as is attested by the fact that the terms chosen use a highly culturalist vocabulary: all languages are designated equally as "languages." Moreover, this formulation is less hierarchizing than that of the previous Republican Constitution of 1931, in which the "national language" was counterposed to the "regional and provincial languages."

The current regulation implies that there exists an official language in all the territory of the state, Castilian, and a second official language, according to what the Autonomy Statutes establish in the territorial area of the Autonomous Communities with their own languages (Catalonia, Galicia, the Basque Country, Valencia, and the Balearic Community). The formulation embodies a model of co-officialdom or of dual linguistic officialdom, which presupposes an equal capacity to make public use of both languages within the Autonomous Communities. The Constitutional Court has clarified the extremely vague concept of "officialdom" saying that a language is official "independently of its reality and its weight as a social phenomenon, when it is recognized by the public authorities as a normal means of communication in and among them and in their relationships to their private citizen subjects, and given full validity and legal effects" (STC 82/1986).

Despite the greater operational difficulties, this approach has the advantage of favoring a greater respect of linguistic freedom. In effect, the core of linguistic freedom revolves around the right of the citizen to choose between one or another official language.

The Autonomous Communities with two official languages (their own and the common language, Castilian) have exercised their legislative authority in approving "laws of linguistic normalization" whose object is the recovery of the normal use of vernacular languages. As of now, the results—though not of the same scope in all languages—have supported an important recovery of the Catalan, Galician, and Basque languages in teaching, legislation, and public administration. Nevertheless, the process has not developed in a fully peaceful way, since there are still frequent "linguistic conflicts" that tend to end up in the Constitutional Court.

NOTES

1. The *Dictionnaire Universel de Antoine Furetière*, published in 1690, recognizes only the original agricultural significance of the term: "Culture: the care one takes in rendering land fertile, by labor, by amendments, to raise a tree or a plant." But a century later, the *Dictionnaire de la langue française, de Littré*, published in 1878, recognizes the modern usage. This metaphorical use was already to be found in the *Diccionario de Autoridades de la Real Academia de la Lengua Espanola*, edited in 1726, which defines culture this way: "Metaphorically, it is the care and application by which something is perfected, such as a young man's instruction, to as to illuminate his understanding." [Ed. note: All translations into Spanish are by author; English translations are based on author's versions.]

2. Article 3 of the Mexican Constitution of Querétaro, of February 5, 1917, referring to education says: "it will be democratic, considering that democracy is not only a legal structure and a political regime, but also a system of life founded on the constant economic, social and *cultural* betterment of the people . . . ; it will be national, insofar as—without conflicts nor exclusions—it will attention to the comprehension of our problems, to taking advantage of our resources, to the defense of our political independence, to the assurance of our economic independence, and to the development of our *culture*."

3. Thus, for example, articles 3 and 20 and the Final Disposition refer to the "languages"; "culture," "cultures," and "cultural" appear in the Preamble and in articles 9, 25, 44, 46, 48, 50, 143, 148, and 149; article 20 speaks of "art," "literature," "science," and "technology," article 44 of "science" and "research"; articles 148 and 149 refer to "museums," "libraries," and "music conservatories."

4. Thus, for example, we find in article 9.2: "It is the responsibility of the public authorities . . . to remove the obstacles that impede or restrict participation by all citizens in political, economic, social, and cultural life"; and in article 48: "The public authorities will promote conditions for the free and effective participation of youth in political, social, economic, and cultural development."

5. Editor's note: *Cuius regio, eius religio*—religion follows the crown. Durham (1993: 451) identifies this maxim with the Peace of Augsburg (1555) and the history of religious liberty following the Reformation: "Under this principle, the secular prince was given the right to dictate the religion of his realm to assure a religiously homogenous population. Dissenters could move to a friendlier domain or possibly practice the 'freedom of the hearth'." I am grateful to Keith Buckley for providing this reference.

6. Editor's note: *Refertur ad universes quod publica fit maiorem partem*—"Anything publicly done by the majority is ascribed to everyone" (as translated from Mommsen's German translation of Justinian's *Digest* by Alan Watson). As above, I am grateful to Keith Buckley for supplying this translation and its source.

7. Otto Bauer and Karl Renner gave personally based cultural autonomy theoretical foundation in their proposal for a "corporative federalism" that they designed

for application in the Austro-Hungarian empire, in which the cultural capacities remained entrusted, separately from other matters, to corporate nationality organizations (*Korperschaften*).

8. Article 2 CE: "The Constitution is based on the indissoluble unity of the Spanish Nation, common and indivisible country of all the Spanish, and recognizes and guarantees the right to autonomy of the nationalities and regions that integrate it and the solidarity between all of them."

9. Article 143.1: "In the exercise of the right to autonomy recognized in Article 2 of the Constitution, bordering provinces with common historical, cultural, and economic characteristics, island territories, and the provinces that already form an historical regional entity accede to their self-government and may be constituted in Autonomous Communities according to the arrangements found in this Title and in the respective bylaws."

10. Article 149.2: "Without prejudice to the competences that the Autonomous Communities will be able to assume, the State will consider support of culture as a duty and essential responsibility and will facilitate cultural communication between the Autonomous Communities."

11. Article 3.1: "Castilian is the official Spanish language of the State. All Spaniards have the duty to know it and the right to use it."

12. References to the basics of this discussion are to be found in the works of Castro (1954) and Sanchez Albornoz (1956). Also important is the study by Ortega y Gasset 1993 [1922]. The most complete study of the broad bibliography on this issue is by Marcial Blas (1989: 119–149).

13. Art. 3: "Castilian is the official Spanish language of the State. . . . The other Spanish languages will be also official in the respective Autonomous Communities according to their statutes."

14. Judgment of the Constitutional Court 49/1984, of April 5, 1984.

15. According to the interpretations of constitutional jurisprudence, the Fundamental Law of Bonn is found to be governed by the principle of *Kulturhoheit* or cultural sovereignty of the *Länder*. The judgment of the Federal Constitutional Court, of 28 of February of 1961, matter *Fernsehurteil*, related to the wish of the Federal Government to create a participatory society exclusively through the Bund in order to profit from a television chain: "in the measure to which cultural affairs could be administered and regulated by the state, in accordance with the basic principles of the Fundamental Law, will be subject to the *Länder*, whenever there do not exist special arrangements or exceptions that favor the Federation."

16. Prisoners "in any event, will have a right . . . of access to culture and to the integral development of their personality" (art. 25.2). "The public authorities will promote the conditions for the free and effective participation of youth in political, social, economic and cultural development" (art. 48.2). In relation to elderly citizens, the public authorities should promote "their well-being through a social service system

that will attend to their specific health, housing, culture and leisure problems" (art. 50).

17. "The Spanish are equal before the law, without discrimination by reason of birth, race, sex, religion, opinion or any other condition or social circumstance."

18. These data correspond to the year 1986.

Chapter 5

Disorderly Differences: Recognition, Accommodation, and American Law

Austin Sarat and Roger Berkowitz

In its January 20, 1992 issue, *People Magazine* ran a story entitled "Die, My Daughter, Die!" (*People Magazine* 1992:71), which described the murder of Tina Isa, sixteen-year-old daughter of Palestinian émigrés Zein and Maria Isa who, with their seven children, came to the United States from the West Bank in 1985. The children had been forbidden to go on school trips, attend concerts, visit friends on weekends, or date. Tina refused to abide by these prohibitions. She took a job as a counter girl at Wendy's fast-food restaurant and dated an African-American schoolmate. In the eyes of her parents, she violated long-standing Arab canons of behavior for young women and brought shame and dishonor on the family name.

Tina and her father had frequent fights. Her father warned her that her behavior was offensive (e.g., allowing herself to be seen in public with her boyfriend), and he threatened to vindicate the family's damaged honor. On the night of Tina's death, Zein again confronted her and accused her of shaming the family. While Maria, Tina's mother, held her down, he stabbed her to death with a seven-inch knife. *People* quotes an anthropologist, himself born and raised in Jerusalem, who said that "the way Tina lived offended her father's sense of honor. " 'Everyone' " he continued, " 'growing up [as Tina had] in the Middle East knows being killed is a possible consequence of dishonoring the family' " (*People* 1992: 75).

Charged with first degree murder, the Isas sought to raise the so-called cultural defense (Sheybani 1987: 751). They claimed that they could not justifiably be found guilty since what they did to Tina would not have been treated as a crime in their homeland. This defense failed, as it generally does, and the Isas were each convicted of first-degree murder and sentenced to death.

In this essay we examine the "us"/"them" dichotomy that the *People Magazine* portrait of the Isas conjures up. "We," the *People* article implies, would never do the kind of thing that Zein and Maria did; "they" do such things (Connolly, 1991). In contrast we want to call into question the ways in which difference is constituted and given meaning in popular culture and, most especially, in the institutional practices of American law.

At one level, Tina's death is a story of difference. The honor code invoked by Tina's parents is an example of the kind of meaningful cultural commitments frequently romanticized by those who seek to retrieve what they perceive to be the lost ideals of community and solidarity. But Tina's story is also an example of difference turned violent. It is a story of what we will call disorderly difference—difference that threatens the allegedly fragile harmony and stability of this nation of immigrants. When acted on, disorderly differences violently and brutally impose themselves on others. Disorderly differences, like the familial honor code that justified Tina's murder, forcefully raise the question of when and how differences can (and should) be recognized and accommodated. Even by framing the question as one of accommodating difference, we have presupposed a hierarchical structure with the authority to annihilate or accommodate difference. Any attempt to address the problem of difference within a legal framework is inevitably forced to establish some hierarchical authority for the resolution of conflicts (Minow, 1990 and 1991). Disorderly differences, we argue, require us to ask whether we can (or should) justify, or excuse, conduct which, while it may seem reprehensible to us, reflects a deeply felt cultural or religious conviction (Spiegelman, 1973).

To be an American is to live an ambivalent relationship to difference. It is to be a neighbor to difference and, at the same time, to harbor suspicions that difference may be our national undoing, that differences can never be bridged, and that without assimilation disorder lurks just below the surface of our national life. As Varenne notes (this volume), the ambivalence is conveyed by the metaphor of the melting pot, which acknowledges and celebrates our differences, but also insists on the painful process of melting down those differences and molding a new and unique society. *E pluribus unum*: Out of many one (Fuchs cited in Delbanco, 1992: 83).

Yet, difference is an integral part of American culture; America is a hybrid nation. Difference, as well as the conflict difference generates, has been a part of the cultural life of Americans since the nation's founding.

Reflecting on the "hostile" relations among Europeans, Africans, and Indians in the United States, Tocqueville (1876: 425) observed that "almost insurmountable barriers had been raised between them by education and law, as well as by their origin and outward characteristics; but fortune has brought them together on the same soil, where, although they are mixed, they do not amalgamate...." The perception and fear that the United States would be a nation of many peoples who would not "amalgamate" has prompted a strong desire for order in the form of sameness and community. This desire for order creates what Michael Kammen calls, "A dialectic of pluralism and conformity... at the core of American life" (Kammen 1972: 128).

Kammen's dialectic of pluralism and conformity is reflected, moreover, in the contemporary dialogue about identity and difference. As the media coverage of Tina Isa suggests, that dialogue grows more—not less—difficult as new groups enter our national life. The more difference is recognized, the more vexing the effort to accommodate difference in our institutional lives and practices becomes (Minow, 1991 and Jardine, 1985). As in the *People* story, difference frequently is made to be the fearsome presence within, rather than the enlivening wellspring of, democratic politics. Difference, for some, is a source of dread, a fear of the unknown, an "apprehension of a future heavy with the possibility of danger" (Craft, 1992: 521).

To understand the dialectic of identity and difference, and the dread that it too often inspires, one must take that dread seriously. One must recognize that disorder is the often unspoken specter that haunts discussion of difference. As Kenneth Karst (1986: 310-311) puts it, "Behind the bland terms 'intercultural relations' lies the menace of violence." If one is to be hospitable to difference, one must learn to think and speak about order as the indispensable partner of the friends of difference.

All too often the friends of difference refuse to speak of order; in so doing they leave the field to others. They leave the definition of order and the constitution of orderly difference unchallenged in the practices of the institutions that define difference. For example, academic reaction to the violence following the first Rodney King verdict rightly countered the media's demonization of the black, Hispanic, and Latino communities living in South Central (Gooding-Williams, 1993). Yet it was the local community and religious organizations that angrily resented the riots and stressed the need to bring order to the area.

It is, we think, necessary to put the problem of order on the agenda of those who seek to understand the way difference is constituted and understood in and by legal institutions. Difference, as this essay argues, is all too often imagined as tantamount to disorder. Thus an insistence on order and orderliness is the institutional counterpoint to all claims for the recognition and accommodation of difference. Only those differences that pose no threat to order, or whose threats can be assimilated into a narrative of predictable change—that is, only those differences that have been sufficiently domesticated to fit within prevailing cultural assumptions and institutional routines—are recognized and accommodated.

For the critics of difference, each claim for exemption or special recognition is seen as always implying others, in a multiplying and unlimitable progression (*United States v. Moylan*). It is as if within every demand for recognition and accommodation there is already the question, If this, then what? As Alison Renteln puts it, "Anarchy would reign if each person could claim a different cultural immunity from prosecution" (Renteln, 1987: 26). Such statements reflect the belief (sometimes reasonable, sometimes not) that the proliferating recognition of difference itself generates an accelerating and potentially destabilizing realignment of institutional practices (see Patricia Williams's discussion of the proliferation of rights; Williams, 1991: 165).

We believe that simply condensing the association of difference with disorder does little to advance the claims of difference or the chance for a politically progressive response and accommodation of difference. Those who would champion difference as an energizing presence in democratic politics must learn to constitute difference in such a way as both to recognize the multiple and contradictory affiliations and identities that give our lives meaning and, at the same time, to tame the specter of disorder. It is only by presenting claims for the institutional recognition of difference in a language of order, that the friends of difference can hope to win institutional respect for and accommodation of different ways of life.

It is the argument of this essay that disorder is the imagined other of difference and that no response to the dilemmas of difference that does not deal with the problem of order and disorder can provide a productive response to those dilemmas. Disorder gives difference its political and juridical meaning. To think about how difference itself is constituted and understood we must attend not only to the cultural lives of citizens and groups, but to the institutional practices through which the claims of difference are recognized and understood.[1]

Difference gives rise to two such claims: claims of rights and demands for protection. The former often take the form of requests for exemption from the reach of state law; the latter take the form of demands for change in institutional practices themselves (Minow, 1991). In American law both are seen through the eyes of a commitment to order and orderliness. If claims for difference that embody the assertion of rights and the demand for protection are to succeed, it is essential that they are not presented as claims made at the expense of order.

In what follows, we will try to develop our claim about the impoverished relationship of order and difference through a reading of two Supreme Court cases—*Reynolds v. United States* (98 U.S. 145 [1878]) and *Wisconsin v. Yoder* (406 U.S. 205 [1971]). Separated by almost a century, *Reynolds* and *Yoder* both involve the claims of distinct religious groups to exemption from the demands of state law. In one of these cases—*Reynolds*—the claim was rejected, in the other—*Yoder*—it was accepted. In the former, the disorder of difference was constituted in such a way as to demand rejection; in the latter, difference was domesticated in such a way as not to appear disorderly at all.

However, we read both cases as exemplifying two ways of denying difference in the name of order (Connolly, 1991: 43). At a time when the illusions of stable and nondiscursive identities are exposed and critiqued in popular culture as well as the academy and when the search for solidarity is revealed in its genocidal potential, the simple formula of either annihilating or assimilating difference must be transcended. Even among those who genuinely welcome difference either as a good in itself or as a useful component of democratic and capitalist societies, the specter of disorder continues to haunt the efforts to effect real change. In short, our vocabulary for speaking about and structuring difference must be changed. Thus, before we proceed to our discussion of order and difference in *Reynolds* and *Yoder*, we briefly review the available vocabularies through which Americans speak about difference. These vocabularies surface with particular vividness in the two cases.

VOCABULARIES OF DIFFERENCE

Notwithstanding a rich historical, literary, and artistic tradition of celebrating difference in the public culture of the United States, Americans speak about difference in a cramped vocabulary. Mainstream discourse gives us few ways of seeing and speaking of difference except to mark its threats or to wish for its end. This observation is not obvious; against it, one could argue that liberal tolerance provides a powerful and proven vocabulary for speaking about difference. Many Americans pride themselves on being tolerant of difference, their tolerance extending even to those who are themselves intolerant. In this essay we invoke "tolerance" not just as a reference to the passive acceptance of difference, but to difference being actively sought out and celebrated.

However, tolerance, as it has been substantively understood and practiced since its inception, is compromised as a minimal vocabulary of difference (McClure, 1990: 362). Tolerance receives its substantive significations through its association with liberalism, and liberalism's major competitor in

American political discourse, civic republicanism (Michelman, 1988 and Selznick, 1992; see also Powell, 1988). For liberals, tolerance serves as the bastion protecting individual freedom from government interference (Rawls, 1972). For civic republicans, tolerance frequently becomes a substantive conception of the civic good to which the republic can aspire (see Cornell, 1992, Michelman, 1988, Stolzenberg, 1993).[2] Further, both liberals and civic republicans imagine tolerance as necessary in a democracy to allow participation and innovation in the collective pursuit of truth (Mill, 1987; Taylor, 1989). Yet, while liberalism and civic republicanism purport to balance the competing imperatives of freedom and order, both, because they construct difference as disorderly, are ultimately deeply hostile to difference. In this section we argue that liberalism and civic republicanism are each committed to understanding difference as the antithesis of order; neither, therefore, can support a substantive conception of tolerance that promotes respect for and the accommodation of differences (Unger, 1984: 242).

Liberalism

Liberalism advances an individualistic conception of human nature that takes the individual as the primary, and the most significant, unit of modern states (Kateb, 1992). Individualism is, in liberal theory, rights-based, but interest-oriented (Macpherson, 1962). Interest-oriented behavior is legitimated and protected through the recognition of negative rights. For a liberal, life at its best consists in being left alone to identify and strive to attain one's own interest. In such a life, what any individual wants represents the full measure of his or her capacity to know the good (Sandel, 1982; Lukes, 1989). As a result, no one—in the prepolitical world as imagined by liberalism—can be justified in prescribing the good for others.

Liberalism is thus deeply suspicious of anything collective, most especially the state. For a liberal, individual personality is defined outside of groups or communities which are, in turn, always seen as the locus of a threatening pressure to conform (Mill, 1987). Values are subjective; indeed values are, in liberal thought, virtually indistinguishable from preferences (Cornell, 1992: 3-8). Thus, the good is inevitably different for different people, and any sharing of values is merely the coincidental matching of preferences. Liberalism can offer no conception of the good except that individuals should be allowed to identify and pursue their own visions of it with minimal outside interference (Sandel, 1982).

In such a condition the best we can expect from each other is tolerance. Tolerance of the rights of others to hold opposing views is considered the "fixed star of American Jurisprudence" (319 U.S. 624, 642) and the bulwark of liberal notions of freedom and fairness. Tolerance is, as any vocabulary for recognizing and accommodating difference must be, a relativist theory of difference. Relativization, or perspectivism, acknowledges difference without making it a sign of moral inferiority (Todorov, 1985: 189–191). As a concept that, at least in theory, allows others to live according to their own moral and religious truths, tolerance is a relativist doctrine that seeks coexistence and moderation instead of the imposition of a simple formulation of virtue (on moderation see Todorov, 1993: 359).

Though relativistic with respect to social values and practices, liberal tolerance cannot escape its own hierarchical aspect. Tolerance is "permission granted by authority" and an "allowance, with or without limitations, by the ruling power," and the allowing of "that which is not actually approved; forbearance; sufferance" (McClure, 1990: 362). Tolerance presupposes a hierarchical relationship between someone who requests tolerance, and an authority that tolerates only if and when it wishes. Tolerance presupposes one power—namely the liberal state—which can decide whether or not to tolerate the activities of other, less powerful, actors.

The complicity between tolerance and power has led some to question its desirability as a vocabulary for organizing difference. Despite its rhetorical association with respect for difference, liberal tolerance, say its critics, has itself become a guarantor of order. For example, Herbert Marcuse argues that tolerance stifles nonconformist attitudes and protects the authority of those whose privilege it is to define the scope of tolerance (Marcuse, 1965; Lorde, 1984: 111). Tolerance, in this sense, may be nothing more than forbearance of a despised people, pending their assimilation (Todorov, 1985). Taken together, these views suggest that tolerance may not offer so rich a vocabulary as its liberal supporters claim. Liberal rhetoric notwithstanding, tolerance presupposes and accepts the legitimacy and authority of the state. Tolerance, then, is less a vocabulary of difference, than an apologetic for order.

The transformation of tolerance into a language of order is a corollary of liberalism's individualist and interest-oriented conception of human personality. Liberalism both celebrates tolerance as guaranteeing the freedoms necessary for the full realization of the human character, and circumscribes the scope of tolerance as encouraging those freedoms that invite conflict and disorder (Unger, 1984: 65). Liberals, therefore, describe societies as comprised of free individuals whose pursuit of their own vision of the good is inevitably disorderly. As Locke and Hobbs assert in different ways, it is only through a collective appeal to a rationally governed civic realm that disorderly differences can be made orderly within the liberal imaginary (Locke, 1988 and Hobbes, 1968).

As a political theory, then, liberalism turns to the state as the only reliable guarantor of order. State law stands as the trope through which legality gets equated with order (Fitzpatrick, 1992). The primary responsibility of the liberal state is to do the job that cannot, or will not, be done elsewhere; that is policing the behavior of its self-interested, utility-maximizing citizens to ensure that each remains free to pursue his or her own good in his or her own way (Mill, 1987). Liberal social institutions are necessary to preserve order; they do not aspire to alter or improve human character, but merely to police and to protect us from one another.

Civic Republicanism

In contrast to liberalism, civic republicanism does not begin with the isolated individual struggling to realize his or her interests in a world of scarcity where others are similarly engaged in the pursuit of their own interests. For civic republicans the primary condition of social life is life with others in the pursuit of the "common good." If liberalism elevates individual difference, civic republicanism seeks to overcome difference in the name of a communal civic virtue (Michelman, 1988; Sunstein, 1988: 1539; Selznick, 1992: 406–427).

Central to the republicans' attempt to define civic virtues for a community, is their belief that subjectivity itself is discursively constructed within communities. For the republican, the liberal individual is inseparable from and unknowable outside of community. For civic republicans individual citizens as well as their communities are constituted through a dialogue about justice (Ackerman, 1989: 5). Political life is a life with others forging commonalty through the shared search for virtue. Life together is just that; it is life together where "personhood and character gain substance; from the experience of belonging to a specific moral community" (Selznick, 1992: 228; see also Sandel, 1982). And community is more thickly constituted than just a temporary association of persons in suspicious and temporary alliances for similar goals. To say that people are members of a community is to say that their very personality, their character, values, and interests are constituted in and through the community of which they are a part. As Paul Kahn (1989: 5) puts it, earlier communitarians were civic republicans. There is no self to understand apart from the community just as there is no community apart from the members.

Difference is a barrier, but not an insurmountable one, to an integrated, harmonious community life. Civic republicans seek to overcome difference through dialogue. In their version, difference ideally can be subordinated in the search for shared understandings (Michelman, 1988). The threat of disorder that plagues liberalism is thought to be overcome as difference itself is overcome. Thus, while contemporary civic republicans often claim to honor dialogue, plurality, and tolerance in the construction of republican communities, they simultaneously affirm the possibility of reaching a societal consensus regarding the normative presuppositions of society itself (Michelman, 1988). For them the normative basis of the common good does not exist outside of the processes through which community is forged and sustained. Instead, it is through the process of founding and creating laws, civic republicans argue, that plural individuals are integrated into a coherent and unified community.

For civic republicans, law plays a critical role in the process of maintaining a dialogue geared to defining the civic virtues within a community. Law is more than a structure of restraint, setting the boundaries within which individuals pursue their self-interest. It is a vehicle for, and an expression of, the shared values of the community (Cover, 1983: 4).

Civic republicanism is, we contend, deeply hostile to difference (Young, 1989; but see Stolzenberg, 1993). It posits values, or the pursuit of values, that can bring unity out of apparent diversity as it denies the desirability of maintaining and supporting meaningful difference. "If individual freedom is subordinated to the community's prescriptive demands, it appears that civic republicanism can only accomplish its goal of establishing communal criteria for moral judgments at the expense of diversity" (Berkowitz, 1990: 11). Disorderly differences are overcome, therefore to the extent that dialogue succeeds in forging a societal consensus concerning the civic virtue.

Both liberalism and civic republicanism confront difference as a problem of disorder, and neither appreciates the way difference may already contain the seeds of its own orderliness. While liberalism anxiously acknowledges and seeks to make the best of difference, civic republicanism seeks to overcome and quiet it. While the former treats difference as the irreducible fact of political life, the latter sees difference as epiphenomenal. Neither uses the fact of difference to reevaluate and revalue order itself, to ask what it means to demand or search for order among diverse and overlapping perspectives, cultures, and values. Neither provides a vocabulary that both welcomes difference and also responds to the legitimate demand for order.

American law sees difference in the cramped vocabularies of liberalism and civic republicanism both of which treat claims of difference as if they were the disorderly assertion of naked individual preferences. U.S. law knows no way to celebrate difference as a site of alternative visions of orderliness, or to recognize the potential within differences to instruct others about useful realignments in existing practices (Minow, 1990). Social theory should respond to this situation not simply by condemning law for its fantastic imagination of difference as disaster or for its repressive, homogenizing preoccupations. Instead, social theorists needs to provide, not only a richer, more complicated vision of difference, but also to develop a richer, more complicated vision of order.

THE LEGAL CONSTRUCTION OF DIFFERENCE

Reynolds v. United States: Imagining the Savage

Over one-hundred years ago, the United States Supreme Court confronted what would now be called a cultural defense claim—though one quite dissimilar from that advanced on behalf of the Isases—in a case involving an admitted violation of the law against polygamy by a member of the Mormon Church (see 98 U.S. 195). The defendant in that case, George Reynolds, claimed that he could not, and should not, be convicted of a crime against state law that conflicted with his religious beliefs and the practices mandated by those beliefs. He noted that it " 'was the duty of male members of . . . [the Mormon Church], circumstances permitting, to practice polygamy . . . [and] that he had received permission from the recognized authorities in said church to enter into polygamous marriage . . .' " (Ibid.: 161). It is crucial, at the outset, to take account of this claim and the language with which it is expressed because it was never taken into account by the Court. In his request for an exemption from the statute prohibiting polygamy, Reynolds embraced not the language of freedom or willfulness, but instead the language of "duty" and "authority." In other words Reynolds's claim for the recognition of difference embraced a claim of order; even as he asserted the limits of the sovereign prerogative of the state, Reynolds claimed not to be free, but to be bound by a different law.

However, in the Court's description of Reynolds's position, his deference to "duty" and "authority" disappeared. The question before the Court was framed by then Chief Justice Waite as whether "one who knowingly violates a law which has been properly enacted [can be found guilty] if he entertains a religious belief that the law is wrong" (Ibid.: 162). This framing was, as is readily apparent, an artful alteration of the question that Reynolds originally posed, as well as a way of framing the difference that Reynolds advocated as a threat to the law itself. Reynolds, in fact, had advanced no view as to whether the law against polygamy was right or wrong in society outside the Church of Jesus Christ of Latter-Day Saints. Instead, he argued that he should be exempt from the law's reach, whether the law be right or wrong, because of the unresolvable conflict between state law and his religious obligations.

Reynolds argued that in the case of marriage, the state claimed an interest and authority that was too expansive and overly intrusive. But here again Waite did not take up the challenge as posed. Instead, Waite merely reiterated the fact that the state did claim to regulate polygamous marriage throughout American society and he argued that while Reynolds was free to believe whatever his conscience dictated about the morality or immorality of polygamy, he was not free to turn that belief into action. The First Amendment, Waite argued, deprived Congress of "all legislative power over mere opinion, but . . . left [Congress] free to reach actions which were in violation of social duties or subversive of good order." But was Reynolds really a subversive? Was he really a radical proponent of the view that each person should be free to decide on the nature and limits of his or her social duties? Or was he instead so immersed in taking his duties seriously that he was prepared to defy what today we might very well describe as a "colonial" legal order?

In the way Waite treated Reynolds's claim we have a powerful example of what Mark Tushnet calls the "reduction" principle (Tushnet, 1986: 702) which converts questions of difference into questions of order. In Tushnet's view, the Supreme Court has, throughout its history, treated religion as a private and solitary act of individual conscience. As a result, the claims of religious difference are just another expression of the kind of idiosyncratic preferences that a liberal society generates and supports. "It matters not," Waite wrote, "that his [Reynolds's] belief was part of his professed religion; it was still belief and belief only" (98 U.S. 167). He treats religious belief like any other belief, with no greater or lesser claim to informing practices. And people are free to believe whatever they want; they are not free, however, to act on their beliefs. All differences are, in the end, merely differences of opinion. None are to be suppressed. But to imagine that such differences could and should be the basis for selective exemptions from the obligations of the law would, again in Waite's words, be "subversive of good order." Here Waite reflects the classic liberal response to religious difference. Liberals separate objective fact and subjective belief and make the former the domain of civil authority and the latter the province of religious, and other, diversity (McClure, 1990: 336).

It is a concern for order and for a limitation as well as an assertion of civil power that drives Waite's unmaking of religious difference into a threatening diversity. For Waite properly religious questions are those that concern salvation. As soon as one's actions are seen to harm another they cross the line from the religious realm into the civil jurisdiction. Freedom of religion is transformed by the vocabulary of liberal toleration from a freedom to live one's life in accordance with the laws of one's religion to a freedom of worship tolerated by a civil law regime, as long as the worship respects its limits and does not result in worldly injuries (McClure, 1990: 336).

Waite constituted the Mormon practice of polygamy as a civic danger in precisely this sense. With figurations and allusions, he presented polygamy as a savage practice and the practice of savages. Resistance to polygamy was, in turn, a mark of the civilizing progress. "Polygamy," Waite confidently noted, "has always been odious among the northern and western nations of Europe, and, until the establishment of the Mormon Church, was almost exclusively a feature of the life of Asiatic and of African people" (98 U.S. 164). As Waite understood it, that savage practice posed a grave threat to the institution of marriage which was, in turn, again figured through the lens of order. Marriage, Waite argued, was the basis on which "society may be said to be built (Ibid., 165)." To honor Reynolds's request for an exemption would then be to threaten society and civilization itself.

To admit of this exemption would, on Waite's account, lead immediately onto a slippery slope, in which savagery would find its place in the midst of civilization. To condone that difference, to welcome the stranger within, would be an invitation to an escalating savagery. Disorderly difference is the invitation to dread, which it is the job of law both to name and to tame (Craft, 1992). Waite's opinion reflects his view that the job of law is first to mark the stranger and then to tame, if not civilize, the stranger by repressing his or her savage difference.

Waite shifts his readers onto the slippery slope by posing two rhetorical questions. "Suppose," Waite asked, "one believed that human sacrifices were a necessary part of religious worship, would it be seriously contended that the civil government under which he lived could not interfere to prevent a sacrifice? Or if a wife religiously believed it was her duty to burn herself upon the funeral pile of her dead husband, would it be beyond the power of the civil government to prevent her from carrying that belief into practice?" (98 U.S. 166). Through these questions Waite again frames the question of difference as a question of civilization versus savagery. His rhetoric suspends the distinctions between Mormon polygamy, human sacrifice, and ritual suicide.

Here law's seemingly harsh rebuke of the duty-invoking, authority-obeying Reynolds becomes comprehensible as a semiotics of colonialism itself. Law's passion for order and for imposing itself against disorderly differences is a passion for "civilization" against a brutal, lawless, "savagery" [it is also a way of reaffirming "our" own sense of identity in oppositional terms (Connolly, 1991)]. The tranquil voice of duty and authority with which Reynolds framed his request for exemption is translated into a series of imagined horrors with which his claim is rhetorically joined.

As Peter Fitzpatrick has observed in another context, "Law and order . . . [are, as in this case,] constantly combined not just in opposition to but as a means of subduing the 'disordered and riotous' savages in their state of lawless 'anarchy'.... [In *Reynolds* as elsewhere] this scenario precisely reverses what was the case" (Fitzpatrick, 1992: 80). The history of western law is the history of a rhetorical inversion, in which the law of colonial states regularly asserts itself against the order of various subcultures and, at the same time, labels itself the champion of order (Fitzpatrick, 1992: chapter 3).

Reynolds must be asked to sacrifice his religious practice to prevent the sacrifice of (ordered) life in the name of religion itself. Religion that sanctions polygamy is imagined to exert such a powerful, mysterious, and ultimately irrational pull that, once it is let loose in the world, it challenges government itself. To sanction the potency that might sustain polygamous marriage would be to threaten the potency of government. "To permit... [a man to excuse his practices to the contrary because of his religious belief] would be to make the professed doctrines of religious belief superior to the law of the land, and in effect to permit every citizen to become a law unto himself" (98 U.S. 167).

Waite reads Reynolds's claim as exemplifying a radically individualist assertion in which each person's preferences assert sovereignty, unless or until checked by a neutral state. It made no difference to Waite that this was not the claim that Reynolds actually made, or that his claim was made as a member of a community, which itself asserted the right to govern his conduct. Reynolds's was precisely not a claim to be a "law unto himself." Instead his request for exemption from the reach of state law was based on a recognition of another kind of obligation, a different sphere of obedience, rather than an assertion of licentious freedom.

The difference Reynolds pressed was a disorderly difference not because it was either anarchic or savage. It was disorderly precisely because it challenged a prevailing institutional practice—monogamous marriage—at the heart of mainstream social life. Reynolds's difference was a disorderly difference because it did not reflect an idiosyncratic or peculiar belief, but rather was the sanctioned difference of an entire subculture. In our view Waite's rejection of polygamy was not in fact a rejection of disorder, but was instead the violent gesture of one vision of order against another (Fitzpatrick, 1992: chapter 3). Waite's response was and remains typical of the way U.S. law marks the different as strange and renders the strange a dangerous, disordering presence in the public's midst. For law to welcome difference under these circumstances, it must code that difference in a way that affirms the taming of its disordering potential. Overcoming the problem of order—in which difference is constructed as disorderly—is thus a legal prerequisite to the recognition and accommodation of difference. An important example of such a legal coding—in contrast to Reynolds—is provided by Chief Justice Burger's majority opinion in *Wisconsin v. Yoder* (406 U.S. 205). While Burger's opinion carves out an exemption that accommodates Yoder's claim for difference, his opinion so completely emasculates the difference claimed by the Amish that, as Burger presents the case, the Amish are not different at all.

Wisconsin v. Yoder: When Difference Is No Difference at All

In *Yoder*, decided in 1971, another request for exemption was pressed by yet another religious group, the Amish. This time the requested exemption again seemed to challenge an important social institution—this time, public education. Members of the Old Order Amish challenged the Wisconsin compulsory school-attendance law that required them to send their children to a certified public or private school until they reached the age of 16. The Amish refused to send their children to a state-sanctioned school after the eighth grade. This meant that most Amish children were removed from school usually by the age of 14. As a result, Jonas Yoder, Wallace Miller, and Adin Yutzy were tried and convicted of violating the compulsory-attendance law.

They challenged that law claiming that it violated their rights under the First and Fourteenth Amendments. Echoing George Reynolds, they argued that compliance with the state statute would require them to violate the commands of their church and also "endanger their own salvation and that of the children (Ibid.: 209) and they noted that their religion required "life in a church community and apart from the world and worldly influence" (Ibid.: 210). In addition, high school and higher education were said to be objectionable "because the values they [public schools] teach are in marked variance with Amish values and the Amish way of life; they viewed secondary school as an impermissible exposure of their children to a 'worldly' influence in conflict with their beliefs" (Ibid.: 211).

Yoder is one of the relatively few cases in the U.S. constitutional tradition in which a request for exemption from valid state law was granted, and in which the claim of difference was apparently accommodated and recognized. However, in our view, it is a misreading to conclude that *Yoder* affirms difference. In Burger's rhetorical figuration, difference is neither recognized nor accommodated; it is made to disappear. The problem of disorder is confronted and overcome by portraying the Amish as an image of sameness, as exemplifying if not sharing fundamental American values, and as being, in their timeless simplicity, the true embodiment of a threatened, yet precious, American way of life (Kurland, 1984: 16).

Burger recognizes and accommodates the claim of the Amish for exemption from compulsory school laws by turning the Amish into living monuments to the Jefferson ideal of the independent farmer. "[T]he Amish communities," Burger contends, "singularly parallel and reflect many of the virtues of Jefferson's ideal of the 'sturdy yeoman' who would form the basis of what he considered as the ideal of democratic society" (406 U.S. 225–226). Unlike Waite's rendering of the Mormons as the savage other, Burger figures the Amish as already a part of "us," a vanishing, but still recognizable, aspect of an American way of life that is important to the sustenance of democracy, even as he criticizes the "requirements of contemporary society" with their relentless insistence on "conformity to majoritarian standards" (Ibid.: 217). Yet, by the time Burger is done describing the Amish there is nothing for them to conform to since they have been made into the living embodiment of values recognizably important in the American tradition. Disorderly difference is tamed as the orderliness of their difference is asserted, and then their difference itself is assimilated—and thereby denied.

In this gesture, Burger does the kind of linguistic violence that Todorov attributed to some of the Christian missionaries who rationalized the colonial ambitions of the Spanish conquest of the Aztecs. Todorov argues that such violence is done by asserting identities and equivalencies as a way of justifying allegedly humane treatment. He presents Las Casas's description of the Aztecs as a characteristic act of erasure in which the other is recognized only in and through an asserted essential identity. "According to Las Casas," Todorov writes:

> the Indians' most characteristic feature is their resemblance to Christians.... The Indians are provided with Christian virtues, they are obedient and peaceful ... Here then is an incontestable generosity on the part of Las Casas who refuses to despise others simply because they are different. But he goes one step further and adds: moreover, they are not ... different. (Todorov, 1985: 163–167)

Violence is done by Burger, as it was by Las Casas, by turning an asserted difference into a comforting and recognizable similarity. Accommodation is premised on identification; difference on identity. What appears initially strange is really, on second glance, quite familiar; what appears different is really quite similar. The outside is already inside. A seemingly challenging other is really a nostalgia-inducing remnant of a past we have regrettably left behind. In contrast to Waite's Mormons who were presented as anarchic and thus savage, Burger's Amish, like Las Casas's Aztecs, are obedient, patient, and peaceful, and thus good Americans and Christians.

Burger's opinion is replete with gestures of various kinds that are intended to be reassuring and whose reassurance takes on meaning in part through their contrast to the rhetorical moves made by Waite in *Reynolds*.

The first of these gestures is the suggestion that the claim of difference that the Amish are making does not pose a challenge to the system of compulsory education itself. Whereas the practices of the polygamous Mormons were portrayed as incompatible with the institution of marriage, the "Amish," Burger tells his readers, "accept compulsory education generally. . . . The Amish do not object to elementary education through the first eight grades as a general proposition because they agree that their children must have basic skills in the 'three R's' . . . They view such a basic education as acceptable because it does not expose their children to worldly values" (406 U.S. 212). Burger insists that there is less difference in the Amish claim than would initially seem to be the case, repeatedly noting that they already embrace the very values that the state seeks to promote through compulsory education.[3]

The reference to worldly values in the language quoted above is one of many in Burger's opinion; the Amish, Burger notes, view secondary education as an "impermissible exposure of their children to a 'worldly' influence in conflict with their beliefs." Moreover, they seek "separation from, rather than integration with, contemporary worldly society" (Ibid., 211). Throughout Burger's opinion, the Amish are portrayed as innocence against a modern worldliness about which Burger himself is, at best, quite ambivalent. Amish devotion to "life, family and home," [Ronald Reagan would have said to "work, faith, and family"], Burger argues, "have remained constant" against the pressures of modernity (Ibid.). Here Burger unembarrassedly sentimentalizes Amish existence, describing their life as "inherently simple and uncomplicated" (Ibid.: 217) and praising their "qualities of reliability, self-reliance and dedication to work" (Ibid.: 224).

Writing at the beginning of the 1970s, Burger embraces the Amish as a living rebuke to the leftish, "hippie" values that had predominated in the previous decade. In this context Burger needs both to praise the Amish for their difference and, at the same time, deny them their difference: As he puts it, "Even their idiosyncratic separateness exemplifies the diversity we profess to admire and encourage" (406 U.S. 226). The problem of disorder is overcome by a mythic nostalgic identity. The Amish, Burger writes, live a "life of 'goodness,' rather than a life of intellect; wisdom, rather than technical knowledge; community welfare rather than competition" (Ibid.: 211). Goodness, wisdom, and community represent the civic republican side of the American vocabulary of difference, a side threatened in an urban, capitalist culture (Lasch, 1979). Refusing to respond to the Amish desire for what Burger sees as a slight accommodation (406 U.S. 236) would be a self-destructive act by one part of ourselves against another.

Burger explicitly rejects Waite's aggressively colonialist response to difference even as he enacts a subtler version of the same thing. Instead of holding out the claim of difference as a mark of an irreducible otherness, he marks the difference that he confronts as a useful reminder of what America once, in his view, was, and might profitably, if improbably, become again. Thus Burger notes, "We must not forget that in the Middle Ages important values of the civilization of the Western World were preserved by members of religious orders who isolated themselves from all worldly influences against great obstacles" (Ibid.: 223). Waite's equation of difference with the uncivilized other is reversed; in *Yoder* the other stands in for civilization itself, for "our values" needing a place of refuge from the dark ages of our own self-made and corrupt modernity. Indeed much of Burger's opinion can be understood as a "ceremony of regret" (Engel, 1984: 580) a lamentation at the conditions of a modernity gone bad.

In contrast to Waite who figured difference as a threat to the state, Burger notes that no such threat is posed in this case. Not only are the Amish the same as "us" and thus not a threat to state authority, but also they are docile, weak, and powerless in the face of the state. "There is no doubt," Burger confidently notes, "as to the power of a State ... to impose reasonable regulations for the control and duration of basic education" (Ibid., 213). Note the reference to power rather than to authority. What Burger wants to say is that the difference that the Amish allegedly represent is neither so disorderly a difference nor so potent a difference as to represent a threat to order itself.

In fact, in what initially seems like some quite extraneous passages, Burger notes that the Amish "have an excellent record as law-abiding ... members of society" (406 U.S. 213), and that "its members are productive and very law-abiding members of society ... [who] reject public welfare in any of its usual modern forms" (Ibid.: 222). Their law-abidingness is a powerful imagistic rejection of the riotous, rebellious violence of the 1960s. Unlike the dope-smoking, draft card-burning students of the 1960s, Amish youth, in Burger's account, capably fulfill "[t]he social and political responsibilities of citizenship" (Ibid.: 225).

In this regard Burger conjures the image of Henry David Thoreau to mark the contrast between the Amish way of life and those who, as modern-day Thoreaus would self-indulgently and self-righteously put themselves above the law. While Thoreau "rejected the social values of his time," the Amish, Burger notes, do not want to allow "every person to make his own standards on matters of conduct in which society as a whole has important interests" (Ibid.: 216).

In the opinions of Waite and Burger we have examples of two different ways American law deals with difference. The former exaggerates the disordering potential of difference as well as the orderly potential of identity in order to justify an overtly colonial response. The latter denies difference even as it seems to embrace it. The problem of order is displaced through a process of identification. If there is a disordering recognition in the confrontation with the difference of the Amish lifestyle it is, in Burger's view, the recognition of a society in decline, a society called back to its true self through the strange confrontation with the living carriers of its abandoned way of life. The disorderliness of difference disappears as difference itself is rendered invisible.

Despite their rhetorical dissimilarity, the opinions of Waite and Burger share an essential commonalty in that "neither engages the enigma of otherness" (Connolly, 1991: 43). The claims for recognition and accommodation of difference represented in *Reynolds* and *Yoder* were interpreted within a vocabulary of difference in which they could be either disorderly (and therefore threats needing to be annihilated) or orderly (and therefore must be assimilated as without difference). In neither case was the difference for which accommodation was sought recognized and addressed in a way that took difference seriously. Neither liberalism (which gives Waite his slippery slope) nor civic republicanism (which gives Burger his nostalgia) provide a vocabulary of difference and order adequate to the task. In our opinion, such a vocabulary does not yet exist.

What is needed is not only a reconceptualization of difference, but also a reconstruction of how we speak about order. Before difference can be recognized and accommodated, difference must cease to be understood as the prelude to disorder. And, order must cease to be understood as exclusive of all difference. In our conclusion we identify one alternative vocabulary for thinking about difference and order that we believe provides a better way to speak about the relations between them.

CONCLUSION

If we are ever to discover the other and to embrace Todorov's vision of different but equal, we must find a vocabulary that constitutes difference in a way that acknowledges and recognizes the claims of order. Such a vocabulary would welcome both *Reynolds* and *Yoder* into Todorov's community of different but equal while, at the same time, holding off and forcefully differentiating the Isas's unacceptable claim to equal recognition of their difference. Neither liberal tolerance nor civic republicanism has met that challenge. As a result, U.S. law either obliterates difference in the name of order, or treats orderly difference as no difference at all.

The vocabulary of legal pluralism meets these criteria.[4] While the advocates of legal pluralism themselves span a wide range of concerns and opinions, they share the conviction that power, order, and meaning are not the exclusive province of hierarchical command-obedience relationships. Power, and the concomitant capacity for ordered social and political institutions, can and does exist outside and separate from relations of coercion and hierarchy. Legal pluralists, consequently, paint a picture of the problem of order and difference that is very different from that suggested by liberal and civic republican theorists. Instead of fearing difference as disorderly and a threat to a central authority, legal pluralism takes the possibility of difference, understood as orderly difference, seriously and intends to honor it. A legally pluralist society is not limited to one civil realm dominated by a neutral state. Instead, the task of maintaining order is dispersed throughout society among different groups who receive wide latitude for group difference.

But, as we discussed earlier, the dilemma of difference requires that not all differences can be honored equally. Simply recognizing differences as orderly does not and cannot give to all differences the equal right to accommodation. There will inevitably be conflicts and disputes within or among societies that will not be able to be resolved except through violence or other means of domination and submission. Thus, even legal pluralists run into the problem of requiring some central authority, possibly a state, to resolve disputes and determine which differences can and cannot be honored.

Some versions of the legal pluralist argument maintain, relying on anthropological research, that different groups can exist within a central conglomeration of power but without the formation of any hierarchical relations privileging a central bureaucracy over diverse groups. Claustres, for example, has argued that among the Tupi societies in Brazil, different groupings existed without any central conglomeration of power and violence (Claustres, 1987: 71). Even as these distinct societies interacted, traded, and "unified" in what Claustres terms a multicommunity social organization, no centralized and hierarchical arrangement between them arose. On the contrary, Claustres argues that the very emergence of such a centripetal force aiming at the crystallization of a hierarchical "floating" structure caused among the various Tupi communities a symmetrical strengthening of centrifugal forces. In other words, the dynamic Claustres describes is *dialectical* in nature; as the construction of the system progressively asserts and defines itself, its component elements react to this change in their status by accentuating their concrete and special nature, their individuality.

Though some have tried, it is hard to imagine how Claustres's model could be transposed onto contemporary states such as the United States of America. While liberal theory may underestimate the order inherent in difference, one should not merely make the opposite claim that conversation and negotiation can adequately resolve all conflicts that arise. As the story of Tina

Isa demonstrates, there remain differences in our society that cannot be resolved except by violent imposition either by the state or by one of the parties. Unless legal pluralists are content to allow these irreconcilable differences to be reconciled in contests among groups determined by power, they must continue to depend on some hierarchical structure with the authority to accommodate claims for the institutional recognition of differences and resolve disputes among diverse orders. Granted there are paradoxes within legal pluralism to be worked out, but even so, what would a legally pluralist society look like?

One model of legal pluralism is associated with the work of Robert Cover (1983: 4). While Cover takes the possibility of difference seriously, he recognizes that legal pluralism need not, and does not, honor all differences. His brand of legal pluralism recognizes and accommodates difference when two conditions are met. First, it does so when difference arises out of and expresses the normative aspirations of an integrated and ordered community, when it exemplifies and expresses a "nomos" (Ibid.). In this sense, Cover's legal pluralism embraces the liberal celebration of multiplicity, but in a way that insists that the claims of difference be linked to the requisites of a richly constituted, normatively engaged orderliness (Sarat and Kearns, 1992).

The second condition for recognizing and accommodating difference also puts order at the fore. Under this condition, legal pluralism insists on the reality of plurality as itself providing a constraint on those versions of difference that would press themselves on us (McClure, 1990). What this means is that the claims of difference need not be honored when they do not themselves honor the principle of difference they assert. Legal pluralism need not require that those of us sympathetic to the claims of difference stand by as all manner of horrors are committed in the name of cultural difference. We can, and should, insist that difference be orderly, even as we invite questions about what order entails. We can, and should, insist that the claims of equal but different honor both principles of equality and principles of difference.

The normative claim Cover makes for legal pluralism orders difference by recognizing and accommodating those differences that arise out of the shared activity of communities of persons united in their pursuit of a particular conception of the good. Cover names this pursuit law (Cover, 1983). Legal pluralism recognizes both the subjectivity of values to which liberalism is sensitive and the aspiration to shared moral engagements, which is at the heart of civic republicanism. In and through a recognition of the claims that difference makes when it subjects itself to law, both greater space for difference and a greater recognition of the need for order can, at least conceptually, be attained.

By showing how claims for the recognition and accommodation of difference can be made consistent with order, Cover has contributed greatly to the development of a new vocabulary for speaking about difference. In considering the claims made by the *Reynolds* and *Yoder* under Cover's model of legal pluralism, we see that in both cases what is sought is the right to live according to a different order. Recognition of that claim does not entail agreement or even sympathy. It is possible to accommodate the Mormons law requiring polygamy or the Amish attitude toward schooling, it is another to welcome them. What Cover counsels against is the feeling or assertion of authority that claims the right to either annihilate or tolerate another's law.

In the end, however, legal pluralism is no more than a different vocabulary for talking about difference, one which is perhaps only useful in engaging a different kind of conversation about difference rather than in assuredly providing satisfying answers to the vexing problems that appreciation of difference inevitably poses. But this is no small accomplishment. As Western nation-states find themselves populated by individuals who identify with international Diaspora cultures ranging from African to environmental, legal pluralism offers a vocabulary by which these cultures can empower themselves. We recognize them as what Claustres calls "nonseparate" legal orders. Each nonseparate law must recognize and respect the other as other, though not wholly alien. The task of social theory is to provide a vocabulary for reconciling the claims of difference with the legitimate demand for order so that occasions for intervention and assertion are minimized and respect for difference encouraged.

ACKNOWLEDGEMENT

This is a much abbreviated version of an essay that appeared in *The Yale Journal of Law and the Humanities*. This essay was presented at the Conference on Democracy and Difference, Indiana University, April 22–25, 1993, and the Annual Meeting of the Law and Society Association, Chicago, May, 1993. We are grateful to participants in those events for their helpful comments and for the advice and criticism of Lawrence Douglas and Tom Dumm.

NOTES

1. The dichotomous relation between difference and order that we construct is one of the typical dichotomies (e.g., freedom/order, difference/identity, good/evil, etc.) found in political theory [McClure, 1990: 361, 372–373 (citing *The Oxford English Dictionary*)]. Differencing, as McClure suggests, establishes "a hierarchical relation between things," Ibid. at 373.

2. Communitarianism has gained popularity of late, as a response to both liberalism's inability to account for the human need for community and republicanism's insistence on homogeneity and to the fear of disorder we have attributed to both liberalism and republicanism. However, simply transferring the problem of order to small self-sufficient communities, cannot solve the problem of plurality. As Roberto Unger puts it, "Once plurality is granted, all the problems of liberal thought seem to spring up again with the difference that they apply to the relations among members of different communities rather than to every encounter among individuals" (Unger, 1984: 282).

3. Moreover, Burger argues that the Amish "have carried the . . . difficult burden of demonstrating the adequacy of their alternative mode of continuing informal vocational education in terms of precisely those overall interests that the State advances in support of its program of compulsory high school education" Ibid., 235.

4. Legal pluralism is fast becoming a field in itself, drawing its adherents from anthropology, political science, economics, and the law. See Cover 1983: 4; Claustres, 1987; Macaulay, 1986; Merry, 1988: 869; Moore, 1973: 719; Fitzpatrick, 1983: 45; Ellickson, 1991; Berkowitz, 1990; Comaroff and Comaroff, 1992: 54–56.

II

The Making of Official Discourses of Identity

Part I established some of the parameters of tension surrounding "diversity" in the liberal democracies of Spain and the United States. Cultural identity becomes "official business" to the extent that culture is perceived to be a source of inequality; however, as we have seen, the effort toward redress is limited by the recursive effects of defining culture in terms that neglect the sources of inequality in society itself. In Part II, authors examine sites where this process can be seen in the making. Yanow's essay on U.S. census categories continues the theme of paradox and denial introduced in Part I, as she demonstrates how the census constructs some categories and precludes others in ways whose net effect divides Americans from each other and their own pasts. Fernández de Rota also considers what is lost in the official categories, as he compares official and unofficial perspectives on Galician identity in the context of Spanish national politics. Analyzing the process by which "the people's point of view" is lost from official discourse, Fernández de Rota appeals to ethnographers to chronicle people's understandings of their own lives—as situated in multiple cross-cutting associations.

In that very spirit, Chock and Azcona consider the political and legislative processes by which the literal and figurative borders between identities are widened and made permeable or impermeable. Chock offers a close reading of the U.S. Senate's debate on immigration reform, dominated by images of unregistered immigrants as unruly, even polluting, in the U.S. landscape. Azcona explores the landscapes of Basque nationalism, tracing the tensions between Basqueness constructed in racial terms (as by Basque ultranationalists) and in terms of sentiment—"feeling" Basque. Urciuoli's essay concludes the section. Her ethnographic research in New York City also considers official discourses, and, developing the theme of contradiction in theory and practice raised by earlier essays, shows how ethnic minorities aspiring to middle-class security cannot escape participating at least partially in the official discourse and its models of "the good citizen."

The common theme in all the essays in this section is the contrast between the complex ambiguity of people's actual identifications (of themselves and others) and the role of the political process in selectively refashioning and singularizing these as official discourses of difference—as well as the value of ethnography as a technique for the recuperation of their complexity. Official discourses of difference have pervasive effects in the organization of daily life, collective histories, and personal subjectivities; however, they do not monopolize the possibilities for public dialogue or positive change.

Chapter 6

American Ethnogenesis and the 1990 Census

Dvora Yanow

In many areas of contemporary administration of public policies, we ask others or are asked ourselves for identification by racial makeup. The categories given in the typical 1990s questionnaire are: White, Black, Hispanic, Asian-American, Native American, Other. Yet identity is complex and multifaceted. Part of that complexity is that although we often use "race" and "ethnicity" to refer to different things, we also use them interchangeably. For this reason I will use "racethnic" in this essay as a single referent for both. This lack of terminological clarity is part of the subject of this essay, in which I explore U.S. racethnic categories as seen in the 1990 Census. The 1990 Census raised problems for many people who found that the categories for race and ethnicity did not reflect their own sense of identity. I consider some of the implications of American racethnic discourse for public policy and administration in addressing the following questions. According to what characteristics are we dividing our population, and why do we choose these characteristics and not others? What characteristics do we leave out? What public discourse is encouraged by this form of categorization, and what discourse is discouraged? I use "policy" to refer both to legislation and to a set of national practices. Taking an interpretive approach to policy analysis, I focus on the meanings made in the creation and use of public policies—in this case, the U.S. Census.

Census categories are not fixed; category names, boundaries, and what they refer to change over time. One property of categories is that they reflect a historical moment with its attendant sociopolitical "realities." However, we tend to reify many categories, forgetting that they are social constructions, treating them as though they were fixed and as if they corresponded to the real world. We use these reified categories as the basis for political judgments and administrative action, forgetting their "as if" quality. At times we justify such action by appeal to these categories, long after the original perceptions of the human world which served as their genesis have changed. When administrative actions are based on categories that no longer fit lived experience, these actions are likely not to solve the problems to which they are addressed. Indeed, they may even be the source of new administrative problems.

THE 1990 CENSUS: CATEGORIES AND CONTRADICTIONS

The 1990 Census asked four racethnicity-related questions.[1] Question 4 asks: "What is. . . .'s race [ellipses in original]?" The answer block printed on the census form provides for the following answers:

—White
—Black or Negro
—Indian (Amer.) (Print the name of the enrolled or principal tribe.)
—Eskimo
—Aleut

Asian or Pacific Islander (API)
— Chinese   — Japanese
— Filipino   — Asian Indian
— Hawaiian   — Samoan
— Korean   — Guamanian
— Vietnamese   — Other API (Print the name)
— Other race (Print race)

Instructions given to the census taker offer the following possibilities for "Other API": "Cambodian, Tongan, Laotian, Hmong, Thai, Pakistani, and so on." The Census Bureau's analysis of the data includes the following additional groups:

Asian	Pacific Islander
Bangladeshi	Tahitian
Burmese	North Mariana Islander
Indonesian	Palavan
Malayan	Fijian
Okinawan	Other
Sri Lankan	
Other	

The enumerator is further instructed, "If response is 'Other race,' ask—Which group does.... consider (himself/herself) to be [ellipses in original]?"

Question 7 asks: "Is ... of Spanish/Hispanic origin?" The census form offers the following as possible answers to the respondent who would respond in the affirmative:

Mexican, Mexican-American, Chicano
Puerto Rican
Cuban
Other

Instructions given to the census taker on "Other" identify "Argentinian, Colombian, Dominican, Nicaraguan, Salvadoran, Spaniard, and so on" as possibilities.

Question 13 asks: "What is this person's ancestry or ethnic origin?" The census form offers as examples: "German, Italian, Afro-American, Croatian, Cape Verdean, Dominican, Ecuadoran, Haitian, Cajun, French Canadian, Jamaican, Korean, Lebanese, Mexican, Nigerian, Irish, Polish, Slovak, Taiwanese, Thai, Ukrainian, etc."

And Question 15 asks, "Does this person speak a language other than English at home?" The examples printed on the form are "Chinese, Italian, Spanish, Vietnamese."

The Census Bureau accepts the "standards on ethnic and racial categories for statistical reporting to be used by all Federal agencies" established in the OMB's Statistical Policy Directive No. 15. That Directive, "Race and ethnic standards for federal statistics and administrative reporting," which took effect on January 1, 1980, established the standards by which federal agencies were to collect racial and ethnic data. It defines these data categories as follows:

a. American Indian or Alaskan Native. A person having origins in any of the original peoples of North America, and who maintains cultural identification through tribal affiliation or community recognition.

b. Asian or Pacific Islander. A person having origins in any of the original peoples of the Far East, Southeast Asia, the Indian subcontinent, or the Pacific Islands. This area includes, for example, China, India, Japan, Korea, the Philippine Islands, and Samoa.

c. Black. A person having origins in any of the black racial groups of Africa.

d. Hispanic. A person of Mexican, Puerto Rican, Cuban, Central or South American or other Spanish culture or origin, regardless of race.

e. White. A person having origins in any of the original peoples of Europe, North Africa, or the Middle East.

The Census Bureau notes that Hispanic origin "can be viewed as the ancestry, nationality group, lineage, or country of birth of the person or the person's parents or ancestors before their arrival in the U.S." and may be of any race.

According to Census publications, "the concept of race the Bureau of the Census uses reflects self-identification by respondents; that is, the individual's perception of his/her racial identity. The concept is not intended to reflect any biological or anthropological definition." Furthermore, "we recognize that there are persons who do not identify with a specific racial group." And so "the 1990 census race question includes an 'Other race' category with provisions for a write-in entry" (Bureau of the Census, 1990).

RACETHNIC CATEGORIES AS SOCIAL CONSTRUCTIONS: COLOR, CULTURE, AND COUNTRY

The Census and OMB labels suggest neat categories with clear boundaries. This does not correspond, however, with individuals' reported experiences of their lives and identities or with analytic exploration of the definitions of race and ethnicity implied by the questions.

For example, 9.8 million Americans checked "other race" in 1990 in answer to Question 4, up from 6.8 million in 1980 (of the 9.8 million, 4 million were from California) (*Washington Post*, 4/29/91, A9). Some people objected to the category name that the Census gave their group. One woman, for instance, was angry that the form did not have "African-American" as the category name and told Census officials that she was neither "black" nor "Negro" (*Newsweek*, 4/30/90, p. 23). Others objected to identifying people as other than generic "American."

Still others found that the categories forced them to make a choice that reflected only a part of their complex racethnic background. The *Los Angeles Times* (1/13/91, E1) interviewed a woman born in Tokyo to a Japanese mother and an American father whose own parents were Blackfoot Indian and African American, who said that the racial categories of Black and Asian American did not capture her identity and experience. She argued for an additional category: "multiracial." Columnist Roberto Rodriguez wrote that as a mestizo—"mostly Indian, part European"—he could not find an appropriate box that fit his racial self-perception. "I tried to check American Indian—but was told Mexicans were not considered *American* Indians." Ruling out Asian left black or white. "[T]he great majority of the people of Latin America are indigenous/mestizo, yet because of colonial legacies of race, are considered white," he wrote (Rodriguez 1990). The choice forced by the Census was apparently so irritating to some people that a reporter for the *San Francisco*

Chronicle (R. G. McLeod, 3/23/90) wrote, an answer of "earthling" to Question 4 will bring the enumerator to your door.[2]

Yet these objections are predicated on the perception of "race" and "ethnicity" as terms that correspond to some objective reality. That they do not—that their meanings are unclear—can be seen from further analysis.

Question 4: Race

In a literal sense, Census Question 4 is about race. But the categories and suggestions given for possible answers indicate that it is asking about something other than the common definition of race as a human group "distinguished... by genetically transmitted physical characteristics" (*American Heritage Dictionary*, 1975, p. 1075). Indeed, this question reflects the historical flux of racial categorizations by color, culture, and country of origin.

Many people schooled in the United States will recall having been taught well into the 1960s (if not later) that there are three races: "Caucasoid, Negroid, and Mongoloid." In more recent public discourse and policy, we have turned these into four categories, reflecting the prominence we accord to skin color within the long list of physical attributes historically measured as racial indicators. Two of the earlier categories are still present in color-based Census labels and in common parlance: White and Black. The Mongoloid group has been replaced by two other color-based categories: American Indians (depicted as "red") and Asian-Americans ("yellow").[3]

From this we begin to see that "race" does not reflect natural phenomena. It is a social construction that we have imposed on the human world around us.[4] In further analyzing Census Question 4, we find that it is not asking about racial groups only in the sense of physiognomy or skin color. It uses "race" also to mean "ethnicity" or culture, as well as geographic origins.

The three categories listed in Question 4 after White and Black/Negro are "Indian (Amer.), Eskimo, and Aleut." "Indian" first appeared as a separate category in the Census count in 1860. Prior to that, they would have been counted among "all other free persons," unless they lived on reservation land (in which case they were not taxed and therefore not of interest to the Census and, hence, not counted). "Indian" became "American Indian" in 1950. Eskimos and Aleuts argued that they are not American Indian "tribes" on the grounds that they do not share the same history, customs, language, and traditions as American Indians. Since 1980, they have been listed separately.

Shared language, religion, foods, customs, traditions, and so forth are commonly referred to as cultural traits or hallmarks of "ethnicity." The Census institutionalizes a distinction between "race" and "ethnicity" on this basis, using a separate question (number 13) about "ancestry or ethnic origin." But in accepting a culturally based distinction among Eskimos, Aleuts, and American Indians in Question 4, the Census seems to be using "race" to mean "ethnicity." We see this same confusion of meaning in non-Census questionnaires that list Hispanic together with White and Black. Since Hispanics may be of any race, by definition, the three used together in this way cannot denote racial groups. This categorical equivalence makes White and Black into ethnicities.

In addition to "color" and "culture," Question 4 suggests another possible meaning of "race." The subcategories listed for "Asian and Pacific Islander"—Chinese, Japanese, Filipino, etc.—are all nation-states, as are all the other possibilities suggested to enumerators and tabulated by analysts (with the exception of the Hmong, a mountain-dwelling group from Laos). Here, "race" appears to mean people who have a common geographic origin (on geography and race, cf. Greenwood, 1984). And so, Question 4, which asks for the respondent's "race," offers and tabulates racial, ethnic, and geographic answers—indicating that in Census Bureau practice, "race" means something other than physical features alone.

Question 13: "Ancestry or Ethnic Origin"

The confusion of color (race), culture (ethnicity), and country (geography) also characterizes the suggested answers to Question 13, which asks about "ancestry or ethnic origin." Despite the fact that it seemingly institutionalizes the distinction between race and ethnicity, Question 13's proposed answers suggest the same mix of category types as Question 4. German, Italian, Croatian (the Census was prescient: Yugoslavian is not on the 1990 list), Cape Verdean, and others refer to specific geographic places. Afro-American, Cajun, and French Canadian refer to peoples who share such cultural elements as a common history, language, cuisine, and other customs (to a point). That means that Questions 4 and 13 are both asking about the same phenomena—country and culture—and using "race" and "ethnicity" to mean both.

But even the cultural sense of "ethnic origin" in Question 13 is not based on clear distinctions. For example, Lebanese and Nigerians come from countries with internal divisions along linguistic, religious, and other lines; hence, it is not clear that either is an "ethnicity," as that term is commonly understood. Similarly, "Irish" includes two religious groups, Protestants and Catholics, whose differences might be reason to have two rather than one subcategory. And not all "Afro-Americans" (the census term) share the same ancestry or "original" history, cuisine, religion, and so forth.

Further real and hypothetical combinations of race and ethnicity emerge from this analysis. The various possible answers to Questions 4 and 13 suggest a distinction between Negro or Black as a "race" and Afro-American as an "ethnicity." By the logic of this distinction, one could be racially "Black" and ethnically something other than "Afro-American." This, in fact, is the claim of immigrants from the Caribbean, who identify their heritage as Trinidadian, Jamaican or, more generally, West Indian. One could also be ethnically "Afro-American" and racially non-Black, according to these categories, which might hypothetically be the situation of someone raised in an African-American family who has "passed" or, by definitional happenstance, of a white African immigrant.

Question 7: "Spanish/Hispanic"

The implied distinction between race and ethnicity is further muddied by Census Question 7, which asks about Spanish/Hispanic origin. Here, too, the possible answers suggested are geographic: Mexican, Puerto Rican, and Cuban are the main subcategories; Argentinian, Colombian, and so forth, the offered additional possibilities. At the same time, by noting that Hispanic peoples may be of any race, the Census appears to suggest that Hispanics are cultural or ethnic groupings. Using "Hispanic" to refer to geographic and ethnic identities raises the question of the overlap between nationality and culture. Yet, "Hispanic" is not included as a possible answer to Question 13, suggesting that it is not an ethnicity or ancestral heritage any more than it is a race. Although included as a racial category in Question 4, unlike Hispanic, Native American is also not included as a possible answer to Question 13 ("ancestry or ethnic origin"). But Mexican and Dominican are proposed answers to both Question 7 ("Hispanic") and Question 13 ("ethnic origin"); and Korean is proposed as an answer to Questions 4 ("race") and 13 ("ethnic origin").

My point in detailing these ambiguities and contradictions is not that we should be more exacting in our use of these two terms, nor am I suggesting that the Census Bureau is somehow at fault. Rather, my focus is on them as reflective of contemporary American discourse: the categories are a constructed text, not an authored text. If we recognize that both "race" and "ethnicity" are social constructions, then we can begin to ask what sorts of features their use highlights and what silences are enabled.[5] Those who argue for adding a "multiracial" category to the Census or who do not find themselves reflected in existing categories confirm not only the constructedness of racethnic categories, but also their decreasing utility as descriptions of present American self-perceptions and experiences. That the categories and subcategories have changed in various ways over time, reflecting contemporaneous domestic and foreign policy concerns, further substantiates their constructed quality.

CATEGORICAL INSTABILITY OVER TIME

Categories have changed over time independently of demographic changes in the United States. Required by the U.S. Constitution and first taken in 1790, the Census was initially concerned with enumerating potential taxpayers, soldiers, and slaves. The word "color" first appears in the 1820 Census, and it is used in reference to freed slaves. (A summary of the early categories may be found in the Appendix.)

In 1850 "color" is first used to refer to whites. Until this point, the "racial" categories had been free whites, all other free persons (including "free colored persons") except Indians not taxed (i.e., living on reservation lands), and slaves. Interestingly, in 1850 color is subdivided into "white, black, or mulatto" for free inhabitants; "slaves" have no color subdivisions.

The word "race" first appears in 1870, with the subcategories white, colored, Chinese, Indian. This Census also tabulates "native or foreign born," which had been asked once before in 1820 as "foreigners not naturalized"; in neither case was gender, race, nor other information requested.

The 1880 Census adds Japanese to the race list. In 1890 "race" becomes "color" as the category label, and "Colored" is replaced by "Negro." In 1900 "Negro" is followed by "(colored)." In 1910 "(colored)" is dropped and "Negro" is subdivided into Black and Mulatto (the latter term reappearing for the first time since 1850). In 1920 the subdivisions of "Negro" are dropped, and the category name is listed as "color or race."

In 1930 new subcategories are added: Mexican and Filipino. These are supplemented in 1940 by Hindu, Korean, and "all other." "Indian" becomes "American Indian" in 1950, and Hindu and Korean are dropped. "Negro" becomes "Negro or Black" in 1960; Hawaiian joins the list, and Korean returns. In 1980 Negro and Black reverse order; Eskimo, Aleut, Asian Indian, Vietnamese, Samoan, and Guamanian are added. No new names were added in 1990.

In general speech as well as in the Census, changing usages of racethnic names reflect social movements and historical moments. "Black" and "Afro-American" are currently giving way to "African-American." "Asian-American" has come into widespread use, although "Oriental" may still be heard on the East coast and in the mid-West. In the 1950 and 1960 Censuses, Hispanics were tabulated in a separate question, identified as "Persons of Spanish Mother Tongue." In 1970 they were listed as "Persons of Both Spanish Surname and Spanish Mother Tongue," and in 1980 the "Hispanic" category was created.

For a while "Chicano" was also in use in general parlance, and is now being generally replaced by "Mexican-American" and "Latino/Latina." "Indian" was replaced for a while by "Native American," although many "American Indians" are returning to that name, and "Alaskan Natives" have established that grouping as a separate category. The Small Business Administration accords "Native Hawaiians" separate standing.[6] Another recent development is that "White" is being contested by "Caucasian" and by "European-American." The term "Anglo" suggests an opposition to "Hispanic," a less charged alternative to "gringo." As shorthand for Anglo-Saxon, it includes Celts, Protestant Irish, English, and Scots, and by derivation, French, German, and Scandinavians. It is not as inclusive as "White," however: "Anglo" excludes Italians, Greeks, and others of Southern and Eastern European origin. Both "Anglo" and "European-American" exclude Arab peoples, who are included in the OMB definition of "white."

The categories, in other words, are neither fixed nor stable. They reflect specific choices, contexts and concerns at particular moments in time. We can see this instability in further detail with each group.

The White category has included people who at other times it has excluded. The Melungeons, whose ethnic history has only recently been detailed, descended from Moors—North African Arabs who had settled Spain and Portugal and were expelled from those countries in 1492 and 1497, respectively, and again in the early 1500s. One group of Moors landed off the South Carolina coast around 1580 and were eventually pushed to Newman's Ridge above the Powell River Valley along the Virginia-Tennessee border, where they have lived for the last 200 years. Along the way they married Cherokee and other Indians and English immigrants. They were originally listed in the Census as "free persons of color." Around World War II, their classification was changed to "White" (*The Herndon (Va.) Observer*, 1/29/93: 1, 4). Racial reclassifications in the United States were by no means limited to isolated incidents. The 1990 post-Census update planned to count Asians and Native Americans as "Whites."

The nature of "Black"-ness is unique in American usage in one respect. Children born of one African-American parent are commonly registered as Black. This is a heritage of the so-called "one-drop rule" that has long operated in this country, which has stipulated that any person with one drop of African blood was to be identified as "Black" (cf. Davis 1991). The *Los Angeles Times* (1/13/91, E1) relates the story of children of a Swedish mother and Black father who are considered to be Black in all official records, to the mother's disbelief and dismay at finding her part of their heritage denied.

The context-specific meaning of "Black" may be further seen by examining its meaning in other societies. In Great Britain, where a census ethnicity question was first asked in 1991, the "Black" categories are: Black-Caribbean, Black-African, and Black-Other, with a space to identify which other.[7]

"Hispanic" or Latino/a identity is a similarly "unstable" category. OMB Directive No. 15 defines "Hispanic" as including those of "South American or other Spanish culture or origin." This could include Brazilians, who speak Portuguese, but not Portuguese-speakers from Portugal unless they consider themselves to come from a "Spanish" culture. Sepharadi Jews come from a Spanish origin; many in the United States and elsewhere have Spanish surnames, and a Spanish-Hebrew dialect may still be spoken by their families, even though their ancestors left Spain in 1492 when Jews were expelled during the Inquisition. Are Sepharadi Jews from the United States, the Middle East, North Africa, Greece, Holland, and Israel, "Hispanics"?[8] "Hispanics" do not share a language, if we include Brazilians and Sepharadi Jews—or a religion, if we include Sepharadi Jews along with the Catholics who predominate. They are neither a race, an ethnicity, nor a geographic group.

READING RACETHNIC CATEGORIES

Since racethnic categories are social constructions that have changed over time, it is reasonable to ask what attributes of racethnicity are reflected in these categories. What characteristics does that discourse highlight, and what does it tend to conceal? The Census case illustrates several features of this discourse: (1) the categories imply a point of view *outside* the system of differences; (2) this external category-maker aggregates groups that mark distinctions among themselves; (3) the resulting "categorical lumpiness" implies and implicitly enforces a unity that in many cases is not supported, and it reifies these categorical divisions as if they were scientifically grounded, thereby masking both their constructedness and the point of view from which they were created.

The Census categories mix people together who by other criteria—language, for example, or religion, or food and other customs—are quite distinct. Let us examine some of the oddities of this lumping, looking first at "people of color."

Categorical Lumpiness and the Modern American Adam

1. The category "American Indian" or "Native American" diverts attention from the sorts of differences that one might anticipate among the 119

tribes recognized by government treaty, suggesting a homogeneity that from another point of view may not be there. The underlying principle of classification seems to be "race," but it is race in the sense of "blood" composition that demarcates Indian from non-Indian. To claim Indian heritage a person must document a minimal percentage of blood or genetic composition, as well as self- or other-identification with a federally recognized tribe. At the same time, although OMB Directive 15 defines Native Americans as "original peoples of North America," Rodriguez found himself excluded as a *Mexican* Indian, as noted earlier.[9]

2. As noted above, the cluster terms "Hispanic" and "Latino" also suggest a cultural homogeneity and a political unity that do not exist in practice (cf. Coughlin, 1991). Here, too, categorical lumpiness implies a homogeneity which, from the point of view of category members, does not exist.

3. The "Asian-American" or "Asian and Pacific Islander" (API) category masks generational and economic characteristics, as well as geographic and cultural ones. It includes fourth generation Japanese, along with a newly arrived immigrant from Pakistan. The Census list of possibilities for API has 25 different countries, covering 6,000 miles and many languages, religions, foods, customs, traditions, and physical features. A visual display of the territory covered by this category would highlight the arbitrariness of where the category line is drawn, as well as the continuity of the peoples involved on both sides of that line.

4. The African-American category similarly masks generation of immigration and country of origin. For example, an African-American from Chicago whose ancestors were brought as slaves and who was raised in the South and a recent immigrant from Ethiopia living in Boston are both "Black," according to the Census, as are immigrants from the West Indies. This suggests another problem with Question 13: How far back in time is an individual to go in tracing "ethnic origin"? As with Native Americans, the principle of classification is blood (institutionalized in the one-drop rule, still a matter of practice in many places, although no longer legal; see Davis, 1991).

In these four categories, then, there is seemingly no common classificatory principle according to which they have been created. The requirements for membership and for "passing" (escaping membership) suggest that while American Indians and African-Americans are categorized by blood, Asian-Americans are classified by geography and Hispanics, by accent. The shared classificatory principle emanates from elsewhere, in the point of view from which these groups are being perceived, a point of view that is unspoken, though implicit in the categorizations. That eye belongs to a contemporary "Adam" who, looking out at the world, describing its inhabitants, and naming them "according to their kinds," sees and defines an "Other."

Note the order in which the categories are typically given. When we want to suggest status equality among categories, we often list them in alphabetical order. This is not the case in the Census (or in most such questionnaires). The list is given in order of difference, of Otherness, beginning with the "normal" category. It is not a historical sequencing: the Pilgrims in Plymouth faced the local Indians before they faced Africans. The list follows a descending order of otherness, reflecting a single-point perspective.

This American Adam is the collective embodiment of a "White" communal perspective. From his perspective (and in most respects, our modern-day Adam has been male) the salient characteristics against which he perceives "Otherness" are white skin, European facial features and hair, and "unaccented" English—the elements that make "passing" possible. More finite distinctions—that there are noticeable physical or speech differences between a "Black" from Chicago or the West Indies and one from Ghana, or between an "Asian" from New Delhi and one from Korea, or between a Navajo and a Mashpee—have typically not been visible to him (even though Whites, especially those East of the Mississippi, make minute judgments of recognition among themselves based on physical features and names with reasonable degrees of accuracy, differentiating among Irish, Italians, Jews, and others). Our Adam is from the East coast or the stretch from the Northeastern industrial cities to Chicago, because his "Other" is mostly "Black": he sees his opposite in the black skin of his historical encounter with slavery, in the Civil War, and in the Civil Rights Movement. This, despite the fact that there have been Asian-Americans in the West for over 100 years and "Hispanics" and American Indians in the Southwest and elsewhere for longer than there has been an America. We cannot yet call him "Caucasian" because he is typically not conscious of "having" a race himself: in his mind's eye, he sees himself as "normal" or regular. (This may be changing, as "white" is emerging as a growing racethnic self-identity.) Until very recently, our Adam has been Anglo-Saxon and Protestant (I will return to this shortly); he still is Christian: Jews are "Other" along with Moslems, Hindus, Bahai's, Buddhists, Shintos, and so forth.

This is the person who supplies the perspective from which Others are labeled. Perhaps because his perspective is relatively undifferentiated, the categories he has created are highly aggregated and "lumpy." They make less sense with respect to the attributed similarities of their members than they do relative to their aggregate differences from him.

White Is a Color, Too

But "White" is also a lumpy category. It is no more fixed or stable than the others. Current usage reflects a changed sense of historical experience.

Until recently, the racethnic identity of the dominant American culture as perceived by themselves and others was not only White, but Anglo-Saxon and Protestant as well. Other non-Anglo-Saxon and non-Protestant "White" groups became "hyphenated-Americans": Irish-Americans, Italian-Americans, Polish-Americans, Jewish-Americans. The hyphen denoted their Otherness. That they were also "white"-skinned Caucasians was not reflected in the categories of the time. Their contrasting features stood out more: physical (that they were redheads [Irish] or swarthy with dark, curly hair [Greeks, Italians, Jews], rather than blonds); religious; cultural (that they practiced other customs and ate different food). For those who grew up in East coast cities and suburbs, the phrase "Irish and Jews need not apply" may still be familiar, along with the memory of streets where owners had pacts not to sell their homes to "Jews and Negroes."

Recent usage of the category "Whites" implies that this distinction between Protestant Anglo-Saxons and Catholic and Jewish non-Anglo-Saxons has broken down. The European ethnics have made their way into the workplace, the boardroom, and the country club. The use of the phrase "People of Color" has strengthened the oppositional categorization "Whites." The turn to hyphenization among other Others—Asian-Americans, African-Americans, Hispanic-Americans, Native Americans (even without the hyphen)—has given rise to a new oppositional category, "European-American." The blurring of distinctions between ethnicity and race has also, of late, fostered the designation "Caucasian" to mean a "White" cultural group.

What have we gained, and what have we lost, by this lumping?

The lumpiness of "Whites" masks recent and continuing discriminations against various "White" subgroups. On the one hand, it evens the playing field categorically: if all Americans are now hyphenated-Americans, are we not then conceptually equal?[10] The once-demeaning hyphen has become almost a mark of status. As essayist Barbara Ehrenreich (1992) recently noted, "it [has] begun to seem almost un-American not to have some sort of hyphen at hand, linking one to more venerable times and locales." This would suggest that European ethnics are no longer "Other." However, David Duke's campaign, intimations linking Mario Cuomo to the Mafia, and concerns about Paul Tsongas's presidential candidacy—"Another Greek?" after Michael Dukakis—indicate that this animosity is not entirely behind us. The City University of New York, for example, includes Italian-Americans in its protected classes for affirmative action purposes. Also, this conceptual equality does not extend to non-European, "white" Muslim and Christian Arab-Americans, whose "Otherness" was made visible most recently during the war against Iraq and in character depictions and lyrics in the popular Disney film, *Aladdin*.

Moreover, this conceptualization of Whites as a uniform group colors the discourse on workplace diversity, where "diversity" is typically used to mean the presence of nonWhites. This implies that "Whites" are either not culturally diverse or, perhaps, do not have "culture." In claiming that such cultural diversity in the workplace is new and unprecedented, those who research the topic also rewrite the history of diversity and discrimination in the 1950s and 1960s when European ethnics were taking their places in the suburbs and the workplace. This denies the experience of non-Anglo-Saxon, non-Protestant "Whites" who have also had to learn to be bicultural (Yanow, 1992).

At the same time, their presence as a separate category implies the existence of a "White culture" (in the same way that the categories also imply the existence of African-, Asian-, Hispanic, and Native American cultures). In creating a "White" (or any) category we engage in a process that Omi and Winant call "racialization," "through which racial meaning is extended to a previously unclassified relationship, social practice, or group" (quoted in Delgado and Sen, 1988:144). In this case, however, Whites are racialized without the cultural hallmarks of common language, religion, foods, customs, and so forth that typically denote ethnic groups. Here too, we can look for the unspoken definer, a mythical Adam "of color"—the counterpart to the WASP Adam who has racialized the other lumpy groups.[11]

We have stripped Caucasian women and men of the cultural characteristics that they defined themselves, as we have done in denying diversity within the other categories. For those who find identity in ethnic cultures, this is a loss. Ironically, it is not only the European ethnics' culture that is lost in the lumpiness of "European-American" or "Caucasian." "English" is also absent as a possible ancestry in Question 13.

In developing a category labeled "European-American," we create an identity that is conceptually equivalent to other hyphenated identities and yet at the same time so distanced from many Caucasians' self-perception that it is devoid of substance. The category "White" serves as an oppositional form to "People of Color" but both are culturally blank.

STORIES AND SILENCES

In part the story told here represents a struggle over who gets to define what an American is. The taxation, military, and labor concerns of the earliest

Censuses are no longer our primary interests. Since the early 1900s, the Census has reflected a growing concern with national identity. And we have come to see racethnic components as the central, if not exclusive, feature of that identity. Why?

In our particular usages of these racethnic categories, we are telling ourselves identity stories of three kinds: stories about group identity, national identity, and national origins. To be without a racethnic identity in the United States today is to be silenced: individuals and groups without category labels cannot tell their own stories about membership in American society.[12]

By lumping at a high level of aggregation, we accomplish an "ethnic deracination," bleaching all members of the lumpy categories of cultural marks. By lumping at this level of aggregation, we seem to deny any but the most superficial cultural identity to all groups. In this way, we accomplish both a nod to difference—although in name only, devoid of cultural substance—and the preservation of the "we" on the other side of the hyphen. We thereby accommodate our fears both of difference and of disunion. As Chock, Urciuoli, and Sarat and Berkowitz (this volume) report, American public discourse associates difference with political disintegration.

Moreover, through categorical lumpiness and the reification of race and ethnicity, we maintain one of the classic areas of silence in American society: the notion of class (see Segal, this volume). By presenting racethnicity as the central component of our identity, we maintain the founding myth that we are a classless society. In accounting for our national origins, we are in accord that our Adam's ancestors, the Pilgrims, came in search of freedom from persecution. We enshrine this origin story in our immigration policy, giving refuge to those fleeing from adverse political and religious regimes (as long as it is in keeping with our foreign policy). But we deny, in all practical senses, that those ancestors brought a social and economic class structure with them and/or developed one on this soil. And in this denial, and in the active embrace of classlessness, we deny ourselves an explanation for status differences in contemporary society. Racethnic stories give us this explanation, at the same time that they mask it. They allow us to maintain the belief that success and failure are in individuals' hands, or are attributes of blood and the soil that nurtured it.

In counting all "Asians and Pacific Islanders" in one category, thereby reporting a statistic that is an average over all subgroups, we divert attention from those groups below the poverty line. Treating "Blacks" without internal differentiation plays on stereotypes that are silent on the existence of a Black middle class. This silence also obscures the existence of poor Whites—agricultural families, for example, who came to the small towns of California's Central Valley during Dust Bowl migrations, whose children or grandchildren in 1998 are the first generation in their family to go to college. They are as "European" as wealthy or middle-class Whites. This choice to make racethnicity the central organizing principle of societal status also confounds immigrants from countries where class was the more important feature. We maintain the fiction that we are a classless society by focusing on racethnic categories, but we empty those categories of substantive meaning. In doing so, we divert attention from economic sources of power and status in this country, which also contribute to the making of American identity and culture.[13]

Policy and administrative judgments require achieving a balance between the group and the individual, or creating possibilities for case-by-case evaluation. This is seen most clearly in the census case. Census categories were not created to allow individuals to express their identities. They have always had clear instrumental purposes.

Today, racethnic categories appear to be statements about social status and class. But since we have inherited a national mythology of classlessness, alluding to class through racethnic labels highlights racial discourse while it silences public discourse concerning economic bases of status. "What we do with difference, and whether we acknowledge our own participation in the meanings of the differences we assign to others, are choices that remain" (Minow, 1990: 390). On the subject of evolving racethnic categories that embody and mask cultural and class differences, we should not be silent.

ACKNOWLEDGMENTS

I thank Mary Irving for research assistance in the preparation of an earlier version of this essay, Davydd Greenwood for his extensive comments on several versions, Carol Greenhouse for her sensitive and sensible editing, and David Rosenhan for his encouragement in its pursuit. Parts of this essay appear in "American ethnogenesis and public administration," *Administration and Society* 27:4 (February, 483–509). Earlier versions were presented at the Fifth National Symposium on Public Administration Theory, Chicago, April 9–10, 1992; the Western Political Science Association Annual Conference, Pasadena, California, March 18–20, 1993; "Democracy and Difference," Indiana University, Bloomington, April 22–25, 1993; the American Society for Public Administration Annual Conference, San Francisco, July 19–21, 1993; and the American Political Science Association Annual Meeting, Washington, D.C., September 2–5, 1993. I thank the participants at these conferences and especially those at Indiana University for their lively responses to this work and for their many personal stories of racethnic identities that confound easy categorization.

NOTES

1. These are the only questions that have direct bearing on racial and ethnic population features. Questions about religion are not included in the Census following the principal of separation of church and state.

2. Apparently, many people greet the Census with responses that range from anger and annoyance to humor. Felicity Barringer in the *New York Times* (4/15/90, p. 12) reported that someone listed a family member's name as Puss E. Cat; his race in Question 4 was listed as Siamese.

3. As I show later, "color" does appear as a category in earlier versions of the Census, beginning in 1820 as "free colored persons" as a separate category from "slaves." Greenwood (1984) elaborates a detailed argument to show that post-Darwinian, supposedly "scientific" concepts of race are, in fact, echoes of ancient Greek and Roman ideas about the four environmental elements and their related humors: fire (yellow bile), air (blood), water (phlegm), and earth (black bile). These correspond with the stereotypical "choleric" or excitable yellow-skinned Asian; the "brave, noble, red" Indian "savage"; the "phlegmatic" white European; and the "melancholic" or lazy black Negro.

4. Anthropologist Stanley Garn (1968: 9) noted that various researchers had found between 2 and 200 "racial" groups. By the 1980s both anthropologists and biologists had given up the idea of a scientific basis for a race and ethnicity. There is, of course, a lengthy literature in these fields on this subject, which I will not reproduce here. See Garn (1968) and Greenwood (1984) for further references.

5. On "color," race, and ethnicity as social constructions, see also Fischer, 1986; Sollors, 1989; and Williams, 1990.

6. The SBA (in its Business Classification Definitions for Disadvantaged-Owned and Controlled) also accords protected standing to Hasidic Jewish Americans. It includes people whose origins are from "the Iberian Peninsula, including Portugal" as Hispanic Americans.

7. The non-Black categories were: White; Indian; Pakistani; Bangladeshi; Chinese; Any other, with a space to identify which other. Mexico, by comparison, has not asked a racethnic question for 70 years.

8. "Sepharadi" Jews trace their ancestry to Spain ("Sepharad," in Hebrew) or Portugal before the time of their expulsion (1492 and 1497), when they migrated to the countries of North Africa, the Middle East, and some European states (typically Greece, Bulgaria, Italy, and Holland). The first Jews in the United States were Sepharadim from Amsterdam who came to Nieuw Amsterdam (later New York) in Peter Stuyvesant's time from Recife, Brazil, where their ancestors had settled. "Ashkenazi" Jews are those whose ancestors came from Germany ("Ashkenaz") and other countries of Eastern and Western Europe to which German Jews migrated (cf. Rita Arditti's comment in Bulkin [1984:201 n.7]).

9. Although the Census allows individuals to register their self-perceptions, OMB No. 15 allows American Indians to be so identified by "community recognition." EEOC policy, however, requires that identification be made according to the administrator's point of view (although this appears not to be uniform practice). This question of "in whose eyes?" has led to problematic court deliberations for Native Americans, usually around land claims. The Mashpee are a well-known earlier case (see Minow 1990, pp. 351–356 for example); but the matter was more recently before the Senate in the case of the Lumbee of North Carolina, which was decided against them (Healey, 1992; *Wall Street Journal* editorial, 3/18/92). I have discussed this question of self-vs-other identification at greater length in Yanow (1995).

10. Buker (1987: 26) made a parallel argument about the category "Black Americans" (or "Blacks"). In replacing "Negroes," it signaled a different status for its members: rather than indicating a nation with a few Negroes, she writes, the new category name implicitly argued that "Americans" included Blacks and Whites.

11. An example of racializing at work can be seen in the present shift from writing "white" and "black" to "White" and "Black." Linguistically, the use of the capital letters moves the terms from adjectives to nouns. As categories, the capitalized words become conceptually equivalent to the other capitalized racethnic terms. This can also be read as an assimilationist story, one that began with undifferentiated Blacks, and is now producing undifferentiated Whites.

12. I elaborate on these ideas in Yanow (1995).

13. See also Steinberg 1989, Williams 1990, and Segal and Urciuoli (this volume) for more extensive analyses of the connections between class, race, and ethnicity.

APPENDIX

Early Census Categories

The first Census, taken in 1790, had six categories for race-related divisions: five of them counted free people (free white males older than 15 and older than 21, free white females younger than 15 and in general, and all others), the sixth, "Slaves." (Steinberg [1989] notes that among the slaves were Indians and Whites as well as Blacks.) The next Census refined these into four categories: age gradations of free white males; age gradations of free white females; all other free persons except "Indians not taxed" (i.e., those on reservation lands); and slaves. In 1820 the list was revised by the addition of "foreigners not naturalized" and "free colored persons." The gender of slaves was first noted in 1820. "Free colored persons," first counted that year, are also tallied by gender.

In 1830 the categories are simplified into three: free white persons; slaves and free colored persons; and "deaf and dumb," divided between whites, and slaves and colored persons. Neither slaves nor free colored persons were counted by gender. Gender tabulation of slaves and free colored persons returns in 1840. This Census adds "blind and insane" to deaf and dumb, separated between white and colored persons. The 1850 Census simplified the count with two categories: free inhabitants and slaves. Each had four subcategories: "age; sex; color; deaf, dumb, blind, or insane, idiotic." The latter disappears altogether as a category after this Census.

The 1860 Census is the first whose categories resemble contemporary ones. There are four: white; free colored; Indians; slaves.

Chapter 7

Difference from the People's Point of View

José Antonio Fernández de Rota Monter

In Galicia, a country situated in the northwest of Spain, people have a strong sense of identity that is clearly distinguishable from those in Spain's other geographical areas. The second half of the nineteenth century saw a rise of so-called regionalist political movements in Galicia aimed at protecting the region from what was considered unjust treatment by Spain as a whole. These regionalist groups initially claimed that the Galician language was a fundamental element of their identity and they have slowly moved toward other nationalist claims. These claims, which now include a wide range of elements, are usually given the generic and rather ambiguous name "galleguismo" (Galicianism). Galician regionalism and nationalism have combined to develop a full intellectual theorization of the identity of Galicia by emphasizing its linguistic, ethnocultural, and historical personality. While Galician nationalists base their arguments on a marked Galician collective identity that is deeply felt in Galicia, most Galicians appear to combine their sense of regional identity quite harmoniously with a feeling of Spanish nationality and a desire to continue to form part of Spain.

At the same time, the revival of customs considered as typical, and love for tradition, speak of a new awareness that accords with new winds of change. Galician nationalists could win support for their claims based on the country's economic inferiority. The argument that the Galician people should be treated with more respect and dignity has also met with approval in certain sectors. However, there is an especially negative attitude toward this movement among the growing, influential circles of Spanish speakers. For the moment, the great silent majority appears to be the most important, anonymous absentee in the nationalist politics of all sides in Galicia.

In this situation anthropology has a role to play in registering the voices, actions, and contexts of political self-expression. Following a review of the main claims by nationalists regarding Galician identity, I will summarize the findings from an ethnographic study of self-identity in one township, El Bierzo. There, investigation shows that, in fact, collective identity appears necessarily to seek support in the elusive frontier world rather than in a stable unit. It is in a dynamic, ambiguous world of levels and degrees of identity that the apparently solid, but always unstable, walls of a recognized nation are built.

Collective identity is not just a category that can be demonstrated in a cold analysis of "objective similarities," but a living experience that is closely related to a person's own self-identity. It is captured in a combination of different levels stretched out between the individual and humanity or the cosmos. Anthropologists try to seek out the particulars of experience in actual, close-up contexts and frameworks; they try to understand people's convictions or skeptical attitudes, their practical compromises, social strategies and specific institutions, their games of acceptances, and the changing coercions and inertias on which identity depends.

NATIONALIST IDENTITY CLAIMS

Let us begin by considering the nationalists' central claims regarding Galician language, culture, and identity against the backdrop of a brief survey of Galicia in the context of the Iberian peninsula and Europe. First from a linguistic point of view, we should pay particular attention to the way in which vulgar Latin was slowly transformed into vernacular languages, in the course of what is generally termed the fragmentation of the Roman Empire. The territory from Finisterre on the west coast of the Iberian peninsula to Trieste on the eastern borders of Italy embodies a continuous map of small variations. According to isogloss graphs, there are small variations in linguistic usage every fifteen to twenty kilometers. Judging from such graphs alone geographic distance corresponds to linguistic difference.

The formal geographical picture of a philological continuum cannot fail to fascinate an anthropologist dedicated to the subject of identity, given many nationalists' claims that linguistic differences form the basis of identity, race or nationality. One could imagine a hypothetical frontier every fifteen to twenty kilometers. Using only linguistic characteristics as a basis, it would be possible to build out of one single nation many hundreds between Finisterre and Trieste. But isogloss abstracts do not provide an accurate view of linguistic reality. In practice, it is possible to find similar linguistic phenomena at distant points on the map, all along the continuum. Thus, although claims linking philology to a broader regional geography are always defensible, they are also always contestable.

Turning to cultural geography, we find a rather different map—though equally available as a resource for both creating and contesting identities. Most of Europe constitutes a huge area of cultural interaction, where for many centuries, similar customs have existed in several widely dispersed cultural fields. To a great extent, the multi-dimensional nature of intense cultural contact over time has made each region of Europe a melting pot of customs. The maps of customs overlap considerably. Even with regard to those particular customs—such as certain components of festivals—which occur across Europe, one should speak of characteristic varieties peculiar to particular regions or even to much smaller areas, rather than to clear contrasts among different regions.

Turning to political history, we encounter the puzzle of medieval feudalism in Spain, as we would in many other European countries. Diminutive kingdoms were not uncommon and alliances, conquests, and hereditary divisions contributed to the creation of a continuous flux of political formations on the map of the peninsula. Subsequently, absolute monarchies and, later the constitution of Spain as a nation-state, gave rise to administrative divisions with ambiguous boundaries. These are now more stable and defined than they were during the last regime. Over the last 150 years, the administrative units and divisions came to have different official shapes in the political, legal, military, and religious spheres, with the political division in the provinces and regions being the most influential in the mental map of Spaniards in this century.

All these historical graphs of border dynamics and the continua of changing coordinates help clarify the rich sources of argument and debate between theorists of different nationalist ideologies which, in accordance with modern European tradition since the Romantics, consume a considerable measure of historical fuel. But nationalist theorists do not rely on academic argument alone. They also draw on popular approaches to collective identity for their starting points.

What are the popular arguments in favor of a collective Galician identity at this more grassroots level? Some nationalist theorists consider themselves to be the true representatives of popular sentiment even when their ideas are at odds with local views—over which they exert some influence. Nationalists point first to language. The first, basic differential element is the "dejo" or lilt, which is the standard way of pronouncing and speaking Spanish, with the added awareness of speaking a different vernacular language, more often than not unintelligible to outsiders from other parts of Spain.

Second, there are a series of "ethnographic" elements that are considered as typical or more typical of Galicia: the corn barns (*horreos*), the clogs, the Dutch oven, music played on the bagpipes and characteristic traditional costumes. To these we could add some gastronomic characteristics and stereotypes that portray certain psychological characteristics and collective forms of behavior.

With respect to the popular distinction between Galician and Spanish (Castilian), the map drawn from isoglosses along a shifting continuum provides a good visual idea of the linguistic situation in the fourteenth and fifteenth centuries. In Spain, the birth of absolute monarchy, forged under the scepter of the Catholic Kings, would gradually ensure the dominance of the educated variation of Spanish used by the court at that time. This language, which soon became the one used in official documents and by educated people, had an increasingly decisive influence on local dialects. Local dialects began to die out over large areas of the peninsula, ultimately reduced to a few secondary variants of a language in ever wider use.

This substitution of standardized Spanish for many dialects progressed steadily outward from central Spain toward the East and West. By the beginning of the twentieth century, this process of language standardization process covered an extensive area in the center of the peninsula. Only here and there did small pockets still exist where the use of local dialects was still dominant, serving as a reminder of medieval fragmentation. In most rural areas in the center of Spain, the old forms were present only in linguistic remnants, and these did not withstand the pressure of Spanish in schooling and communications. Only the extreme east and west corners escaped the destructive advance of Spanish across the countryside.

This advance is still visible under the different conditions that prevail today. In the northwest corner (the subject of my analysis) it is still possible to draw a line—from the western tip of Asturias to the west of the provinces of Zamora and Leon—separating the rural communities, where practically only Spanish is spoken at home, from those where local dialects predominate. In several villages just to the west of this line, only the elderly now speak the local dialect, while the young only understand it or are even totally unfamiliar with it. As far as we can gather, at the beginning of this century, the dividing line would have been drawn several kilometers farther to the East.

Thus, from the point of view of Spaniards in this century, in so far as the West of Spain is concerned, only Galicia and some of the neighboring areas preserve a form of speech that is clearly distinguishable from Spanish. For this reason, it is logical to accept the popular stereotypic synthesis that classifies this collection of local dialects as "Gallego," quite apart from any academic consideration of a philological nature.

Regarding popular customs, although it is true, as we have already mentioned, that a great many of these customs could be found in large areas of Europe, there is also no doubt that several have gradually and completely died out. Today, the practice of these customs has been reduced to small islands that stand like sentinels of the past. Not withstanding this trend, various ethnographic traits found in popular Galician tradition can be found in many other neighboring areas.

Finally, the administrative divisions of modern times and especially the last century and a half, despite all their ambiguity, have helped to set the territorial limits around an older, more shadowy concept, Galicia. Galicia was a concept that already existed in the Middle Ages, when the Northwest of Spain was the Kingdom of Galicia.

So far we have spoken from the vantage point of the popular theorists of Galicia. Let us turn now to the politicians who support Galician nationalism.

THE POLITICS OF THE GALICIAN MOVEMENT

At present, within the Galician movement, there is a powerful sector with strong convictions who are ready for action and ideological proselytism. They firmly believe in the idea of Galicia as a nation and in the self-determination of the Galician people. Within this sector there are two distinct political parties, grouped together in two main coalitions: Bloque Nacional Popular Galego and Esquerda Galega. While differences in their attitudes and nuances of their programs are sometimes important, their general aim is to make Galician the official language of the region and to promote its use generally so that it should become the language normally used by Galicians at all levels "by turning spontaneous Galician speakers into conscious Galician speakers and encouraging Spanish-speakers to consciously adopt the Galician language in their way of life. In this respect, education is expected to play an important role in our country because, through the use of our language, we will be able to achieve a real identity, denied to us daily, as Galicians."[1]

These political trends attract large groups of fervent militants, in particular young teachers and university students, and also well-known Galician nationalists of older generations. However, so far, they have not met with much electoral success. At present (1989–1993), of the seventy-five members of the autonomic Galician Parliament, only two belong to Esquerda Galega and five to the Bloque Nacional. Neither of these coalitions is represented in the Spanish Parliament in Madrid.

In addition to these Galician coalitions, there are also Galician Nationalist wings in the main political parties: the conservatives, the center, and the moderate left. These moderate nationalists emphasize the importance of being Galician and speaking the language by focusing on their ethnic identity as a means of economic, political, and cultural development in a depressed country. Some defend the present system of autonomous communities while others aim to achieve a complete restructuring of our federal system. Generally, they consider the coexistence of both languages, Galician and Castilian,[2] in Galicia as beneficial, and they are working to revitalize Galician, traditionally discriminated against in both social and cultural circles. All this is aimed at helping the Galicians rid themselves of the "inferiority complexes" that have historically limited their possibilities.

Some of these moderate nationalists have formed their own political parties but these usually lack unity inside and have mediocre or totally disastrous results at the polls. Frequently they have joined coalitions or have been fully integrated in the most important Spanish national parties who have had excellent electoral results: Partido Popular (PP) and Partido Socialista del Obrero Español (PSOE).

Within these majority parties, the Galician nationalists represent only a minority, but nevertheless sometimes constitute an influential group, as is the case in the PSOE (Socialist Party), which at present forms the core of the coalition in power. In general, the large number of voters who support these moderate parties and, in particular, the majority conservative party (as well as the majority of those who abstain) consider Galicia to be part of Spain and reject their claims to self-determination.

In spite of this majority opinion, the parties representing these groups are implementing policies for standardizing Galician in official circles and in the schools.[3] Why have these decisions been made contrary to the majority opinion of the electorate? Respect for the different languages and characteristics of the various regions of Spain was one of the main concerns in the attempt to find a consensus and balance of opinions during the peaceful transition to democracy. The aim was to correct many of the repressive aspects of the previous dictatorship and to do so in as moderate a manner as possible, thus avoiding the radical attitudes and tensions that caused the Second Republic to dissolve into the Civil War.[4] In the case of Galicia, the nationalist groups formed a minority, and popular backing was weaker than in Catalonia and in the Basque Country. However, in the nationalists' logic, if the constitution considered Catalonia and the Basque Country "Historic Nations," then Galicia, even against majority opinion within the region, should be considered a nation by the very same standards. The politicians could also invoke the Galician situation as demonstration that autonomy does not go against a deep feeling of Spanish nationalism. Autonomy, from this point of view, is not a concession to nationalist groups, but a statement that there are many ways of being Spanish. In this way, the conservative democrats champion a much more advanced form of autonomy for Galicia than that requested by the majority, thus neutralizing the opposition of extremist nationalists and absorbing or winning the support of more moderate nationalist groups.

Added to this situation were the facts that the main conservative political leader at the time was Galician, and that he managed to obtain very good electoral results among his own countrymen. Over the last few years Galicia has become the main conservative stronghold, yet this party has at all times shown its special interest in defending Galicia as an autonomous community integrated into the national structure. In view of the fact that the Socialist Party, with its Andalusian leadership, was taking over in Madrid, the Conservative Party could achieve an important publicity advantage by underlining its Galician interest in contrast to the centralist focus of the Socialists.

The result of this interplay was that all the political parties in Galicia have made considerable efforts to show themselves officially to be Galician nationalists. In compiling their winning strategy, the silent majority and its representatives in official political life constitute a prudently quiet majority. Even the non-Galician nationalist sectors of the Socialist Party—who are in some respects freer in this ideological field since they cannot truthfully be accused of "Francoism"—also usually maintain attitudes that are prudent. Thus, consensus is emerging in which several political forces decide to act and express themselves in certain areas in ways that either go against or are irrelevant to their own beliefs.[5]

LEGAL SUPPORTS FOR GALICIAN IDENTITY

Let us consider how these concerns have been reflected in the basic institutional norm of Galician Autonomy, the "Estatuto" (Statute of Autonomy).

The Statute echos one of the fundamental articles of the 1978 Spanish Constitution, which states that "Catalonia," the "Basque Country," and "Galicia" are "historical nationalities." Once awarded the status of a nationality, the autonomous community "takes on the main task of defending the identity of Galicia and its interests and promoting solidarity amongst the Galician people." The territorial limits included the four provinces that have been part of Galicia for the past century and a half, thus accepting pre-existing boundaries. The Statutes also state that "the language of Galicia is Galician," while recognizing both Galician and Spanish as official languages. A pledge is also taken "to promote the use of Galician in all walks of public and cultural life, including the media."

Once the Statute was drawn up, it was submitted to a referendum. The great majority of the population did not turn out to vote; however, 24% did vote in favor of the Statute, which proved to be a higher percentage than the negative votes. This made it possible to pass the Statute and obtain ratification by the Spanish Parliament. On the one hand, calculations regarding the voting intentions of the electorate reveal that most of the negative votes came from nationalist sectors seeking a more radical approach to autonomy. On the other hand, the remaining negative vote and a high percentage of the abstentions can be interpreted as a rejection of or skepticism with respect to autonomy. We could say that the Statute was passed despite there being a majority against it.

The Statute's mandate with respect to language confronted certain problems. The various pro-Galician groups aim to purify the popular "Galician" language by making it more clearly different, in other words, authentically Galician. To what degree do Spanish and Galician match? To what extent are they different? What practical problems are involved in the purification of language?

A certain sector of radical Galician nationalists is trying forcefully to speed up the reconstruction of a hypothetical Galician language free from the powerful influence of Spanish. The Galician language is understood to be the "natural language" of all Galicians. In this context, natural means spontaneous, beyond the reach of political pressures from outside Galicia, as it would have developed historically in its "natural" state in a spontaneous manner following its own course of evolution. An example used is the evolution of Portuguese after the separation from Spain. Accordingly, nationalists think they must resort to "much older Galician forms," as it is much more likely that the more modern ones have suffered from the pressures of Spanish.

Backed by these arguments, these nationalists consider that Galician should be understood as the language of "Galicia." This includes not only the Spanish Autonomous Community of Galicia but also Portugal, Brazil, Angola, Mozambique, and so on. In these terms, Galician should be understood as "the language of our people" and the aim should be to try to find, within the wide geographical boundaries already mentioned, those forms that are most authentically Galician. This logically presupposes that the speech forms normally used in Galicia have been influenced by Spanish and are, therefore, adulterated. For this reason, "The linguistic geography and spatial neolinguistics will be extremely useful in determining true Galician forms by eliminating intrusions."[6]

Meanwhile what views are officially defended by the autonomous government with respect to these issues? The official orthographic and morphological rules, by which administrative documents are usually governed, and which are expected to be used in the teaching of Galician, were preceded in the statute by a brief introduction on their basis in certain theoretical principles. These reflect the Galician nationalist ideals, although they have been smoothed over and formulated in such a way that various interpretations are possible. They say that "the norm is to favor a Galician language which is true unto itself and free of all spurious elements which may have come embedded in the living language as a result of pressures from Castile."[7] This means "that everyday language should be as Galician as possible, but standardized without pressures or dependency, with scrupulous attention to the linguistic structure and characteristics of Galician."[8] They also say that "the principles chosen should be in harmony with those of other languages, especially romance languages and in particular Portuguese."[9]

In spite of the large effort the Galician government is investing in the standardization of the language, the results in no way meet nationalist expectations. Socio-linguistic studies reveal a clear, progressive decrease in the use of Galician. Even though Galician is still widely spoken in rural areas, it is used only by a minority of the younger generation now living in these districts and in the small market towns. Migration to city suburbs has further reduced the number of Galician speakers.

THE PLURAL WORLDS OF EL BIERZO

At this juncture, let us add to our considerations the question of what role the anthropologist should play in dealing with the type of problem I have sketched in the preceding synthesis. I take anthropology to be a research activity that attempts to understand the concrete "worlds" where people live, as well as what these people and the things in those "worlds" signify. The anthropologist's prime interest lies in these plural "worlds" and their plural truths.

In our large-scale, anonymous societies, those in power or in charge of our economy or "culture" are only interested in numbers and abstractions. Only a very few attempt to investigate and understand our world from the bottom up. This is the exceptional position of the anthropologist. Our duty is to establish where the people are. Our method focuses on details that are ignored or inaccessible to other approaches. Within the limitations of the scope of individuals' efforts, our job is to exemplify processes through well-crafted, specific cases—as an answer to the vague, dehumanizing or generalizing abstractions of politics.

In support of the arguments of this essay, I shall briefly refer to some aims and reflections of anthropological team research that I have been directing personally over the last six years. In previous work, we have tried to explain the problems of Galician identity by means of detailed analysis of the borders of Galicianism. We investigated specific areas around the geographical frontiers of Galicia, outside the administrative unit of Galicia but considered as Galician-speaking. We have also researched small market towns and city suburbs, in an attempt to gain some insight into the conflict between tradition and modernity in the most significant settings.

I will try to summarize some of the findings from our fieldwork in certain parts of El Bierzo, an area bordering on the Eastern limits of Galicia. Political opinion regarding El Bierzo embodies almost all of the logically possible political positions.

One group of "Bercianos" accepted the present official organization of El Bierzo as belonging to the Community of Castile and León. A second group believed that El Bierzo is León and not Castile. Some of them consider that León is made up of three provinces—León, Zamora and Salamanca—and others just one—León. A third group believes that El Bierzo is Galician and should form part of the Galician Autonomous Community. El Bierzo should be the fifth Galician province, as there is a natural unity with the district of Valdeorras in the Province of Orense. Some living at the western limits of El Bierzo do not accept that El Bierzo is a unit and believe that the Galician-speaking municipalities in the West should become part of the province of Lugo. The last group believes that El Bierzo is clearly separate from the surrounding areas. Some would like to see it become a province in its own right and perhaps in the future even an autonomous community. Others would be satisfied if Ponferrada, the capital of El Bierzo, were delegated some powers from the provincial capital.

If we move from these general political arguments to an analysis of the opinions existing in the different geographical areas of El Bierzo, the variety of opinions also proves to be significant. On the one hand, in Villafranca, a rival of Ponferrada, there is strong pro-Galician feeling. On the other hand, in rural Galician-speaking areas close to the official Galician border, people tend to consider themselves not as Galicians, but as belonging to León. They may be considerably influenced by a general attitude that undervalues the Galician language and everything Galician which, in their small rural circle, they associate with poor mountainous regions. However, in one of these bordering villages, thought by those living around it to be the poorest, people have traditionally felt great solidarity with the Galicians and think of themselves as Galician to a great extent.

Nevertheless, when people are asked direct questions, their answers are ambiguous. They often used expressions of "being" or "belonging," "leaning" or "being drawn" toward one direction or another. The different levels of identity also combine differently, with more emphasis on one or another or even through the formulation of degrees of identity. For example, a person could be more or less Galician. The same group of people could sometimes behave in a more Galician manner than at other times.

THE SEMANTICS OF INDENTITY IN EL BIERZO

In my fieldwork, I concentrated on Galician-speaking areas as the ones with the greatest complexity of identity, together with the towns of Villafranca and Ponferrada. In conversation, Bercianos used a series of verbs that helped them to express their feelings on identity with ease. Of course, the verb "ser" (to be) is necessarily one of the main ones. On many occasions we were told "somos leoneses" (we are Leonese), although generally speaking, this statement would not have been said so definitively.

Frequently, a less controversial verb was used: "Pertenecemos a León" (We belong to León). The verb "pertenecer" (to belong) appears to refer mainly to the official administrative territorial scheme. On still other occasions, they would state "nosotros aquí nos considermos leoneses" (those of us here consider ourselves Leonese).

Very often when the verb "ser" is used, riders are also attached. So, for example. To be Leonese loses force as the geographical proximity to Galicia increases, "to be . . . well, we are Leonese . . . but we are situated on the very edge of the province . . . We sit right on the border, but Galicia is sitting right on top of us." If being on the edge, on the very boundary, implies a geographic marginalization regarding being Leonese, having Galicia pressing down from above seems not just proximity to another being, but actually being threatened by it.

The fact that they think of themselves and their customs as similar to those of the Gallegos makes the proximity of Galicia all the more manifest. This is conversationally reflected when people (of El Bierzo) say we are near to Galicia. In other conversations, where there was an affirmative viewpoint, people said "nos *consideramos* más gallegos que leoneses" (we feel more Galician than Leonese) or "nos consideramos más gallegos" (we *consider* ourselves more Galician) and even "*somos* más gallegos porque hablamos gallego" (We *are* more Galician because we speak Galician). The verb most often employed to indicate the degree of "Galician-ness," however, is the verb *tirar*. The most concrete meaning of this verb is to pull something physically or to draw something toward oneself. I, for example, pull or draw the table toward me, or oxen pull the cart. Metaphorically, this dynamic image establishes one of the verb's more abstract meanings. If, for example, a person feels attracted to something, we say they feel drawn to it (le tira aquello), an apt usage for conveying the idea of being "drawn" to the place where one was born, to one's family, or to one's blood.

There is, in addition, a third meaning of the verb I would like to consider, one which plays an important role in the cases to which I will be referring. It implies that, within a continuum, as in a range of colors, there is a greater similarity to one or another color, as, for example, when one says "el color de este jersey *tira* a rojo" (the color of this sweater tends toward red).

My informants have often used these two deeply rooted popular meanings together with the metaphorically dynamic notion of traction to explain their situation: "nosotros aquí tiramos para Galicia" (Galicia draws us), or "Tiramos más a Galicia" (Galicia pulls us more) or "tiramos mucho a Galicia" (Galicia really pulls upon us). *Tirar*, to pull or draw, implies movement between the poles of Galicia and León. The movement may be based as much on similarity (We are more like the Galicians) as on attraction (We feel attracted by all that is Galician). Neither expression demands *being* exclusively one thing or the other, it is a situation of almost but not quite.

At times, that same ambiguity seems to affirm: "No se si somos de León o de Galicia que más da una cosa u otra, lo importante es vivir y tirar palante" (I don't know if we are from León or Galicia, what's the difference anyway? What does matter is to get on with living). Or, "Que más da que seamos una cosa que otra, todo es lo mismo" (What is the difference, one way or the other, it is all the same). Or, as I was told, "Nos sentimos más leoneses, pero somos gallegos iguales" (We feel more Leonese, but we are also equally Galician). And someone would reply, "No, somos bercianos" (No, we are from Bierzo); and the final words were "Casi da igual" (It is practically the same) and this was clarified with the final explanation that "Pero ni en Galicia eran tan esclavos" (But not even in Galicia were they as enslaved as we).

The conversational contradictions about *being* or *not being* take on particular relevance in conversations with shopkeepers in the aristocratic town of Villafranca. Asked whether they were Galician or Leonese, one replied without hesitation "Más gallegos; la mayor desgracia de Villafranca fue pasarla a León, todo el comercio va hacia Galicia" (More Galician; Villafranca's greatest misfortune occurred when it was transferred to León, because all the business goes toward Galicia). After emphasizing that Galician is spoken in the town, in some of the outlying communities, and also at the Tuesday market, he concluded "comercialmente, en costumbres, en espíritu, somos gallegos. Nos tira más la gaita que los tambores de Astorga, la gente vibra con lo gallego" (In business, customs, and spirit, we are Galician. The bagpipes draw us more than do the drums of Astorga [León], the people dance to anything Galician).

Shortly after these emphatic statements, one of my chief informants went on to say "en Madrid me *decían* gallego por el dejo, *no es* que *sea* gallego ni lo tenga en menos, cada uno es lo que es, yo pertenezco a León. Nos gusta lo gallego, nos tira, nuestras costumbres son gallegas o los gallegos copiaron de nosotros, no sé. No es que esto *sea* Galicia. Villafranca fue provincia propia" (In Madrid they called me Galician because of my accent. It's not that I am Galician or that I would mind being one. Everyone is what one is, and I belong to León. We like everything that is Galician, we feel drawn by it, our customs are Galician, or the Galicians copied them from us. Who knows? It's not that this could be Galicia. Villafranca was once itself a province.).

In another conversation, in response to my question as to whether they were Galician or Leonese, I was told "Somos gallegos, tenemos la misma lengua, la misma forma de comer, las mismas costumbres. Yo estudié en una escuela de Madrd y había varios gallegos, pero El Gallego era yo, mi padre era de la Rúa, vino aquí de 10 ó 12 años y casó con una villafranquina. Yo nací aquí. Si nos preguntan ya decims que somos gallegos" (We are Galician, we speak the same language, eat the same foods, follow the same customs. I studied in Madrid, along with some Galicians, but among them, I was "The Galician" because my father came from Rúa [a village nearby in Galicia]. He came here about ten or twelve years ago and married a woman from Villafranca. I was born here. When asked, I always say, we are Galician.).

Did he mind, I insisted on asking, being called Galician in Madrid: "No me molesta nada que me llemen gallego porqué ma había de molestar; si preguntan más o se habla, se explica que somos leoneses, pero si no para que explicar tanto" (I do not mind at all being called Galician. Why should I? If the conversation goes on, we might end up explaining that we are Leonese, but if it does not, why bother?).

When, in a third round of questions with this same informant, I asked about Bierzo's political party, he replied "En realidad sabemos que esto es un snob, que nosotros *somos* leoneses, que llevamos siglos y no va a cambiar" (In fact, we know that this is nothing but snobism, we *are* Leonese, we've been here for centuries and that's not about to change). Afterwards, he went on to say "Yo hablo castellano en case, hablamos lo que somos, pero también sé hablar gallego" (I speak Castilian at home, we speak what we are, but I also know how to speak Galician). The principle of identity shifts back and forth until in the end, at one and the same time, they seem to be asserting that they both *are* and *are not*.

THE CAMPOSOS

In more detailed fashion, I will now look at a particular case of identity in this zone, a case that offers a special shading to this sociocultural analysis of contradictory terms. The case concerns a Bierzo township whose lands form part of the boundary with Galicia. Its people, the Camposos, are viewed in the area as quite singular, living in two different places over the course of the year. In the winter they live in the valley of Aira da Pedra and live the rest of the year in Campo del Agua, up a steep track about five kilometers away. To be sure, others from nearby villages also graze their stock in summer grasslands known as "alzadas" where there is relatively flat, arable land. In their summer houses, by accumulating manure, they were able to fertilize the nearby fields. Up on the mountainside, there were fewer houses than below and only some of the members of the family spent the summer there. "Los camposos" held hardly any land in the valley, most of it being up in the mountains. So almost all the inhabitants went up and down constantly, spending most of the year cultivating their lands and only taking refuse to Aira de Pedra during the worst of the winter. Each family would load up their cart with farm tools, kitchen equipment, and even furniture, along with the hens and pigs.

Even bearing in mind the extreme characteristics of the area, for the anthropologist, there is one outstanding feature: each village has its own church, patron saint, a local holiday, and its own cemetery. So we have two different villages for the same inhabitants whose identity is distanced as they go up or down the mountains according to the season. This village, with a double life, preserves an origin myth that explains this.[10] The villages are considered to be as different as night and day by the inhabitants themselves. Their topography, house styles, and climate are markedly different from each other. Furthermore, for them, the customs of the upper village were much more Galician than those of the lower one. "Aira da Pedra no *tira* tanto para Galicia como Campo del Agua" (Aira da Pedra is not drawn so much by Galicia as Campo del Agua).

Campo del Agua is closer to the Galician border. The Camposo shepherds live with those from the Galician villages in the summer pastures. Most of the houses in Campo del Agua are thatched while in the bottom of the valley, they are slate roofed. In Campo del Agua, there are several "horreos" (granaries) but in Aira da Pedra there are none. In Campo del Agua people slept in straw spread on wooden platforms in almost promiscuous proximity to the animals, while in Aira da Pedra, they slept in bedrooms. In this way the Camposos moved each year from being more Galician to being less Galician and vice versa, materially dramatizing the stretching of the Berziano spirit. To be Gallego or to be Leones are two opposing realities, but they themselves live by going up and down between the two.

Let us now return to the general analysis of identity in El Bierzo. Undoubtedly, a fundamental component of the ambiguity in identity in the western rural area is the fact that Galician is spoken in spite of the fact that the area belongs administratively to León. Although it would be difficult to find anyone who would categorically state that what is spoken there is Galician, they will perhaps say that "se habla gallego mezclando" (we speak a Galician mixture) or "se habla un chapurriado" (people speak a hodgepodge) or "lo que se habla aquí no sé lo que es" (I do not know what you would call what we speak here.) In answer to my question about whether they speak Galician, they sometimes say, "Hablamos muy mal pero hablan peor por arriba" (We speak very badly but they speak far worse up there) or "hablamnos cincuenta palabras mal y una en castellano" (We speak fifty words badly and one in Castilian).

It might be easier to accept as something in the past "aquí se hablaba gallego, aunque estamos lejos de Galicia" (We used to speak Galician here, although we're a long way from Galicia). In Villafranca, people spoke enthusiastically about the Galician language although it was pointed out that Spanish was usually spoken in the town and Gallego in the mountain villages. Farther north, people tended to say "El deje es más parecido al asturiano y que el gallego que se habla por ahí en los Ancares" (The accent tends to be like Asturian and the Galician that is spoken there in Los Ancares). Some even classify the different areas into linguistic zones, saying that "el Berciano tiene un deje parecido al asturiano; en este pueblo (Vega de Espinareda) parecido al gallego; en Balboa, es gallego-gallego y por Suárbol más gallego que aqui" (The Berciano speaks with an accent like the Asturians; in this town [Vega de Espinareda] we speak like the Galicians; in Balboa, it is Galician-Galician and in Suárbol, more Galician than here).

On the other side of the language barrier toward the east, people admitted that "el deje es gallego" (the accent is Galician) and for that reason "dicen que somos gallegos ... nos llaman gallegos" (they say we are Galicians ... they call us Galicians). On the other hand, over the border toward the Galician Autonomous Community, the completely opposite opinion holds among the locals. They consider that the villages close to El Bierzo "son más gallegos aún que nosotros" (they are even more Galician than us), "dicen que no hablan gallego pero hablan un gallego más cerrado aún" (they say they don't speak Galician but they speak a more pure Galician). "son gallegos en todo, en nada se diferencian" (they are Galicians in everything, they don't differ in anything).

With this set of degrees of difference and ambiguities as a starting point, there are those who present their situation as a juxtaposition of elements. On a parallel with their linguistic hodgepodge, we were told, "Nosotros somos una mezcla" (We're a mixture), "Somos un intermedio entre Galicia y León" (we are halfway between Galicia and León), or they may even insist that is what they are and that they speak a mixture of Galician, Asturian and old Leonese.

The area in between where this mixture is to be found is called El Bierzo; however, there are a number of points of view to be taken into account when considering El Bierzo as a unit. The people in the mountain areas often talk about going down to the villages in the valley as "Voy al Bierzo" (I am going to El Bierzo), or they give a geographical description about something being in El Bierzo ("Bierzo adentro") or about what you can find if you go down to El Bierzo ("bajando al Bierzo"). In some of the lower villages, we were told about the time "antes se hablaba de esto como del Bierzo" (before people referred to this area as El Bierzo) although it is generally considered today that the mountainous valleys such as Los Ancares are also El Bierzo. In some districts, once municipalities but now part of the borough of Villafranca, people told me that they, too, are from El Bierzo because they belong to the borough of Villafranca del Bierzo.

The situation of self-identity also appears to have different generational connotations. Older people are more likely to accept their similarities with the Gallegos; sometimes they even value the moral qualities of the Gallegos: "Son mejores los gallegos, son más honrados, más leales. Los leoneses son más fulleros" (The gallegos are better, they are more trustworthy, they are more loyal. The Leonese are more crooked). It was the old people who were loath to choose between León or Galicia and who said, "Es lo mismo una cosa que otra" (One thing or the other, it's all the same). "Casi da igual" (It's almost the same) or, "Qué más da ser una cosa u otra" (What does it really matter, being one thing or the other). It was mainly among themselves that they admitted to feeling more Gallego. In spite of all this, the overriding view in this area was the assertion—although sometimes accompanied by certain reservations—that they *are* or *consider* themselves Leonese or that they *belong* to León.

Obviously, as one moves toward the East, the geographical hierarchy or the fact that Gallego is not spoken provides the country folk with further clear arguments in favor of their identity as Leonese. In the end, it is only the Galician lilt or accent that leads to confusion about identity: "Aquí no se habla gallego pero el dejo gallego lo llevamos todos, no lo podemos quitar" (No one speaks Gallego here but we all speak with a Galician accent, it's something we can't get rid of). When asked if they got upset if they were taken for Gallegos, they replied: "Hay quien se ofende y quien no, hay de todo, aunque nos gusta lo gallego" (Some do, some don't, there's a bit of everything, although we like everything Gallego). Another interviewee gave his own opinion this way: "No se lo llame a la gente que hay quienes se enfaden" (Don't call people that because there are some who would get angry).

A very different situation exists in the old aristocratic town of Villafranca. For eighteen months in 1822, it was the capital of the Province of Villafranca, which included El Bierzo and Valdeorras. Ever since then, it has become a tradition in Villafranca to campaign for a return to this situation. The memory of that leadership still lingers on amid the external signs of a glorious historical past to be found in the churches, palaces, and narrow streets, as well as in the fortress-castle of the Marquis of Villafranca. At present, their rival, Ponferrada, which is twenty times larger, has managed to attract all the economic and administrative activities of the area, thus leaving the old capital out in limbo. The logical escape for Villafranca, the main town in the Galician-speaking area and wholly committed economically to Galicia, is to aspire to being included in the Galician Autonomous Community—a remote possibility which would free it from being under Ponferrada and Leon. Despite the fervent wish on the part of many of the inhabitants to come closer to Galicia, the two representative dialogues I analyzed previously are full of ambiguity and have been presented in my argument as a good example of the almost simultaneous statement of being and not being.

In general, it was difficult to come across a clear statement, "Somos gallegos" (We are gallegos). In the few cases where this statement did occur, there were always further explanations: "Si nos preguntan ya *decimos* que somos gallegos" (If we're asked we always say we're Gallegos), although when questioned more closely "Explicamos que *somos* leoneses" (We explain we're Leonese). On the other hand, you do hear at times the categorical "Somos leones" (We are Leoneses) or even "Pertenecemos, nos consideramos y somos leoneses. Yo no quiero saber nada de gallego" (We consider ourselves and we are Leoneses; I want nothing to do with anything that is Gallego). Administrative division and contempt for everything that is Gallego seem to have come together here. To speak Gallego and to look like a Gallego, sometimes in combination with various local interests, emphasizes the other pole where other terms are used—for example, to be drawn (tirar) to Galicia, to feel like (sentirse) a Gallego or even to be more (ser más) Gallego. All this implies that, within the bipolarity, despite being Leonese, they are less Leonese. It is not a question of being or not being but rather one of moving up or down from one extreme to another.

CONCLUSIONS

In identity questions, there is considerable significance to the relationships and hierarchies of prestige between one area and another, as well as local rivalries and antagonisms. Traditional administrative boundaries are very relevant. The fact of belonging or not to a province implies, in practice, the existence of certain conditioning forces. We could also say that, in this game of ambiguity and acceptance, there are also high levels of inertia and coercion.

With regard to this point, let us go back to an idea that we consider fundamental to the nationalist cause, examples of which we presented earlier relating to linguistic standardization: a defense of the spontaneous evolution of culture and language against external coercion. In the case of El Bierzo, for example, the strongly pro-Galician groups take the contempt felt for the Galician language or their own status as non-Galicians as a result of a systematic policy used by teachers and people of influence in previous times to undermine these values. Groups with an opposing ideology say that it is the pro-Galicians themselves who pressure people by trying to inculcate in them the idea that their popular dialects, common throughout the Province of León, are Galician and that they, contrary to popular belief, are Galician.

In reality, coercion forms an integral part of historic reality. So-called popular spontaneity does not exist as an autonomous or independent reality; however, it is not all pure coercion or pure inertia. There is some dialogue emergent from by the initiatives of people and groups—never themselves "pure." Moreover, these initiatives have elements of creativity produced by the people themselves, as we have seen in the case study, as they engage with these conditions.

It is important for my effort to emphasize, in contradistinction to dichotomous formulations, how the feelings of these protagonists move between different levels of identity that are combined in differing ways, underlining at different moments and in different circumstances one thing more than another or even formulating gradations within their own collective identities. Even the same group could behave sometimes as if more Galician and at others as if less Galician.

This is, of course, the analysis of an area that is viewed as a border area. But not infrequently the groups that have an apparently more clearly defined identity surprise us with similar ambiguities and show us analogous paths in the always shifting and uncontrollable movements of collective being.

The conjunction of the plurality of spatial and temporal perspectives, conflicting local interests, ambiguous sentiments formulated over dichotomies, and the dynamic forms of expression supported by differing verbal forms together produce a strong impression of movement and fluidity: the assertion of an identity is, in practice, a connection between identities. Such connections are made possible by present circumstances and the long history of variety and change that has shaped the maps of Galicia, Spain, Europe, and beyond.

Democracy, political tension, and the need for amicable compromise within the framework of states and peoples, all require abstraction. Democracy's abstractions consist of anonymous, artificial, generalizing syntheses. Such syntheses must be justified before the people and, paradoxically, in so doing, they dilute the people's authentic diversity.

NOTES

1. Associaçom Galega de Lingus (AGAL), 1983.

2. English speakers refer to Castilian as Spanish.

3. At the present time, as a result of Conservative party policy decisions, the number of hours per week of Galician language and literature now matches those devoted to Spanish in all primary and secondary schools. Moreover, it is now also compulsory to use Galician to teach other subjects, in particular those connected with social issues, where language is so important. Official documents, as well as bureaucratic forms are usually always written in Galician, although forms in Spanish are handed out if they are expressly requested. In a minority of cases, the forms are written in both Spanish and Galician. Generally speaking, politicians and official authorities speak Galician in public and their subordinates are encouraged to do likewise. There is a great deal of campaigning in favor of the standardization of Galician. Programs on the local Galician television channel are normally broadcast in Galician.

4. These corrective measures included, in particular, special concessions to Catalonia and the Basque Country, both with strong nationalist traditions. These areas were also highly industrialized and, therefore, powerful regions in comparison with the rest of the country. In the case of the Basque Country, there was also the added threat of the nationalist terrorist group, ETA. One of the main arguments used in defense of the ethnicity and cultures of these two regions was the fact that they both possessed languages that are different from Castilian.

5. Of course, this does not win the approval of the more extreme Galician nationalist political forces. Although the content of the decisions is very often in accord with the political ideologies of these minorities, they consider it all as a strategy to put a brake on the authentic Galician nationalist movement. In this way, decisions which, if taken by them, would be highly acceptable can become extremely dangerous precisely because they are taken by the opposition.

6. Associaçom Galega de Lingua (AGAL), 1983.

7. Instituto da Lingua Galega—Real Academia Galega, 1982.

8. Ibid.

9. Ibid.

10. Formerly, the two villages were entirely separate, a fact which is proved for them by each having its own church and cemetery and their being a boundary stone halfway up the track marking the boundary between the two municipal districts. The top village, the larger of the two, once contained two hundred houses and a population of 1,300, while the lower one had only 70. A plague wiped out the district, leaving just five survivors in the high village and three below. They decided to join forces as one village, spending the summer in Campo del Agua and the winter in Aira de Pedra.

Chapter 8

Porous Borders: Discourses of Difference in Congressional Hearings on Immigration

Phyllis Pease Chock

> *Our border with Mexico is almost completely out of control.*
> —Badham (CA: H9716[1])

> *That Statue [of Liberty] never looks south.*
> —Gonzales (TX: H9717)

Sen. Alan K. Simpson (WY) was one of the principal authors of the Immigration Reform and Control Act of 1986. In 1984, while the bill was still moving through the United States Congress, he wrote about what I take to be the heart of his concerns:

> [I]llegal immigration threatens to dilute public support for our present, generous immigration policy. In addition, scoffed at and unchecked, substantial illegal immigration may portend much potential harm to our country—to American values, traditions, institutions, and our public culture: the things that make us truly unique and sought after around the world. (Simpson, 1984: 489-490)

In Simpson's view America itself was threatened by illegal immigration.[2] In the public debate that swirled for more than a decade around what became known as the illegal immigration crisis, visions of America were called into question. The country, it was argued by many, would have to regain control of its borders. "Porous borders" became a key metaphor for the crisis, and when the Immigration Reform and Control Act of 1986 (IRCA) reached the floor of the House of Representatives for the final speeches before the final vote in October 1986, speaker after speaker appealed for support of the measure in order to regain control of American borders.

What follows in this essay is a cultural analysis of the discourse in which the public debate about "the illegal immigration crisis" took place. Initially it examines terms, images, narrative forms, and mythic themes in which speakers on all sides of the issue spoke. The party affiliations of speakers are not given, nor are indigenous labels such as "conservative" or "liberal" used. Participants, regardless of their affiliations, spoke a common language. The aim of this part of the analysis is to describe that language and its uses to formulate legislation. Later the analysis turns to examine how speakers tried variously to negotiate understandings of order, differences, and nation that were inscribed in IRCA's provisions for "amnesty" and "employer sanctions."[3]

A shift in the use of images and narratives with which to render the "crisis" of illegal immigration occurred between 1975 and 1986. The goals of hearings as settings for public talk about immigration also changed. In 1975 illegal immigration was defined as a public problem, and participants had struggled to grasp what the nature of the problem was. The U.S. House of Representatives Subcommittee on Immigration, Citizenship, and International Law (of the Committee on the Judiciary), for example, had largely sought information, and the testimony focused on unemployment and on the questions of how many illegal aliens there were and whether they were taking jobs away from Americans (see Chock, 1991). One prominent approach to these questions was to call for further efforts to find out the exact number of illegal aliens, and for increased enforcement through improved technology, expanded budgets, and more personnel, for agencies such as the Immigration and Naturalization Service (INS) and the Border Patrol.

Also in 1975 there was a narrative that enabled some people to make provisional, if contested, connections between (at least some of the) illegal aliens and national visions of immigrant "opportunity," in which immigrants are seen to have found opportunities to become "new men." The American bicentennial was approaching and in the public talk about the American nation, myths about ancestral immigrants were being retold and sometimes revised. These narratives operated on a problematic category, "illegal aliens," and transformed them into individual men (not women) who could seek their fortunes in America.

In response to this narrative tack, there were charges, often from districts where unemployment was high, that the opportunities of Americans were being stolen by illegal immigrants; and, significantly, from districts where agribusiness was dominant, came accusations that controlling illegal immigration would take away the opportunities of farmers, who were not able to find workers. Finally, there was one subversive, and unheeded, voice of a spokesman for a Latino organization, who said that all the opportunities were those of business and that the government had consistently seen to it that that was so. Who was to have "opportunity" was not resolved. The "crisis" was still viewed from Washington as mainly a regional one for the Southwest.

In 1981 the Select Commission on Immigration and Refugee Policy had made its report, after extensive hearings, with specific recommendations about what legislation was needed. By the early 1980s there were complex immigration bills before subcommittees in Congress, to which the bills' authors and proponents had by then made substantial political investments in what they perceived to be a high-risk political topic. Consequently, they sought from witnesses reactions and proposals pertaining to the provisions of their bills. The bills were documents whose language attempted to mediate opposing, even contradictory conceptions of "the problem" and what could be done about it. Talk in hearings was constrained by this language, and as we will see, witnesses who tried to use other terms were sanctioned by legislators; nevertheless these witnesses did challenge the terms of the legislation and its vision of democracy.

"POPULATION": GENDER, RACE, AND CLASS ELIDED

"Porous borders" is an image that directs attention to who or what is coming through the borders. "Population"[4] was one key term of the talk about border-crossing. It offered speakers a frame of ideas entailed by biology in which to think about and act on immigration issues. "Population" suggested that unambiguous numbers and such seemingly gender-free, class-free, race-free notions as "resources" could be used to clarify what was happening. "Population" also brought speakers to the verge of denying humanity and culture to illegal immigrants in favor of their biology and nature. Illegal immigrants were being transformed by images suggested by "population" into animal populations, or worse, vermin or insects. Such images distanced illegal immigrants from the speaker and subordinated them to the social hierarchies of business or law. Through the use of such images threats to a social order could be reconstituted as a natural order that had to be mastered by technology and new vigilance.

In the 1980s more use was being made of "population" metaphors in public talk about illegal immigration, and border control became population control; speakers claimed that America was being inundated by a flood of illegal immigrants across the border.[5] Zero Population Growth (ZPG), the Federation for American Immigration Reform (FAIR), and the Environmental Fund (EF) got a hearing in 1983, before the Subcommittee on Immigration, Refugees and International Law, though their arguments left congressmen irritated. Spokespeople for these groups insisted that the United States and its "resources" such as land, clean air, and water, were being overwhelmed by immigration—legal and illegal—so that a strict annual cap of 425,000 immigrants was needed. That limit, it was proposed, would be "reviewed periodical[l]y ... [so] that the ceiling [could be] reset on the basis of a system to evaluate the adequacy of U.S. resources of agriculture, forest land, water, minerals, and others required to support our populace" (Thomas McMahon, EF, U.S. House of Representatives [USHR],[6] 1983: 738).

"Carrying capacity," "resources," and immigration limits were terms offering unambiguous lines with which to redraw the border, unlike stories about present and past immigrants to which many other witnesses appealed. People were coming to this country to get jobs, it was argued, and they had to be stopped; the situation was "like a huge electromagnet. When you turn off the switch, there is no more attraction" (McMahon, EF, USHR, 1983: 768-769). These were, however, unsatisfactory terms for the subcommittee members, in a political hot-seat, who testily asked how they were to decide who the 425,000 were to be.

Some of the more troublesome social categories in American public speech—gender, race, and class—were being effaced by the reliance on "population" as a key metaphor with which to conceive of social transformations. Other speakers used "population" to diagnose what were conceived of as social ills being brought about by illegal immigration. Women, for example, entered the talk as those who were bearing large numbers of children who would have claims on the United States; and class was submerged as references to those women and children, who were, and would be, it was assumed, making claims on the "welfare" agencies and budgets of states and local jurisdictions. Some witnesses, then, were haunted by a specter of large numbers of illegal alien women giving birth to tiny United States citizens in public (or "welfare") hospitals.

> The district I represent. ... is but a few hours away from the porous United States-Mexico border ... Approximately 70 percent ... of the babies born in country [sic] hospitals are to undocumented alien women. These babies are automatically American citizens, and are therefore

> eligible for all the welfare benefits available to any U.S. citizen. (Dannemeyer, CA; H9729)

> I am told 80 percent of all children born in Los Angeles County public hospitals are born to illegal alien mothers—80 percent! (Reid, NV [comment added to transcript]; H9775)

Women were multivocal signs, but never subjects in this talk. On the one hand, they were the nameless ones who were having babies (perhaps uncontrollably, some seemed to fear) at the public expense. Women and children figured as signs of social disorder. They brought together what, in this imagery, should be kept apart—what was messy, irrational, and uncontrollable from what was rational and market-driven.[7] That is, women's reproduction of labor power inside the United States, and not outside its borders, was problematical. It violated a "transnational" spatial separation of the sites of the purchase and use of labor power (controlled by the market and reason) and the sites of its reproduction (natural, instinctual [?], and irrational) (see Kearney 1991: 59).

On the other hand, women were also necessary, despite being nameless parts of the nuclear families who, as neighbors, classmates, church members, looked to some like Americans. Then speakers could be sympathetic; nuclear families were read as signs of stability and of blameless, law-abiding, married people with children, who were earning their "equity" in America. Amnesty was conceivable for such people.

> Registry . . . allows case-by-case amnesty. It allows anybody here prior to 1976 to come forward to indicate they are married, that they have kids, that they go to school, they work, they are law abiding [sic], they have not been in trouble, and they can become permanent residents and then become citizens. That is fair, and I think that is compassionate. (Daub, NE; H9727)

> The strange thing is, most people are against illegal aliens; . . . but those same people will say: "By the way, Congressman Lungren, . . . this person I know down the street . . . the woman who works in my house, the children who go to school with my children . . . Will you do something for them?" . . . [M]ost . . . are good people. . . . and when we know them, we in most cases like them and we will go out for them. (Lungren, CA; H9711)

That is, a "person," unlike a "population," had a character and motivations that could be evaluated.[8] "Good people," who collectively were good persons—that is, law-abiding and not in trouble—were able to be judged worthy (or not) of residence and citizenship. But families were also worrisome units in which to think about immigrants, because they could force a speaker to reconsider what was entailed by population:

> If you look at the issue of population control, . . . you are going to have between 10 and 20 million people legalized and if only half of those people come forward and take advantage of general amnesty and you multiply that times the chain of seven relatives who will be eligible for entry into this country, then you are looking at between 50 and 100 million new faces that will be added to the population flood to this country. (Daub, NE; H9727)

Arithmetic applied to population multiplied the "new faces"—without names or characters—whom Americans would find in their midst. The arithmetic of population probably also conjured visions of crowded and unruly urban spaces for this congressman from the Great Plains.

Workers, nevertheless, were clearly needed, some argued, if only they could be realigned in space. Some viewed migrant labor—a category crosscutting "legal" and "illegal"—as a fact of natural order to be mastered by policy:

> MR. MAZZOLI: . . . [It] is tough to get a guy to move from Bangor, Maine, to Fresno. His roots are in Bangor, Maine. . . . All of the enticement in the world, all of the pay may not get him out there. There is traditionally migrant labor, either U.S. citizen or non-U.S. citizen, willing to go with the sun, to follow mother nature's time clock. (Mazzoli, KY; USHR, 1983: 456)

"Population flood" was a natural sign of threats to the nation as "the breadbasket of the world" (McMahon, EF, USHR 1983: 739-740). But to stop the flood equally meant damage to . . .

> the perishable crop industry. . . . Today the reality is that 85 percent of . . . those who work in agriculture are undocumented aliens. These workers . . . are often abused, live in fear, or exploited and have no rights. That is a bitter reality. . . . The farmers, those who are trying to raise the crops, are subject to random raids that disrupt their operations. . . . It is a bitter reality. . . . (Panetta, CA; H9719)

Rep. Badham, CA, contended that "we must provide a stable work force to sustain our vital agricultural industry by instituting a new and carefully monitored guest-worker program" (H9716). Thus, two "bitter realit[ies]" collided—abused workers and harassed farmers. Sympathy was extended to workers, but concern focused on farmers. A romance of ripe crops configured some of the talk about illegal immigration throughout the decade of debate. (See also, e.g., USHR 1983: 562-567; USHR 1975: 41, 171.) Ripe crops were threatened by rot, just as farmers and agribusiness were vulnerable to government interference with labor supply to farms. Vulnerable farmers were to be understood as metonymic signs of a vulnerable nation. Both could be saved only by preserving opportunity for farmers to do business. The border had to be rebuilt, it was argued, so as to furnish them what was needed. Talk about ripe crops, like talk of population, used images of nature to render what was amiss on the borders.

SOCIAL DISORDER: CRIMES ON THE BORDERS

By the mid-1980s there was even more emphasis than there had been earlier on borders as places of crime, disorder, and inhuman conditions. "The border" was a space in which fundamental understandings of what was "American" were being seen as subject to question. A congressman who had been part of a congressional search for information about illegal immigration for almost a decade, noted in 1983 that the United States had to regain control of its borders. "[I]mmigrants," he said, "have been a great source of this country's strength. . . . But huge numbers of illegal aliens rushing past our borders may have already started to blur that understanding [by the American people]" (Fish, NY; H9711). His district, another representative said, overlooked this scene of blurred verities; it was "a few hours away from the porous United States–Mexico border . . . " (Dannemeyer, CA; H9729).

Bringing what was a blur into focus was the object of much of the talk about borders. An eyewitness account of "the border" was always a galvanizing narrative. Those who were unable (or unwilling) to tell stories about immigrant antecedents, could tell them about the border and move their listeners:

> MR. HALL: I do not care what you put in this bill, if you do not have people patrolling that border, and I mean down on the border where the Rio Grande flows—sometimes it is as wide as this room, sometimes you can step across it—if you do not have people patrolling and watching it, as long as these push factors remain, . . . people are coming across. (Hall, TX, USHR 1983: 776)

The above passage is from the comments of a representative who objected to the contentions by witnesses from FAIR, ZPG, and the Environmental Fund, who saw the setting of unambiguous numerical limits to immigration as the solution to the population flood. The image of a border only a step across called into question the possibility of setting immigration limits. Another congressman charged that witnesses' relying on a numerical ceiling meant only that he and his colleagues would be left to "do the dirty work" (Smith, FL; USHR 1983: 776) of restoring borders. Numbers furnished no assurance that the border would be or could be controlled. Eyewitness accounts of the border were also compelling because they depicted assaults on social order not only on the space of the border, but within America itself. Borders were places where those in authority—border guards, but also even visiting congressmen—had to take extraordinary action to maintain their authority ("respect for law") in the face of challenges from illegal aliens, whose disrespect for law and ridicule of social hierarchies was palpable to those in charge. Congressional representatives and witnesses called for sealing the border against lawlessness, epitomized by drug traffic and terrorists. What had become a zone of crime and defiance of law required measures to provide more border patrol personnel and high-tech equipment, but stopping short of a Berlin-like wall, an "armed camp," or use of the military (e.g., comments of Scheuer, NY, Reid, NV: H9775), because those would smack of authoritarian states. The dilemma was how to be authoritarian without seeming to be.

The subversion that was possible on the border, in the words of one congressman, "the whole situation there," was summed up by his testimony of having witnessed an "international . . . B.A. [bare ass]." This congressman, like many other speakers, was telling his story of the border and reading signs there of a more pervasive disorder, of things and people dangerously out of place.

> Now, down there at that border I saw American territory controlled by people who are not Americans, standing there, 1,000 of them. One of them turned around, he did not know there was a Congressman there, he probably would have laughed if he did. He just thought I was one of the border guards again. He turned around and dropped his pants and gave us the international—to use the western acronym, a B.A. . . . It kind of symnbolized [*sic*] for me the whole situation there. (Dornan, CA; H9719)

The congressman re-established his authority to control the situation from the air; shining his spotlight from a border-patrol helicopter, he enacted mastery of place and people, watching from above both their fear and their disorder.[9] From the air, those on the ground lost personhood and were transformed into scurrying, if sometimes insolent, creatures:

> At night when I got into a helicopter... and controlled the spotlight down on these guys, you know we are all good with spotlights on cars in California—I was pretty good and in a few minutes I was able to track all these people running around, some of them like scared people, others just giving other international signs. (Dornan, CA; H9719)

The ambiguous character of population and person images came to a head in these eyewitness testimonies. Back on the ground, Dornan saw "nice clean holding pens" that contained the disorderly elements; "pens" suggested domesticated animals and contradicted the scene he also described, of people enjoying a homely meal:

> How about when I walk into one of those nice clean holding pens where they are eating Ritz crackers and tomato soup.... We are being inundated, and there has got to be a humane way to close this border. (Dornan, H9719)

Rep. Badham (CA) straddled the same conceptual dilemma—were these people, or were they insects headed for Americans' suburban homes—as he looked out upon this zone of disorder and viewed them through "night vision binoculars"?

> [O]ur border with Mexico... is almost completely out of control.... I saw first hand thousands of illegal aliens crossing into the United States virtually unimpeded.... I watched... as scores of men, women and children gathered in open fields.... As I looked through night vision binoculars, I saw dozens of people dart through our porous border fence... into a suburban San Diego County residential area. (H9716)

The proposed immigration bill would give Americans "the ability to enforce our laws.... To seal our borders and protect this country from illegal aliens" (Smith, FL; H9716). Illegal immigrants, it was claimed, took lawlessness with them into the heart of America, threatening its most vulnerable parts:

> In my district made up of San Diego County and Orange County we have had a tragic increase in drugs, crime, prostitution, and social problems.

Now I read ... that the aliens are preying on our schoolchildren by stealing their lunch money. (Packard, CA; H9732)

But, equally, illegal aliens, who were "living in a jungle today," were being "preyed upon by ruthless people" (Dannemeyer, CA; H9729). But there lay behind this concern a sense that illegal aliens had somehow brought the jungle with them. Illegal aliens were signs of social disorder, of statuses, hierarchies of authority, institutions, and ultimately a nation, in disarray.

IRONICAL RIPOSTES

Rep. Dornan's depictions of the sources of this disorder were challenged in the 1986 floor speeches by his House colleague:

MR. GONZALES [TX]: I was just curious ... if after he was with this rather motley assortment of Congressmen if any immigration officer stopped the gentleman for looking suspiciously alien?
MR. DORNAN [CA]: Suspiciously Norwegian.
MR. GONZALES: That is only the point I wanted to make. (H9719)

While Dornan's response trivialized Gonzales's ironical query about pragmatics of ethnic identification, Gonzales pointed out that there was more order on the border than Dornan had observed. The BA challenge could not override the cultural processes that made "suspiciously Norwegian" oxymoronic, nor the social hierarchy that was being preserved by the immigration officer's ability to avoid violating cultural rules that shaped social enforcements. Dornan's status as a congressman and as one with a unmarked ethnic identity, who could control the Border Patrol's spotlight without being challenged, had not been seriously shaken by the alien's "B.A."

POLICING PERSONHOOD

Threats to law were also seen to stem from the prospect that amnesty for illegal immigrants would mean short-changing those who had sought legal entry by waiting patiently in line, and thereby reducing "the meaning and value" of American citizenship (Combest, TX; H9731).

[A]mnesty tells the world that the way to get into America is to break the law, cheat and come here because you can get permanent residence and then you become a citizen.... [I]t cheapens the value of American citizenship. (Daub, NE; H9727)

Amnesty, and certainly citizenship, ought, it was said, to be a prize "strictly limited, with eligibility based upon demonstration of a working knowledge o[f] the English language and desire to become a productive contributor to the economy" (Badham, CA; H9716). But illegal aliens are "people who came here and lived unprotected, in limbo, exploited, and unable to advance and climb up the ladder as millions of others before them had done" (Schumer, NY; H9724). That is, illegal aliens who are exploited were perceived to be denying the myth of the ladder of opportunity that transforms immigrants into "new men" (Chock, 1991). So it was deemed desirable, indeed necessary, by most speakers to "permit [undocumented aliens with years of U.S. residence] to come out of the shadows and contribute more to our country" (Fish, NY; H9711).

Coming out of the shadows was possible, however, only for individuals with socially bestowed personhood. Congressmen's stories about constituents making special pleas on behalf of illegal immigrant neighbors or maids—"this person I know"—tapped into this understanding that personhood both constitutes and is constituted by belonging to a community. Creating personhood for illegal immigrants was a matter of evaluating an immigrant's character; one had to be judged worthy of either amnesty or citizenship. One argument was that amnesty ought to be awarded on a "case-by-case" basis, that is, to individuals, not as a "blanket" measure to a "population" that would confound individual identities and measures of worth. Applicants should be eligible only, for example,

after living 1 year in the United States in good character and after demonstrating basic citizenship skills.... Even then, each permanent resident alien will have to wait at least 5 years before applying for citizenship, during which time the applicant must live a blameless life ... [And be] ineligible for welfare benefits. (Mazzoli, KY; H9713)

"Amnesty" and "employer sanctions," then, were used by these speakers to resolve contradictions that porous borders displaced onto illegal immigrants. In the eyes of the immigration reform bill's co-author, Rep. Mazzoli, these two measures made the bill one of "symmetry and balance and humanity and compassion" (USHR 1983: 938). For Mazzoli and Rep. Hall, these mediating terms meant avoiding "the racist rhetoric that is normally associated with immigration issues." But neither man noted the conjunction of personhood and policing that the two provisions entailed, creating persons who were simply caught in the bind of living illegal but otherwise blameless lives. On the one hand, legislation of amnesty provided that the INS and "volags" (voluntary agencies) would weigh evidence that particular people had indeed led worthy lives of building equity by receiving paychecks and paying rent. That is, illegal immigrants' passage into the American community was to be officially reviewed and endorsed as conforming to immigrant-opportunity narratives. On the other hand, the much-touted employer sanctions against "knowingly" hiring illegal aliens used increased policing of immigrant and ethnic communities to restore social order and to banish unworthy and disruptive interlopers. Employers were to be appointed to keep an eye on those who passed through their fields of vision.

The two provisions of "amnesty" and "employer sanctions" inscribed into IRCA years of contentious negotiations about immigration. Amnesty brought together assumptions about a moral/social personhood (e.g., "character," "good people," "roots") that made an immigrant a worthy member of the nation, with jural existence[10] (legal residence) that was to be conferred on an immigrant by the state. Employer sanctions extended surveillance of persons by the state[11] to employers, who were to adjudicate employees' identities. Proponents of employer sanctions assumed that jural existence (the legal status of a job applicant) was unambiguous (e.g., "illegal is illegal" [Lewis, FL: H9789]), which it is not. That is, they assumed that employers' making judgments about applicants' legal status would be simple, error-free tasks and would not be confounded with their making judgments about applicants' personhood (including those based on ethnicity, gender, race, or class).[12]

Those who glimpsed the contradictions generated by the "symmetry and balance and humanity and compassion" of such provisions tried to describe how invidious borders of race, language, and class (less of gender in these hearings) were less than porous. Their arguments assumed that personhood and legal residence were always conflated. For example, Althea Simmons, spokesperson for the National Association for the Advancement of Colored People [NAACP], noted that Black-Haitian-Cuban conflict in Liberty City (Miami) exemplified the problem of closed internal borders of race and class that would not be addressed by extending amnesty to people trapped by the porous borders, though she had endorsed that American generosity:

> MR. SMITH [FL]: Yesterday in Miami, there was another riot in Liberty City ...
> [W]e may be putting people out of work who are already going to be grandfathered into this country and have a situation where when those American, native American born jobseekers get back the jobs we then put people on the social welfare programs, because they can't get the jobs?

> MRS. SIMMONS. . . . [T]he Miami situation, Mr. Smith, is one that we forecasted 10 years ago to the mayor of the city and suggested . . . reading the Kerner Commission report.
> MR. SMITH: . . . If we are going to put black youths in jobs that are now held by Haitian refugees, we will discriminate against Haitian refugees. . . .
> MRS. SIMMONS: We need more job creation. (USHR 1983: 836–837)

The questions posed by subcommittee members more than once tried to play off supposedly competing and conflicting interests of ethnic groups against each other. This discursive process displaced contradictions of class and culture on reified groups and interests. Smith's questions to Simmons, for example, probed for fissures between Blacks and Haitians and (by implication) Cubans/Hispanics, and set the scene for the difficult testimony that followed.

Witnesses for "Hispanic" organizations and "Asian" organizations appeared on the same panel, and, more important, their testimony had been placed within a frame of ethnic stereotypes that the congressmen had already set up. The witnesses' respective stances toward the legislation would likely only enhance and confirm the stereotypes to the congressmen. Acquiescence of a kind, then, was being required of both sets of witnesses. In order for them to resist this frame, it would be necessary for them to find words for the conceptual and political dilemmas with which the frame confronted them. John Huerta, spokesman for Mexican American Legal Defense and Education Fund [MALDEF], for example, tried to defer judgments of personal and ethnic worth in his written statement to the subcommittee, commenting that "the undocumented immigrant" is not "a saint or a sinner" (USHR, 1983: 863).[13] Then, alluding to the classic immigrant opportunity narrative, he note:

> While there are always exceptions, generally the undocumented worker who comes to this country is not different from our forefathers who came seeking a better life, hoping to invest something of themselves in America so that their children [can] benefit from their toil. (p. 863)

Moreover, Arnoldo Torres, League of United Latin American Citizens [LULAC], tried to untie American perceptions of illegal immigration as "an Hispanic phenomena [*sic*]"[14] (USHR, 1983: 906), in part by reading from a trial transcript in which the arresting (local police) officer was questioned about his apprehension and jailing of a Mexican-American citizen:

> Q: Now is this the normal routine that you follow when you arrest Mexicans in Grand Prairie?

> A: Are you speaking of an illegal alien or a Mexican?
> Q: Well, how can you tell the difference? . . .
> A: . . . When I can't determine, that's why I put them in jail for investigative charges. (p. 924)

Mazzoli refused to heed the concerns voiced by these representatives (Huerta and Torres, and earlier, Martinez [see n. 16]) of Latino organizations (MALDEF and LULAC) about the double bind in which the proposed legislation put their constituents. IRCA, they had seen, increased surveillance of Latino communities without altering the terms (e.g., illegal alien = Mexican, and illegal immigration = crisis) that made them marginal to the nation. And the IRCA did not offer them better regulation of the more problematic social hierarchies, of employers and employees (e.g., USHR, 1983: 942). IRCA instead required their complicity in the bitter quandaries of the status quo. The spokespeople noted, for example, that "enforcement of labor laws is a more viable approach" (Torres, LULAC: 942) than employer sanctions.[15]

Mazzoli lashed out at these spokesmen for their being uncooperative[16] ("Nothing but criticism, negativism, not a positive word" [USHR, 1983: 944]) and simultaneously praised ("to your fantastic credit" [p. 944]) the spokesmen (Benjamin Gim, Organization of Chinese Americans, and Norman L. Kee, U.S.-Asia Institute) from "Asian" associations for their contributions to the discussion. On the one hand, using ethnic stereotypes Mazzoli had placed the latter "model minorities" as worthies somewhere inside the American community; he had heard their reference to "the American dream" (p. 940). On the other hand, he exiled the former to the margins of America; they were willfully not participating, he charged ("that answer is no answer at all" [p. 944]).

POPULATION, IMMIGRANT NARRATIVES, AND BORDER-MAKING

Talk of a "crisis" of illegal immigration marked an ambiguous cultural space[17] in which state and nation were conflated. The image of "porous borders" provided both challenges to meanings of community and nation and possibilities to make new meanings. To challenge meanings or to make meanings is actors' cultural work. Participants brought cultural categories and some pre-assembled cultural forms, such as immigrant stories, to the hearings. With these, witnesses and representatives tried to create images with which to understand the social transformations that they apprehended in fragments. That there were unwanted newcomers, that some Americans were unemployed, that some school systems and public welfare budgets were being affected, were some of these partial glimpses of change. A natural history frame of interpretation, which entailed images of nature, including "population," was one within which understandings of such phenomena could be explored and lodged. "Personhood" was another frame in which participants examined social changes for their meanings of and for community and nation.

"Population" afforded some treacherous avenues of conceptualization of this cultural space. Official discourses tried to reduce the ambiguity to concerns entailed by population, such as rational determination of exact numbers of people, setting levels of technology and personnel of control, and calculations of costs. "Population" also offered terms in which to glimpse the fears provoked by changes that were being conceived of as social disorder. It also opened up a possibility of viewing social differences of nationality, class, and gender as species differences to separate Americans unambiguously from illegal immigrants. But in doing so, it recalled enduring national dilemmas of race used as a ground on which to build social partitions.

The "personhood" frame brought its own contradictions. Immigrant narratives that create persons were preliminary measures in the immigration reform debate to re-creating community that included illegal aliens, who were to be magically transformed into "new men" (Sollors, 1986; Chock, 1991). In the context of the American "success story," for example, an immigrant seeks and finds opportunity for a new and better life in the New World. Generations of immigrants have been conceived of, through the recital of these myths, as having measured up to this American ideal. Population images, by contrast, made such a transformation of illegal immigrants into American persons incomprehensible and even unthinkable.

But such understandings are constantly being renegotiated. Immigrant myths make persons of particular kinds. These narratives can be used to deny "natural" differences of race, class, or gender, in that the "new men" are understood to have shed their pasts, foreign cultural baggage, and encumbering social ties. As opportunity stories, they historically have been used by those whose voices are heard to scold "minorities" for falling short, to affirm the upward mobility of descendants of immigrants, and to size up newcomers against these pioneers. For IRCA's legislative sponsors and for others whose principal concerns were with restoring social and cultural order, IRCA's provisions for amnesty and employer sanctions mediated contradictions between personhood and enforcement of laws.

However, from communities, networks, and neighborhoods come challenges to these stories' denials of differences by speakers who have contextualized knowledge of others in their communities, from alternative nonhegemonic immigrant narrative forms (Chock, 1989), from local exchanges and negotiations across actors' differences (Urciuoli, 1991) and oppositional political action (Gregory, 1993), and from speakers' stumbling over the narrative's ideological contradictions (Chock, 1989). Undocumented immigrants' own attempts to renarrate their liminal circumstances on borders of the community problematically and provisionally use elements of the opportunity myth (Chavez, 1991).

National renegotiations are more problematic. In national settings, such as congressional hearings rooms, the dominant immigrant story can be and often is both text and context. To tell it is to affirm America and to affirm the speaker's authorization to tell it. Some speakers, though, used irony as a rhetorical device with which to mark and challenge the myth's otherwise unnoted suppositions about social categories. For some legislators, including Reps. Gonzales and Frank, for example, whose concerns were less those of social order than of justice, such rhetorical and narrative devices could be used to contest a bill's provisions for order. Other speakers used immigrant opportunity myths to shift attention away from the Rio Grande toward internal borders of class, language, and race, and to the means by which those borders are patrolled. This kind of cultural work by witnesses and legislators in the hearings interrogated one of Americans' most powerful and solemn communal myths. It located silences about cultural and social differences within this myth. It rearranged some of the myth's themes, particularly those of personhood. Multifarious "persons"—who in these witnesses' parlance were "real people," that is, persons situated by class, gender, language, or ethnicity—had to be and could be connected in new ways, to new situations on borders. That is, some of the speakers subverted and provisionally transformed the immigrant opportunity myth, and with it they attested to unfinished negotiations inscribed in immigration law.

ACKNOWLEDGMENTS

I thank Catherine Allen, Jon Anderson, Mary Jo Arnoldi, Anita Cook, Susan Coutin, Jean-Paul Dumont, Mark Leone, Daniel Segal, and Bonnie Urciuoli for critical readings of various drafts of the manuscript. I also am grateful to Stephen Schneck for inviting me to give a colloquium based on this work in the CUA Department of Politics, and to Bonnie Urciuoli for inviting me to give a lecture based on the manuscript at Hamilton College. An early version was given as a paper in the session "Imagining Other Communities: Reflexive Discourse and Collective Identity," organized by Jonathan Boyarin, at the Annual Meeting of the American Anthropological Association, Chicago, November 1991. Finally, I owe much to the participants of the

"Democracy and Difference" conference for their critical insights on ideas in this essay, and in particular to the organizers, Carol Greenhouse and Davydd Greenwood, for inviting me. *Editor's note:* Selected passages of this article also appear in *Policy Sciences*, and are used with permission of Kluwer Academic Publisher.

NOTES

1. "H" references hereafter are to Congressional Record.

2. In 1981 Simpson asked, "[I]s it not odd that we are the most desirable country of access [for immigrants] and have the least desirable law?" (U.S. Congress, Senate [USS], 1981: 35). Simpson asserted that rather than a "national immigration policy,"

> it is more of a national nostalgia or mystique of immigration that comes from our feelings about the Statue of Liberty and the remarkable praises of Emma Lazarus. . . .
> [T]he actual name of the statute [*sic*] in the harbor is "Liberty enlightening the world." It is not "Send us your huddled masses." It would be difficult to enlighten the world if we were truly overwhelmed by illegal immigration and unlimited legal immigration. (p. 35)

That Statue, in Simpson's eyes, did not face Wyoming but the world needing enlightenment. Chinese and European immigrants left no marks, only nostalgia, on Simpson's view of the Western landscape.

Further, Simpson's rhetoric, like that of much American public speech, thoroughly conflated nation and state, denying the possibility that the state might have interests different from those of the nation ("America," "the American people"). See also Simpson's writing and speech elsewhere, as a member of the Select Commission on Immigration and Refugee Policy (U.S. Select Commission, 1981: 407–481), as a sponsor of immigration legislation (Simpson, 1984), and as a Senate Judiciary Committee member conflating his career, nation, and state (1993 televised confirmation hearings of Zoë Baird).

3. "Culture" in this analysis is defined as both constructed and constructing relations among meanings. Culture is constructed in that meanings have particular histories. Meanings of social differences such as race, gender, or nationality, which are so powerful, yet unstable in the talk about immigration, are products of a colonial, industrial, patriarchal history (see, e.g., Wade 1993 on "race"). Culture is also constructing; categories, meanings, and ideologies of race, gender, or nationality were, explicitly or implicitly, already there in the setting of the hearings rooms in that they were implicated in the language, the unequal relations between participants, and the

routines of action there. But such meanings are unstable because, through their practical and ritual performances, social actors create, contest, negotiate, or reproduce meanings in particular social scenes (see, e.g., Gregory, 1993).

4. I will not analyze here some appearances of biblical or religious images—of the immigrant as sojourner or pilgrim, for example—except to remark that a biblical framework in these hearings was used almost exclusively by witnesses representing various church or religious associations. Their joining of frames of religion and immigrant narratives is a significant example of a discourse that runs deep in American culture (e.g., Sollors, 1986; Susman, 1984; Rischin, 1965).

5. In hearings in 1975, one witness (John Tanton) from Zero Population Growth (ZPG), for example, had claimed that the root causes of illegal immigration, including exploding populations in the developing world, were like an incurable disease. He asked representatives to consider "the limitations of how many people we can provide for" (USHR, 1975: 255). He feared population growth in the United States meant "further constrictions on our individual liberties" (p. 259). But the use of terms such as "population" for thinking about "illegal aliens" had been dismissed by House subcommittee members; representatives could not see a relationship between civil liberties and population (pp. 260–261).

6. "USHR" citations hereafter are to U.S. House of Representatives 1975 or 1983.

7. Thanks to Bonnie Urciuoli for pointing out to me the importance of "reason" as opposed to the "irrational" in discourses of difference in the U.S.

8. My proximate debt here is to David Schneider's (1968) cultural analysis of "person" in his American kinship work.

9. The use here of the B.A. image also suggests both impotence before threats from illegal immigration and homophobia in the image of a feared, sexualized immigrant. I thank Susan Coutin for bringing these meanings to my attention.

10. Thanks to Susan Coutin, who helped me clarify this distinction between personhood and jural existence.

11. See also Rouse (1992: 35–36) on how police surveillance of neighborhoods inflicts "proletarian discipline" through "non-discursive means" of patrols of scenes where Mexican immigrant men gather.

12. Legislators' repeated consideration of requiring a "counterfeit-proof" identification card rested on the assumption that identities conferred by the state could be made to be unambiguous. The U.S. Civil Rights Commission was concerned that employers' verification of employees' immigration status was not a simple task. The Commission reported that even officials of a California state enforcement agency "were unsure of the proper method" (Dimas et al., 1980: 64); an official had testified in Commission hearings that "I can't say that [employers] did [understand what to screen for], because I really didn't understand it totally" (p. 64).

For analyses of ambiguities embedded in such categories as "citizen," see, for example, Shklar, 1991; Sapiro, 1984; Nelson, 1984; Fraser, 1989; and Young, 1990. For witnesses' arguments that assumed that ID cards are multivalent tokens of social/legal identity, see n. 16.

13. In previous, joint hearings (U.S. Congress, Senate and House of Representatives [USSHR] 1981) MALDEF spokeswoman Vilma Martinez had been closely questioned by representatives and senators, and she had argued along the same lines. She drew on personhood of immigrants ("real people") in her objections to a "guest worker" program:

> Ms. MARTINEZ: ... I submit that people good enough to come and work here ought to be good enough to come here as real people, as you [Rep. Barney Frank] called them yesterday, with permanent resident alien status on a track toward citizenship. (USSHR, 1981: 248)

14. Maldef had similarly tried in 1981 to unhook "immigration" and "crisis":

> Ms. MARTINEZ: ... I fear those traditions [of scapegoating and deportations of Mexicans] and I fear that the climate, the tenor of the discussions that immigration is out of control, that there is nothing positive in immigration, there is nothing positive about these people. (USSHR, 1981: 246)

15. But the oral testimony of both men, it is very possible, did not make these cases; exchanges in the question period focused on Maldef's and Lulac's perceived unwillingness to make positive contributions to the IRCA bill. The transcript of the 1983 hearings (USHR, 1983) contains only the written statements of these witnesses and the exchanges between witnesses and representatives, but not the statements that witnesses gave orally.

16. The same accusation had been made before, if less vehemently. In 1981 Vilma Martinez, Maldef's spokeswoman, had eloquently argued against employer sanctions, even "with any kind of ID card" (USSHR, 1981: 161). Her grounds were that people do not have uniform experiences with sanctions and law enforcement. She said that while Fr. [Theodore] Hesburgh might have found carrying ID cards not to give him trouble, people who look different, who are not members of Chase Manhattan's board, or who live in other parts of the country, do not have such benign experiences. ID cards, for some, bring "stigma" and "people will hassle you" (p. 243), she said. Mazzoli nevertheless complained, "[I]t would be so much more helpful to us, if you could give some wisdom, instead of just simply saying that everything that has been presented..., you cannot go along with" (USSHR, 1981: 245). Also compare the rejection of another Latino witness's argument in 1975 (Chock, 1991). The Select Commission's recommendation of a social-security type card to alleviate potential discrimination by employers was an attempt, common to official discourses, to create unambiguous signs. Sen. Simpson (WY) insisted, for example, "What we are talking

about [is] something that is presented at the time of seeking employment by every single American, every single person" (USSHR, 1981: 244). Rep. Fish (NY) referred to "a foolproof ID card carried by every person in the country (p. 245), In contrast, I understand Martinez's argument to say that signs are always used in context and that contexts differ, in part based on appearance, or memberships, or region.

17. The U.S.-Mexico border is a powerful trope of cultural ambiguity and social disorder that deflects attention from social transformations that have created "transnational" zones. The growing literature that details these characteristics and processes includes, for example, Bustamente, 1983a, 1983b; Cockcroft, 1986; Kearney, 1991; Nagengast and Kearney, 1990; Thomas, 1985.

Chapter 9

To Be Basque and to Live in Basque Country: The Inequalities of Difference

Jesús Azcona

Basque culture is more an invention constructed for contemporary purposes than a heritage handed down from the past. The social dimensions of this creation are paradoxical in that, on the one hand, they make possible a collective identity, and on the other, they stigmatize inhabitants of the region who come from other regions of Spain. This situation is acute in the Spanish Basque Country because of the large number of "foreigners" (immigrants) and because of the great cultural pressure created by the Basque movements.

Anthropologists have contributed more than any others to the process of "creating" Basque culture, and consequently the inequalities it produces. The present essay explores the relations between anthropology and nationalism and the changes that have occurred during the recent decades of this complex relationship.

Ethnographically and historically the Basque Country is composed of seven provinces. Politically, however, these never formed a nation and even less a state in the modern sense. Ever since Spain and France have existed as nation-states, four of the provinces have belonged to the former and three to the latter.

EUZKADI: THE SEVEN BASQUE PROVINCES

Although a feeling of ethnic belonging is very strong and of very long standing, the Spanish Basque provinces were never politically unified. In this century, several attempts to create a united Basque political entity inside the Spanish state ended in disaster, due to internal conflicts and to the preferential treatment the Spanish state gave to the Province of Navarra. Even today, after the strong, united struggle against the Franco regime, the new Spanish Constitution of 1978 still endorsed two self-governments rather than one in the area: the Basque Autonomous Community (Vizcaya, Guipúzcoa, and Alava) and the Foral Community of Navarra.

If in earlier times, the political, social, and cultural differences between the three provinces and Navarra were considerable, today they have become even greater. The unique constituencies of the two home-rule communities, the political and economic differences between the areas, and the percentage of immigrants in each makes them quite dissimilar. Basque culture also has a different weight, there being large sections of Navarre (particularly in the southern area) that show only modest Basque influences.

In this essay, I do not attempt to account for these differences. I take them as givens in order to focus on another point. My emphasis is on an examination of the when, why, and who behind the fact of Basque cultures special power in the life of the inhabitants of the Basque Autonomous Community only.

While the present cannot be understood solely through the past, we must know the past to understand the present. Thus I begin by offering a brief account of the principal anthropological traditions or tendencies that have affected the region.

ANTHROPOLOGICAL TRADITIONS

Studies of Basque people and Basque culture have a long history. At least from the seventeenth century onward, there has been an ongoing interest in knowing the biological origins of "primitive" and "modern" humans and the origins of certain characteristics of cultures, both past and present. Wilhelm von Humboldt (1767–1835) was the first to ascribe great antiquity to Basque culture and language. More important, he was the first to include the Basques within the purview of the newly emergent anthropological "science." Basque people and Basque culture were considered to be an ancient European legacy, the study of which could enable us to discover the most ancient and original cultural roots of the continent. In Humboldt's time, the archaic and ancient in European culture was converted into an object of meticulous and thoughtful research.

By the end of the nineteenth and the beginning of the twentieth centuries, anthropologists, archaeologists, and folklorists interested in the Basques had formed numerous cultural societies. They focused on a search for explanations of the origins and persistence of Basques and Basque culture, but their specific goal was to discover elements from the past that could be used to create a new social order. This reformist intent explains the fervor with which they threw themselves into the study of Basque rural society, its the political and social institutions, music, literature, and the plastic arts. They were trying to discover which of these features was due to the Basque "genius," in the terminology of this period as used by the organizer of the first Congress of Basque Studies in 1918, Luis de Eleizalde (cited in Urla, 1987: 33).

Two new institutions arose from this Congress: Eusko Ikaskuntza (the Basque Studies Society), and Euskalzandia (the Basque Language Academy). Their aim was to learn the essential features of Basqueness and to formulate programs for the reform of society in accord with those features. "They conceived of their role as that of artisans of a new society which, while retaining its cultural distinctiveness, would also be reformed to meet new norms of what constituted a healthy population and environment" (Urla, 1987: 35).

The Basque Studies Society's enthusiasm for social engineering contrasts with the more nostalgic and catholic traditionalism one can find in the writings of the founder of Basque nationalism, Sabino Arana, and in the ethnographic and anthropological works of some of the most important figures of this century, Telésforo Aranzadi (1860–1945) and José Miguel Barandiarán (1889–1991). For these anthropologists, Basqueness was a question of ancestry: to be Basque depended on the "purity" of one's blood, measured by the number of Basque surnames one possessed. "True" Basque culture could be distinguished by its greater antiquity compared with more recent influences. Race, language, and culture were understood as a unity, in the double sense that "the Basque speaks his language and only he speaks it" (Jaureguiberry, 1962: 16) and that Basque culture survives because Basques have always lived in the same territory (Barandiarán, 1978, XII: 66; 1976, XI: 356).

This anthropological tradition, important before the Spanish Civil War (1936–1939), was reinforced by the physical presence and teaching of Barandiarán at the Catholic University of Navarra—an Opus Dei institution—between 1965 and 1975. His teaching had a specific, underlying theme: the Neolithic era and rural Basque culture constitutes the authentic basis of present-day Basque culture and society.

Aranzadi and Barandiarán's research results can be summarized as follows:

1. The Basque race is unique and clearly differentiated from other races. It is a product of autonomous evolution within a specific territory, the Basque country (Aranzadi, 1967: 171; Aranzadi and Barandiarán, 1948).
2. Basque culture is unique. It was formed in the Neolithic era and survives today in popular beliefs and customs (Barandiarán, 1976, XI: 397–425; 1978, XIII: 106).

3. Basque people and Basque culture have a characteristic orientation toward history and language. The essential characteristic is *gizabidea* or humanism. (Barandiarán, 1980: 16)

Despite the dominance of this trend, other views were articulated in the Basque Country. The work of Julio Caro Baroja is particularly relevant in the context of arguments about the conception of "the Basque" (*lo vasco*) and of "the Basques" (*los vascos*) as unique (Azcona 1982). Davydd Greenwood has observed: "The integration of history and anthropology realized by this scholar [should serve as an example] to be developed and applied in our studies of Europe" (Greenwood, 1971:80). Caro Baroja's work constitutes a bridge that links the efforts of prehistorians and archaeologists with studies of contemporary cultural reality; however, built on an antipositivist and anti-essentialist view of sociocultural reality, Caro Baroja's work centers on a conception of time and history that was out of favor in the Basque Country:

It is not that Caro Baroja denies the existence of the Basques, of their language, of their customs and even of "the peculiarities of their character" (this last point, to my mind, a difficult one to demonstrate and that corresponds to a type of anthropology that is scarcely practiced today). Rather he denies that the persistence of a uniform Basque culture over considerable geographical area and throughout all time is shown by the mere fact that, here and there, a few vestiges were found that pertained, or rather were attributed to a Basque cultural cycle.... (Azcona 1989: 27)

The notion of "vestiges" was central to the Viennese historical school or *Kulturkreislehre* and to the work of Barandiarán and Aranzadi.

Rather, as Caro Baroja maintains, the existence of a multiplicity of eras and meanings, always the times and meanings of specific, concrete people, makes legitimating the present by reference to the past or the past by reference to the present impossible. This view cuts directly against the nationalist claim to political rights through the archeological and anthropological research on the uniqueness of the Basques and Basque culture.

EUSKADI TA ASKATASUNA (ETA)

During the Franco regime, as noted now twenty years ago by the sociologist J. J. Linz, "one of the most complex lines of cleavage in Spanish society lies between the dominant Castilian-speaking culture and power structure and those in the periphery who identify, in different degrees of identity, with local language and traditions" (Linz, 1973: 240). In the Spanish Basque provinces in the early 1960s, the political opposition became both more culturally defensive and politically aggressive than in other regions. As a consequence, Franco's deliberate policy of imposing the Castilian language on the Basques and the regime's refusal to permit any public expressions of Basque culture were aggressive and brutal. The very term *Basque* became synonymous with resistance and, what was worse for the regime, of opposition to the unity of the Spanish nation and state. The Basque cultural self-affirmation was transformed automatically into the work of an enemy essential to destroy to safeguard the sacred, indivisible unity of the one, great and free Spain, as was the standard shout after singing the Spanish national anthem.

The aggressiveness of the Franco regime produced numerous social reactions. One of the most important in the political and cultural reality of the Spanish Basque Country was the founding of Ekin (Action) by a group of students in Bilbao in the early 1950s. Engaged initially in study sessions and consciousness-raising activities, they eventually opted for a hard-line approach and founded ETA (Euskadi ta Askatasuna), Euskadi and Freedom.

In my view, the greatest success of ETA in the 1970s was that this small armed group was able to develop a social representation of Basque culture and Basque history based on myth, heroism, and tragedy. ETA developed a history to support its struggle a history centered on a view of the Basques, their language, and their culture as unique. This vision of history and culture made it possible for them to construct time, space, and community in direct opposition to the community the Spanish state was seeking to impose on the region. Their life and death struggle was given a specific meaning in this context (J. Azcona, 1984: 139–163).

This sense of belonging was built up through the use of the most intimate, affective links in their society. Little villages, families, parishes and *cuadrillas de amigos* (groups of friends) formed the front line of cultural resistance and also a major channel of communication about Basqueness at that time. Basqueness became a social classification that divided radically what was Basque from what was Spanish. Homogenized for public presentation, this "Basque culture" permeated the leisure and work time of many people, projecting new light on the old-fashioned customs, beliefs, and lifestyles that could no longer be found in the industrial or semi-industrial regions of the country. The *baserri* (farmstead), sociologically insignificant and in decline, became the reservoir for an idealized view of the Basque culture of the past. The personal experiences of political violence and their ideas about freedom were couched in discourses about the transformation and collapse of the rural economy, familial organization, customs, and worldview, together creating a coherent image and social representation of the ideal Basque society. These images also became the raison d'etre for the ongoing violence:

> A fundamental dimension of ETA's violence consists in promising a revolutionary solution to the political estrangement of Basque society by creating the image of an independent Basque nation. The premise is that after the achievement of this radical "freedom" Basques will be in a position to build their own political institutions, which can alone prevent the country from falling into historical and cultural alienation. (Zulaika, 1988: 134)

ETA's ideology encountered two other organizations through which it could transmit the message: the Basque rural and urban youth movements, *Baserri Gaztedi* (Baserri Youth) and *Juventudes Obreras Católicas* (Catholic Working Youth). Without these channels, it would be difficult to understand the speed and extent of the diffusion of the model of society put forward by ETA. These movements had adopted the famous Christian method of action: "See, judge, act" (*Ver, juzgar, actuar*), in contrast to the traditional maxim "See, listen, be silent" (*Ver, oir, callar*) and soon were transformed into Basque social movements. The new generation of priests, educated in the seminaries in the 1950s and 1960s, were already conscious of the Catholic church's collaboration in acts of cultural repression. As a response, they decided to learn and teach the Basque language, and take some responsibility for the political pursuit of Basque nationalism. As an expert on the Catholic movements states:

> The principal motivations were social and moral at the outset (focusing on) the relation between faith and trade union negotiation . . . Over time the problem of Basque people displaced this social problem. (Personal interview)

The process of developing a nationalist consciousness was described by a priest who was the rector of the seminary of Pamplona at that time:

> I believe that people did not understand what was happening in Navarra. The principal issue was religious, but a religious problem accompanied by many other things. When our generation discovered that we were ignorant of recent past history, when we learned what had happened to our people, it generated a kind of repulsion, disgust, or shame, a kind of collective justification that linked the religious to the sociopolitical

situation. "Basqueness" was the third element in this consciousness; it came later. (Personal interview)

At the outset, the model of society put forward by ETA assimilated basic constructs from Sabino Arana, the founder of Basque Nationalist Party (PNV) at the turn of the century. "The idealization of the rural world . . . (in which) the *baserritarra* (farmer) turns into the archetype of the primitive Basque" (Elorza, 1978: 186), is one of the most important links. It was a matter not of protecting the interests of Basque rural society but of creating a mythical model, in the first place " . . . to set against the negative aspects of the industrialization around Bilbao" (Zulaika, 1988: 134) and in the second place, to establish the basis for a Basque democratic system. "The Basque democratic system was based on the *etxeko-jaun* (lord of the house) as the holder of active suffrage" (Documentos, 1979, 2: 68). For ETA and for Sabino Arana "Euskadi remains Euskadi in race, language and territory" (Documentos, 1979, 1: 92), in spite of the fact that it suffered from the influences of neighboring peoples, the invasion "of another race," the Aryan imposition, and the battles against the Celts.

SYMBOLOGIES OF BASQUE NATIONALISM IN POLITICAL CONTEXT

In a significant shift from Arana's early nationalism and from Basque Nationalist Party teachings, ETA increasingly made the Basque language the cornerstone of the nationalist argument. It was proclaimed to be an essential condition for Basque identity—"a Basque for whom the problem of *euskera* (the Basque language) is not decisive is a traitor" (Documentos 1979, 1: 104). Language use was transformed in the *sine qua non* condition of Basqueness and into one of the core elements in the strategies for the liberation of the Basque people.

> From the estrangement and invasion Arana's and from the recuperation of any historic and folkloristic elements that survived in the rural society, the new vision set the emphasis in the oppression of the Basque Workers' People and in the strategies for their liberation." (Azcona, 1984: 114)

The loss of the language is only one among many elements, but it remains the most important.

ETA's cultural heritage was adopted by *Herri Batasuna* (Popular Unity), a party founded in the early 1970s and that extended its influence over the four Spanish Basque provinces. Ever since Arana, one of the crucial aims of Basque nationalism was the creation of an ethnically differentiated community. This task required:

> on the one hand, to lay the foundations of the perception of difference and to define the others sociologically as different; and on the other, to create a single structure of communication through which interaction itself can achieve the maintenance of the differences." (Gurrutxaga, 1985: 48)

The same task can be viewed in other arenas. For example, the problems in the formation of a symbolic center of action

> finds a political expression in the search for a conflictual and political institutionalization of each "we." In Western modernity, the necessary political dimension of "we" is created in the transition from personal forms of political authority to impersonal and territorial forms or, what amounts to the same thing, to forms of legal-national legitimation. The disappearance of the symbolic dimension of the personal political bond presupposes a symbolic base for political authority as the expression of the will of the community, and thus, assumes the existence of a community, of one "we." (Pérez Agote, 1987: 1)

The success of Arana's symbology was to achieve this multiform task, and it was just as successful in the 1960s and 1970s as it had been in the first three decades of the twentieth century—the two most important periods in the history of Basque nationalism. In the first period, the infrastructure that created the framework for an ethnically differentiated society inside the Basque country were the *Batzokis* (community nationalist clubs of the PNV), the *EuskoGaztedia* (Basque Youth/EG), the *Mendigoitzale Bazkuna* (Mountaineering clubs), the *Solidaridad de Obreros Vascos* (Basque Workers' Solidarity), and the *Emakume Abertzale Batza* (Association of the Patriotic Women/ EA). In the second period, the infrastructure was provided by the church, the family, and the so-called associative world—the village (*pueblo*), the quartier (*barrio*) and the groups of friends (*cuadrillas de amigos*), which transmitted the symbolic capital of nationalism.

It was also a period of the active prohibition and repression of any Basque cultural and political expression. The Franco regime imposed the so-called society of silence on the Basques, giving rise to a "a collective clandestinity" where only:

in the intimate space of the family, in the refuge of the "cuadrilla," in the backrooms of the cultural associations, of mountaineering clubs, folklore groups, in the daily round of the "*poteo*" (wine drinking); were produced and subsisted nationalistic forms of consciousness were produced and maintained through these means and they shaped an affective and collective support structure for violence as the possible reaction to imposed silence. Violence and collective experience of the violence were thereby reinforced. (Pérez Agote, 1987: 199)

The public expression of this silence and violence took place in the 1970s. At this moment, "collective life is made public, politics and political action become a daily intersubjectivity. The street becomes the ritual setting for politics" (Pérez Agote, 1987: 200).

At this moment, three political and cultural processes made spectacular gains in intensity and scope. On one side, a single process unified a whole range of heterogeneous groups and individual opposed to Francoism and they united to reiterate demand for democracy and Basque national rights. On another: This period also witnessed an extreme polarization of all aspects of Basque public life and political activity. Political parties, artistic production, amnesty organizations, historical research, economic enterprises, schools, newspapers, public projects, popular festivals, publishing houses, and so on, were forced into the mutually exclusive categories of *abertzale* (patriotic), *españolista*/nonnationalist, Basque/anti-Basque. Through the insistent pressure of this polarization the boundaries demarcating the Basque nationalist community and its exclusive institutions became explicit, consolidated and impermeable (Heiberg, 1989: 110–111). At this moment too, the same collective associations, schools and academic organizations, called on anybody who knew something about anthropology to reinforce these political claims.

Since the principal thesis of the then hegemonic anthropology and the nationalist creed linked the Basque territory with the Basque race and the Basque ethnic group with Basque culture, another exclusionary category demarcated the inhabitants of the country: the true Basques and the false Basques. While exclusivistic political categories might be removed through acts of personal will, racial-cultural categories are independent of the individual's will. In the context of this framework, Basque surnames continued to be a key differential characteristic of "true Basques." For immigrants, the insistence on overcoming their lack of true Basque descent manifested itself in their adoption of more extreme political attitudes against all that Spain and its police forces represented. It also more frequently caused them to mask their own regional sentiments, folklore, and traditions, and to take on actively the label of all that signified "Basqueness." Learning *euskera* was the most typical expression of goodwill toward and support for the endangered cultural condition of the Basque community.

In the 1970s and early 1980s, despite the segmentary and heterogeneous character of the political and social realities, two essential features remained: Basque voters did not accept the legitimacy of the Spanish state and the reaction of Basques toward non-Basques became more antagonistic. One result of the social pressure on the immigrants and of the internal conflicts between true Basques and false Basques was the silencing of both groups. By the end of the 1980s, neither the non-Basques nor the Basques openly expressed their true opinions about Basqueness. The public political debate focused on issues of a different sort. Only a few politicians occasionally made references to Basqueness in terms of its constructed aspects. Thus Basqueness disappeared from political and public debates.

BASQUENESS TODAY: AN ETHNOGRAPHIC SURVEY

After sixteen years of democracy, including fourteen years of home rule since the first elections for the Autonomous Basque Parliament in 1980, Basque nationalists have controlled all political institutions. This situation is very different from anything previous. The changes that have taken place are remarkable in all fields, including the transformation of much of the industrial landscape into wasteland, the increase in unemployment to around 25 percent, and an increased rate of drug abuse. Except for some sectors of the *abertzales* with ETA at their center who claim that nothing fundamental has changed—and for some intellectuals who hold that Basque nationalism is grounded on a mythical reading of a century-old past—the majority of the population and the intellectuals are aware of the changes in Basque society that have occurred in this brief period. The world of Basqueness is theirs.

These changes are seen primarily in the content and the contexts in which the people speak about Basqueness. Perhaps we will have to wait some years to see the real effects of these changes on the society, but I believe that the Basque society is in the process of becoming a society based on a new legitimation of the collective identity of the people that live there.

To my mind, these changes in Basqueness have occurred very rapidly. If in the 1970s and 1980s, Basqueness was associated more frequently with Basque race and with other interrelated sets of symbols such as *euskera*, Basque customs, the Basque character, and Basque history, in the 1990s, these elements have begun to lose their interconnections. In 1994, some of these, such as the Basque race and Basque character, are collapsing. Even *euskera* is losing its role as the cornerstone for the construction of Basque community. I base these conclusions on the responses of two groups of students—around three hundred—from the University of Basque Country, to questions asked in 1990 and 1994 about the elements they considered essential to defining Basqueness. I will now analyze the principal features of their responses and quote from their answers.

A considerable number of students questioned in 1990 answered by linking race, language, and culture; however, Arana's supreme symbol and one of his principal "anthropological" realities, the Basque race, is beginning to lose its exclusionary function and role as a moral category. By this time, the Basque race has become primarily a neutral category of differentiation and a legacy of tradition. "To my mind [writes a student] to be Basque, to have a culture, a language and a race centers on differentiation. Without falling into radical nationalism or into racial concepts, the Basques, the Basque race are different." For another "to be Basque is to form part of a social group. This group depends on some characteristics that makes them different of another groups. These characteristics are related to origins and traditions." Only one student makes Basqueness a exclusive category: "It is impossible to belong to two different ethnicities or nations."

For two students, the Basque race and Basque language are connected to the sentiment of belonging to a nation. For others, the Basque language becomes a characteristic independent of race: "*Euskera* is one of the most important cultural facts ... The majority of people that can speak *euskera* find a different meaning in Basqueness from those that cannot speak it." "My friends, my family and I, [says another], believe that the differentiation of the Basques from other groups lies in language, not in race. First of all, this is because we are not sure what our race is, and secondly, because we perceive clearly that this is a sign of racism." For others, the Basque language is an emblem of community membership: "It is a common belief that persons who have not acquired some of the objective characteristics, such as the language, are members of an inferior category in the community, just as if they are not full members of it." "Language and ethnicity [writes another] bear a very strong relationship because the authentic Basque is one who speaks the Basque language."

The majority of students are of the opinion that Basqueness has only to do with the feeling of belonging to the Basque community: "Today it is not important to have six Basque surnames but to feel that one is Basque." For many students, however, this feeling is not entirely free of doubts, contradictions, and even suffering. It is particularly a problem for the sons of immigrants. The strong feeling of being discriminated against makes the need to find an accommodation with Basque community imperative for them; for them, it is the fact that they were born in the Basque Country that makes them Basques. The feeling of belonging to the Basque community is mixed with self-exclusion from both Spanish and Basque nationalities, and the consciousness of discrimination is related to the desire to have genuine "Basque" blood. This student's statement could not be more significant:

> I do not know if I am Basque, but I believe that nobody can know it. This is a matter of feeling. Naturally I feel that I am Basque... The majority of definitions exclude me. Where are the fourth of Arana's Basque surnames? And all those ancestors disappeared from Euskadi's history? Really, I was born in Euskadi and I grew up here. (That's my point.) They say that language is important too. Although I claim the use of *euskera* because I am *euskaldunberri* (a new Basque), I have continued always to be a Spanish speaker, at most being bilingual. My first language was Spanish but what is a surprise is that I do not consider myself Spanish. (What is more, I reject strongly the possibility of becoming Spanish)... Frequently they have rejected me, and my condition as a Basque because of the racial question (based on those genes that I do not have). I, too, believe too much in race. I would not like give it a weight that it does not have, but I do and I exclude myself. It would fill me with pride to discover the possibility that Martínez had his origins in Euskadi and García dated back to Navarra's kings. Even more, I would get excited to hear that my great-grandfather was an illegitimate son of a Basque woman who copulated in Salamanca. So, at last, I would have 6 percent of Basque blood to claim.

A very important thing to notice is the changes in consciousness that many of the students' statements reveal. There is, at first, a shift of emphasis about Basqueness between old and young people. While the former emphasize race, language, and culture as a set of objective and indivisible characteristics, the latter put the emphasis on education and self-awareness as social elements that can or cannot decide membership in one or another community. Neither race nor surnames alone make Basqueness. Purity of ancestors is not important to becoming a Basque. Second, they distinguish clearly where these different conceptions of Basqueness are used: "It is the familial circle that maintains the old conception that race, culture and language are the same thing... while in the circle of friends, this is not taken it into account."

In the brief period of four years, these tendencies have become accentuated. To speak about Basqueness is a polemical theme among friends. One of them may believe in the Basque race. Another may think that there are several degrees of being Basque. But for the majority that think this way, this reality is not opposed to being Basque without speaking *euskera*. The following statement summarizes perfectly this position and shows how the new vision of Basqueness prevails over the parental generation's version:

> We, yes, we speak about the Basque race with pride, especially my father. We, my brothers and I, are a little more shy in speaking about the exploits of the Basques because we are living in times that are not very heroic for the Basque race. For me, Basque race and Basque culture are completely linked. A Basque with a pedigree carried with him a set of traditions, teachings, etc., of their parents, which is the Basque culture. Those who do not belong to the Basque race but carry Basque culture with them, either because they were used to it or because they were interested in learning it, they are for me as Basque as anyone.

Another student speaks from a distinct point of view, that of an immigrant's son: "There are Basques by blood and Basque by spirit. What do I mean by that? Many are identified with the Basque race and with Basque culture because they have their origins there, and many others, among them I include myself, are identified with all that which is Basque, although our past generations did not belong to Basque race. Even we feel 'Basque in spirit.' "

The new generations are not obsessed with their surnames nor are the immigrants' sons seen as carriers and representatives of Francoism, as personifications of an oppressive state intent on destroying Basque life. The immigrants' sons are not Spanish; they are and feel themselves to be Basques: "Personally, my environment is more than Castilian enough (but not Spanish). I speak Castilian; I have Castilian surnames, my friends are sons of Castilian parents but we feel ourselves to be Basques." Or as another with Basque surnames says, "Today we do not hear about the Basque race. There is talk about Basque culture as a combination of language, history, customs, etc., all elements that can be shared and in fact are shared by thousands of persons that do not pertain to the O blood group and whose cranial shape is not mesocephalic. For me they are all Basques who feel Basque."

The older Basques and immigrants claim that they occupy a distinct sociocultural world that is disappearing. Only a very few feel the urge to know who is Basque or have the desire for a Basque genealogy; in addition, a few place a high value on *euskera* and race as essential characteristics of Basqueness. The majority think that in order to belong to the Basques, it is enough to know and to feel Basque culture.

Under these conditions, Basque culture has now become the concept and the term that reproduces the apparent objectivity of the old-fashioned concept and term "Basque race." Basque culture is viewed as if it possessed primordial qualities that persist through time:

> To be Basque [says a student] is to belong to a millennial culture that in spite of everything and in spite of all the forces that tried to conceal or to bury it, to minimize it or even deride it, not only has it not disappeared but it has had a revival and has come to form an active part of society.

The emphasis they put on Basque culture is as a sign of distinctiveness from other peoples:

> For me, to be Basque, [says another], in addition to finding oneself identified with the territory, is to be identified with a specific type of culture and to feel it as your own, to put into practice the values of this culture and to defend it even when you have to move among other cultures.

CONCLUSION

Particularly important in popularizing this naturalized and objectified concept of culture are José Miguel Barandiarán and Basque nationalism. Basque nationalist parties were closely strenuously linked to the kind of anthropology Barandiarán embodied, as I noted ten years ago (Azcona, 1984). On the one hand, from the moment he began writing in the decade after 1910, Barandiarán took up the methodology and principles of the Viennese historical school as his main analytical tools. His enthusiasm for this approach explains the fervor with which he threw himself into the study of Basque rural society and the manifestations of the earliest Basque past. These Neolithic and early historical rural Basque societies, in his view, constituted the very basis of present-day Basque culture. Where still found, these earliest manifestations mattered because they provided something close to the "true nature" and "divinity" of Basque culture. By contrast, technological and urban culture were seen as nothing but degeneration and decadence.

Not surprisingly, Basque nationalism's perception and vision of Basqueness complemented rather than replaced the social and moral perceptions and worldview expounded in this kind of anthropology. As William Douglass has noted:

> The question is not if all or some of these [anthropological] interpretations could pass the test of a deeper investigation, but how this bloom of scientific energy furnished Basque nationalism with much more than remote mythical claims (although, as we have seen, it had plenty of them, too). In fact, it is possible to argue that the mutual understanding between Basque nationalism and this autochthonous Basque anthropological tradition was even deeper in the sense that one canceled the other. That is to say, if scientific discoveries strengthened the nationalist claim of the Basque uniqueness, the same movement influenced, and it is still influencing, the scientific notebook. (Douglass, 1989: 108)

This conception serves today as a point of reference for many people of the Basque Country and particularly for the inhabitants of the Basque Autonomous Community. This outcome was not central to Barandiarán's academic research interest, but it is no less a real achievement for all that. While he was alive, Barandiarán's person embodied and symbolized this reality. Basque culture may have been wiped off the rural scene and turned into an urban culture, but Barandiarán contributed more than anyone to the refounding of this culture through a particular type of anthropological research. Seen in this way, Barandiarán was the founder and the inventor of present-day Basque culture.

Chapter 10

Acceptable Difference: The Cultural Evolution of the Model Ethnic American Citizen

Bonnie Urciuoli

INTRODUCTION

U.S. national ideals have come to be embodied in the person of the citizen, and, in particularly interesting (if problematic) ways, in the ethnic citizen. The good citizen epitomizes hard work, the will to better oneself, the desire to achieve, the ability to produce. These qualities provide a validating frame for ethnic/race difference: the good ethnic citizen is the person whose country or culture of origin provide the moral wherewithal ("family solidarity," "work ethic," "belief in education," etc.) to "make it" as an American. Within this frame, one's name, how one looks, where one is from, and so on can be safely nonwhite or non-Anglo. Without the frame, safety disappears. This frame, then, provides a set of containers for acceptable difference.

The good ethnic citizen as a model of acceptable difference has evolved slowly from a time when citizenship was restricted to whites. Immigration and naturalization laws provide a useful guide to contemporary models of citizenship at various points in U.S. history. Racial specifications were defined, redefined and eliminated in 1965, along with quotas. Character requirements for naturalization have changed little in two centuries. A person must prove, subject to examination, his or her

> good moral character, understanding of and attachment to the fundamental principles of the Constitution of the United States, ability to read, write and speak English. (U.S. Code 1952)

While these character requirements are by law independent of race, too many Americans have embedded them in a cultural model of the white Anglo for too many years. The result is a racially ambiguous model of good citizenship, in which race and class have been mapped onto a person's character, beliefs, and abilities. The good ethnic citizen is measured against this model, with the worth of one's ethnicity hanging in the balance: good Italian-American or low-class Sicilian? hardworking African-American or underclass black? Enter publications like *Hispanic Magazine,* which carefully craft models of Hispanic-American achievers in business, politics, the arts, education, and research.

The good ethnic model makes it is easy to imagine that, despite categories of difference, the same embracing social truths must hold for everyone, and there is no such thing as a conflicting perspective. In an "ethnic" world, without the displacements of race and class, everyone (ideally) has the same chances and should "naturally" succeed. Everyone will be the same in ways that are definingly American, with differences neatly and safely contained. The only problem is that race and class do exist. Achievement and progress are not always up to the individual. And the good citizen model leaves little room for understanding why that is.

THE EVOLUTION OF THE CITIZEN

Over the course of U.S. history, defining the citizen has run aground several times on ambiguities about what the citizen should be: who is eligible, what is the cultural ideal. Ideas about citizenship in the United States grew from the concept of the subject, framed by the idea of membership in the nation as a matter of volitional allegiance. In this way, the idea of *naturalization* predates and frames the idea of citizenship in the United States. If by the 1760s native and adopted subjects "shared the same status and . . . rights, could not one conclude that their allegiance too was the same—contractual, volitional, and legal rather than natural and immutable" (Kettner, 1978: 128)?. In the Articles of Confederation and the Constitution, the early United States moved unevenly toward a sense of national community: "The individual citizen was the basic irreduceable unit." But of what? A national community or individual states (ibid.: 285–286)? This was not resolved until the fourteenth and fifteenth amendments (1868 and 1870) accorded citizen status to ex-slaves. U.S. citizenship was not to "be denied . . . on account of race, color or any previous condition of servitude" (Amend. 15, sec. 1). Citizens of states became citizens of the nation, which meant all citizens came under the jurisdiction of the Bill of Rights. Black and white native-born U.S. residents were equally citizens of state and nation (ibid.: 344).

Whatever constitutional amendments may say, the cultural opposition between slave and citizen had been indelibly mapped onto race and entrenched in U.S. culture. Judith Shklar (1991) argues that the American citizen is conceptually located between two noncitizen, non-American extremes: aristocracy, who do not earn because they need not labor; and slaves, who do not earn because their labor has been appropriated. The American citizen sells his (the concept is gendered) own labor or, ideally, is self-employed. The slave's status is fixed by law as chattel. The citizen is mobile, with the right, indeed the moral duty, to rise in life. By the early nineteenth century:

> Independent citizens in a democratic order had now not only to be respected for working, they also had a right to self-improvement, to education and unblocked opportunities for self-advancement. These rights were partly a fulfillment of the promise of equality enshrined in the Declaration of Independence, and partly they were a necessary corollary of the duty to contribute to the progress and prosperity of the republic. For the individual citizen, this also meant that socially he was what he did as an earner at any given moment in his life. One was what one did in such a world. (ibid.: 68)

These cultural connotations of "citizen" were in place well before the fourteenth and fifteenth amendments, and they go well beyond the legal framework to consolidate the moral basis of citizenship. Slavery ended but the classifications embedded in slavery did not. Race remained a social (though never a biological) fact, a "natural" explanation of social place.

The ideal of citizenship has been legally codified in two separate areas: naturalization procedures and race restrictions[1] on eligibility. From 1868 to 1965, the race restrictions were bitterly argued, recodified, strengthened, mitigated, and finally revoked altogether, while the basic procedures, the beliefs, and knowledge that one had to demonstrate to become a citizen changed very little. Meanwhile, under the terms of the Fourteenth Amendment, people whose parents were racially ineligible for naturalization were themselves born into citizenship. As a result, the legal and moral bases of citizenship have been linked in complex, sometimes ambiguous, even paradoxical ways.

The legal codifications of citizenship make explicit the defining terms of ideal citizenship. Indeed, the naturalization procedures specify the *moral* ideals of citizenship, so it is particularly interesting that what one must demonstrate to become naturalized has changed so little in two centuries. Petitioners since 1795 have had to demonstrate support for the Constitution, proof of good moral character, and competence in English.[2] In other words, the ideal citizen demonstrates rectitude in politics, personal character, and language—three defining areas of American morality that are inextricable from the central notion of the ideal American citizen as a producing person.

Race restrictions on naturalization first shifted in 1870 when, in addition to "free white persons," people of African nativity or descent also became eligible (Kettner 1978: 345). This left open the question of who was "white." Japanese, Afghans, and Hindus [sic] had been variously allowed or denied eligibility at the discretion of local judges, until they were categorically barred by 1922 and 1923 Supreme Court decisions, as were Filipinos, Koreans, Hawaiians (until the whole territory was naturalized), Chinese, and Indians (Gettys, 1934). Admitted as "white" were Syrians, Armenians, "a mostly Indian Mexican and a Parsee" [*sic*] (ibid.: 62). These exclusions remained in effect until 1952. Meanwhile, immigration restrictions were legislated that further limited the influx of "nonwhite" aliens (and thus limited the potential number of nonwhite children to be born into citizenship). The 1882 Chinese Exclusion Act barred labor immigration from China. Japanese immigration was excluded by the Immigration Act of 1924, which also set forth immigration quotas by nationality origin, heavily restricting southern and eastern Europeans. The Chinese Exclusion Act was repealed in 1943. The Japanese restriction was removed in 1952.

Because the terms of naturalization can be legislated, they reflect contemporary ideas of what is most truly American, what the *real* qualities of citizenship should be. The "good" alien exemplifies what a person can become given the opportunities that life in America has to offer. The question is, how much is this "ideal citizen" morally defined, how much is it racially defined, and to what extent are race and morality seen as inextricable? The dominant position, represented by innumerable media stories, politicians' speeches, and science or social science theories informed the exclusions and restrictions of the 1880s through 1920s, culminating in the provisions of the 1924 Immigration Act. (The quota numbers were based on the 1890 census and were meant to reflect the "original" U.S. race/nation demographics.) A recent *Newsweek* (8/9/93, p. 20) story provides a striking example of the race-is-morality position in a letter from President Hoover to Congressman Fiorello La Guardia, describing Italians as "predominantly our murderers and bootleggers . . . foreign spawn [who] do not appreciate this country."

The thinking on this was by no means monolithic. An "Americanization Studies" series published a volume sponsored by the Carnegie Corporation, *Americans by Choice* (Gavit, 1922) that passionately argued this perspective. Gavit cites a Professor Franklin Giddings of Columbia University: an American is loyal, "plays the game," takes pride in country and community, takes moral and civic responsibility to better conditions and (since all good citizens of all countries have these qualities) an American also has "a certain sensitiveness to the finer values in life . . ." (ibid.: 9). Gavit stresses that none of this is race-specific, and that the "true" American is characterized by "absence of exclusive racial marks" and "is the product of *all* races" (ibid.: 10), susceptible only to moral definition.

This position prevailed to the extent that at least some judges distinguished *individuals* who had the wherewithal to be model citizens were it not for the misfortune of their birth:

> There was . . . one striking example of non-admission to citizenship of a Japanese who had resided here for 20 years and who was a graduate of an American high school and college. The court, in barring him, considered him "well qualified by character and education for citizenship" but excluded him for racial reasons. (Gettys, 1934: 177)

The naturalized citizen as moral example stands in contrast to the birth citizen who may be neither moral nor exemplary. The Fourteenth Amendment in 1868 made citizens of all children born in the United States. From then on, children of "racial undesirables" (as they were no doubt perceived) were now citizens. To people believing that racial restrictions on naturalization preserve the moral quality of the citizenry, such birth citizens are not "real" Americans. Moreover, entire populations were naturalized, including residents of territories like the Philippines or Puerto Rico who became citizens through territorial acquisition instead of individual effort and who were by no means considered "white." These factors add up to second-class citizenship.

The racial constraints on naturalization were lifted by the 1952 Immigration and Nationality (McCarran-Walter) Act, which dropped the ban on "Oriental" immigration but kept the 1924 quotas more or less intact. The quotas were finally dismantled by the 1965 amendment to McCarran-Walter. The 1964 testimony concerning this amendment, at this point House Resolution (HR) 7700, nicely illustrates the range of positions taken in discourses about what makes a good citizen. Congressional Representatives, Cabinet officials, and spokespersons for U.S. civic organizations sorted themselves into a range of opposed positions, which can be summarized as follows: dropping quotas meant flooding the United States with the kind of people who cannot make good citizens; or, immigrants have already proven themselves to be model citizens and dropping quotas will bring in more good citizens.

Mark M. Jones, speaking for the National Economic Council, opposed HR 7700, gives this rationale for retaining quotas:

> The problem of assimilation—of molding an individual into a productive and responsible social unit, capable of self-control, self-direction and self-development—has not been solved in this country for our own population.... We have more people who consume more than they produce.... Instead of more consumers the paramount need is for producers. (USHR, 1964: 689)

Being a producer—supporting oneself and contributing to the nation—are key constructs in U.S. citizenship, as Shklar (above) argued. The proofs of character and ability required for naturalization set one up to produce: good personal character is proof of self-control; learning English signifies a willingness to learn whatever it takes to advance; upholding the constitution and forwearing anarchy and polygamy are proofs of the ability to embrace the controls inherent in a democratic order. None of this is possible if people remain part of an "undigested lump" (as another witness put it): immigrants must transform ("assimilate") into individual, productive, responsible units. The people who do not do this include what Jones goes on to describe as the "avalanche of Puerto Ricans and other Caribbeans that have inundated the Atlantic seaboard" (ibid.) as well as Mexicans, legal and illegal. He sees none of these as producers and the fact that Puerto Rico "is part of the Nation" (ibid.) clearly sticks in Jones's craw. Without quotas, there is no way to contain nonassimilative nonproduction. Similar positions were taken by, for example, the Daughters of the American Revolution, the American Legion, and the Veterans of Foreign Wars.[3]

Exactly the opposite point of view is taken by groups like the Sons of Italy or the Japanese American Citizens League who assert precisely the fact that they have contributed, bled for the polity. As John Papandreas of the Nationalities Service Center (Cleveland, Ohio) stated, "Immigrants have been producers" furnishing both "raw manpower" and "skilled technicians" (ibid.: 698). A revolutionary twist on the idea of "producer" is presented by Edward Dubroff, of the Association of Immigration and Nationality Lawyers, who spoke of seeing "more Americanism in the horny hand of an immigrant who dug our subways, laid our railroads ... than possibly you might find in the well-educated, native-born citizen" (ibid.: 861). He goes on:

> To have a concept that a person cannot make a good American unless he can speak, read and write English is measuring a man's worth by his education rather than by what he is. We want citizens for what they are and not for what they seem to be superficially. (ibid.: 861)

The key element of contrast between Mr. Jones's and Mr. Dubroff's visions of citizenship is the intersection of race/nationality and class. What Mr. Jones outlines is a middle-class ideal: someone self-directed, self-developed, and self-controlled sounds a lot more like someone who went to law school than does someone who dug subways. Mr. Dubroff sees manual labor as production. He also sees English competence not simply as an individual ability but as the product of privilege, of education.[4]

Control and sacrifice as informing themes of citizenship resonate through these hearings. Pro-quota witnesses often talk about individual effort, stressing the need for limiting immigration to those who can motivate themselves. Antiquota witnesses usually talk about immigrants overcoming hardship, working long hours and difficult jobs, fighting and dying for the United States in World Wars I and II (the spokesman for the Japanese American Citizen League poignantly developed the latter theme).[5] Pro-quota witnesses stress the need for order, arguing that quotas provide protection against an influx of Communists, disease (especially tuberculosis), crime and unemployment "from those nations highest in crime," as the Doorstep Savannah witness put it (ibid.: 664–667). Above all, quotas keep out the kind of immigrants that "tend to create isolated communities and do not assimilate our language nor our culture" as the witness for the Greenwich Women's Republican Club put it, offering Puerto Ricans as a paradigm case (ibid.: 817). While this is hardly a subtle reference to race, it is less explicitly name-calling than Hoover's depiction of "foreign spawn."

Evolving through the 1965 hearings, albeit unevenly, are ways of talking around race and class. As Chock has shown in studies of Congressional hearings on immigration between 1975 and 1986 (Chock, 1991; this volume), talking around race and class (and gender) has become central to U.S. political process; my analyses of the 1965 hearings draw from her approach. Race, class, and gender issues are increasingly reframed in rationalist and natural history terms: the 1986 Immigration Reform and Control Act hearings are heavily dominated by tropes of "population" and "control." In such a frame, Chock argues, it is increasingly difficult for people to challenge restrictive attitudes if doing so appears to oppose a logical or rational order. These reformulations are instrumental in the transformation of what used to be thought of as "race" into what is now called "ethnic."

ETHNICIZING AND RACE-MAKING

The naturalized citizen has evolved legally from white to racially unmarked, otherwise remaining a morally upright English speaker who supports the constitution. Nevertheless, through the decades that racial restrictions on citizenship have been legally mitigated, race continues to matter deeply to many of those legislating America. Meanwhile, what used to be seen as race has been mapped onto other frames of reference in public discourse.

The naturalized citizen is an idealized citizen and in many ways personifies the United States as nation. The racial status of this ideal citizen remains ambiguous. The rationalism, self-control, goal-orientation, and patriotism attributed to the ideal citizen also resonate with the figure of the white Anglo. There has been an increasing sense that the generic American is middle class. Sennett and Cobb (1972) capture this dynamic in *The Hidden Injuries of Class,* when they speak of class mobility as the only way for a person to "get respect." Class mobility has come to define individual worthiness, especially with the post-World War II mobility of "ethnic whites." This American cultural model of the middle class (see, e.g., Rapp, 1987; Newman, 1988; DeMott, 1990; Ortner, 1991) is, again, not specifically white but many Americans, especially racially minoritized Americans, map what they typify as middle-class behavior onto whiteness.[6]

All this plays merry hell with "imagining America" according to Anderson's (1991) idea of nation as imagined community. Race is undeniably if not always explicitly part of the imagining despite Anderson's assertion that race and nation are mutually exclusive constructs. Segal and Handler (1992) argue (contra Anderson) that not seeing race for what it is contributes to just the essentializing nationalism that Anderson proposes to deconstruct. In the shift from monarchic to national imagining:

> the hierarchical differentiation of those persons had to be placed under erasure. Thus, a pre-condition of national identities . . . was "individual equality" . . . (which) did not sequentially replace medieval hierarchy but was coeval with, and constituted in relation to, an exteriorized hierarchy.
> . . . it was in racial terms that hierarchy was inscribed beyond the boundaries of what thereby became the collective, racial self—"the European." (ibid.: 59-60)

"Imagining" the U.S. happens in a Euro-American social and historical context. If quotas were institutionalized to reflect a time when the U.S. population was largely northern and western European, many Americans, especially legislators, imagine "the (Northern) European" as part of their imagining of the United States.

Thus, race is now analytically present in and ideologically elided from the vision of the rational producing citizen. In fact, race can be elided *because* the citizen is idealized as a self-motivated producer. Production can be ascribed entirely to *individual will and resourcefulness*, regardless of the structural elements that constrain people's actions and options. This makes possible a mitigating discourse, a way to shift the vision of citizen from "racial exclusion" to "ethnic inclusion." I posit "race-making" and "ethnicizing" as contrasting processes with a specifically American cultural sense. Take the following example from Jonathan Rieder's *Canarsie: The Jews and Italians of Brooklyn Against Liberalism*. Rieder quotes a local Jewish merchant:

> Face it, the Haitians and Jamaicans and the other islanders down in Flatbush don't consider themselves black. These island people are producing people, they're up early sweeping their stoops and taking care of their homes. They're producing people like we are! But the black lower element don't contribute to society, they just take. In my view, you should get what you put into. You have to contribute. (1985: 105)

The "black lower element" are race-made; the Haitians and Jamaicans are ethnicized. All have equally African ancestry; it is what they do with their ancestry that assigns them their social place—for which they are ideologically responsible *as individuals*. Being able to do this turns on the idea of self-controlled agents in charge of their own destiny. Those in the situation of the "black lower element" are there because they have not gotten themselves out of it. They contrast sharply with the Haitians and Jamaicans who, according to this informant, "don't consider themselves black."[7]

"Race" and "ethnicity" in the United States have become naturalized as neutral descriptive properties of groups. This obscures their processual nature. Their oppositional nature is obscured by the ambiguity with which both terms are currently used. My approach to race derives partly from Stanfield's (1985) discussion of race-making, a naturalized stratification of human relations built into Euro-American nation-building. Omi and Winant (1986) similarly see "racialization" as a historically contingent process of stratified classification. In U.S. race-making, a people's cultural worth depends on their social location, including how their mode of entry into the polity is still seen, that is, as slaves or as highly proletarianized labor. Over decades or centuries of public discourses, the group's name becomes a metonym for their social location, that is, becomes a race term. *Chinese, Irish, Italian, Polish,* and *Jewish* have all been race terms. If a group's racial status remains low, it is seen as a result of not trying hard enough. In this model, working-class status is a place to start from, not a place to stay.

My approach to ethnicity draws from Williams (1991) who sees the tension between "race" and "ethnic" labels as politically motivated. The principle she outlines in her study of Guyana also works in the United States insofar as ethnicity reflects the ways in which people "conceptualize their contribution to the development of a sociocultural order" (176). People ethnicize when they prove their worth to the polity by "progressing" out of the working class, by bleeding for the nation in times of war, and by relating their progress and sacrifice to the nation from which they came (though few such points of departure were nations when the European migrations began). Entry into the United States is transformed into a "new beginning," as Segal puts it, with the pre-immigration experience "placed into a past that is enclosed and complete" (forthcoming: 2). *Irish, Polish, Italian*, and so on move from race to ethnic terms when they can be hyphenated -*American*, when their bearers can reinforce their credit as Americans by an "old country" that is also a nation with a national culture. Qualities attributed to an old country heritage (work ethic, family closeness, etc.) hasten the group on its way of ethnic progress, and so are equally "American values." Class disappears as anything other than a point of departure ("we were poor") and a measure of mobility and individual effort ("but we made it").

None of this simply happens. Unionization, consolidation of political power, opportunities for mobility after World War II (especially the G.I. bill) all created structural openings and clout for "white ethnics." Ethnicizing requires structural shifts; it also requires the interpretation of those shifts as part of a natural story. The commemorative expression of ethnic values as American values is strongly framed by the growing ethnic presence in business and the professions in what Bodnar (1992: 69) calls "the middle-class offensive in commemorative events on behalf of respectability and Americanization." This respectability is exemplified by participation in political process: the "good" ethnic has *earned* the right to vote and exercises it as a citizen should. Voting links the individual to the state, to upholding the constitution. Voting signifies the existence of the citizen as a *unit* of democracy and is the ultimate leveler: the laborer's vote counts exactly as much as that of the President's.[8] Ethnic voting is symbolically important as the vote that rewards sacrifice. It is instrumental in building ethnic representation.

The model for ethnic labels is the national referent: *Irish, Polish*, and so forth. (This is no litmus test: *Mexican* has certainly been a race-making referent.) In her examination of the *Harvard Encyclopedia of American Ethnic Groups,* Chock (1991a) points out the resultant "splitting and lumping" principle: European ethnicities are split into national groups, non-Europeans tend to be lumped into, for example, *Asian, Hispanic, African-American, Caribbean,* and so on, all of which also have racial referents, making them subject to an interpretation that is at best ambiguous. Nor do those thus referred to have much choice in how they are labeled. Many people from Spanish-speaking Central or South America or the Caribbean might prefer to be known by their nationality than by *Hispanic* but in the United States, *Hispanic* is what works in most media, political and academic discourse. The burden is on the bearers of the term to "ethnicize" it and elide its race overtones. Representation and celebration are important venues for showing good citizenship. So is the ethnic media.

ETHNICIZING DISCOURSE: CONTAINING DIVERSITY IN *HISPANIC MAGAZINE*

Hispanic Magazine is of particular interest because it is an English-language magazine for a Hispanic U.S. audience. There are a few other Hispanic-issue magazines in English, but they are oriented toward academics, engineering, business, education, or literature; *Hispanic* is the only general interest magazine (Katz and Katz, 1992: 656), covering news, finances, sports, political representation, education, arts, and entertainment. It is aimed at a career oriented, upwardly mobile readership. The table of contents for January-February 1993 lists these features: Presidential Promises (what Clinton has to offer Hispanics); New Beginnings (resolving to make 1993 a better year); Getting into the Game (sports); New Faces in Congress (Hispanic members); Creative Spirit (artist's profile); Classically Puerto Rican (a ballet company); 1993 Hispanic 100 (the companies that provide the most opportunities for Hispanics); Catch Them If You Can (the most eligible single men and women); The Straight Rap (Hispanic *raperos*). Regular departments include: From the Editor; Letters; This Month (political, art, and entertainment events involving or affecting Hispanics); Cars; Careers; Money; Travel; Business; Reviews; La Buena Vida; People; Hispanic Calendar; Forum.

Each feature or department is an arena that showcases an aspect of good citizenship: political process and the power of the vote (electing those who will uphold the constitution); education and achievement (English literacy as prerequisite to both); moral character (these are people to admire and emulate). To draw on the Lakoff and Johnson (1980) idea of the container metaphor, each feature of the magazine is a kind of container fitted with an implicit scale, a kind of cultural measuring cup designating levels of achievement.[9] The stories are about Latin success models, people who earn respectable salaries, win awards, become educated, start their own businesses, perform in arts and entertainment, become mayors, Congressional representatives, Chamber of Commerce chairs, doctors, and lawyers. Success within most of these areas is quantifiable by years of education, number of votes, performances given, awards achieved, amount of earnings, or annual sales. Even fame can be scaled as "more" or "less."

In each case, the measurement of success is authorized by and contained within legally defined parameters. By law, becoming a doctor or lawyer requires extensive and expensive training, so simply becoming one is a sign of "progress." Their activities are carefully regulated, beginning with the licensing procedure, so the things one does to be successful are very specifically ordered. Business activities are regulated by law and founded in charters of incorporation; salaries and benefits are subject to legislative control. Education, the starting point for business and profession pursuits, is legislatively mandated through public schools, and state and city colleges and universities. Doing what it takes to be a good citizen may seem like a private pursuit, but it can only happen in a detailed framework of legislation:

> The legal structure, meaning and character of these transactions are public, and they affect the whole republic. Economic exchanges and entitlements are ultimately subject to public sanction . . . Earning and spending are hardly private in the sense that prayer and love might be. (Shklar, 1991: 63)

The magazine's advertising reinforces its messages about structured mobility. There are 74 advertisements in this issue, only about a third of which urge individuals to consume products. Most target minority recruitment or sell business services. The emphasis on the career ladder is quite clear. Most advertisements are in English; those in Spanish are marked with a single asterisk (*), those in English with a few Spanish words are marked with a double asterisk (**). Hispanics are targeted through images of people much more than through Spanish (though, interestingly, all tobacco and alcohol advertising is in Spanish). Three quarters of the ads showing people show dark haired, often dark skinned people with Spanish names. This is no accident: literacy in English is a prerequisite for the upwardly mobile young citizens targeted by major corporations.

> *Companies urging readers to consume their products:*
> Insurance/Investment: Allstate Insurance, State Farm, Charles Schwab Investment, American Family Life Insurance
> Electronics/Telecommunication: IBM, AT&T, Apple Computer
> Travel: United Airlines
> Cars: Cadillac, Dodge, *Toyota, Ford, Lincoln, Buick, Geo Prizm, Pontiac, GMAC SmartLease, **Honda, Ford
> Appliances: General Electric
> Clothing: *J.C. Penney
> Entertainment: **Columbia House (Latin music)
> Beer/Liquor/Food: *Budweiser, *Miller Lite, Goya, *Johnnie Walker
>
> *Ads urging small/minority businesses to use their services:*
> Insurance/Banking: Travelers Insurance, Nacional Financiera (Mexican Bank)

Travel/Transport: American Airlines, **Wells Fargo
Communications: Pacific Bell, MCI Telecommunications
Military Recruitment: **U.S. Air Force, U.S. Army Civilian Employment

Companies soliciting applications for minority hiring programs:
Investment/Insurance/Banking: Dean Witter, Blue Cross Blue Shield, New York Life, Union Bank
Electronics/Telecommunications: Xerox, Northern Telecom, IBM, Electronic Data Systems
Transportation: Federal Express
Food: **McDonald's, Kellogg
Medical: **SmithKline Beecham Laboratories, Paramedics
Petroleum Products: Exxon, Chevron, Rustoleum
Chemical/Textile Engineering: ARCO, Monsanto
Vehicles: John Deere, Honda
Aerospace: Lockheed, Rockwell

Companies declaring their sensitivity to minority needs and possibly (but not explicitly) seeking minority applicants:
Insurance: TIAA-CREF, John Hancock
Electronics/Telecommunications: AT&T, Digital, Pitney Bowes
Petroleum: Texaco
Chemical Enginerring: Hoechst Celanese
Personal Care Products: **Colgate-Palmolive, Johnson & Johnson, Gilette
Tobacco: *Philip Morris, *R.J.R. Reynolds
Food: Sarah Lee, Coca-Cola, Pepsico
Vehicle Manufacture: General Motors
Entertainment: Time Warner, Readers Digest

Just under half the pages in the issue carry advertising. 32 advertisements urge individual or corporate (small business) consumption, mostly of insurance and investment services, electronics and telecommunications, autos and travel services, with a few ads for appliances, clothing, music, food, and drink. The stress is clearly on movement, communication, and long-range planning. forty-two ads are explicitly or implicitly recruitment ads. Those explicitly recruiting stress investment, insurance, electronics, telecommunications, movement (of people or goods), and the military. The companies that advertise themselves as friends-of-minorities cover the same territory as well as a few personal consumption areas (food, drink, tobacco). All in all, the magazine seems to aim at a readership just starting up the career ladder into corporate life.

The stress is not on product consumption as an expression of lifestyle. Few material products are advertised, aside from autos and even here the stress is on practical knowledge and technology, not luxury. Aside from the one Cadillac ad, the advertised autos are mid-income-range practical: Ford, Toyota, Buick, Honda, Dodge, Geo. The practical but expensive makes, the Volvos and Saabs, are conspicuously absent. Of the remaining consumption-oriented ads, half are about organizing one's path through life: learning skills, making rational decisions, making long-range plans, managing money, providing security against the future and life's accidents.

The areas in which diversity is safe are those that do not impede this path of rational action and achievement. Acceptable differences include one's name, place of origin, skin color and hair texture (so long as the hairdo is relatively contained). An "ethnic" personal style within a limited range of clothing, hair arrangements (including mustaches on men), and accessories is allowed. Personal histories telling of poor beginnings are acceptable but illegitimacy, jail records, and drug use are risky. Speaking Spanish is acceptable so long as it does not "interfere" with one's English: a slight accent is allowed, as are occasional emblematic Spanish words. Grammar irregularities ("mistakes") are not allowed. These "ethnic" signs are relatively safe because they are "natural" signs of origin, beyond the control of the individual and therefore not subject to assessment. Indeed, since it is known that these are signs against which some uncitizenly Americans are prejudiced, these signs may be badges of pride: "With all this, I achieved."

When skin color, name, immigrant history, and a language other than English are seen as "underclass signs," as bad character and bad language, as impediments, the sense of safety disappears and the signs become race-makers. Judging from the letters page, this is a major concern to readers, many of whom write about how Hispanics appear to non-Hispanics, praising or criticizing the magazine's efforts to present a creditable picture of Hispanics. One reader criticized a recent story on Hispanic business dress styles for making Hispanics appear to overemphasize looks (and, implicitly, underemphasize skill and knowledge). Other readers praised a story that had critically spotlit the way several leading newspapers reported stories involving Hispanics. One reader, herself a college professor, praised a feature on U.S. Hispanic writers who might serve as exemplars for her students.

The magazine is above all aimed at "the Hispanic community," a community reified by the U.S. Census as 20,000,000 (or so) checkmarks in one of the "yes" boxes following the question, "Is this person of Spanish/Hispanic origin?" This was followed by questions about income, occupation, housing, education, the containers for achievement that define the community's worth. The answers establish guidelines for affirmative action, determine qualification for federal programs, provide data on home mortgage lending patterns, determine whether financial institutions meet credit needs, review state districting plans, assist minority-owned small businesses, plan school construction, assess health needs, and assess fair juror selection (U.S. Department of Commerce, 1990). In short, they set up categories of ordered, legally delineated community activity, coherent with the articles and advertisements in the magazine.

What makes this problematic is the peculiarly U.S. sense of *community* which emphasizes likeness, not relationships. It is, as Varenne puts it, a group of individuals who "live together, who act together, and above all who develop a shared state of mind" (1986: 224). The archetypal community is the small town or neighborhood that develops a shared consensus. Shared consensus is the key feature of the American notion of community because it informs usages like *ethnic community*, *Hispanic community*, *Italian community*, and so on. The very usage *community* is ethnicizing: *black community* is synonymous with *African-American community*, not with black in a racial sense. The consensus implicit in these uses of *community* emphasizes similarity of individuals over structure and relationships, making conflict atypical and problematic rather than a common dimension of human relations. At the same time, there is a sense that each individual community member carries that consensus consciously and deliberately. What results is a construct in which the whole community is the individual member writ large. The consensus is essentialist, arising from a replication of units, not from human action full of compromises, complex motives, and politics. To some extent, the consensus model is imposed on a social group by the expectations of the larger society, whether people want to be seen as a "community" or not (ibid.: 226). This is frequently the case with "ethnic communities" who are too often depicted by media, academics, and policy makers as embodiments of "cultural" traits: language, customs, food, music, and so on. Rarely are "ethnic communities" depicted in terms of the political and economic dynamics that set its "members" apart from the larger society. Class is effectively elided; individual achievement foregrounded.

One of the hidden costs of this idea of community is that it opposes the "ethnic community" to a race-made mass of disorder, a population out of control. Hispanic good-citizenship is valued insofar as it distances images of a disordered Hispanic underclass. Ironically, in a society that so praises the individual, the idea of an ethnic community leaves little room for individuation, for "ethnic individuals" to appear as unique selves to the larger society. "Hispanic community members" are responsible for "successes" that can offset the "failures" of Hispanics who live below the poverty line, draw welfare support, never finished school, live in deteriorated neighborhoods, work at dead-end jobs, or have no jobs—the antithesis of citizenship and community that, as articles about the "underclass" put it, feeds on the nation-state without contributing to it. There is little room to be an average citizen, neither a success nor a failure.

Much welfare legislation represents state control over the lives of private citizens (Piven and Cloward, 1971). The very act of becoming eligible for welfare is read as a forfeiture of personal control over money, relationships, even one's own time. Yet the clients are responsible for knowing how to handle the bureacratic system. The irony is that the social dynamics that turns people into clients undermines their sense of control over what they do know: if they "get it wrong" they lose services. As I found in fieldwork among Puerto Rican bilinguals in New York, women who were quite comfortable in English with neighbors and family found themselves unable to trust their English in dealings with social bureacracy. Both bureaucrats and clients, especially bureaucrats, ascribe miscommunication to defective English much more than they ascribe it to the highly politicized imbalance of class, race, and gender. People in such a position can much too easily come to epitomize anticitizens (doubting their own worth into the bargain) because "their English was bad," a defect they should be able to fix with enough effort. English, depoliticized and decontextualized, becomes a defining measure of social worth.

When a population is seen in the polarized terms of success and failure, a great deal of success is required to offset the vision of failure. A "community" is validated through its high points and there are few higher points than presidential recognition. The cover story for this issue of *Hispanic* is "Presidential Promises: What Will Clinton Do for Hispanics?" Administrative titles are a valuable frame for a Spanish name: "Frank Cota-Robles Newton, Executive Director of the National Hispanic Leadership Agenda" (p. 24). Without these high points, non-Hispanics will only see poverty, crime and "bad" or no English—none of which adds up to a "community." Rags-to-riches stories are necessary to suggest that if some make it, more may follow even if it takes some time: "While the Hispanic community is pleased with the appointment of Henry Cisneros and Federico Pena, there is strong concern that there is a paucity of Hispanic appointments at the sub-cabinet level" (p. 24).

Given the limits inherent in discourses about community and good citizenship, it becomes vital to build media pictures of a "Hispanic community" that can show the 20,000,000 census responses to advantage and recast perceptions of undocumented Mexican migrants as parasites on the polity, or of Puerto Ricans as anticitizens who cannot or will not "assimilate." But it is up to the ethnic to recast those perceptions in suitable terms. There are few solutions available in U.S. public discourses beyond the rags-to-riches story. *Hispanic Magazine* works hard to cast Hispanics as successes but does not change the original cultural script. The old model of the nonwhite as the un-American anticitizen is always lurking, and can only be fended off by constant exemplary effort.

The homogenization of difference, each ethnic group "different" only in ways that contribute to the polity, is a fundamental process in U.S. culture, and the tension between ethnicity and race lies at the heart of it. The fault lies not in the ideals of citizenship, of sacrifice and achievement, of individual effort rewarded, but in the hegemonic perspective that success or failure are ultimately up to the individual.

ACKNOWLEDGMENTS

This essay is based on a paper presented at *Democracy and Difference: An International, Interdisciplinary Conference on Cultural Diversity and Democratic Processes*, organized by Carol Greenhouse and Davydd Greenwood, at Indiana University, April 1993. Thanks to Douglas Ambrose and Hervé Varenne for their most helpful comments and criticisms of early drafts of this manuscript.

NOTES

1. These are codified partly as race and partly as nationality but what they add up to are race restrictions.

2. There have been recodifications of residency requirements and the time periods involved in the application procedure. At one point, it as necessary to foreswear polygamy and anarchy.

3. The spokesperson for Doorstep Savannah Inc. also singled out Puerto Ricans as anticitizens: "Forty thousand Puerto Ricans migrating into New York City each year depress wages, increase crime rates, complicate already complex health and education problems, and cost New York's taxpayers $35 million a year in welfare costs" (USHR, 1964: 664).

4. Some people took intermediate positions. Some followed the line "My group was good for the U.S. and should have their quotas dropped, but some of those other groups are not good for the U.S. so keep their quotas." Others followed the line taken by Mr. Sam Baccala, Americanism Chairman for the Baltimore American Legion, who said that while he was proud of his Italian family, he spoke as an American first, and that dropping quotas, even for Italians, would not be good for the United States (USHR 1964: 934).

5. One witness did not locate himself in this citizenship discourse: His Highness Galumalemana Vaiinupo Alailima, president of the Organization for Preservation of Samoan Democracy and special representative for various villages of American Samoa. He asserted that U.S.-Samoan relations had been defective for sixty-four years. U.S. immigration law pertaining to Samoa did not take account of local political and kin organization and thus barred from immigration people whose relations to local chiefs should make them eligible. He then cited language to correct these defects in HR 7700, which he hoped would end the "unnecessary hardship and inconvenience" now experienced by Samoans hoping to migrate to the United States (USHR, 1964: 931).

6. See Fordham and Ogbu, 1986 on race/class attitudes of African-Americans students. I stress "cultural model" because the now prevalent sense of a generic American middle class does not correlate with specific structural elements of class.

7. Ironically, while African Americans are citizens by birth, Jamaicans and Haitians are often seen to act "more American" than Americans, a theme developed in a *Newsweek* story (August 8, 1993) about a gifted Haitian student.

8. See Shklar (1991) on voting and citizenship.

9. Lakoff and Johnson argue that people conceptually organize the less tangible areas of reference around the more tangible, reifying abstractions and experience as if they were things or people ("Life is tough" or "History tells us") and orienting themselves accordingly ("in trouble," "under indictment," etc.). Container metaphors— experiences or concepts as things that can be filled and measured— are endemic in U.S. conceptualizations.

III

Official Discourses and Professional Practice

From the previous sections' concerns with the sites and media by which official discourses are made, and made to matter in social life, this section turns to the process of social inquiry itself. The three essays gathered here clarify the reproduction of official discourses over time, and their reflexive implications for ethnography. The section opens with Velasco's critical account of the discipline of folklore in Spain, and the evolution of its absorption by the Spanish state. Carefully tracing the construction of performance in rural areas (e.g., in oral, artistic, and artisanal practices) as manifestations of a collective regional ethnic subject, Velasco's account traces a complex map of remembering, forgetting, and reconfiguration in the modern liberal state. Mertz also asks us to consider the significance of the ways experience is acknowledged or silenced through speech in the public sphere, or at its edges, in the simultaneous projects of maintaining a profession and a nation. She takes us to U.S. law school classrooms, where her analysis of classroom conversations between students and teachers shows an official discourse of difference in the making—as students' prior understandings are pruned to the particular shapes the law recognizes and validates. Comelles takes up the theme of recognition and denial, as a means of relating the history of ethnography in Spain and the United States in terms of the way the state opens or forecloses markets for particular forms of knowledge, understanding, and conscience.

Each of the essays in this section explores a fundamental aspect of the contingent status of ethnographic inquiry with respect to the politics, market forces (including professional marketplaces), and constructions of subjectivity in the modern liberal state. Their common theme is ethnography's importance as a counterdiscourse in precisely these circumstances—and its marginal status as a mode of inquiry. But before ethnography can fulfill its potential in this respect, its reflexive conundrums must be reconnected to their roots in the tensions within liberal democracy itself over the possibility of justice in a multicultural world, and ethnography's role in shaping those very tensions at various junctures. Comelles's account of the crossed histories of democracy and ethnography, and their ongoing challenge to ethnographic practice, doubles as the volume's conclusion.

Chapter 11

The Role of Folklore and Popular Culture in the Construction of Difference in Spain

Honorio M. Velasco

Even today it might seem surprising that on November 4, 1883, Antonio Machado would address an article entitled "Spanish Folklore" in *El Globo* to "Spanish politicians" and, in particular, to the heads of the political parties.[1] In it, he urged them to take on folklore studies as a great national effort capable of uniting all:

> I believe first of all that it must be evident to all of us that a nationality constitutes such a strong and high community of interests that not even the natural conflict among opposed factional interests within it can break it up. Without this dimension, true national unity can never exist, in my judgement, a unity that we must seek, beyond the community of race, territory, and basic language—indispensable in all nations, as noted by the famous historian A. Herculano—in a community of ideas and goals, and of course, in a project that is of interest to all. Without that community of vision and thought, without the project provided by great works of general interest, nations end up disappearing in history or seeing themselves subjected to the yoke of more intelligent and vigorous peoples.

This article had been preceded by another, entitled "The Folklore of Madrid," in which he presented a general questionnaire on the "customs of the Castilian people in the different spheres of their life" as a first step in folklore studies. His aim was to encourage an "awakening among all Castilians of the desire to create [*formar*] the folklore of the two Castiles."

That the article was directed to Spanish politicians is less surprising if we appreciate Machado's conviction about the transcendence of the work he was proposing. The audacity that is taken for granted in this gesture was no more than a reflection of the passion with which he, like many other European folklorists, put themselves to the task of developing and spreading folklore.[2] It is possible that the impassioned tone undermines a bit the transcendence that he advocates in the quote. Still the founding and organization of Folklore Societies and the early participation in them by eminent politicians and scientists of the period and the actions undertaken at the outset are certainly revealing. The publicity that he sought through the press had another objective as well, that folklore become known to newspaper readers, with the unequivocal intention that they too would join the effort.

In the published articles, the addresses of the president and secretary of the Society are given so that prospective collaborators could send them information. It is no accident that the presentation of folklore was made by means of the publication of a survey, because through this, Machado was trying to provide the basic work tools that were need to build the collection of materials, his first and principal mission. The involvement of university professors, literary figures, and scientists from various branches of learning noted in the newspapers, not only attempted to earn prestige for folklore and to legitimate it as another branch of knowledge, but also served to stimulate the participation of others and, in particular, of those called to perform the informant's role.[3] Some questionniares were directed at priests, doctors, and schoolteachers on subjects appropriate to their particular specialties.[4] The Folklore Societies tried to have corresponding partners in all the towns and cities, which could then be subdivided into provinces, subregions [*comarcas*], and localities. This does not mean that the folklorists did not themselves engage in field research, but they were aware that the magnitude of their effort demanded broad social participation, especially by the literate sectors (with institutional connections) who could gather good quality information about oral traditions and the customs of different places.

Perhaps it could be said that the penetration of folklore into the social fabric was a methodological requirement. Whether or not this is true, the project was proposed in such a way that particular social sectors came to see themselves as directly implicated in it. Thus it is not so surprising that the article was directed to Spanish politicians.[5]

Offered as a "great national work," it gave informants and collaborators the satisfaction of contributing to a high cause because it was a common cause, to the point—and it is more surprising that they would believe it—that the fact of participating in it could overcome party and business differences. If it seems a naive methodological proposal to try to gather such materials through a simple invitation to priests, schoolteachers, and doctors in the newspapers, it is even more so as a political proposal. The design of this kind of folklore had a greater political or social twist than would any mere scientific activity.[6]

That the importance of the work Machado proposed was based on a criticism of the essentialist conception of nation should not be ignored. The attention of the politicians is directed toward folklore as common task and toward its contents. It is not that it offers—we would say today—elements of identity to justify nationalist decisions, but rather some common "ideas and goals." Later in the same article, Machado stated how "the community of religious ideas made possible the unity of the country in times of the Catholic Kings." The emphasis is on the idea of "community," not on "religious ideas."

This proclamation—made in Madrid—had an antecedent in the presentation of the Society of Spanish Folklore, founded in November, 1881, in Seville, especially in the circular that *El Folklore Andaluz* (the first of its efforts) directed "at the Andalusian provinces" (note the generic reader in contrast with the prior example).[7] The first circular praises the Andalusian region, mentioning some of the illustrious men that it gave to the Church and the country, and then presents the apparently modest task of collecting tales, proverbs, *romances* [a poetic form], and so on, from the populace—making explicit the goals of the project: "to collect material for the true history of these provinces, up until now, like that of Spain, not yet written..." and "... to make manifest to the whole world the soul of this privileged and very original Andalusian race, whose most secret motives and most beautiful qualities underlie this anonymous poetry and knowledge." Thus the work proposed in creating the Society of Andalusian Folklore was a "an eminently moral and civilizing effort" and one "of transcendental justice," since it was going to

> recognize the right of the people to be considered an important factor in human history... The work that we are undertaking [the circular continues] is completely separate from all political viewpoints and philosophical schools; this barely known effort has already had the effect of linking men of the most diverse views and political parties around a common idea, and is eminently educational.

This effort—and the proclamation explains this later—"will teach the lovers of the past affection for the modern generations and respect for past generations to the lovers of the present." The circular continues:

A work of true social importance because it causes us to recognize all men as brothers without distinction of party or views, everyone has a place in it and we call on everyone to carry it out; from the most humble peasant to the most aristocratic lady; from the most modest craftsman to the person occupying the uppermost social position; all have, as Andalusians, the right to live below this beautiful sky, the right to hold a position in the Society of the Andalusian Folklore; we call on everyone because we need them all; this is everyone's enterprise, we are all interested in it prospering and flowering.

By citing both proclamations, I want to emphasize not just the rhetorical capabilities of Machado and his companions, or their knowledge of subtleties that permitted them to make their message more acceptable to politicians or to the people, but also an assemblage of intertwined dimensions of their substantive ideas. These can be synthesized in the following points:

1. Folklore was presented as a scientific task (the reconstruction of the history).
2. It was also presented as a work of national and social transcendence. Its transcendental character does not reside so much in its scientific character but rather: a) in its returning historical agency to the people, and (b) in its ability to overcome party and class divisions, which, in principle, must affect everyone. It is formulated as a work of formation or consolidation of a nation. The mentioned social divisions are as much a universal condition of human beings in general as they are a part of the more restricted condition of Andalusians or Spaniards.
3. Everyone is invited to participate in this scientific work as informant. It is the mission of the Folklore Societies to compile the materials that created by the support of the literate correspondents from all over the country.
4. The organizational structure of the Folklore Societies (according to paragraph 29 of its by-laws) has a territorial basis and treats the regions as differentiated units (though they are included within in an overall unity—Spain—that, at the same time, is included in yet another unity, Humanity).

There is a double and important superimposition here. On the one hand, folklore is presented as a scientific task, but not one reserved only to the intellectuals. Rather it is offered as a social activity open to all whether they be informants or compilers. On the other hand, the territorial structure responded to the requirement that the organization centralize widely dispersed information, since it is necessary to include even the smallest groups, in part as an element in the logic of the projection of the superordinate unifying categories that can motivate the participation of all in the effort. This peculiar mix of methodological requirements and sociopolitical conceptions gave folklore a set of equivocal meanings that it still bears.

It should not be forgotten that Machado reproduced (or at most re-adapted) the definition of contents, objectives, and organization from the Folklore Society of England and took on the ideas of Spencer on the reconstruction of the history of the humanity and the Tylorian concept of survivals.[8] And, as the journal *El Folklore Andaluz* shows, he understood the work of all the regional societies that he contributed to founding as part of a scientific movement that he believed all European nations were participating in—a scientific movement impregnated with evolutionist theories.[9]

The passion with which Machado and other folklorists in Europe committed themselves to folklore was stimulated by a strange mixture of universalism and particularism. Folklore began to be formalized as a common language in which to express national, regional, or local uniqueness. It was forged as shared code to express territorial differences. And furthermore, it was one of those few domains of knowledge within reach of all. While it is possible that its scientific character was compromised by its link to social action, possibly no other domain of knowledge became as popular as "popular knowledge."

Machado did not succeed in gaining the attention of politicians, the proposed questionnaires were hardly used, and the Folklore Societies were dissolved a short time after their founding. Machado himself abandoned folklore and apparently fell into a depression.[10]

But not many years afterward (1901), on the initiative Joaquin Costa, the Academia de Ciencias Morales y Políticas and the Ateneo de Madrid circulated vast questionnaires on customs having to do with the life cycle. These institutes also supported the preparation of monographs about agrarian collectivism, customary law, and so forth, that relied on the participation of numerous local compilers. Compilers interviewed rural informants or they themselves acted as informants (attorneys, doctors, local historians, priests, and schoolteachers).[11]

This project never ended—as Guichot y Sierra noted in 1921 and Luis de Hoyos pointed out in his *Manual de Folklore* in 1947; thereafter, it is evident in the *Revista de Dialectología y Tradiciones Populares*. On the one hand, it was a strictly academic activity centering on philologists, musicologists, and to a lesser degree, on ethnographers. But, on the other hand, it was converted into and ended up being maintained as an activity of amateurs (generally part-time), involving numerous groups of people from the most diverse professions and ideologies. Indeed, it could be said that this group should be recognized as the disciples of Machado, except that they generally lack organization, and act in isolation with very little transmission of information among them. They were and are distant from the new theoretical currents in anthropology, reproducing instead old methodological habits, mainly consisting of questionnaires (or even inventories).

Strangely, with respect to academic activity, folklore lost its identity and was absorbed as an element in philology (or of musicology—though here, folklore retained part of its identity[12]), but the amateur practitioners rarely rejected their identity as folklorists or as lovers of popular traditions. The compilations they made generally are not even systematized; rather they are either collections or just separate notes on diverse topics.

The old aim of reconstructing history was forgotten—and supplanted by an objective that had been announced at the very beginning: the documentation of customs that were disappearing or whose memory would soon be lost. The early scientific character of the activity was obliterated while, at the same time, the territorial specificity of the compilations to different national, regional, provincial, or local places increased.

Folklore did not become a national project (at least not in the sense that Machado had intended), but many folklorists believed they contributed something through their actions to the aggrandizement of their nation, region, province, or locality or at least to the demonstration of its singularity. The recent development of the history of anthropology in Spain shows that the process is quite complex and not generalizable in the same form to all regions and nationalities.[13] In this sense, folklore was being converted not only into a storehouse of elements of uniqueness but also into a code for the expression of differences between peoples rooted in particular territories.

Folklore contributed to the crystallization of a concept of *the people* that was inseparable from the idea of the *nation-state*, and, for this reason, it was also inseparable from particular territories. The folklorists took for granted the substantivation of territorial boundaries that were made thus to appear as collective entities. In their works, the concept of the people always emerged, re-elaborated not in terms of class, resources, activities, parties, or other references to social divisions, but rather in terms of genius, soul, race, that is to say, of a joint nature ("nation") and through shared territories different from those of others.[14]

This apparently simple and objective methodological task, taken on exclusively by the folklorists and whose result was the creation of collections, proved to be an effective way of transmuting the peoples within delimited areas into collective entities. The treatment of the materials from oral tradition—the main objective of what was understood to be folklore—followed these criteria:

1. a text appears in a collection as unique, even when it may have been obtained from several informants;
2. a text appears in its complete version and it is believed to be the task of the investigator to compose it, when the available records from different informants are fragmentary;
3. a text has to be entirely specific, thus homogenizing the speech that gave rise to it;
4. a collection should be exhaustive;
5. the value of the text was higher if it dealt with a singular instance, that could be taken as a privileged example;
6. the collections, however, were selective, eliminating those that were not considered publishable;
7. the texts from the oral tradition were written down following pseudo-phonetic conventions that permitted the recognition of speech differences;
8. the texts were artificially ordered in dictionary form; and, finally,
9. they had to be authentic, that is to say traditional and popular.[15]

The collections unified, homogenized, and normalized the materials from oral tradition, decontextualizing them and thus transforming them into a single discourse. It was a process of reduction of the multiple to the singular, of the plural to the common, that made it possible to attribute it to a single collectivity. As a discourse, it referred to particular linguistic-territorial locations. The collective subject that emerged was not only monolingual, but also "monospoken" and discursively fused with a territory.

This double differentiation was reinforced by the singularity of the expressions found in the collection. "Authenticity" was the central issue. The collective subject emerged as the basis for not distinguishing among the informants who became anonymous, democratizing it in the radical sense ("the people") to make it thus more homogeneous, obscuring all features of social distinction (and especially literary education that was understood to be not only disruptive of oral tradition but also individualizing).[16] Its role in the intergenerational transmission process (tradition) was underlined, instead of focusing on the process of manipulation, recreation, and re-elaboration of the text in particular contexts. It also included them within a demarcated territory that served as much to designate a place of origin as to refer to community, a double meaning reflected in the Castilian word *pueblo*.

The emergent collective subject was no less than a hypostasis of the traditional speaker, an "imagined community," if you will. And if the "imagined communities" were created through a normalized language, as Anderson (1983) says, folklore was a second *normalized* language superimposed on this language, a language of and for "imagined communities."

The treatment of the materials from the oral tradition that appears in these collections reproduced, in certain measure, the normalizing treatment—both rationalizing and universalist—of a language; such treatment could be extended and attributed to collective subjects in any territorial location. The primordial effects of this normalizing treatment are found in the configuration of a common language in which to express national, regional, provincial, subregional, commercial, and local differences and similarities.

The concept of normalization invoked here refers to an institutionalized generalization of certain modes of expression that permit self-recognition and recognition of others' differences. It also permits a process of socialization, or of education, to which the folklorists felt called—but one that showed itself to be susceptible to absorption into political movements. Ultimately, that process was absorbed into public institutions and the state itself. Said another way, the study of popular culture—folklore, as Machado wanted it to be in principle—resituated individuals and groups in the overall history of the "people." It also served to make certain territorial schemes unquestionable, given that the differentiated entities were assumed to be not just acceptable but desirable, subsuming other kinds of social difference. Its redesign of pluralism took a form that could justify irreconcilable divisions as well as politico-administrative units that were enriched by the variety of their components. We should not forget that the role of the collections of oral tradition, as in the case of museums of material culture, was fundamentally dissemination and education.[17] Indeed, one can refer to museums as unifying and homogenizing collections of objects as demonstrations of a collective subject.

For decades, the objective of amateur folklorists was this: Apparently they were trying to distinguish the territorial entity to which their collections referred, partly in response to similar works by other authors who had done this with their respective territorial entities.[18] Possibly, they also contributed to the assimilation of their countrymen into the joint subject of which they believed themselves to be a part. And they were the best demonstration that folklore could offer of the manifold and almost inexhaustible possibilities for the configuration of a collective subject.

It is necessary here to consider the paradigmatic identification of the "people" imagined by the folklorists using the inhabitants of the rural areas or the typical neighborhoods of the cities. Folklorist iconography reproduced insistently individual or paired figures of country people generally dressed in their regional garb in a festive setting or in family groups at home. This iconography contrasts with the real identity of the compilers whose own biographies and lifestyles were drawn from the educated, bourgeois classes. One could imagine that if the inhabitants of rural areas were used as the image of the "people," it was not only because these helped objectify territorial differences, but also because there was an intention to assimilate and integrate others into this collective subject. This was an assimilation and integration that was not necessarily moved by the "people" so much as by compilers and by the social sectors to which they directed their works and the institutions that supported them.

The "people" represented authenticity since, in reality, they served to demonstrate territorial differences. They were converted into prototypes of the collective subject, though in most cases they were not part of nationalist movements and indeed were marginal to the state. Their incorporation into modernity was at the cost of making them represent the past. They were made into the speakers of a language that even they did not understand completely—folklore—but that made them into protagonists, at least in appearance. Partly modifying their role in the society at large, they ended by progressively accepting—even at the cost of being partially subjected to it themselves—the image of themselves that had been forged by others.

It is possible that folklore contributed to redirecting the attention of the bourgeois classes toward rural zones. It could be, among other things, a show of nostalgia and the uprootedness of people who immigrated to the cities and to other countries, as a counter to the context of homogenization or to the framework of progressive industrialization. Still, for all that, it remained a certain kind of incorporation of marginal areas into the state, one of the ways by which modern societies configure themselves as plural societies.

But the Folklore Societies were not the only organizational model, nor are their activities as compilers and their files the only ones to scrutinize. In contradistinction to anthropology and other domains of academic knowledge, popular knowledge was gradually being configured not just as an ideal utopia but as a realizable one. The approach to work and the organizational structure created by the many excursion societies that had emerged—some of these being contemporaries of the Folklore Societies—was somewhat different.[19] These associations worked on a more strictly regionalist (localist) model, representing a variety of intellectual interests and operating in a fundamentally participatory way. For them, folklore was only one of the activities, though their activities always implied a move to a particular area and some period of time living with area's inhabitants.

Such societies were formed by city people from diverse professions, though the majority were students. For this reason, the excursions were basically of an educational character. In some cases, as those promoted by the Institución Libre de Enseñanza, they represented a major innovation in teaching (De Lecea, 1982: 68; Tunin, 1967). Like the folklore societies, their main tasks were compiling and filing, and their members served as an auxiliary for the completion of inventories. But they also included activities of cultural reproduction, mainly musical and dance activities and participation in festivals. For members, such activities probably constituted proof of their own belonging and of their personal involvement in the territorial entity (national, regional, subregional, or local) that was the object of their interest.

The activities involving the conservation of living or reborn culture developed increasing importance—to the point of requiring not just familiarity, but also an apprenticeship. In this sense, folklore was not merely a discourse, but a group of elements that had to be internalized. In this way, amateurism gained another dimension. Though it was a general attitude among many of the branches of learning (archaeology, geography, art history, musicology, etc.), it was completely justified as both knowledge of and love for the country or nation, for the territory, and for the people. Folklore was one more activity, integrated with the rest, for some individuals and groups. And it was a specialty that lasted for a long time.

It is worth highlighting certain revealing dimensions within these activities:

1. Recuperation or conservation consisted of recovering or conserving elements of tradition. Besides the compilations and inventories, the members of these groupings—first one section and then the whole groupings—called themselves "folkloric," and devoted their efforts to salvaging, re-creating, or reprocessing elements of a traditional culture in particular rural zones, including songs, dances, clothing, and objects. In this way, they began to make folklore into something that became as important (or more important) than the collections of stories, legends, riddles, or sayings: it became a form of "popular" action.

    This is the first dimension of what I have called the "internalization of folklore"—its conversion into a social activity that undertook and made the effort public, one that soon occupied space in festival programs and became part of leisure time activities. Through this process, folklore was no longer the work of compilers, scientists or amateurs that relegated others to the role of informants; rather, it converted everyone into potential actors or amateurs, even if certain contexts and stages were still reserved for the better *performers*.

2. These actions were widely distributed, gaining not just the acknowledgment and plaudits of society at large, but also stimulating their reproduction by individuals and groups from the most different social sectors. This range of participation generated a phenomenon that has not been sufficiently

considered, that of the incorporation of individuals and groups with special abilities in these domains of activity from the rural areas and marginal social strata into the roles of "interpreters" for society at large, thereby creating a means of social mobility.[20] This is the sense in which we speak of "popular" activity, in such a way that it could be converted into a common practice that overcame class distinctions, permitting a certain general sense of identification under the common category of the "people." These communities were "imagined" thanks, too, to broad participation in folklore studies as a joint activity. To the degree that the meaning of "people" was associated with a territorial unit as a point of reference, instead of being seen as a "national effort" as Machado proposed, folklore was converting itself into a national activity—but also regional, or even provincial, subregional, or local—given the broad broad correspondence of practices and customs across territorial units within the same area.

In reality, folklore always maintained a double axis of distinction: on the one hand, showing respect for the forms of "erudite" and formal culture, and, on the other, respecting corresponding and analogous forms of behavior by other "peoples." We tend to understand the first axis of difference as having remained chained to contexts and historical times in which differences between nations or other entities are the focus. But the discourses of modernity cannot say that folklore is foreign to "high" culture, but rather that it is a curious projection of that culture into what apparently is its opposite, the "popular."

3. Folklore as an activity was carried out following the same criteria discussed above regarding the homogenization and normalization of the compilations. The treatment of songs, dances, costumes, objects, and festivals treated each as unique, complete elements (eliminating variants and incomplete forms and fixing them in specific forms of action). It conceived of them as singular (denying in some cases their similarity or the existence of identical forms in other places). And there was a special selective and transformative treatment given to them. It is not easy to prove that we are dealing with intentional selection nor is it possible, in the majority of cases, to identify the groups or elites that made the selection decisions. Some traditional elements gained greater "popularity" than others, and were then transformed to the point that in some cases it would be better to speak of "invented traditions." They were adapted to the needs of mass spectacles in modern society, on the one hand, and on the other, to the accepted image of the collective subjects who were said to be represented.

The history of the *sardana*, the *jota* or the regional costume of Extremadura or of particular songs or holidays are clear examples of these processes.[21] The selection process assumed that a local variant would gain power until it was converted into a representation of a whole nation or region, subsuming or eliminating other local variants. This occurred in the course of the element's transformation through a process of refinement or complication, with the intervention of artists or individual interpreters. In the end, oddly, it was not understood as an individual creative work; once artists or interpreters were widely known and accepted, they became known as "popular."

In contrast to collections in which a collective subject is configured by an accumulation of elements, the collective subject in these actions or folkloric objects is made manifest through representation. The meaning of the representation is double and is applied to both the interpreters and the forms. The forms were understood as true educational instruments for the development of a national or regional sentiment and participation in this implied integration into the collective subject. The "image" of the joint subject takes shape in these groups and their features are sculpted through the sounds of the songs and the movements of the dances.

It is difficult to doubt that the effectiveness of the localist model of folklore that throughout the twentieth century has given rise to so many and such lasting and diversified groups: professional, educational, festive, leisure, immigrants, returnees, etc. And we cannot we doubt the political power of "popularization" that made it into the subject of political manipulation.

4. But folklore is a form of dissociated cultural action. The decontextualization that has been imputed to most of the collections and compilations was not unique among the symptoms of the dissociation that was built into folklore studies from the beginning. Materials from the oral tradition were extracted from their context and organized in the form of consultable records, yet they were expressive of collective subjects from specific territorial locations. Properly speaking, this is not decontextualization but rather a different codification that, in a sense, installed these elements in fictitious contexts in which they acquired new meanings. I refer not only to the effectiveness of the transcriptions from the oral tradition, but also to a recodification that converts them fundamentally into expressive forms—thereby restricting their multiple communicative functions and subordinating these to expression.

In the same way, one can refer to the decontextualization of folkloric activities: their extraction from festive rituals, work environments, and social relations in their places of origin for reproduction onstage or as leisure activities. Perhaps it is better to see this process not as one of decontextualization, but as the insertion of these forms in new "fictitious" contexts, using different codings.

In spite the theoretically holistic formulation of Machado and the other folklorists, folklore was delimited more and more in modern society. The category of "cultural" applied to folklore involves ambiguities and contradictions. On the one hand, in the academic model, the acknowledgment of its role in "culture" was a responsibility of folklore, since its realm was coextensive with the broad way Tylor had defined culture, at about the same time. On the other hand, another element in the folklore project was the attempt to create folklore as a science or an art and, thus, to achieve its acceptance within the narrow concept of culture that modern societies have forged.

In this way, folklore was almost always in a paradoxically multiple cultural categorization. A large part of the intellectual elite resisted recognizing as "culture" what was considered a field of superstitions and ancient customs, some even adverse to progress, that is, those things characteristic of an uneducated "pueblo." It is certain that the folklorists undertook strong efforts not only to achieve an acknowledgment of their labors, but also to make others see in their material the same features of knowledge, wit, and aesthetic meaning that were used in appraising the works of writers and artists recognized as "cultured."

But it does not appear that they ever fully achieved their goal. Folklore as a putative science did not achieve the status of a stable academic institutionalization and only developed some level of acceptance as an art form in the fields of music and dance.[22] The efforts of numerous amateurs—which to some extent is a consequence of their lack of academic acceptance—were not only unproductive but made academic acknowledgment even more difficult. Put another way, the folklorists, in spite of using the broad Tylorian concept of "culture," treated and appraised the materials of the oral tradition that they compiled according to "erudite" cultural criteria used by the elites. Perhaps it could not have been otherwise since they adopted these very schemes in order to get these materials and their own work recognized as "culture." The concept of "popular culture" perhaps emerged as hybrid forms of acknowledgment that permitted both meanings of culture to appear to coexist: the broad notion of culture, as well as the restricted conception of "erudite culture."[23]

Despite this, doubt rarely was cast on the importance of folklore as an expression of national, regional, or local feeling. And, beyond this, it was extremely and unconditionally exalted as "culture" by nationalistic, regionalist, and localist movements. The localist model attempted above all to gain an acknowledgment of the national character of folklore and understood as "culture" only that which was unique to the national culture. The relative success of folklore as a form of activity was based, in reality, on its reduction to a group of limited elements (songs, dances, etc.) that tried to give real dimensions to a "pueblo"—something like a cultural essence, especially given its strong sense of representation.

Relegated to specific contexts and to particular events, folklore as a form of activity became dissociated from other areas of culture and social life. Eventually, it was unequivocally counterposed to economic, cultural and social exchanges, and it adopted fixed, normalized forms that appeared to correspond more fully to the concept of tradition. In this way, it intentionally re-created the meaning of folklore as a "survival" while it assumed, at the same time, folklore to be a reflection of attitudes and values that contrasted with the modern urban industrial form of life. It emphasized internal homogeneity as contrasted with the heterogeneity of urban society, authenticity as compared to appearances, spontaneity as compared to formalism, groups contrasted with aggregates, community contrasted with individualism, social equality contrasted with social differences—and, always, difference in contrast to other "pueblos." Rural society, claimed as the origin of these ideas and the point of contrast with urban society, in reality provided only a pretext, since folklore was a re-creation, a re-elaboration of rural origins. In a certain sense, rural society had to learn to recognize itself in these folkloric re-creations.

Folklore's dissociation as an activity developed after it became limited to leisure-time activities and, thus, separated from the hard core of social life. It was distanced from the disciplines and practices of high culture, ignoring even its promise of the power to develop national representations. In this sense, its dissociated and marginal character offset the utopian ingredients and radicalism that has almost always lay within it.

This dissociated character reveals the double contradiction that folklore carries within itself. On the one hand, there is the contradiction that arises from the tension between plurality and unity in modern states. The terms of the contradiction could be stated as follows: folklore is offered as a unitary enterprise, but on the other hand, it appears to provide motivations and legitimations for the fragmentation of a historically consolidated state.

It is not that folklore lacked some of the subversive connotations of popular culture—the culture of the people—exploited in the period prior to and during the Civil War (1936–1939), but that these were eliminated by another strategy that configured a particular folklore as the national culture. The joint project became that of mutating the code of difference. The concept of culture was by then already institutionalized in the modern state and it was owned by "erudite" culture, so the task of the folklorists became to reconfigure folklore as "culture" and to recover the "pueblo" as the subject of history. This was tried in a way that agreed with models of scientific rationality and also with politico-administrative models. The joint cultural work had to construct a collective subject whose contours reached the frontiers of a territorial entity. Since it was elaborating a new code of difference, it could question those already set forth. And, thus, folklore became the discourse of the nation-state and of the nations that wanted to become states.

The homogenization and normalization that were effective as unifying possibly also enhanced the representative quality of particular cultural elements that were unique—as if there were confidence in the universalizing capacity of rationality, but only insofar as it implied a reduction of pluralism and diversity. Thus they were denying the difference within the collective subject they had configured in order to claim difference in the face of foreign others. This mutation of the code of difference appears have been accomplished with the intent of rationalizing diversity, but the cost was the upset of some of the formative principles of the modern nation-state.

Another contradiction shows the weak plot with which the apparent transcendence of folklore was being moved along. Attributing to folklore the possibility of making the "pueblos" more dynamic could not be accomplished without simultaneously underlining the permanent risk of sullying and undermining the object that is inherent in such a project. As a putatively scientific and social movement, folklore could have been nothing other than a kind of mythical discourse and ritual action that did not fit well with the modernization processes to which industrial societies were committed. As a "retrofitter" of culture, folklore ultimately ended up with a small and separate territory and was relegated to "traditional culture" or to "popular culture." And as a promoter of social activity, it appears to have achieved no more than establishing itself as a dissociated, unique activity, like many others, limited to leisure time, consumerism, and tourism.

It is probable that in Spain, as in other modern European societies, the code of socioterritorial differences that folklore contributed through its transformation of certain social pluralisms could have founded a set of practices and knowledge that would have made such pluralism acceptable. It is even possible that folklore contributed to creating a certain basic tone in democracies, salvaging "cultural" minorities from their inevitable fate of assimilation into universalizing projects.

NOTES

1. The previous day, in the same newspaper, another article appeared with the title: "Folklore of Madrid I." Machado y Alvarez had moved from Seville to Madrid in that same year, and accompanying his father, with special fervor, took on the task of presenting folklore. In the weekly, *La Epoca*, September 26, he had published the

"Bases of Spanish Folklore." In the October 8, 15, and 22 , November 12, and December 3 issues, he published a variety of articles on folklore. Other work had appeared in *El Globo* (October 16). On the same November 4, *El Progreso* reproduced a copyrighted article, "The Folklore of Colors," previously published in the journal *El Folklore Frexenense*. And on the November 11, the "Folk Questionaire for the Collection of Materials on the Customs of the Castillian Pueblo in the Different Spheres of his Life" appeared. On those same dates, the journals *La Ilustración Española y Americana* and *La Ilustración Universal* reproduced four other previously published articles from Sevillian journals. The one directed at the Spanish politicians was also reproduced in *La Ilustración Universal* and in the journal *El Folklore Frexenense*. See Guichot y Sierra (1984: 181).

2. The tone of the article is heated, accusatory, condemning: "Should we not count on you today, not as individuals, but as party chiefs, with sufficiently broad and sophisticated ideas what to vouch for the fact that national unity will not be destroyed the day, perhaps not distant, in which social unrest will put a yoke on the neck of the mesocracy and destroy completely the already fragile bonds that bind to the people to the aristocracy and the middle classes?" "The actually embarrassing and ridiculous nomenclature of our political parties, that classifies men as nocedalistas, canovistas, sabqastinos, moretistas, zorrillistas, salmeronianos and pigmargalistas, shows, not in you, but in the social forces that you represent, a complete lack of these high ideas that give the pueblos their own physiognomy and give to them a right to occupy a place among the civilized nations. What is the current mission of Spain in Europe? What is its providential destination? To civilize Africa, or to continue in a state such of divisions that it will be possible that Africa ends up civilizing us? To instigate a war with foreigners to give brilliance and splendor to the reigning monarchy and to reclaim again that we are worthy descendents of El Cid and of Pelayo?"

3. *El Folklore Castellano* is constituted November 28, 1883, and becomes part of this society (*El Globo*, November 30, 1883): Gaspar Nuñez de Arce, José Ferreras, Maximum Laguna, Joaquin Sama, Alfredo Escobar, Rodrígo Amador de los Ríos, Francisco Giner, Baltasar Ortin de Zárate, Laureano Calderón, Ignacio Bolivar, Romaldo González Fragoso, José Cano, Pascual Vincent, Manuel B. Cossío, Gumersindo Azcára, Agustín Ondovilla, Joaquin Costa, Francisco Quiroga, José Inzenga, Gabriel Rodríguez, Leopoldo Ascención González, Francisco Durán, Eugenio Olavarría, Jacobo Laborda, Hermenegildo Giner, Aniceto Sola, Federico Rubio, and Antonio Sendrás y Burin.

4. On December 29, 1883, a circular appears in *El Globo* from *El Folklore Castellano* aimed at priests, doctors, and teachers. The priests are invited to collect information about baptisms, marriage, burial, mourning, the lottery of quintos, the feast day S. Juan, S. Antón, and so on, chants, hermitages and sanctuaries, honors, superstitions, invocations, ghosts, witches. The teachers were asked to collect songs, Peges, riddles, children's games, children's mythologies (the bogey man, etc.), children's language, ideas about numbers, and so forth. To the physicians were given household medicines, childbirth, the moon and its influence, color, and the numbers 3 and 7, and local names of diseases.

5. Machado was inciting them to mobilize in the countryside: "Do not worry about forgetting that adoring cohort that esteems you, more than for your merits than for the employment and carrers that you can provide to them. Leave politics aside for once in order to be politicians, and from your high position, and from the heights of the gran meseta of the Guadarrama, where all the vapors born in the valleys condense and are turned into the copious rain that fertilizes the fields, direct your authoritative voice to all the provinces so that they take part in this great national enterprise" (*El Globo*, November 4, 1883).

6. After perceiving in the disagreements among the politicians a "lack of ideals among the Spanish people," Machado proposed the following:

> I do know, it is clear, like you, and much more than you, the remedies for such great evils, but I believe the Spanish people, if it is to cure itself, as the first condition, to do a serious examination of its "conciencia" [author's note: "conciencia" is both conscience and consciousness in Spanish] and to learn about its character and aptitudes, in whcih, as in the qualityof its lands, we find all the energies that are needed for its regeneration and cure. This first necessity can be dealt within the sphere of action of the institution of Folklore through which we can study *what we have been* and our customs and *what we still are*, through it, we can reconstruct your past history, know and set the course of our future history. In this enterprise, the lovers of tradition and the lovers of progress join together, in it the different social classes come together and *are obligated to deal with each other* and different countries, breing brought together in an enterpriese that awakens, by making clear the community of traditions, the love and fraternity among peoples and finally, by putting us into a continual ever more intimate relationship with the local people, it arouses in us the desire to cultivate and thus to enrich and better the earth of our fatherland.

7. This call was published in the appendices of the journal *El Folk-lore Andaluz*, 1883, pp. 503–505, after the bylaws of the Sociedad del Folk-lore Español, Reissued in Madrid, 1981, Edit. Three, Fourteen, and Seventeen.

8. See Guichot 1984 and Aguilar 1990: esp. Chapter V.

9. See Velasco 1988.

10. For a description of these developments as reported by one of their protagonists, see Guichot, 1984.

11. Regarding Costa's role in these projects, see Del Pino, 1992.

12. The work of Menéndez Pidal, however, never was recognized as folklore, though he was a staunch compiler of oral tradition, following the approach of the folklorists, cf. Cid, 1992: 127. This is a clear example of the restricted acceptance of folklore in these specific fields.

13. The recent development of the history of anthropology in Spain shows that the process is quite complex and not generalizable in the same way to all the regions and nationalities. Cf. Prats, 1987a; Prats, Llopart, and Prat, 1982; and Prat, 1991. These authors maintain that in Catalonia (as well as in Galicia and the Basque Country) the emergence of folklore was closely linked to the regionalist and nationalist romantic movements (or rather the late romantics, as were Machado and his group) who exalted traditional popular and religious values. For this reason, these movements were quite remote from the Anthropological Societies, which took their inspiration from scientific Darwinisim, societies among which we should frame the Folklore Societies that Machado promoted and that furthermore were aspiring to reconstruct the history of the country (Spain). It is true that maintenance of the interest in folklore in the three cited cases was something more vigorous, linked as it was to the regionalist/nationalist discourses in those three areas. But it is no less certain that Machado also conceived of folklore as inextricably linked to territorial delimitations and that he tried intentionally to encourage nationalist, regionalist, or even localist discourses through it. However, the later fate and the vicissitudes of folklore in Catalonia, the Basque Country, and Galicia were not necessarily parallel.

14. See especially the work of G. Cochiara, *Storia del Folklore en Europa*, Torino, 1952, Edizíone Scientifiche Eillandi, for the Herderian notions and their influence in folklore.

15. I have developed this codification in Velasco, 1990.

16. The issue of homogenization has been discussed by Gellner (1983) as both a consequence and condition of nationalism. His thesis states that a modern industrial state "requires both a mobile division of labour, and sustained, frequent and precise communication between strangers . . . transmitted in a standard idiom" (p. 34). The emergence and implantation of folklore takes place at the same time as the transformation of a predominantly agrarian society into a predominantly industrial society; the fields and the landscape are rediscovered at the same time that general literacy and cultural standardization is extended—and popular culture is rediscovered. Indeed, folklore as a social, scientific, and political movement is a homogenizing movement, if we understand this to mean codification according to common criteria of difference.

17. The constant argument with which the collections (and the museums) were justified alluded to the deterioration and loss of materials from traditional popular culture and the necessity of stanching these losses by educating people about them and publishing them for general benefit. And, in good measure also, the aim was to reinsert them into the schools with the hope that the younger generations would learn them, serving both to give them and then strengthen their love of their fatherland. The projects designed by Martínez Torner (1965) and Larrea (1966) respond to these aims.

18. In good measure, the very diffusion of folklore in Europe and in the regions of Spain responded, not only to the desire of participating in an effort that needed everyone, but also as a reply and reacion to the enterprise that characterized other collective entities. For example, one perceives among many folklorists who did

compilations a spirit of competition, trying to demonstrate with their work the greater richness (or uniqueness) in their locale than in others.

19. Initiated in the 1870s, but generalized, at least in terms of their practices at the beginning of the twentieth century, the associational schemes had different strength in the various zones of Spain. See Prats, 1987b and 1991: 77.

20. The genesis and development within "popular culture" of what is generally called the "Spanish song" and "Spanish dance" regrettably is not a well-studied phenomenon. Nevertheless there is an abundant literature about its stars.

21. See, for example, Brandes (1985) and Díaz, 1988.

22. Nevertheless, it has deserved other modern forms of recognition in the field of crafts and the theater (masks, disguises, and festive rituals).

23. For a study focused on this topic, see Velasco, 1992.

Chapter 12

Linguistic Constructions of Difference and History in the U.S. Law School Classroom

Elizabeth Mertz[1]

In this essay I examine the way in which an underlying structure in legal discourse enforces a powerful epistemology that encompasses—but also neutralizes—concepts of difference and of historical specificity. My focus is the law school classroom, where students are trained to this structure through a pedagogy that embodies that epistemology in discourse often rife with role-taking and cospeech, forms that impute motives and remake persona for the students. A central feature of this reformulation is that the students' new roles and motives exist out of social and historical specificity; the students' attention is trained on legal arguments and doctrinal categories deemed to be somehow apart from or above the particular circumstances of the parties in any particular case. At the same time, race, gender, politics, and (on rare occasions) class enter through the backdoor known as "the equities" of the case, and through occasional fragmented and marginal realist commentary on the backdrops of the cases.

It is my argument that this method of bringing together abstract legal categories and sociohistorical context is no accident—that it provides a crucial combination of apparent openness to (indeed, at times, a voracious gobbling-up of) change with deep-structural abstraction that neutralizes as it consumes the social "stuff" of legal cases. Without its flexibility and openness, legal discourse would lose its ability to serve as a locus for the translation of virtually all arenas of social life into a common language. However, that translation involves a crucial move out of cultural and historical specificity, into legal doctrinal categories that at once develop from specific contexts, yet also effectively deny their roots. One source of legal legitimation is precisely that the heated specifics of particular places and people are somehow cooled and neutralized as they are "run through" the abstract legal categories that are supposed to ensure "equal" or fair treatment across dazzling array of differences. This fairness is to be achieved by rising above the sway of particulars, emotions, and contexts—by learning to use rather than be moved by these local phenomena. The combination of apparent attention to social contextual detail and a deeper structure that abstracts away from context is precisely what renders legal language a credible and effective medium for the resolution of divisive issues in a democratic society in which differences must at once be acknowledged and yet also overcome. Students are trained to that language in a classroom discourse that also combines apparent concern for detail with an abstracting deep structure.

It would perhaps seem more a propos to an examination of social diversity and difference, were I to use a Constitutional Law classroom as my example. The general approach to reading legal texts that I have described thus far takes on a peculiar shape when the "stuff" of the legal categories at issue is social categorization; to a larger extent than in many "core" U.S. law school classes, Constitutional Law forces overt consideration of the history, sociology, and even anthropology of social classification that is often bracketed-off in other courses. However, my study concentrates on Contracts courses, in which it is possible for students to read cases for an entire year without ever confronting issues of gender, race, class, or social classification. Nonetheless, the Contracts course, precisely in its silences and in the limits of those silences, speaks to the issue of democracy and difference in legal pedagogy and epistemology in a more indirect, but important way. By exemplifying the possibility and character of a silence about social specificities, the Contracts class illustrates a key way in which standard legal approaches to reading, taught through many areas of law, deal with difference. And, of course, the areas of law that avoid explicit attention to issues of difference are not somehow outside of social context, bereft of these considerations. Indeed, feminists and critical race theorists in the legal academy have been relentlessly uncovering the hegemonic character of legal readings in many such areas, which so frequently assume the "unmarked" (white, privileged male) position as neutral and prefigured.[2]

With that introduction, then, let me step back and explain further the concepts of legal reading and epistemology that inform my approach to the classroom materials. I will then present some detailed examples from transcripts of law school classes.

"LEARNING TO READ LIKE A LAWYER": THE ROLE OF SOCIAL CONTEXT

The research from which I draw here is a study of the language of Contracts classrooms in eight different schools, using tapes, transcripts, in-class coder notes and interviews with participants to elucidate legal pedagogy. One reason for including more than the usual two or three schools of most previous studies of law school teaching is precisely an attempt to tap diversity across kinds of schools and differences among students and professors. Initial work seems to suggest that there are indeed differences among schools, professors, and students that result in widely variant styles; at the same time, there are interesting commonalities.

The most striking commonality is the shared approach to texts and reading that emerges across many differences. Hence, my contention that a key function of U.S. legal pedagogy, particularly in the first year, is to impart a way of reading (and talking about) legal texts. I would argue that it is no coincidence that a particular orientation to text is what widely diverse classrooms share, for learning to read "like a lawyer" involves a subtle but crucial change in orientation toward social contexts and events. I talk about this orientation as an epistemology, and it is an epistemology that depends crucially on language as a key mediator and way of knowing about the social world. Further, this orientation or epistemology is expressed not only in the content of the language but in its form, doubly complicated in the classroom by the fact that the classroom discourse itself mirrors aspects of the reading it seeks to teach.[3]

From the initial classes, students are taught to read the "stories" of the cases they are assigned in a new way, breaking down previous "semantic" level readings of text. Thus, rather than focus on the dramatic (or boring) events of the case, students must learn to focus upon what linguists would call the pragmatic structure of the case. Presented at the beginning of the semester, for example, with a case involving a patient whose nose has been badly disfigured by a surgeon who promised her a beautiful new face, students will frequently direct their attention to the content of the story, only to find themselves repeatedly interrupted by professorial questioning focusing on doctrinal and procedural framing of the narrative:

Example 1 (P1):

1 P: How did this case get to the appellate court?

2 S: Well the um the the patient was a woman who wanted a—

3 P: How did this case get to the appellate court?

Using a questioning style that itself teaches not through content or semantics as much as through its very structure, professors train students to bracket the content and emotionality and specificity of the stories in the cases, focusing their attention instead on the narrow legal issues framed by the procedural stance and doctrinal categories of the case (see Mertz, 1992, n.d.). These frames are part of any legal text's claim to authority; for example, because only certain issues are appealed, the authority of an appellate court's text is limited to the issues properly before it. Similarly, because only certain issues are relevant to doctrinal categories, a court's writing must usually maneuver successfully within those categories to carry authority.

At the same time, professors bring in issues of social context at the margins of legal reading. After the basics of doctrinal and procedural framing are established, or before moving into the serious and systematic legal analysis, there is room for social specifics, framed as humor, place-setting, or courtroom strategy. Thus the professor might mention as an aside that even if a doctrinal requirement is not met, occasionally judges and juries can be persuaded by the particular circumstances of cases to overlook doctrinal difficulties, so as to avoid results that seem manifestly unjust. Or, alternatively, the professor might mention in passing that social context or prejudice at times affect legal outcomes; when case results are hard to reconcile with the prevailing doctrine, social context often emerges as the "wildcard" that explains these apparent anomalies.

Consider, for example, the way in which "ethnicity" is problematized in one classroom, by a Euro-American male professor addressing a Euro-American male student:

Example 2 [5/10/2]:

1 P: Mr. S. is [student's last name] Greek, by any chance?

2 S: No, it's Polish, sorry.

3 P: All right.

4 *(class laughter)*

5 P: Well, for the moment we're going to assume that it's Greek.

6 Go on.

7 *(class laughter)*

8 S: Okay. Mr. Ganas was a Greek and he uh was a waiter on—

9 P: Is it significant that Mr. Ganas was a Greek?

10 S: I don't think it is. It shouldn't be.

11 P: Well, let's decide which it is.

12 (class laughter)

13 S: Um.

14 P: Is it significant, or is it that you think it shouldn't be?

15 S: Mmm ... I think it shouldn't, he shouldn't—shouldn't matter.

16 P: It shouldn't matter.

17 S: No.

18 P: What a wonderful, absolutely American perspective. Just
19   like a World War I movie. It shouldn't matter, you suggest, where
20   you come from. It shouldn't matter what your ethnic group
21   is. Let me disillusion you just a little.

22 (class laughter)

23 P: One of the wonderful rules in interpreting common law
24   cases is, whenever you have a party whose name ends
25   in a vowel, rule against that party.

26 (class laughter)

27 P: Watch carefully, see if that doesn't work out in practice.
28   There is something rather interesting going on here. Okay,
29   he's a Greek, it shouldn't make a difference.

Note that there was considerably more discussion of social context in this classroom than in most of the others in the study. The class discussion then moves on from this humorous introduction to focus on questions pertinent to doctrinal issues: Had the Greek servant's amorous feelings for his employer's wife constituted a breach of the contract between servant and employee? Could the employer's estate use these feelings on the servant's part as a defense to the servant's eventual request for restitution damages? Did it matter whether the amorous feelings had actually interfered with the servant's performance of his duties, and so on? Ethnicity is presented as a stereotypic background factor that might affect the reaction of the court in a way that is somehow apart from systematic analysis of the sort the class is centrally occupied with:

Example 3 [5/10/3]:

1 P: ... Why did they tell us he's a Greek?

2 S16: I don't know. I guess they were just interested in that.

Linguistic Constructions 223

3   (class laughter)

4 P: Why are they interested in that? Why tell us that he's
5   a Greek? What if he were French, what if he were Polish,
6   would it make a difference? What is it about Greeks?
7   Yes, uh. Ms. uh?

8 S11: "C."

9 P: Ms. C.

10 S11: After reading *Zorba the Greek,* I would say maybe
        because of their reputation as lovers or—

P: There's this zest for life.... There is something
        going on and there's all kinds of hideous things about
        the Greeks that the Americans sometimes think. Indeed,
        there are horrible things to think about virtually every
        ethnic group you can name. At least that was in the
        good old days when you admitted that sort of thing. We
        don't do it anymore. But this court involved in the
        casebook, seems to feel it necessary to tell us that
        Ganas is Greek. And you can bet that it was plastered
        all over the opinion, right? There is this thing, we'll say
        for the moment, putting as neutral a face on it as
        possible, about Greeks in love. Go on.

There is no attempt to deny that social factors might be decisive in legal outcomes; indeed, this particular class provides one of the best examples in the study of a direct discussion of the potential impact of such factors. In other classrooms in this study, professors covered similar cases with no mention whatever of ethnicity, stereotypes, or prejudice. At the same time, even in the former class there is no sustained or systematic analysis of the effects of social factors.

Later in the same class, as the professor turns to another case, there is another allusion to ethnicity—this time apparently simply as humorous punctuation:

Example 4 (5/10/13):

1 P: Here we are, by the way, with another interesting
2   ethnic group. Swedish Evangelical Lutheran. What do we
3   know about them? The answer: absolutely nothing! But
4   they want a church apparently. Go on.

The class again moves on to systematic consideration of legal issues: whether the builder's failure to construct a church to meet certain specifications constituted a breach of the contract, justifying the church's decision not to pay the builder; whether defects in construction provided the church with an adequate defense against having to pay the builder damages. The cotextual reference to the previous discussion ("another interesting ethnic group") underlines the sporadic and seemingly haphazard effect of social contexts on legal results.

Perhaps not surprisingly, in the classes I have analyzed to date, issues of gender and race appear to come up more directly and more frequently in classes taught by women and by men of color. (Interestingly, it appears that students as well as professors are responsible for this.) However, even when these topics are brought up more frequently and discussed at greater length, professors generally retain a structure that places such issues at the margins of the truly "legal" discourse, sometimes overtly cautioning students against moving too wholeheartedly into consideration of social context. In the following excerpt, an African-American professor responds to an African-American woman, a student in his class, when she raises the possibility that a case outcome might reflect racial bias:

Example 5 (2/3/37):

1 P: It could have. Th— and it may have been complicated. It
2   could have been important to the decision-making. And, in
3   fact, I mean you could imagine that all of this legal
4   gobblygook is simply a cloak for, you know, an— racial
5   animus. It's a possibility. On the other hand, it could
6   have been this person simply put down the fact that the, ah
7   this is a, quote Negro, simply out of a reflex. Out of a,
8   you know, this race being important for the moment, . . . a
9   reflex. And it really didn't have anything to do with the
10   ultimate outcome of the case—that in fact if this guy
11   Skinner had been white, same result. Tough sort of get
12   beneath the—the um the ah . . . the materials at hand.
13   It's not, I mean it could have been important, then again
14   it might not have been important. Tough to tell.

This summary statement had been preceded by several turns of dialogue in which the professor fully accepts the possibility that social contextual influences beyond strict application of the doctrinal categories—here, racial animus—might affect, or even determine case outcomes. Similarly, in a class taught by a Euro-American woman, the issue of racial bias is brought into view only to be dropped when the more "legal" analysis begins:

Example 6 (3/12/8):

```
 1 P: I think, it was one of the first occasions in which there
 2     was gonna be an interracial fight, and, therefore, one
 3     of the reasons clearly not articulated, clearly not
 4     arguable to the court, would be some racism that would
 5     enter in ah some concern on the part of the court that
 6     ah maybe people wouldn't pay, that they would boycott such
 7     a fight or maybe that they would, maybe they would pay
 8     more. Racism is not the kind of thing you would argue in
 9     the court but it may have been a factor certainly in the
10     the court's refusing to let the issue go to the jury.
```

Just as in the first example, there is no attempt to hide or deny this possibility; and indeed, any such attempt might risk rendering the system implausible. Instead, there is a fascinating combination of a complete willingness to accept social impacts on case outcomes, with an ongoing evasion of systematic inclusion or analysis of those impacts. This brief allusion to racism is followed by a lengthy discussion of, in the professor's words, the "damage issues arising under Dempsey." As in the first example, the implication of this recurring discourse structure is that social influences on legal outcomes are something of a mystery, moving in at random and difficult-to-predict moments to cause fluctuations in the more systematic treatment that could be/often is afforded by "simple" application of the legal categories. And students are continually refocused on those categories. Who knows what the actual decision reflects, they are cautioned—but in the legal categories is a framework that you can know about and work with systematically. This move also entails a push out of emotionality, a distancing, as students are urged to step back from and bracket the influences of heated social/cultural issues, focusing instead on a fairly abstract categorization process: Was this statement a misrepresentation? What features are arguably evidence of misrepresentation? Can not telling someone/silence be misrepresentation? Under what circumstances? Was there such a silence here? What are the arguments for? against? In this distancing act of breaking down and categorizing the social interactions at issue in the case comes a safe, "professional" stance, a new distinctly "legal" perspective on the familiar stuff of human interactions.

ACONTEXTUAL CONTEXT:
A PECULIARLY LEGAL "SUBJECT"

By focusing on instances in which professors actually bring up aspects of social and historical context, I may be giving a misleading impression of the frequency with which such issues come up at all in law school classrooms. Even in the schools in which there was a higher degree of mention of such contexts, they remained a relative rarity. And in several schools an entire semester went by with only a few brief allusions to the possible role of social context in any of the cases. However, in looking through these schools for discussions of situated social context, we began to see some fairly common alternative forms of contextualization.

One of the more striking recurring forms of contextualization in the classrooms of the study locates the cases within fairly abstract contexts generated by political philosophical categories or by general occupational or legal categories rather than specific social settings. Thus, in a discussion of limitations on remedies in cases of breach of contract, quite frequently discussion centered around a "standard average" farmer who decided about breaching based on various strategic considerations:

Example 7 (8/10/18):

1 P: Alright. If you think about what we're worried about
2   is, on the one hand, the farmer is going to go out
3   there as soon as the price rises, alright, make more
4   money off his wheat, alright, thinking that he'll be
5   hedged, alright, he's trying to make a profit out of
6   his wheat, okay. And I suppose in that particular case,
7   what might the farmer be hoping, assuming that, and this
8   is part, my problem when I start talking like this. I
9   have a problem with it because, of course, I'm assuming
10   the farmer, that the farmer will know the law, alright,
11   but in fact, you don't need to know the law. What might
12   the farmer be hoping would happen? In fact, the law might
13   favor the farmer on this one. Notice, why is it the
14   farmer doesn't perform? One reason is, the market's gone
15   up, but you say, but wait a minute, what good does it do?
16   He still has to pay the damages. What might the farmer
17   be hoping? Yeah?

18 S: The buyer'll find cover.

19 P: To find a substitute and what else?

Here we even have an unusual realist aside, pointing out that the "average" citizen need not/probably does not know the law. But note also that the farmer is not situated in terms of time or place; we are working with a stereotypic "abstract" individual whose main characteristics are a set of (economic) strategic considerations given by his occupational situation. The differences between small farmers and large agricultural enterprises, regional/cultural differences among farmers, the influence of long-term relational (or other kinds of) ties within communities and between participants in markets are not salient here. At times this abstract individual loses even the specificity of occupational categories, and becomes simply a buyer or seller, a promisor or promisee, a "party" to a transaction:

Example 8 (5/24/21):

1 P: And we know that the question we have to ask here is,
2   is this a valid bilateral exchange of promises? And we
3   know, that then we have to ask are these promises good
4   considerations for each other? And we're asking in
5   particular, is a promise, "if I buy the land, I'll sell
6   it to you," you can forget about the details, that's
7   the basic idea: "if I buy the land, I'll sell it to
8   you." Is that an illusory promise or not?

9 S: I guess, it is, because the, he doesn't have to buy the
10   land.

11 P: No, he doesn't have to buy the land, but if he does, he
12   has to sell it to the other party. What happens in the
13   [student's name] theory of consideration here?

14 S: Well, there wasn't a thing where—I will buy the land or—

15 P: Let's put it slightly differently. Is the party making
16   the promise "If I buy the land, I'll sell it to you"
17   surrendering any legal right?

Here people and problems are located in individuals operating against the odd acontextual context of a legal geography, two contracting parties interacting with one another—even speaking in the first person singular ("If I buy the land . . .)—against the backdrop of legal rights and doctrines. One wants to buy land, one may conceivably buy some land and would like to sell it—except for (presumably reflexive unmarked usage of) gendered pronominals we have no sense of these actors as people beyond these postulated attitudes toward property.

Professors also locate the issues and people they discuss in terms of broad political and philosophical traditions:

Example 9 (8/14/8):
1 P: Now what would a more fierce judge—a generous judge
2 says to you, Okay, They're trying to manipulate you,
3 all right, into relying. Okay? What might a fierce—
4 Holmes, Hand—judge do?

5 S: [inaudible]

6 P: Hey, don't sit around relying. Do—what?

7 S: Get a contract and make a bargain.

8 P: Get the bargain. Make the contract. By relying, you're
9 doing what?

10 S: Being unreasonable.

11 P: Hmm?

12 S: You're being unreasonable, the reliance is not reasonable,
13 because the other person doesn't know that you have
14 decided to rely.

The professor goes on to describe the "fierce" judge's position as the "market" or "business" position, which she opposes to the "generous" or "bleeding-heart" position. Notice that the student is here, through the use of second-person pronomials, inserted into the role of one of the abstract strategizing individuals who are parties to this bargain. He is asked to imagine himself caught between these two conflicting ideologies, responding to a judge who is berating him for his approach to the bargain. The issue is triply contextualized in a single vivid move; we have at once the context of the abstract legal "subject" bargaining, of conflicting political-philosophical traditions in Anglo-American jurisprudence, and of the student as role-player in a classroom drama. Let us now look at that final modality of contextualization, one which is ubiquitous in these classrooms, in more detail.

"LEARNING TO TALK LIKE A LAWYER": CLASSROOM EXCHANGES

Another aspect of contextualization in these classes is that students are situated as actors in imagined legal dramas. The new "distinctly legal" perspective imparted to law students, evident both in the reading of texts to which students are trained and the dynamics of classroom interchange, is in part inculcated through more subtle aspects of the dialogue such as role-playing dynamics, selective use of the first-person plural inclusive ("we") and other features. In role-playing, for example, students are encouraged to take parts that represent positions in a legal argument rather than situated people. In this excerpt a Euro-American male professor situates a student, also male and Euro-American, as a speaking subject—and not surprisingly, the speaker is an attorney whose discourse and identity are framed by his position in a legal dispute:

Example 10 (5/5/11):

1 P: Okay. What do you think, Mr. B? You are the lawyer for the
2   company that's seeking to fire her. What are you going to
3   say to argue that she should have accepted the position as
4   appliance clerk?

Students are also located within the cases in terms that again encourage them to orient themselves in terms of (and identify with) legal institutional structures and categories, as in this exchange between a Euro-American male professor and a Euro-American male student:

Example 11 (4/13/16):

1 P: Put it like this, is it the only mortgage on the cottage?

2 S: We don't know.

3 P: We don't know, it could be a second. But, where is it?
4   Where is the cottage?

5 S: In Michigan.

6 P: In Michigan. Where are we in the case?

7 S: We're in Wisconsin.

8 P: We're in Wisconsin. Does that raise any problems?

The first "we," introduced by the student, assumes a shared identity based on his common predicament as a reader of a text that gives only limited information. Here he and the professor situate themselves as a "we" defined by their roles as readers of this (casebook version of a) legal text. The second "we," introduced by the professor, moves into and beyond the shared reader role to a position defined by the legal institutional setting from which the written case text was generated; the professor is asking the student the location of the court that wrote the opinion, but note what use of the "we" accomplishes here:

1. It again unites professor and student, both as readers, and now as legal professionals who read the text for certain (contextual, pragmatic) technical framing information, of which the location and kind of court issuing the opinion counts among the most important.
2. It places the student and professor in the case, as it were, uniting them now with the authoring court, creating a momentary equation that allows the student to imagine himself as an authoritative legal source (note also that it elides the case as written and the case as enacted in court—"in the case" referring to both).
3. It foregrounds the location of the court (as opposed, e.g., to other places that are loci for the story unfolding in the case).

Interestingly, in several of the schools, geography seemed to be the main focus of any social contextualization of cases, with professors asking if there were any students in the class from the state in which the events of a particular case took place. The use of generalized stereotypes of parts of the country as a form of in-class (personalized) contextualization of the cases, like the use of "standard average" exemplars of certain occupational categories, fits well with the ideas of acontextual context and abstract individuals, discussed above. Use of role-playing in class reinforces this approach by locating students in these legal landscapes, asking them to imagine how they would strategize as parties, or how they would shape the law as judges or policymakers. While role-playing appears to bring students down to the level of "actual people" in interactions, it also carefully omits the social particulars that usually shape social interactions of all kinds.

CONCLUSION

In sum, we have seen a pedagogy that at once fully accepts that it might matter if you're "Greek" or "Black" and yet centers attention on meeting the tests of abstract doctrinal categories, so that the initial admission loses any power to structure the discourse. As students are trained to this reading, social context and classification are in a sense commodified, made relevant only as the "wild cards" that on odd occasions can be strategically useful. Rather than seeing history and society as moving the doctrines, this reading runs specificities through the abstract mill of doctrinal and procedural categories, or presents them on the margins of truly legal discourse, dulling or hardening the students to the difficult and often painful stories about particular people within the bracketing frames.

At a broader level, if we think of law in the United States as a semiotic nexus, a universalist language capable of translating almost any conceivable event or issue into a common rhetoric (see Mertz, 1993; Mertz and Weissbourd, 1985; White, 1990; Williams, 1991), then this approach to law school pedagogy makes a great deal of sense. In the classroom we see this ideology of universal translatability conveyed in a discourse that neutralizes and marginalizes social specificities, imparting a professional distancing that permits students to handle the heated and potentially emotional particulars of cases (including aspects of social context and classification) in a new, more removed way—running specificities through the abstract mill of doctrinal and procedural categories. This removal is a crucial feature of legal legitimation more generally, affording an appearance of neutrality or fairness to legal outcomes.

Thus the handling of social context in law school pedagogy opens a window on a broader legal epistemology central to law's legitimacy in U.S. culture. This fits well with work on social epistemology in capitalist systems generally,[4] which has repeatedly pointed out the central importance of this kind of abstracting logic. There are a number of implications of this. First, the logic of classroom discourse may be centrally connected with the logic of the legal language it inculcates. This means that there are no easy answers regarding how best to reform classroom discourse, because professors are in a sense trapped by their need to socialize students effectively to the system within which they will be working. Second, the study demonstrates the way in which legitimacy—both in professional identity and of legal language in the wider society—may hinge on a profound denial of the systematic and sustained effects of difference, despite appearances to the contrary. Recognizing this as a problem may be an important first step toward formulating a legal language that does not found democratic legal forms on the effective erasure of difference.

NOTES

1. This project was funded by the Spencer Foundation and by the American Bar Foundation. I have been very fortunate in having a dedicated crew of research assistants who have been invaluable in collecting and analyzing the data presented here. I would like to thank Nancy Matthews and Susan Gooding, who served as Project Managers, Leah Feldman, Kay Mohlman, Jerry Lombardi, Shepley Orr, and Christine Garza; I would also like to thank Jacqueline Baum, Janina Fenigsen, Carolee Larsen, Mindie Lazarus-Black, Nahum Chandler, and Rob Moore for their contributions at earlier stages of the work. Diane Clay has been the backbone of the transcription and data entry processes; Zella Coleman and her group also helped a great deal with transcription.

2. See, for example, Delgado, 1982; Fineman, 1991; Frug, 1992; Matsuda, 1986; Minow, 1990; Williams, 1991.

3. In my focus on form, I build on work from the Prague School tradition see, e.g., Garvin, 1964; Whorf, 1956; Silverstein, 1985, 1992; and other anthropological linguists. In approaching the classroom as a forum for language socialization, I draw on work by Schieffelin and Ochs, 1986, and their colleagues.

4. See Postone, 1993, for a discussion of capitalist epistemology generally; critical race theorists and feminists have more specifically detailed the way in which this abstracting character of U.S. legal discourse functions to divert attention from important aspects of social and political contexts. See also Mertz, 1993.

Chapter 13

From Ethnography to Clinical Practice in the Construction of the Contemporary State

Josep M. Comelles

To Cristina Larrea

> *More than learning to build social equality, our singularly human problem is probably learning to tolerate social and cultural diversity.*
> —Leach 1980: 388–389

It is sometimes said that the process of secularization of Western societies, which led to the development of so-called civil society and the democratic state, was built on the ruins of a religious society. Enlightenment and rationality ended centuries of darkness, it is further said, due in large part to the work of scientists and philosophers. This conventional wisdom has been much criticized, and today we have a clearer understanding of both the role of science and the context of scientific and technical work.[1] For one thing, we know that the modern process of secularization is not unique. A similar one took place in the ancient city, in which scientific discourse, and medicine in particular, played a decisive role in the legitimation of a new political practice. The hegemony of Christianity itself was built on this secular substrate. In either case—desacralization-secularization or sacralization-desecularization—the role of the intellectual or scientist, civil or religious, was as central as it is today.[2]

Framing the question of modernization in this way opens up a fresh perspective on the political significance of expert discourses. Professional practice is not merely an applied task, but equally a struggle for hegemony over other practices—as organic discourses competing to mediate between subaltern and controlling classes. Within the canonical scheme, the professions emerged out of new technical, scientific, or ideological discourses—each discourse delimiting a "good" to be placed within a cultural market.[3] Importantly, such projects were based on claims of universal scientific, philosophical, or religious paradigms. Beyond their rhetorics of universality, intellectuals and professionals (including the clergy) developed their modes of practice in specific historical and political contexts in which they sought to legitimize particular forms of social political consensus around their particular interest group goals.[4] Organic intellectuals are not enlightened apostles of a new humankind, in other words, but members of local corporate groups with a sense of common identity and purpose.[5]

Indeed, there is a paradox in the presumption of universality contained in scientific, philosophic, and religious discourses, in that this very claim clashes with quotidian and concrete *realpolitik* of professional groups in practice. In Western societies, Christianity, scientific thought, capitalism, and democratic states posit a universal utopia of an integrated and homogenous civil (or religious) society. Such claims (whether religious or neoliberal) are at odds with the social reality of an extremely diverse cultural, social, and linguistic mosaic.

Enlightenment constructions of political utopias precluded cultural or ethnic diversity below the level of the nation state. The process of homogenizing the European nation-state probably reached its height between 1880 and 1970. Paradoxically, simultaneous with homogenization in the economic and political spheres was an extraordinary expansion of cultural diversity, especially at the level of small groups. But diversity was not the main concern for emergent liberal states; rather, liberalism was founded on the struggle against inequalities. Cultural differences were perceived as the consequences of inequalities—corollaries of hunger, poverty, sickness, and feudal oppression. Given the construction of diversity in these terms, the move toward democracy implied a choice between fighting against social inequalities or respecting minority cultures; however, the possibility of advancing in both areas was rarely proposed.

In this essay, I want to explore the role of experts in the construction of the liberal state and the influence of their discourses in the concealment or misunderstanding of cultural diversity. My hypothesis is that part of this misunderstanding has been the consequence of the displacement of ethnographic techniques and methodologies by quantitative and clinical ones. Further, a global regard for society and culture has been preempted by an individual-centered view. I explore this process by examining the role of ethnography in medical and anthropological practice, and its abandonment by physicians at the dawn of the welfare state. At that point, ethnography was appropriated by anthropology. I also consider the nature and circumstances of that appropriation, and some of its comparative implications. These highlight differences in the processes of democratization in Europe (and in Spain) and the United States.

MEDICINE AND ANTHROPOLOGY

My starting point is in the observation that ethnographic practice, though appropriated as a hallmark of the *classical anthropological model*, was never its exclusive inheritance. The anthropology which emerged in the eighteenth century as a natural scientific, vocational discourse about humanity and the domains of nature, culture, and the transcendental was developed by physicians, jurists, theologians, psychiatrists, and philosophers. They needed it to explain the local world in which their practices were rooted. It was fundamental to the development of the factual foundations of their discourses and key to their intellectual and political efficacy.

Significantly in this regard, historians of anthropology have never been interested in the ethnographic practices of physicians. As this essay shows, neglecting this aspect of the history of ethnography means missing important connections—both to earlier traditions and to the status of anthropology in the contemporary world.

As one component of the process of secularization in Western countries, medicalization can be described as a lengthy historical process beginning in Europe toward the end of the Middle Ages and culminating at the end of the nineteenth century with the configuration of the medical model, structured on the hegemony of clinical practice and a specific model of professionalization. In this process, doctors played an important role as brokers between political discourse and local worlds (see Comelles, 1996). Ethnography was integral to that role.

Considering the history of ethnography in medical practice means calling into question anthropology's contemporary constructions of its own professional history. Anthropology presents itself as a discipline established during the Enlightenment, dedicated to humankind and its biological, social, and cultural differences. But anthropology was not fully professionalized until the twentieth century—and then almost exclusively in the United States as a critical reaction to the practice of amateurs and armchair ethnographers (Menéndez, 1977). The discipline's professionalization took shape as the *classical anthropological model*. Some characteristic features of this models include a professional identity based on the personal study of problems and subjects under investigation through a lengthy stay in the field, the refusal to accept a hierarchical division between the investigator who gathers data and the one who analyzes it, and the orientation of research toward "other" cultures (Menéndez, 1991: 22).

Medicine and anthropology construct their respective genealogies. In comparison with the solidity of medicine's claim to origins in technical Greek medicine and its very specific model of practice and professionalization (Peter,

1992), the origins of anthropology are inexact, confused, and far from adequately contextualized.[6] Its objective appears limited to legitimating the classical anthropological model—which (as I shall argue in the conclusion) is only one professional option—by allying it to positive science. The history of the discipline (and the classical model itself) construct an organic role for the discipline in terms borrowed from democratic and liberal discourses of tolerance and respect for cultural differences. As I argue at length here and elsewhere, the appropriation of ethnography as the main feature of this ex post facto construction of the discipline's past has had the effect of relegating other modes of ethnographic practice to a subordinate position—in some cases as amateur work, in others as practices not fully recognized as ethnographic (Comelles, 1996).

THE HIPPOCRATIC FUNDAMENTALS OF ETHNOGRAPHIC PRACTICE

Modern readers would recognize the descriptions of ethnographic practice presented in the Hippocratic treatise, *Airs, Waters, and Places*, written around 400 B.C.[7] The text was designed to orient medical practice toward the systematic observation of the environment and the conduct and temperament of cities and villages. It also offered an interpretive approach to diagnosis, applying an environmental theory and comparative methodology. Unlike current ethnography, the Hippocratic corpus documents curative practices based on a direct commitment of the physician and technician to the patient and his or her context in a collectivity. It also chronicles the physician's learning, beginning with his training, and including his study of texts and his subsequent experience at the sick beds of his patients (Laín Entralgo, 1964: 33–100).

As field reports, these texts are filled with precise observations about the terrain (geography, climate, fauna, and botany) as well as nutrition, culture, and the condition of individual patients. Combining protocols of observation and questioning, such clinical histories comprise the nucleus of the *Epidemias*.[8] Most important for our purposes, the combination of the general and the specific observations was the basis of patients' treatment. Hippocratic ethnography combined a holistic and comprehensive view of the microsocial environment together with the particular clinical experience at the patient's bedside.[9]

This text's wide distribution in Antiquity and its articulation with other Hippocratic theories (Lopéz Férez, 1986: 14–15) can be explained by the political, social, and cultural hegemony of Hippocratic practice, which became an organic discourse when it naturalized the etiology of misfortune and pestilence. Hippocratic discourse links ethnographic practice with politics and places the physician in the position of broker between technical and popular knowledge.[10] In this discourse, the responsibility of patients for their own health is transferred to that of citizens for their actions, and to the incipient government for the health of the destitute—culminating in the institution of the public physician.[11]

ETHNOGRAPHIC AND POLITICAL PRACTICE IN MODERN EUROPE

Drawing on classical sources, the Renaissance recovered ethnography as an instrument of political practice. In sixteenth century Spain—one of the first experiments with a centralized modern state bureaucracy—the religious orders wrote ethnographies as instruments of evangelization, as did the state, developing instruments of government.[12] Christian (1981) has explored the wealth of information about religious practice contained in *Relaciones Geográficas*, and López Píñero (1989: 17-21) has emphasized the influence of Hippocratism in many of the survey's questions.[13] The use of surveys, in context, signifies a preference for integrating the data in the holistic spirit of Hippocratism, and the investigators' belief that the presence of the observer assured the reliability of the data.

The appropriation of ethnographic practice by clergy, doctors, and politicians shows the growing influence of natural philosophy during the Renaissance and the awareness of creditable information in making political decisions. For example, in the sixteenth century, Francisco Toledo sent this report from Peru:

> Understanding what is important to the S.M. order and the seating and maintaining of these reigns in Perú, and in order to establish Christian doctrine and the evangelical light in its natives, and for the good government of its republics and to see the order which can be obtained . . . as well as to provide to the general inspector all I am doing in his provinces until I arrive in the city of Cuzco, I ordered to make a report with the number of one hundred witnesses of these natives, of the oldest and elders of most understanding which I have been able to find." (Fransisco Toledo, *Informaciones acerca del Señorio . . . de los Incas* in Palerm, 1982: 230)

The importance of the observational method of physicians was emphasized by the clergy themselves as a useful instrument in the practice of confessor. Palerm quotes Bernardino de Sahagún:

The physician cannot apply medicines to the patient with certainty [until] he first knows from which nature or cause the disease stems; for this reason a good physician benefits from being knowledgeable in his understanding of medicines and diseases in order to apply the appropriate medicine to each illness ... To cure spiritual diseases it is helpful to have experience in spiritual diseases: the preacher in vices of the republic, in order to use them in preparing his doctrine; the confessor, in order to know how to ask the right questions and understand what is appropriate for one in that office to say.... (Sahagún quoted in Palerm, 1982: 159)

The narrative genre most characteristic of the ethnographic literature of physicians in this period was the *medical topography*.[14] These are monographs about villages and cities, in which the authors assemble all of the characteristics of the place: geology, geography, flora, fauna, climate, resources, the description of material goods, dietary practices, styles of dress, and customs of birth, life, and death. They attempt to relate the material with social and cultural life, the airs and the temperaments. They offer a dense view of reality that requires profound local understanding, a lengthy observation period and a theory that structures the presentation and analysis of the data. As in classical Greece, the observer combines general and comprehensive observations with experience at the patient's bedside: "The skillful man takes a look at what is around him, and in an instant arranges it within one point of view, nothing escapes him, and then, understanding the interconnectedness of the parts which make up the whole, he deduces from them indisputable truths and consequences" (Porta, 1845: 10–11).

This monographic practice was intended to help physicians navigate cultural contexts imagined as distinct from their own, to support their role as educators as well as their social and political commitments in what was understood as a process of social transformation. This personal commitment was inescapable in a profession that recognized the limits of its practice, and constructed its identity (and to expand its professional space) in competition with other healers. Its construction of medical practice as a direct communication between the physician and the population became the basis of its hegemony.

The monographic tradition constructed medical practice around observation, cultural distance, and authority. In these constructions, experts were expected to assume their own status as apostles of a new culture in a world of equals, their condition akin to that of foreigners among aboriginal peoples: their own abnormality in the context of their normality. Professionals were necessarily liminal—and this is an asset, as their task requires them to enter into the daily life of the observed subjects through a helping relationship (Ware, 1849: 8).

Ethnographic practice was constructed as a juncture of two worlds. Importantly, critical distance emerges from the narrative itself. The ethnographer writes to be seen writing, and so that others in the future will learn from him (Ware, 1849). His authoritative charisma is constructed as the extension of the hegemony of the written word over the spoken, the dense ethnography asserting a more systematic understanding than the visit or the questionnaire.

Ethnographic practice was an apparently a secondary concern to some physicians, but it did play a decisive role in their commitment to politics and reform (Peter, 1975). Ethnography provided the foundations on which to construct a theory relating disease to poverty and social injury. Further, it supported a political discourse offering happiness and well-being through the satisfaction of material necessities: food, clothing, housing, and freedom from bearing the masters' burdens: "The slave population is a cachectic population," Frank was to say (Frank, 1790, in López Piñero, 1971).

Similarly, ethnography was the basis for a construction of poverty as the result of ignorance, to be remedied by education and medicine:

> The democratic state desires the well-being of all of its citizens, and recognizes the same rights for all . . . Since the basic conditions of well-being are health and education, the State is responsible for facilitating the means of maintaining and encouraging in all ways possible, health and education through public hygiene and official teaching. (Virchow, R. 1848, *Die offenlichte Gesundheitspflege* quoted in Rosen, 1984: 215)

The priority of the democratic state was not diversity but equality of "basic conditions of well-being." Ethnographic practice was integral to defining the state's interest in cultural diversity as a means to this end.

THOSE THAT DANCE WITH WOLVES

The ethics of Hippocratic ethnography cannot be separated from suffering and daily drama. The rural or suburban physician was expected to share the dramatic experience of a patient's disease without the hope of maintaining a distance from that grief when describing in minute detail the patient's condition. Subsequently, many physicians turned from miasmatic interpretations of the effects of the natural substrate, climate or winds, to other theories that posited the roots of human suffering in the woundings of civilization itself: the misery of working-class neighborhoods, inappropriate technology, or the exploitation of factory workers.[15]

Such frames of reference led physicians into alliances with revolutionary movements or militancy in worker parties (Rosen, 1984; Rodriguez Ocaña, 1987). Engels conveys the commitment of the ethnographer and the impact of the context on his subjectivity: "Stop it! Slums like this one are the rule behind the river Irk... The habitations are dirty, like the streets. People cannot be clean!" (Engels, 1968 [1849]: 34).[16] The spirit of his exclamation is parallel to the style of commitment of many medical topographies.

When Engels is cited as the antecedent of sociology and medical anthropology, it is not for his qualities as a "professional," but as an able and educated person. This amounts to a denial that for topographers or for Engels himself the ethnographic narrative is not merely conjecture, but a product nourished by numerous technical repertoires which spell out how it should be composed and written. Deep down, perhaps, we prefer to resist acknowledging the ethnographic professionalism in these forms, for they are alternative forms. Indeed, this world of filth and misery so close to our own is unwelcome. Historians of anthropology who seek to emphasize the apollonian dimension of the classical model look for its antecedents among the aborigines, in the south, and in faraway lands—between the Rousseauian and the romantic, in which the history of Lafitau is intermingled with the romances of Manon, the episodes of Atala and René or the misfortunes of the Last Mohican.

In North America, the narrative genres expressive of the commitment of ethnographers to their subjects of observation emerged in the context of studies of aborigines. Ethnographic practice regarding Indians initially had a specific meaning in the configuration of the political identity as nation-state in American democracy. Pearce summarizes the climate in the midnineteenth century:

> Civilized men, of course, believed in themselves; they could survive... only if they believed in themselves. In America before the 1850's that belief was most often defined negatively in terms of the savage Indians who, as stubborn obstacles to progress, forced Americans to consider and to reconsider what it was to be civilized and what it took to build a civilization. Studying the savage, trying to civilize him, destroying him, in the end they had only studied themselves, strengthened their own civilization, and given those who were coming after them an enlarged certitude of another, even happier destiny that manifest in the progress of American civilization over all obstacles." (Pearce, 1988: xvii)

In order to construct this idea, facts were indispensable and could be obtained solely through rigorous scientific verification regarding what constituted a savage; this scientific activity took ethnographic form (cf. Pearce, 1988: 105).

Methodological rigor in observations that led ethnographers to work for years or even decades among the aborigines also required them to share the daily dramas that resulted from the aborigine's subordination, deportation and the crisis of their eradication and cultural disintegration. Sustaining cold and distant scrutiny may be possible over a short period, but it is impossible once friendships and mutual understandings develop. Morgan, Bourke, Cushing and many others, who went to the field to collect only objective facts, ultimately acquired personal and intellectual commitments with individuals who had initially been merely objects of study. Their new commitments led them to revise the purely intellectual objectives of their task; by "purely intellectual," I mean a curiosity without any apparent relevance to the people under study.

The biography of John Gregory Bourke perhaps best illustrates the ethnographer's contradictory commitments. As a soldier in the Indian wars, Bourke developed an intellectual and personal commitment to his Indian informants and moved toward a consciousness of his mission that distanced him from his military career and made him skeptical of federal Indian policies (Porter, 1986). But Bourke—along with Cushing, Boas, and Morgan—remained among an uninfluential minority. It was only a later political context that offered Boas the opportunity to fashion such conversions into the basis for a profession. More generally, in the United States, as well as in Europe, the innovative experiments of physicians, lawyers, and psychiatrists—constructed as the good works of whites—took place across lines of deep social division and were aimed at resolving inequalities ascribed to the effects of poverty, hunger, and disease.[17]

CLINICIANS AND ARMCHAIR ANTHROPOLOGISTS

Physicians eventually abandoned ethnography, a development paralleling the progressive hegemony of the anatomic-clinical method and medical model during the second half of the nineteenth century.[18] These displaced the "gaze" and medical practice from the collectivity to the individual body, and replaced the social and cultural field with the hospital, as the site for the formation and reproduction of knowledge. In the hospital, dissection, clinical observation, sanitized statistics and later, the laboratory acquire maximum importance. In the laboratory, personal commitment to the social drama of illness diminishes to the point of disappearing.

The anatomic-clinical method is built on the separation of individuals from their social and cultural context. On the one hand, the Hippocratic ethnographer observes nature, culture, society, and disease; the clinician, on the other hand, removes the subject of observation from society and resituates him or her in a professional space. In the clinical model, the subject of observation is an intruder in the observer's space. The observer attempts to strip him- or herself of subjectivity and is not expected to be interested in the subjectivity of the subject. Clinical practice and its correlate, the medical model, dehistoricizes disease, relegating it to a biological substrate and permitting a political practice based on individualized education or the therapeutic correction of each individual case.

The shift from ethnography to the anatomical-clinical method can be explained in Europe by the position that physicians, psychiatrists, and criminologists occupied in the new society of the late nineteenth century, as well as by the conditions under which they exercised their roles. In an already consolidated State, they are no longer authors of general discourses about society, but managers of social problems. New channels of communication and brokerage transfer observations from the office or hospital, to the university, and to the scientific societies.

The professional profile of the prestigious physician was not that of the rural physician on horseback making house calls, but rather the scholar in charge of a hospital service, a member of anthropological societies, and perhaps a member of the House of Representatives or the Senate.[19] These armchair clinicians, who move sedulously through political and cultural circles in Europe and the United States, are also at times armchair anthropologists. Yet the social conditions they address remains far from the gaze of these organic intellectuals in the new society.

Universities also have a part in this story. Nineteenth-century scholars were far removed from general practitioners, and were equally distant from local ethnographers. Indeed, a wide gap surfaced between them.[20] Society, culture, and daily life ceased to be the contexts of scientific inquiry and knowledge. At best, the two were connected to the extent that knowledge acquired in institutions could be applied to people in their everyday needs. Encyclopedic knowledge won out over the ethnographer's local knowledge; the skill of the erudite built on the accumulation of knowledge won out over experience conferred by practice.[21]

Ultimately, ethnography ceased to reflect the commitment of physicians to transform society. It became a marginal task with which some rural physicians managed to accede to the annual prizes of the Medical Academy and profit from their penchant for writing (Larrea, 1994: 75 ff.). Ethnography acquired an aura of amateurism through which missionaries, members of the military, physicians, lawyers, or travelers could be seen to have passed the time in exotic countries or Europe. Academics, however, sent out questionnaires to these amateurs—questionnaires intended to capture the knowledge deemed essential for sustaining their theoretical arguments with comparable data.[22] These questionnaires, completed by correspondents, provided intellectuals with the basis of their syntheses.[23] The emergent division of labor between data gathers and analyst/theorists erected a barrier shielding compilers from their immediate social reality. Behind that shield, critical conscience dissolved and with it, the commitment that had been nourished by the immediacy of ethnographic practice.

The evolution toward armchair practice occurred in Spain as well, with some delay. In the second half of the nineteenth century, anthropological ideas were introduced in the course of debates over evolution.[24] Ronzón (1991) shows this dispute to have been cultivated by physicians, theologians, anatomists, and zoologists. The discussion was at the core of an ideological and political confrontation about the confessional state. Anthropological evolutionism was an optimal discourse for left-wing intellectuals, who ridiculed biblical theories of the origin of the world and stripped the Church of authority. But the intellectual context of the dispute limited them—and with them, anthropology—to an academic ghetto from which it never escaped. Only one professorship in physical anthropology was created for the entire Spanish university system.[25] Armchair anthropology was just a cultural footnote in nineteenth-century Spain.[26]

A decade ago, I attributed the obstacles to the development of academic anthropology in Spain to the Church, the absence of a colonial policy, republican militancy among the majority of armchair anthropologists, and the ideological purifications characteristic of the Spanish university model of the period (Comelles, 1984). More recently, I have revised this assessment, in view of the complexity of the Spanish social, political, and cultural structure as a particular platform in which distinct constructions of the state clash (Comelles, 1987; Comelles and Prat, 1992). These confrontations allow for distinctly instrumental uses of ethnography and anthropology. But any arguments regarding Spain should not make of it too particular a case, since a critical analysis of French, German, British, or Italian anthropologies would show them to be substantially similar in this regard. Between 1875 and 1936, Spanish science—just as that of France, Italy, Great Britain, and Germany—completely accepted the paradigms derived from degenerationist theories, the anatomic-clinical model of medicine and lombrosian criminology.

Moreover, an assessment of Spain as having failed to institutionalize anthropology must be relative to a particular model of anthropology—the classical anthropological model. Clearly, Spain lacks a significant ethnography of aboriginal societies, or one that uses the parameters of structural-functionalism—but these, too, are assessments that begin in a model that emerged from another country's particular circumstances. I ask myself where the current history of anthropology would be if we started from another hypothesis, presenting the anthropological classical model as the result of North American historic particularism—itself derived from the particular circumstances of an immigrant-based nation-state constructed on a culturally complex substrate of aboriginal populations, together with important minority populations of African-Americans, Latin Americans, and Asians. No European state, democratic or not, has this history.

To pursue this hypothesis further: I believe that the institutionalization of Boasian anthropology acquires a fuller meaning when it is understood as a progressive development in the United States (as the hypothesis implies). Stocking (1976) notes the increasing presence (and significance) of social scientists in political and academic life during the thirties and especially with the eruption of the Second World War, by which time social scientists occupy positions in a multitude of interdisciplinary and applied fields in the United States. In contrast, the European panorama is very different. Malinowski and Radcliffe-Brown project rapidly and intensely in the United States, but very little on the European continent. On the European stage, the classical model of anthropology was a less important and residual event, subsumed by the general expansion of the sciences, techniques, and universities. In Spain in the 1920s, there were perhaps a half dozen professional anthropologists; in England or France, two or three dozen at most.[27] Among them, the Frazers, Brocas or Mausses were more common than the Malinowskis and Radcliffe-Browns.[28] European anthropologies in the twenties were in French medical schools or schools of natural science; in Spain, in departments of dialectology or philological institutes, and in departments of prehistory or archeology.[29]

The difference between France and Great Britain, on the one hand, and Spain, on the other, is the relative success of the few French and British anthropologists in integrating North Americans, for better or for worse, into their disciplinary projects through the network that linked Durkheim, Mauss, Radcliffe-Brown, Malinowski, and their respective disciples. Meanwhile, the tradition of German cultural history and the historical school dissolved with the German crisis in 1933, its foundational theories remaining neglected by ethnology until only very recently. The functionalist and structuralist schools rejected German historicism in favor of an antihistorical empirical post-Boasian and post-Malinowskian anthropology. The Spanish, schooled mostly in German cultural historicism or archeology, neither contemplated nor acknowledged this theoretical evolution.[30] These are some of the reasons I suggest we consider armchair anthropology a model of professional practice; doing so allows us to understand how its institutionalization has followed a path distinct from that of the classical anthropological model.

In the debate between culture and biology, North Americans opted for culture and professionalized a culturalist anthropology. In Europe, in order to assure a university position, they did the opposite and professionalized, if you will, an anatomical clinical anthropology. The debate over multiculturalism beginning with the Treaty of Versailles was absent in Europe. The objective of European anthropology continued to be the analysis of the causes and effects of inequalities. But that debate was carried out in terms of biological or genetic roots and/or their effects on the development of insanity, crime or ideological deviations. Practice focused on individual cases and the health care system, which unfolded in the community and took as its model the fight against tuberculosis. In this struggle, Europeans chose physicians, psychiatrists, criminologists, or epidemiologists, not ethnographers.

THE BIRTH OF CLINICAL ETHNOGRAPHY

Notwithstanding these trends, there were some ethnographers in Europe. They were not narrators of the relationships between the milieu and social inequalities. Rather, they described the survivals of peasant cultures, and their resistance to acculturation. Their ethnographic task gave sustenance to folklore.

Amades, one of the great Catalonian folklorists of the twentieth century wrote these lines in about 1955: "[Folklore is] the science concerned with gathering and studying the popular tradition and investigating and cataloging the knowledge of the village and establishing the culture of the ignorant, the illiterate and the people who have not finished higher studies" (Amades, 1980: 1263). For Amades, education was the frontier separating modern from traditional society. But this border was not clearly marked.

Lis Quibén, an important Galician folklorist, was also unable to understand the resistance of peasants to medicalization, but he did understand the ambiguity of the border between popular medical practices and biomedicine. He wanted to clarify it using the concept of superstition: "Superstition is a ridiculous and fanatical science concerning religious matters and the distinct procedures which the vulgar employ in the healing of their diseases" (Lis Quibén, 1949: 15). Two sciences and two worlds, the second a world foreign to medicine but familiar with religion: The duty of the ethnographer is not to judge but to document things in their purity. Lis Quibén masterfully detected the problem. The limits of medicalization were not only superstitions, but the Church, as well. The ethnographer delimits his space and—centuries too late—suggests that the Church do the same (see Del Río, 1611).

Lis Quibén followed the methodology developed by Giuseppe Pitré (1896), a rural general practitioner and folklorist.[31] The problem Pitré faced in trying to organize his data on popular medicine was that it contained not only "superstitions," but also practices, techniques and wisdom which could reasonably be incorporated into clinical medicine (Pitré, 1896: viii). Only a physician would be capable of separating this wheat from the chaff, applying positive medicine as the organizing criterion (Pitré, 1896: xi). But at the same time, lengthy field experience caused Pitré to qualify the rigidity of some of his categories, and to relativize his comprehension of local attitudes and practices (Pitré, 1896: xiii-xiv).

The empathic folklorist, such as Lis Quibén or Amades, did not imply a specific commitment to transformative social action or politics. Rather, their commitment was to friendship and the more or less paternalistic relationships they developed with their subjects of observation. In this "tactical" comprehension, I believe we must recognize the Hippocratic methodology.

Observing the data where it is produced, as Pitré and Lis Quibén demonstrated, means establishing a profound relationship of confidence and respect, a lengthy field stay and a high degree of participation. But the new methodology of Pitré's positivist folklore, derived from clinical analysis, dissociated this dimension from the pure and objective data. The data would be used to develop patterns, permitting the definition of some clearly marked cultural limits between popular medicine and the biomedical models and practices. The resulting narrative, insofar as it followed a radically positivist model, erased this subjectivity from the text: from this point of erasure ascends the anatomical-clinical model. The erasure is essential to understanding the anatomical-clinical model, and its copy, the medical model, as ahistorical, radically positivist, antisocial, and restricted to issues of pragmatic efficacy.

When folklore lost its historical and dialectic dimension, cultural diversity was no longer an interpretable reality but became constructed and reified as the practices of the ignorant—a world to be combatted with the universalization of mandatory education and free health care facilities in a welfare state. From this perspective, if such facilities could be provided to citizens, there would be no further relevance to ethnography.

Indeed, positivist ethnography and folklore refused to take part in organic discourse regarding cultural diversity. The development of a scholarly anthropology as an autonomous discipline in the European welfare state was closed off. The professionalization of anthropology was finished, in part, at the point where folklore and ethnography might have sustained a discourse over ethnic identity and people's rights to self-determination. In the contemporary states of Western Europe—in democracies or in the authoritarian periods—ethnographic practice was necessary as a first phase for diagnosing social ills and emphasizing a politics of social inequality. A political practice based on complex mechanisms of social protection inspired systematically by clinical models has found no lack of holistic ethnographers who make social contradictions evident and, in ethnographic narrative based on experiential participation at the site of observation, express their newfound conscience and ethical commitment to society's ills. Perhaps it is enough to have clinicians capable of ending the crises and planners who prioritize those at-risk groups for intervention.

GATHER YOUR ROSEBUDS WHILE YOU MAY

I contemplate this panorama that has led us from the epidemics of ancient times through the early itineraries of Bourke and up to Pitré in an attempt to understand the meaning of ethnographic practice in the construction of the liberal capitalist state, the process of democratization, and the society in which it is our lot to live. I find in this history not only the Apollonian signs with which hegemonic anthropology constructed its genealogy in the United States, but also other models with their own histories of experimentation, promise and denial. It seems that the rhetoric of the Other, together with affirmations of relativism, have obscured ethnography's absence from immediate social realities, and served as a curtain shielding anthropology from its own fear of taking on the challenge of critical contemplation. It *is* difficult to accept that our hegemonic models of professional practice have emerged less directly from the principled rejection of the excesses of materialism (as our hegemonic origin myths imply) than they do from the need to domesticate the expressive and revolutionary force of ethnographic testimony when it was engaged in our own times. It *is* difficult to accept that our discipline's models of practice arise from a constructed need to eliminate the subjective experience of conscience so as to create an illusion of distance between the observer and the subjects of observation—ironically, in order to allow us to claim that, through others, we see ourselves. The anthropology that was able to professionalize itself chose one path from among several, but it never explained what moved it in that direction. Some refused to see the aboriginal reservation in which those interned were interviewed by force; others refused to explain why ethnography was supplanted by clinical practice.

I would have concluded this essay here, but while sorting my notes, I came across a document which, in my judgment, exposes the contradictions, the denials, and the fears of the revolutionary burden of ethnography in the context of the contemporary state. It was written in 1916 by Sanchís Banús, a Kraepelinian neuropsychiatrist associated with the Ramón y Cajal school and a militant socialist—while Malinowski was in the Trobriands becoming the Conrad of anthropology and Boas ruled at Columbia. He sought to understand and explain to society as well as alert politicians to the causes of an act considered banal in any time, any city, any place:

> The abandonment of a child can be disguised in a multitude of different ways. First, there is the orphanage. The worker's home has as its sole economic base the work of the father, and it often disintegrates at his death. The lower class woman almost never is trained to confront the imperious need to sustain her family. When she valiantly seeks to fight her circumstances, she finds herself compelled to work in ominous conditions, which despite protective laws, modern industry imposes upon its workers. This practically forces the woman to work beyond her strength and her own organic weakness becomes an insurmountable limitation, she quickly loses her life to any of those infirmities which are the inheritance of organic impoverishment. As a result, the children, without the aid of any public beneficence, which is never based on right but on the most impudent of favoritisms, find themselves abandoned at the mercy of all adverse action within the social environment. They are hungry and to satisfy that hunger they are forced almost always to turn to illicit means. When these prove insufficient, the entire field of crime opens itself to them. At best, if their impulses are oriented in the least damaging social sense, they will meander in their rags through the city, rebellious and independent, because life has taught them that only by their own effort will their needs be satisfied. (Sanchís Banús 1916:182)

I doubt Sanchís Banús's text enjoyed much success, but finding it among the documents I was digging out to write this essay, I felt, as I read it, the ethnographer's magic. I felt the implacable power of his analysis, especially in relation to what were the more hegemonic approaches of his own day. But I also felt his enormous sensitivity to the horror he observed, and the depth of his personal commitment. Seventy years later, the text could describe a reality present also in Sarajevo, Barcelona, or New York, where sometimes alongside the skyscrapers, there are dramas we tend to associate more often with Calcutta, Mexico City, or Rio de Janeiro. This sort of ethnography makes us uneasy because its speaks of *us* when we want to believe we have entered into a democratic, post-Fordian and opulent society in which such dramas cannot take place. It makes us uneasy because we recognize that this reality is also ours, and we feel as impotent and as full of rage as the author in not knowing what to do. Yet we know it is our world. For such reasons, I can understand how in the context of the so-called welfare state—in the context of the affluent society of post-Fordian democracies—a technique that inevitably leads to commitment must be relegated in favor of others that allow more distance between the subject and the observer, reducing the former to an object or a mathematical figure.

ACKNOWLEDGMENTS

The first draft of this essay was presented to the conference "Democracy and Difference" at Indiana University in Bloomington (1993). Prompted by seminar discussions and lengthy reflection, I have written a new essay that comes closer to my original intentions and recovers, I think, the polemical spirit that inspired the seminar. For this I must thank Carol Greenhouse and Davydd Greenwood for their warm reception, and the group of participants for their suggestions, with a special compliment to Carol Greenhouse for her editorial work. This essay owes much to the personal and intellectual influence of Davydd Greenwood, Eduardo Menéndez, Joan Prat, Oriol Romaní, Marta Allué, Oscar Guasch, and especially Enrique Perdiguero and Cristina Larrea to whom I owe my interest in physicians' ethnographies. I am also indebted to a long collaboration with Angel Martínez, which sketches a few of the ideas presented here (Comelles and Martínez, 1993; Martínez y Comelles, 1994). Inci Bowman and Sara Oertling kindly received me at the John Blocker Rare Books Collection of the Moody Library in Galveston, Texas, where I carried out some of the documentary investigation for this article, and which was financed in part through two grants by the DIGYCIT in Spain.

NOTES

1. See Weber, 1987; Gramsci, 1986; Rosen, 1974; 1984; Foucault, 1963, 1979, 1990; Freidson, 1970; and Stocking, 1982.

2. Gramsci (1986) distinguishes between philosophers (*intelettuali*) and the clergy. Assimilating priests' practices to those of a modern profession allows us a better understanding of its significance within the market for corporate and political goods. I have developed this subject more extensively in Comelles (1994).

3. Cf. Rosen (1984) and Peter (1975), for their emphasis on the attempts of physicians to "make a new place for themselves in the world." See also Halpern (1988), Comelles (1988), and Medina y Rodriguez Ocaña (1994).

4. See Peter (1975) on physicians' interests in the establishment of the *Société Royale de Medecine* at the end of the eighteenth century. See also Peset, 1994: 71–123.

5. I have discussed the case of psychiatric professionals in Spain in Comelles (1991). On anthropology in Spain, see Greenwood (1992) and Comelles and Prat (1992).

6. The historiography of anthropology does not amount to nearly the level of attention and development brought to the history of medicine. For critical discussion of the historiography of anthropology, see Stocking (1968) and especially Stolcke (1993).

7. Miller (1962), Lopez Férez (1986), Caro Baroja (1983: 109–113), and Greenwood (1984: 36–40).

8. The term *epidemiai* has been interpreted traditionally as "visits abroad," and comes from the experience of traveling physicians who went from city to city to observe the outbreak of disease at its source. For other authors it signifies "passing through" or being "caught by surprise," which reflects the current medical usage of the term (Garcia Novo, 1989). The notion of ethnography is a neologism of the eighteenth century (Vermeulen, 1994: 39–42). See also Hodgen (1964), who identifies ethnography with unbiased observation, and Boon's critical response (Boon, 1982: 28–30).

I have used the Spanish translations of the *Epidemias* by Andre Piquer (1761, re-edited in 1987), and the recent version introduced by Elena García Novo (1989).

9. Evidence found in *Epidemias* (*Tratados Hipocráticos*, 1989, V), a compendium of clinical histories. For the experiential dimensions of the relationship between physician and patient see Laín Entralgo (1964), and Good (1994).

10. In her seminal text on the history of anthropology, Margaret Hodgen (1964) points to other antecedents of the discipline in encyclopedic compilations such as Pliny's *Historia Naturalis* (among others) that proliferated during the Middle Ages and Renaissance. In my opinion, Hodgen's use of sources reflects the ideal type of the discipline in the 1960s; she lumps together texts and materials whose meanings and purposes were very distinct, even contradictory. Most crucially for our purposes, Herodotus, the Hippocratics, and the Roman or medieval compilers established fundamentally different relationships of distance between authors and objects of study. Hippocratics began with direct field observations over a lengthy period; Roman and later compilers worked with secondhand data. Moreover, the Hippocratics' work was in political and medical practice, and constructed a *practitioner's* identity. In contrast, the compilations constructed a *scholar's* identity.

I should note that the term "practitioner" is anachronistic here. I use it to emphasize the orientation of medical experience toward its subjects of observation.

11. See Dupont (1984), in which he explores the transition from religious hegemony to natural philosophy in the context of the practice of politics in the polis, initiating with the interpretation of the causality of epidemics, Terray (1990: 79–153) on the connections between political discourse and the physician, and Miller (1985) for the emergence of public medical practice. Also, Peter (1992) emphasizes the process of the supplanting of the clergy by technical medical practice.

12. In the religious sphere, examples include the *libros de ánimas* (books of souls), which registered testimony gathered from confessions and official inspection visits. In the governmental sphere, examples include fifteenth-century Catalonia, where the monarchy introduced major reforms in the social protection laws in favor of the municipalization of hospitals and pious works, within which physicians began to have a marked presence (Comelles, Daura, Arnau, and Martín, 1991). The same occurred elsewhere (see Lopez Piñero, 1989: 13-17). See also Cipolla (1993) on urban Italian health councils during the Renaissance.

13. *Relaciones de los Pueblos de España* of 1575, was inspired by *Relaciones de Indias*, and the editors introduced questions inspired by the hippocratic treaty (see Lopéz, 1989: 21 and 63–68). Palerm (1982) emphasizes the ethnographic and political interests evident in the reports of public officials found in the Indian chronicles.

14. The first was Clermont (1672) *De aere, locis et aquis terrae Angliae*. London. In Spain, the *De morbis endemiis Caesar-Augustae* (1986) by Nicolas Francisco de Juan y Domingo (Balaguer and Ballester 1981). Larrea (1994, 1997) has carried out a penetrating study on theoretical-practical dimensions beginning with the Catalonian medical topographies, a body of more than one hundred manuscripts preserved in the Reial Academia de Medicinal in Barcelona and edited between the end of the nineteenth and the beginning of the twentieth century. It relates the significance of topography as field observation. See also Urteaga (1980). Balaguer, Ballester, Bernabeu, and Perdiguero (1990); Prats (1989); and Carrasco (1989). In France, the *Société Royale de Médecine* encouraged the systematic editing of *memoires* regarding the situation of the municipal *campesinos* (Peter, 1975). The persistence of this textual tradition well into the twentieth century calls into question the affirmation by Harris (1978: 36–37) that Hippocratism died out in the seventeenth century. For analyses of the modern impact of Hippocratic theory, see Rosen (1984) on eighteenth and nineteenth century hygienism, and Greenwood (1984), on contemporary Western thought.

15. On inappropriate technology, for example, Larrea (1994: 209) describes the refusal to accept flush toilets because the excess of water results in less valuable human waste fertilizer. Murillo Palacios (1918 [1878]: 142) evokes the exploitation of factory workers: "Taylorism is admirably calculated to obtain maximum production from the machine and its attachments, but human flesh is not made of steel and from a principle which does not understand its laws or demands, it is not logical to expect anything beneficial for health."

16. Editor's note: This is the author's translation of the Catalan version of Engels's *The Condition of the Working Class in England* cited in the text: "Prou d' això! Els barris d' aquesta mena abunden al llarg de l'Irk . . . la brutícia dels interiors d'aquests habitatges correspon perfectament a la brutícia que els envolta. Com pot anar neta la gent que els habita!"

17. Rothman (1971) explores the radical change in the view of poverty and misery, a subject of little interest during the colonial period, but which appears as one of the main tenets on which new governmental action (and social investigation) developed subsequently.

18. On the introduction of the anatomical-clinical model, see Foucault (1963) and Ackerknetch (1986). It developed in France during the first half of the nineteenth century, but was not generalized until the end of the century. For its introduction in the United States, see Rosenberg (1989).

19. Such paradigms of prestige are in France (Broca or Quatrefages) and Spain (González de Velasco or Olóriz). See Ortiz and Sánchez Gómez (1994) for specific references to Spanish authors.

20. Again, the case of Bourke is illustrative. After twenty years of field ethnography, the military allowed him a sabbatical during which he returned to his writings and reworked them with an "intellectual" formation (Porter 1986: 267 ff.).

21. A broad perspective on the political significance of the practice of armchair anthropologists can be found in Peset (1984) and Stocking (1987).

22. This was the origin of *Notes and Queries*. Stocking (1992) reconstructs the subsequent significance of this document in the genesis of intensive case studies. In Spain, the questionnaires distributed by societies such as *El Folk-Lore Español* or *El Folk-Lore Frexnense* are well known. Lisón (1970) discusses the survey of the Ateneo of Madrid in 1902. Hygiene manuals were put together on the basis of responses to questionnaires sent to correspondents (Larrea, 1994).

23. In Spain, the use of questionnaires was the major inspiration for (and activity of) folklore societies. For examples of their questionnaires, see *Folklore Frexnense and Bético Extremeño* ([1883–1884] 1987: 351–365). The best known folklore survey in Spain is the *Información promovida por la Sección de Ciencias Morales y Políticas del Ateneo de Madrid, en el campo de las costumbres populares y en los tres hechos más característicos de la vida: el nacimiento, el matrimonio y la muerte* (Ortiz and Sánchez, 1994: 117 and Lisón 1970). Various compilations have been put together based on these materials, the best known being that of Salillas (1905) on "mal de ojo" in Spain. There is no interpretation or contextualization of many records, nor are their authors known.

24. This period has received much attention from Spanish historians. See Lisón (1970), Glick (1982), Puig-Samper and Galera (1983), and Ronzón (1991), which review the intellectual background of nineteenth-century anthropologists.

25. Julián Calleja (1892) vehemently defended this institutionalization in his discourse on entering the Academy of Sciences. Ronzón (1991) relativized this defense in that behind him were the interests of the Faculty of Medicine of Madrid.

26. Anthropology did not occupy this bleak landscape alone. The trajectory of psychiatry during this period was similar. At the end of the nineteenth century there were only three dozen analysts in the entire state (see Comelles, 1991). This relates to nineteenth-century Spain's painfully slow scientific development in some respects, with correspondingly slight attention to some disciplines. The first psychiatric professorship in Spain was created by the autonomous Catalan government in 1932.

27. In reference to Malinowski, Stocking (1982) masterfully shows the marginal status of ethnography in the generation of Haddon, Rivers, and Seligman within the British academy. What would have become of Malinowski and Radcliffe-Brown without their North American reception in the 1920s? Can anyone imagine what would have happened if Malinowski had continued writing in Polish and had not had the opportunities that allowed him to entrench himself in an Anglosaxon culture on both sides of the Atlantic?

28. Mauss never did fieldwork, though he did author an ethnographic manual.

29. A few years ago, I reviewed the minutes of the *Sociedad Española de Antropología, Etnografía y Prehistoria*. Its roll registered few physical anthropologists or ethnographers; prehistorians and amateurs dominate. See also Ortiz and Sanchez, 1994: 645). In this context, it is worth recalling that in France, the rehabilitation of Van Gennep had to wait until the 1960s.

30. Durkheim's *Suicide* (1927) was translated by a penologist and published by the editorial house of the General Counsel of Law. Ortega y Gasset, one of the grand masters of the Spanish intelligentsia, considered it a "piece of Jewish nonsense," as Caro Baroja recounts in his memoirs (Baroja, 1972). Ortega y Gasset was not much interested in psychoanalysis. Because of this lack of interest, there was no psychoanalysis either. Instead, German phenomenology emerged. By contrast, in Italy, De Martino—with a formation in German historicism and influenced by Croce—developed a synthesis with the Marxism of Gramsci. De Martino is an essential bridge for understanding the evolution of some current orientations in anthropology. I expect that the retrieval of De Martino by anthropologies in the United States and Great Britain will establish him on the anthropological Olympus with Radcliffe-Brown, Malinowski or Boas within a very few years. See, for example, De Martino 1966, 1980, 1983a, 1983b, and 1985.

31. Pitré was a rural Sicilian physician who carried out ethnographic fieldwork over a period of more than thirty years. He was a friend of Lombroso and Mantegazza, but his work influenced European ethnography considerably in the twentieth century. In Spain, references to his work are frequent and his questionnaires were used continually, although often without citing the author. On Pitré see Bronzini (1983) and Martínez and Comelles (1994).

References

Ackerknecht, Erwin H. (1986). *La médecine hospitalière à Paris 1794–1848*. Paris: Payot.

Ackerman, Bruce. (1989). "Why dialogue." *Journal of Philosophy* 86: 5–22.

Aguilar, E. (1990). *Cultural Popular y Folk Lore en Andalucía (Los orígenes de la Antropología)*. Seville: Dip. Provincial.

Allen, Theodore W. (1994). *The Invention of the White Race*, Vol. I. London: Verso.

Alonso Ponga, L. and Diéguez Ayerbe, A. (1977). *Bases para la Unification das Normas Lingüísticas do Galego*. Santiago: Ed. Anaya and Universidad de Santiago.

———. (1984). *El Bierzo*. León: Ed Leonesas.

American Ethnologist. (1989). "Tensions of Empire" (special issue) 16(4).

American Ethnologist. (1991). "Representations of Europe: Transforming State, Society, and Identity" (special issue) 18(3).

Alvarez Roldán, Arturo. (1994). "La invención del método etnográfico. Reflexiones sobre el trabajo de campo de Malinowski en Melanesia." *Antropología* 7: 83–100.

Amades, Joan. (1980). *Folklore de Catalunya. Costums i creences*. Barcelona: Selecta.

Anderson, Benedict. (1991). *Imagined Communities*, 2nd ed. London and New York: Verso.

Appadurai, Arjun. (1990). "Disjuncture and difference in the global cultural economy." *Public Culture* 2(2): 1–24.

Appiah, Kwame Anthony and Henry Louis Gates, Jr. (1995). *Identities.* Chicago: University of Chicago Press.

Aranzadi, Telésforo. (1967). "Síntesis métrica de cráneos vascos" (Orig. Imp. de la Diputación, San Sebastián 1923). In T. Aranzadi, J. M. Barandiarán, and M. A. Etcheverry, *La raza vasca* I, Auñamendi: San Sebastián, pp. 71–171.

Aranzadi, Telésforo and Barandiarán, José Miguel. (1948). "Excavaciones de la cueva de Urtiaga 1928–1936." *Eusko Jakintza* II, pp. 285–330.

Assier-Andrieu, Louis. (1993). "In the eye of the law." *Journal of Legal Pluralism* 33: 179–194.

———. (1996). *Le droit dans les sociétés humaines.* Paris: Editions Nathan.

Associaçom Galega de Língua (AGAL). (1983). "Estudo critico das 'Normas ortográficas e morfolóxicas do idioma galego'." A Dorunha: AGAL.

Atkinson, J. Maxwell and John Heritage, eds. (1984). *Structures of Social Action: Studies in Conversation Analysis.* Cambridge: Cambridge University Press.

Azcona, Jesús. (1982). "La delimitación antropológica de lo vasco y de los vascos." *Cuadernos de etnologia y etnografia de Navarra* 40: 753–802.

———. (1984). *Etnía y nacionalismo vasco: Una Aproximacion desde la Antropologia.* Barcelona: Anthropos, Editorial del Hombre.

———. (1989). "On time: Notes regarding the anthropology of Julio Caro Baroja." In William A. Douglass, ed., *Essays in Basque Social Anthropology and History.* Reno: University of Nevada Press, pp. 9–42.

Bahloul, Joëlle. (1994). "The Sephardic Jew as Mediterranean: A view from kinship and gender." *Journal of Mediterranean Studies* 4(2): 197–207.

Baker, Lee. (1994). "Location of Franz Boas within the African-American Struggle." *Critique of Anthropology* 14(2): 199–217.

Bakhtin, Mikhail. (1981). *The Dialogic Imagination* (Tr. C. Emerson and M. Holquist). Austin: University of Texas Press.

Balaguer, Emili and Rosa Ballester. (1981). "La primera 'topografía médica moderna' en España: De Morbis endemiis Caesar-Augustae (1686) de Nicolás Francisco San Juan y Domingo." In A. Albarracín, L. Piñero, J. Maria and L.S. Granjel, eds. *Medicina e Historia.* Madrid: Universidad Complutense, pp. 45–62.

Balaguer, Emili, Rosa Ballester, Josep Bernabeu, and Enrique Perdiguero. (1990). "La utilización de fuentes antropológicas en la historiografía española contemporánea." *Dynamis* 10: 193–209.

Balibar, Etienne and Immanuel Wallerstein. (1991). *Race, Nation, Class: Ambiguous Identities.* London: Verso.

Barandiarán, José Miguel. (1952). "La prehistoria en el pirineo vasco Estado actual de su estudio." *Actas del Primer Congreso Internacional de Estudios Pirenáicos, San Sebastián (1950)*, Vol. IV, Sección III. Zaragoza: Instituto de Estudios Pirenáicos, CSIC, *Obras Completas* XIII, pp. 77–111.

———. (1976). "El hombre primitivo en el Pais Vasco." (Orig. Ed. Etxaropena 1934). *Obras Completas* XI. Bilbao: Ed. La Gran Enciclopedia Vasca, pp. 335–457.

———. (1978). "Antiguedad del pueblo vasco." (Orig. Eusko enda 1, Bayona 1939). *Obras Completas* XII. Bilbao: Ed. La Gran Enciclopedia Vasca Bilbao, pp. 63–67.

———. (1980). "¿Qué es ser vasco?" *Muga*, 10, pp. 14–19.

Barkan, Elazar (1992). *The Retreat of Scientific Racism: Changing Concepts of Race in Britain and the United States between the World Wars.* Cambridge: Cambridge University Press.

Battaglia, Debra. (1996). *Rhetorics of Self-Making.* New York: Routledge.

Bauman, Zygmunt. (1991). *Intimations of Postmodernity.* New York: Routledge.

Behar, Ruth. (1992). "Arroz con MacArthur," *Chronicle of Higher Education* (November 4).

Bekker, Balthasar. (1694). *Le Monde Enchanté ou examen des communs sentiments touchant les esprits, leur nature, leur pouvoir, leur administration ou leurs operations et touchant les effects que les hommes sont capables de produire par leur communication et leur vertu.* Amsterdam: Pierre Rotterdam.

Benedict, Ruth. (1934). *Patterns of Culture.* Boston: Houghton Mifflin.

Benhabib, Seyla, ed. (1996). *Democracy and Difference: Contesting the Boundaries of the Political.* Princeton: Princeton University Press.

Berger, Peter and Thomas Luckmann. (1966). *The Social Construction of Reality.* New York: Doubleday.

Berkowitz, Roger. (1990). "Community and difference: The political theory of legal pluralism." Unpublished manuscript on file at Amherst College.

Bhabha, Homi. (1994). *The Location of Culture.* New York: Routledge.

Black Public Sphere Collective, ed. (1995). *The Black Public Sphere.* Chicago: The University of Chicago Press.

Blanckaert, Claude. (1989). "Introduction." In P. Broca, ed. *Memoires d'Anthropologie.* Paris: JeanMichelPlace.

Boas, Franz. (1940). *Race, Language and Culture.* Chicago: University of Chicago Press.

Bodnar, John. (1992). *Remaking America: Public Memory, Commemoration and Patriotism in the Twentieth Century.* Princeton N.J.: Princeton.

Boon, James A. (1982). *Other Tribes, Other Scribes: Symbolic Anthropology in the Comparative Study of Cultures, Histories, Religions, and Texts.* Cambridge: Cambridge University Press.

Bourdieu, Pierre, (1990a). *The Logic of Practice* (trans. Richard Nice). Stanford: Stanford University Press.

———. (1990b). In Other Words: Essays Towards a Reflexive Sociology (trans. Matthew Adamson). Stanford: Stanford University Press.

Brandes, S. (1985). "La sardana como símbolo nacional catalán." *Revista de Folklore* 59: 162–166.

Bronzini, G. B. (1983). "Antropologia e medicina popolare: Note sugli studi dei positivisti italiani." *La Ricerca Folklorica* 8: 13–17.

Brown, Peter. (1988). *The Body and Society.* New York: Columbia University Press (Spanish translation: 1993, Barcelona: Munchnik).

Buker, Eloise. (1987). *Politics Through a Looking-Glass.* NY: Greenwood.

Bulkin, Elly. (1984). "Hard ground." In Elly Bulkin, Minnie Bruce Pratt, and Barbara Smith, eds., *Yours in Struggle.* Brooklyn: Long Haul Press.

Bureau of the Census. (1990). *200 Years of U.S. Census Taking: Population and Housing Questions, 1790–1990.* Washington, D.C.: U.S. Government Printing Office.

Bustamente, J. A. (1983a). "Mexican migration: The political dynamic of perceptions." In C. W. Reynolds and C. Tello, eds., *U.S.-Mexico Relations, Economic and Social Aspects.* Stanford: Stanford University Press.

———. (1983b). "The Mexicans are coming: From ideology to labor relations." *International Migration Review* 17: 323–431.

Butler, Judith and Joan W. Scott, eds. (1992). *Feminists Theorize the Political.* New York: Routledge.

Calleja, Julián and Joaquin González Hidalgo. (1892). *Discursos leidos ante la Real Academia de Ciencias Exactas, Fisicas y Naturales en la recepcion publica de Don Julian Calleja y Sanchez.* Madrid: Imprenta de Don Luis Aguado.

Capetti, Carla. (1989). "Deviant girls and dissatisfied women: A sociologist's tale." In Werner Sollors, ed., *The Invention of Ethnicity.* New York: Oxford University Press, pp. 124–157.

Caro Baroja, Julio. (1972). *Los Baroja.* Madrid: Taurus.

———. (1983). *La aurora del pensamiento antropologico. La antropologia en los clásicos griegos y latinos*. Madrid: Consejo Superior de Investigaciones Cientificas.

Carrasco, Silvia. (1989). "Assaig de Reconstrucció d'un passat alimentari: Sabadell cap el canvi de segle." *Arxiu d'Etnografia de Catalunya* 7: 113–137.

Cartas Edificantes . . . (1754). *Y curiosas escritas de las Missiones estrangeras de Levante por algunos misioneros de la Compañia de Jesús, traducidas del idioma francés por el Padre Diego Gavin de la misma Compañía*, vol. 4. En Madrid, En la Imprenta de la Viuda de Manuel Fernández y del Consejo Supremo de la Inquisición.

Castro, Americo. (1966 [1954]). *La Realidad Histórica de España*. Mexico: Editorial Porrua.

Chatterjee, Partha. (1993). *The Nation and Its Fragments: Colonial and Postcolonial Histories*, Princeton: Princeton University Press.

Chavez, Leo R. (1991). "Outside the imagined community: Undocumented settlers and experiences of incorporation." *American Ethnologist* 18: 257–278.

Chenaut, Victoria and Maria Teresa Sierra, eds. (1995). *Pueblos Indigenas ante el Derecho*. Mexico, D.F.: Centro de investigaciones y Estudios Mexicanos y Centroamericanos.

Chock, Phyllis P. (1980). "Key symbols and social categories in Greek American ethnicity." In R. Landman, ed., *Anthropological Careers*. Washington, D.C.: Anthropological Society of Washington, pp. 110–122.

———. (1981). "The Greek-American small businessman: A cultural analysis." *Journal of Anthropological Research* 37, 1: 46–60.

———. (1989). "The landscape of enchantment: Redaction in a theory of ethnicity." *Cultural Anthropology* 4: 163–181.

———. (1991). "'Illegal aliens' and 'opportunity': Myth making in Congressional testimony." *American Ethnologist* 18(2): 279–294.

———. (1995). "Culturalism: Pluralism, culture and race in the *Harvard Encyclopedia of American Ethnic Groups*." *Identities* 1(4): 301–323.

Christian, William. (1981). *Local Religion in Sixteenth Century Spain*. Princeton: Princeton University Press.

Cid, J. A. (1992). "La tradición moderna y la edición del Romancero Hispánico: Encuestras promovidas por Ramón Menéndez Pidal en Asturias (1911–1920)." *Revista de Dialectología y Tradiciones Populares* 47: 127.

Cipolla, Carlo M. (1992). *Miasmas and Disease: Public Health and the Environment in the Pre-Industrial Age*. Saybrook: Yale University Press.

Claustres, Pierre. (1987). *Society Against the State.* New York: Zone Books.

Cochiara, G. (1952). *Storia del Folklore en Europa.* Torino: Edizíone Scientifiche Eillandi.

Cockcroft, James D. (1986). *Outlaws in the Promised Land: Mexican Workers and America's Future.* New York: Grove Press.

Comaroff, Jean and John L. Comaroff. (1991). *Of Revelation and Revolution,* Vol. 1. Chicago: University of Chicago Press.

Comaroff, John L. and Jean Comaroff. (1992). *Ethnography and the Historical Imagination.* Boulder: Westview Press.

Comelles, Josep M. (1987). *Hacia una Antropología de la Antropología en España.* Alicante: IV Congreso de Antropología, Mimeograph on file with author.

———. (1988). *La Razón y la Sinrazón. Asistencia Psiquiátrica y Desarrollo del Estado en España.* Barcelona: PPU.

———. (1991). "Psychiatric care in relation to the development of the contemporary state: The case of Catalonia." *Culture, Medicine and Psychiatry* 15(2): 193–217.

———. (1994). "Fe, carismas y milagros. La sacralización de la práctica médica en la sociedad contemporánea." In A. González Alcantud and S. Rodriguez Becerra, eds. *Creer y Curar.* Granada: Diputación provincial.

———. (1996). *Local Knowledge and Medical Practice.* Shizuoka: First Tanigushi Symposium on Comparative Medicine East and West.

Comelles, Josep M., Angelina Daura, Marina Arnau, and Eduardo Martín. (1991). *L'hospital de Valls. Assaig sobre l'estructura i les transformacions de les institucions d'assistència.* Valls: Institut d' Estudis Vallencs.

Comelles, Josep M. and Angel Martinez. (1993). *Enfermedad, Cultura y Sociedad. Un ensayo sobre las relaciones entre la Antropologia Social y la Medicina.* Madrid: Eudema.

Comelles, Josep M. and Joan Prat. (1992). "El Estado de las Antropologías. Antropologías, Folklores y Nacionalismos en el Estado Español." *Antropología* 3: 35–61.

Comisión Lingüística. (1980). *Normas ortográficas do idioma galego.* Santiago: Publ. Xunta de Galicia.

Condit, Celeste M. and John Lucaites. (1993). *Crafting Equality: America's Anglo-African Word.* Chicago: University of Chicago Press.

Congressional Record. (1986). United States House of Representatives, 99th Congress, Second Session, H.R. 3810, Daily Record, October 9.

Connolly, William. (1991). *Identity/Difference: Democratic Negotiations of Political Paradox*. Ithaca: Cornell University Press.

Cooper, Frederick and Ann L. Stoler. (1989). "Tensions of Empire: Colonial Control and Visions of Rule." *American Ethnologist* 16(4): 609–624.

Cores Trasmonte, B. (1991). *El Estatuto de Galicia (Actas y Documentos)*. Santiago, Librigal.

Copans, J. and J. Jamin, eds. (1978). *Aux Origines de l'Anthropologie Française. Les Mémories de la Société des Observateurs de l'Homme en l'an VIII*. Paris: Le Sycomore.

Cornell, Drucilla. (1992). *The Philosophy of the Limit*. New York: Routledge.

Coughlin, Ellen K. (1991). "Political Survey Notes Differences among Latinos." *Chronicle of Higher Education*. September 11, 1991.

Cover, Robert. (1983). "Foreward: Nomos and narrative." *Harvard Law Review* 97: 4–68.

Cox, Taylor, Jr. and Stella M. Nkomo. (1990). "Invisible men and women: A status report on race as a variable in organization behavior research." *Journal of Organizational Behavior* 11: 419–431.

Craft, Gretchen. (1992). "The persistence of dread in law and literature." *Yale Law Journal* 102: 521–546.

Crenshaw, Kimberlé. (1992). "Whose story is it, anyway? Feminist and antiracist appropriations of Anita Hill." In Toni Morrison, ed., *Race-ing Justice, En-gendering Power: Essays on Anita Hill, Clarence Thomas, and the Construction of Social Reality*. New York: Pantheon, pp. 402–440.

Crispell, Diane. (1991). "How to avoid big mistakes." *American Demographics*. March, pp. 48–50.

Davis, F. James. (1991). *Who Is Black?* University Park: Pennsylvania State University Press.

De Martino, Ernesto. (1966). *La terre du remords*. Paris: Gallimard.

———. (1980). *Furore Simbolo Valore*. Milan: Feltrinelli.

———. (1983a). *Morte a pianto rituale. Dal lamento funebre antico al pianto di Maria*. Turin: Boringhieri.

———. (1983b) *Sud e magia*. Milan: Feltrinelli.

——— (1985). *El Mundo Magico*. Mexico, D.F.: Direccion de Difusion Cultural.

De Mott, Benjamin. (1990). *The Imperial Middle: Why Americans Can't Think Straight About Class*. New York: William Morrow & Co.

De Witte, Bruno. (1983). "La pluralité ethnique et l'autonomie culturelle. Etude comparative." In Yves Meny, ed. *Centres et périphéries: le partage du pouvoir.* Paris: Economica, pp. 97–126.

Del Pino, Fermín. (1992) "Joaquin Costa como etnógrafo: Una visión panorámica." *Revista de Dialectología y Tradiciones Populares* 47: 45–73.

Delbanco, Andrew. (1992). "Pluralism and its discontents." *Transition* 55: 83–92.

Delgado, Gary and Sen, Rinku. (1988). "Shades of Race." A review of Michael Omi and Howard Winant, *Racial formation in the United States from the 1960s to the 1980s. Socialist Review* 18(3): 143–148.

Delgado, Richard. (1982). "Words that wound: A tort action for racial insults, epithets, and name-calling." *Harvard Civil Rights-Civil Liberties Review* 17: 133–181.

Del Rio, Martin S. J. (1611). *Les Controverses et Recherches Magiques de. . . . divisées en six livres, auquels sont exactement et doctement consultées les Sciences curieuses, les Vanitez & les superstitions de toute la magie, avecques la manière de proceder en justice contre es magicients and sorciers, accomodée a l'instruction des confesseurs. Oeuvre necessaire et utile a tous theologiens, juriconsultes, medecins et phylosophes.* Paris: Reginald Chaudiere.

Delumeau, Jean, (1992). *La confesión y el perdón.* Madrid: Alianza (French ed. 1990, Paris, Fayard).

Dewey, John, (1966 [1916]). *Democracy and Education.* New York: The Free Press.

Díaz, L. (1988). "Identidad y manipulación de la cultura popular. Algunas anotaciones sobre el caso castellano." In L. Díaz (ed.) *Aproximación antropológica a Castilla y León,* 2nd ed., Barcelona, Anthropos, pp. 13–27.

Dimas, Nicasio, Jr., Donald Chu, and Phyllis K. Fong. (1980). *The Tarnished Golden Door: Civil Rights Issues in Immigration.* U.S. Civil Rights Commission, Washington D.C.: U.S. Government Printing Office.

Domínguez, Virginia R. (1986). *White by Definition.* New Brusnwick, N.J.: Rutgers University Press.

Dostal, Walter. (1994). "Silence in the darkness: German ethnology during the National Socialist period." *Social Anthropology* 2(3): 251–262.

Douglas, Mary. (1966). *Purity and Danger.* London: Routledge & Kegan Paul.

Douglass, William A. (1989). "Crítica de las últimas tendencias en el análisis del nacionalismo." In A. Pérez Agote, ed., *Sociologia del nacionalismo.* Universidad del Pais Vasco/Gobierno Vasco, pp. 95–110.

Dubois, W. E. B. (1962 [1935]). *Black Reconstruction in the United States, 1860–1880,* 2nd ed. New York: Russell.

———. (1968 [1940]). *Dusk of Dawn: An Essay toward an Autobiography of a Race Concept*, 2nd ed. New York: Schocken Books.

Duchet, Michèle. (1971). *Anthropologie et Histoire au Siècle des Lumières*. Paris: Flammarion.

Dumont, Louis. (1977). *From Mandeville to Marx: The Genesis and Triumph of Economic Ideology*. Chicago: University of Chicago Press.

———. (1991). *L'idéologie allemande: France-Allemande et retour.* Paris: Gallimard.

Dupont, Florence. (1984). "Pestes d'hier, pestes d'aujourd'hui." *Histoire, Economie et Société* 4: 511–524.

Durham, W. Cole and Alexander Dushku. (1993). "Traditionalism, secularism, and the transformative dimension of religious institutions." *Brigham Young University Law Review* 1993(2): 421–465.

Durkheim, Emile. (1928). *El Suicidio.* Madrid: Editorial Reus.

Duster, Troy. (1991). "Understanding Self-Segregation on the Campus." *Chronicle of Higher Education*, September 25.

Ehrenreich, Barbara. (1992). "Cultural baggage" *New York Times Magazine*, April 7, 1992.

Eley, Geoff. (1994). "Nations, publics, and political cultures: Placing Habermas in the nineteenth century." In Nicholas Dirks, Geoff Eley, and Sherry Ortner, eds., *Culture/Power/History: A Reader in Contemporary Social Theory*. Princeton: Princeton University Press, pp. 297–335.

Ellickson, Robert. (1991). *Order Without Law*. Cambridge: Harvard University Press.

Elorza, Antonio. (1978). *Ideologías del nacionalismo vasco*. L. Haranburu, San Sebastián.

Estatuto de Autonomía de Galicia. (1991). Santiago: Xunta de Galicia.

Estudo crítico das normas ortográficas e morfolóxicas do idioma galego. (1983). La Coruña: AGAL.

Engel, David. (1984). "The oven bird's song: Insiders, outsiders, and personal injuries in an American community." *Law and Society Review* 18: 551–582.

Engels, Friedrich. (1968). "La situació de la classe obrera a Anglaterra (1844)." In O. W. Henderson *Aportacions a la historia del moviment obrer.* Barcelona: Edicions 62, pp. 23–102.

Erikson, Erik. (1970 [1950]). *Childhood and Society,* 2nd ed. New York: W. W. Norton.

Euzkadi Ta Azkatasuna. (1979). "Euskera y patriotismo vasco." *Documentos* 1. San Sebastián: Hordago, pp. 104–109.

———. (1979). "Un bosquejo de la historia vasca hasta 1512." *Documentos* 1. San Sebastián: Hordago, pp. 91–92.

———. (1979). "Instituciones politicas vascas." *Documentos* 2. San Sebastián: Hordago, pp. 67–73.

Fabian, Johannes. (1986). *Language and Colonial Power.* Berkeley: University of California Press.

Ferguson, James. (1994). *The Anti-Politics Machine: "Development," Depoliticization and Bureaucratic Power in Lesotho.* Minneapolis: University of Minnesota Press.

Fernández de Rota y Jose Antonio Monter. (1987). *Gallegos ante un espejo. Imaginación antropológica en la historia.* La Coruña: Ed do Castro.

———. (1990). "Linguistic correction and semantic skills." In Michael Byram and John Leman, eds. *Bicultural and Trilingual Education: The Foyer Model in Brussels.* Philadephia and Clevedon: Multilingual Matters, Ltd.

———. (1991a). *Identidad y recreación histórica en Galicia,* Revista de Antropología Social No. 0.

———. (1991b). *Identité et culture dans l' experience "Foyer" pour éleves espagnols.* In Johan Leman, ed., *Intégrité, intégration.* Brussels: Editions Universitaires De Boeck.

Fernández de Rota y Monter José Antonio, ed. (1991). *Nos lindeiros da Galeguidade.* Santiago: Consello da culture Galega.

———. (1994). *Etnicidad y Violencia.* La Coruna: Universidade da Coruna Servicio de Publicacions.

Ferro Ruibal, X. (1987). *A igrexa e a lingua galega.* Santiago, Consello da Cultura Galega.

Fineman, Martha. (1991). *The Illusion of Equality.* Chicago: University of Chicago Press.

Fischer, Michael M. J. (1986). "Appendix: Work in progress—Ethnicity as text and model." In George E. Marcus and Michael M. J. Fischer, eds., *Anthropology as Cultural Critique.* Chicago: University of Chicago Press, pp. 173–177.

Fiske, John. (1989). *Understanding Popular Culture.* Boston: Unwin Hyman.

Fitzpatrick, Peter. (1983). "Marxism and Legal Pluralism." *The Journal of Law and Society* 1: 45–59.

———. (1992). *The Mythology of Modern Law.* London: Routledge.

Fitzpatrick, Peter, ed. (1995). *Nationalism, Racism and the Rule of Law.* Aldershot (Hants) and Brookfield (Vermont): Dartmouth.

Folklore Frexnense y Bético Extremeño (1883–1884).

Fontana, Josep. (1988). *Historia de Catalunya V. la fi de l'Antic Regim i la Industrialitzacio (1787–1868)* Barcelona: Edicions 62.

Fordham, Signithia and John Ogbu. (1986). "Black Students' School Success: Coping with the 'Burden of Acting White.' " *The Urban Review* 18: 176–206.

Foucault, Michel. (1963). *Naissance de la Clinique.* Paris: PUF

———. (1975) *The Birth of the Clinic: An Archaeology of Medical Perception* (trans. A. M. Sheridan Smith). New York: Vintage.

———. (1990). *La Vida de los hombres infames. Ensayos sobre desviación y dominación.* Madrid: Ediciones La Piqueta.

Foucault, Michel, ed. (1979). *Les Machines à Guérir. Aux Origines de l'Hôpital Moderne,* Brussels: Atelier Pierre Madarga.

Fraser, Nancy. (1989). *Unruly Practices: Power, Discourse, and Gender in Contemporary Social Theory.* Minneapolis: University of Minnesota Press.

Frazer, Elizabeth and Nicola Lacey. (1993). *The Politics of Community: A Feminist Critique of the Liberal-Communitarian Debate.* New York: Harvester/Wheatsheaf.

Freidson, Eliot. (1970). *Medical Profession.* New York: Free Press.

Friedman, Jonathan. (1992). "The past in the future: History and the politics of identity." *American Anthropologist* 94(4): 837–859.

Frug, Mary Joe. (1992). *Postmodern Legal Feminism.* New York: Routledge.

Fumaroli, Marc. (1991). *L'Etat culturel. Essai sur une religion moderne.* Paris, Éditions de Fallois.

Galego 1. (1984). Santiago: Instituto da Lingua Galega, Universidad de Santiago.

Garn, Stanley. (1968). *Readings on Race,* 2nd ed. Springfield, Ill.: Charles C. Thomas.

García Novo, Elena. (1989). "Introducción." In *T. Hipocráticos, Epidemias.* Madrid: Gredos, pp. 7–44.

Garfinkel, Harold. (1967). *Studies in Ethnomethodology.* Englewood Cliffs, N.J.: Prentice-Hall.

Garvin, P. J. (1964). *A Prague School Reader on Esthetics, Literary Structure, and Style.*

Gavit, John Palmer. (1922). *Americans by Choice.* New York: Harper & Brothers.

Geertz, Clifford. (1973). "Person, time and conduct in Bali." In Clifford Geertz, *The Interpretation of Cultures: Selected Essays.* New York: Basic Books, pp. 360–411.

———. (1989). *El antropólogo como autor.* Barcelona: Paidos.

Gérando, Joseph Marie de. (1978 [1803]). "Considérations sur les diverses méthodes à suivre dans l'observation des peuples sauvages." In J. Copans and J. Jamin, eds., *Aux origines de l'Anthropologie française.* Paris: Le Sycomore, pp. 127–170.

Gellner, Ernest. (1983). *Nations and Nationalism.* Oxford: Basil Blackwell.

———. (1987). *Culture, Identity and Politics.* Cambridge: Cambridge University Press.

———. (1988). *Naciones y nacionalismo.* Madrid: Alianza Universidad.

Gettys, Luella. (1934). *The Law of Citizenship in the United States.* Chicago: University of Chicago Press.

Glazer, Nathan, and Daniel Moynihan. (1963). *Beyond the Melting Pot: The Negroes, Puerto Ricans, Jews, Italians, and Irish of New York City.* Cambridge: The M.I.T. Press.

Glick, Thomas. (1982). *Darwin en España.* Barcelona: Peninsula.

Good, Byron. (1994). *Medicine, Rationality and Experience.* Cambridge: Cambridge University Press.

Gooding-Williams, Robert ed. (1993). *Reading Rodney King/Reading Urban Uprising.* New York: Routledge.

Gordon, Robert J. (1992). *The Bushman Myth: The Making of a Namibian Underclass.* Boulder: Westview Press.

Gramsci, Antonio. (1971). *Selections from the Prison Notebooks* (Quentin Hoare and Geoffrey N. Smith, eds. and trans.). New York: International Publishers.

———. (1986). *El Materialismo histórico y la Filosofía de Benedetto Croce.* México: Juan Pablo Editor.

Greenhouse, Carol J. (1986). *Praying for Justice: Faith, Order and Community in an American Town.* Ithaca, Cornell University Press.

———. (1996). *A Moment's Notice: Time Politics Across Cultures.* Ithaca: Cornell University Press.

Greenhouse, Carol J., Barbara Yngvesson, and David Engel (1994). *Law and Community in Three American Towns.* Ithaca: Cornell University Press.

Greenhouse, Carol J. and Davydd J. Greenwood, eds. (in press). *Cultura, Poder y Representación en los Estados Unidos y España.* Madrid: UNED Press.

Greenwood, Davydd J. (1971). "Julio Caro Baroja: Sus obras e ideas." *Ethnica* 2: 77–97.

———. (1978). *Community-Region-Government: Toward an Integration of Anthropology and History.* In J. A. Carreira, M. Gutiérrez Esteve, R. Rubio, eds., *Homenaje a Julio Caro Baroja.* Madrid: Centro de Investigaciones Sociológicas, pp. 511–531.

———. (1984). *The Taming of Evolution: The Persistence of Non-evolutionary Views in the Study of Humans.* Ithaca, NY: Cornell University Press.

———. (1985). "Castilians, Basques, and Andalusians: An historical comparison of nationalism, 'true' ethnicity, and 'false' ethnicity." In Paul Brass, ed., *Ethnic Groups and the State.* London: Croom Helm, ch. 6.

———. (1992). "Las Antropologías de España. Una propuesta de colaboración." *Antropología* 3: 5–33.

———. (1989). "The anthropologies of Spain." Working paper 2. Spanish Studies Round Table, University of Illinois at Chicago.

———. (1993). "Cultural identities and global political economy from an anthropological vantage point." *Indiana Journal of Global Legal Studies* 1 (1): 101–117.

Gregory, Steven. (1993). "Race, rubbish, and resistance: Empowering difference in community politics." *Cultural Anthropology* 8: 24–48.

Grosz, Elizabeth. (1994). "Difference and the problem of essentialism." In Naomi Schor and Elizabeth Weed, eds., *The Essential Difference.* Bloomington: Indiana University Press, pp. 82–97.

Guichot y Sierra, A. (1984 [1922]). *Notica histórica del folklore. Orígines en todos los países hasta 1890. Desarrollo en España hasta 1921.* Seville: Hijos de Guillermo Alvarez, 1922. Reprinted Seville: Junta de Andalucía, 1984.

Guinier, Lani. (1991a). "The triumph of tokenism: The Voting Rights Act and the theory of Black electoral success." *Michigan Law Review* 89: 1077–1154.

———. (1991b). "No two seats: The elusive quest for political equality." *Virginia Law Review* 77: 1413–1514.

Gurrutxaga, Ander. (1985). *El código nacionalista vasco durante el franquismo.* Anthropos, Barcelona.

Gusfield, Joseph. (1963). *Symbolic Crusade*. Chicago: Illini Books.

Habermas, Jürgen. (1976). *Legitimation Crisis* (trans. Thomas McCarthy). Cambridge: Polity Press.

———. (1989). *Moral Consciousness and Communicative Action*. Cambridge: MIT Press.

Halpern, Sydney A. (1988). *American Pediatrics. The Social Dynamics of Professionalization 1880–1980*. Berkeley: California University Press.

Harris, Marvin. (1978). *El desarrollo de la teoria antropologica. Una historia de las teorias de la cultura*. Madrid: Siglo XXI.

Harrison, Faye V. (1992). "The Du Boisian legacy in anthropology." *Critique of Anthropology* 12(3): 239–260.

Hartog, François. (1980). *Le miroir d'Herodote. Essai sur la representation de l'autre*. Paris: Gallimard.

Harvey, David. (1973). *Social Justice and the city*. Oxford: Blackwell.

Hauser, Philip. (1987). "Madrid bajo el punto de vista medico-social (1902)." In E. Rodriguez Ocaña, ed. *La constitucion de la Medicina Social como disciplina en España (1882–1923)*. Madrid: Ministerio de Sanidad y Consumo, pp. 83–96.

Healey, Jon. (1992). "Lumbees Don't Get Status of Tribe." *Wall Street Journal*, February 29, 1992.

Heiberg, Marianne. (1989). *The Making of the Basque Nation*. Cambridge: Cambridge University Press.

Herzfeld, M. (1987). *Anthropology Through the Looking-glass*. Cambridge: Cambridge University Press.

———. (1992). *The Social Production of Indifference*. Providence: Berg.

Hinsley, Curtis. (1983). "Ethnographic Charisma and Scientific Routine: Cushing and Fewkes in the American Southwest, 1879–1893." In G. Stocking, ed., *Observers Observed*. Madison: University of Wisconsin Press, pp. 53–70.

Hodgen, Margaret. (1964). *Early Anthropology in the Sixteenth and Seventeenth Centuries*. University of Pennsylvania Press.

Historia de Galiza. (1980). La Coruña: Caixa Galicia.

Hobbes, Thomas. (1968). *Leviathan*. C. B. Macpherson, ed. New York: Penguin Books.

hooks, bell. (1981). *Ain't I a Woman: Black Women and Feminism*. Boston: South End Press.

Hymowitz, Kay S. (1993). "Multiculturalism is anti-culture." *New York Times*, March 25, 1993.

Instituto da Lingua Galega—Real Academia Galega (ILG-RAG). (1982). "Normas ortográficas e morfolóxicas do idioma galego." Vigo: ILG-RAG.

Jacob, François. (1982). *The Possible and the Actual.* Seattle: University of Washington Press.

Jardine, Alice. (1980). "Prelude: The future of difference." In Hester Eisenstein and Alice Jardine, eds. *The Future of Difference.* Boston: G. K. Hall and New York: Barnard College Women's Center.

Jaureguiberry, Pierre. (1962). "Consideraciones acerca de la raza vasca" (Orig. Considerations sur la race basque, Bourdeaux, 1947). In P. Jaureguiberry, T. Aranzadi, R. Ganzarain, et al. *La raza vasca* II, Auñamendi: San Sebastián, pp. 9–103.

Johnstone, Barbara. (1990). *Stories, Community, and Places: Narratives from Middle America.* Bloomington: Indiana University Press.

Kahn, Paul. (1989). "Community in contemporary constitutional theory." *Yale Law Journal* 99: 5–85.

Kammen, Michael. (1972). *People of Paradox: An Inquiry Concerning the Origins of American Civilization.* New York: Knopf.

Karst, Kenneth. (1986). "Paths to belonging: The Constitution and cultural identity." *North Carolina Law Review* 64: 303–377.

Kateb, George. (1992). *The Inner Ocean: Individualism and Democratic Culture.* Ithaca: Cornell University Press.

Katz, Bill and Linda Sternberg Katz. (1992). *Magazines for Libraries,* 7th ed. New York: Bowker.

Kearney, Michael. (1991). "Borders and Boundaries of State and Self at the End of Empire." *Journal of Historical Sociology* 4: 52–74.

Kettner, James H. (1978). *The Development of American Citizenship 1608–1870.* Chapel Hill: University of North Carolina Press (Institute of Early American History and Culture).

Kluckhohn, Florence and Fred Strodtbeck. (1961). *Variations in Value Orientation.* Evanston, Ill.: Row, Peterson and Co.

Krzeminski, Adam. (1994). " 'More humility, fewer illusions'—A talk between Adam Michnik and Jurgen Habermas." *New York Review of Books* 41(6): 24 (3/24/94).

Kuper, Adam, ed. (1992). *Conceptualizing Society.* New York: Routledge.

Kurland, Philip. (1984). "The religion clauses and the Burger court." *Catholic University Law Review* 34(1): 1–18.

Laín Entralgo, Pedro. (1964). *La relación médico-enfermo. Historia y Teoría*. Madrid: Revista de Occidente.

Laitin, David. (1986). *Hegemony and Culture: Politics and Religious Change Among the Yoruba*. Chicago: University of Chicago Press.

———. (1992). *Language Repertoires and State Construction in Africa*. Cambridge: Cambridge University Press.

Lakoff, George and Mark Johnson. (1980). *Metaphors We Live By*. Chicago: The University of Chicago Press.

Larrea, A. (1966). *El Folklore y la Escuela*. Madrid: Consejo Superior de Investigaciones Científicas.

Larrea Killinger, Cristina. (1994). *Los Miasmas: antropologia historica de un concepto médico*. Tesi de Doctorat, Universitat de Barcelona.

———. (1997). *La cultura de los olores. Una aproximacion a la antropologia de los sentidos*. Quito: Abya-Yala.

Lasch, Christopher. (1979). *The Culture of Narcissism: American Life in an Age of Diminishing Expectations*. New York: Warner.

Latour, Bruno. (1993). *We Have Never Been Modern* (Catherine Porter, trans.). Cambridge: Harvard University Press.

Lazarus-Black, Mindie and Susan Hirsch. (1994). *Contested States*. New York: Routledge.

Leach, Edmund. (1980). *L'Unité de l' Homme et autres Essais*. Paris: Gallimard.

Lecea, Rodrígu de. (1987). "La escuela de la institución." *Revista Historia* 16(49): 68.

Lévi-Strauss, Claude. (1971). *L'Homme nu*. Paris: Plon.

Linz, Juan. (1973). "Opposition to and under an authoritarian regime: The case of Spain." In Robert A. Dahl, ed., *Regimes and Oppositions*. New Haven: Yale University Press, pp. 171-259.

Lis Quiben, Victor. (1949). *La medicina popular en Galicia*. Pontevedra: Graficas Torres.

Lisón Tolosana, Carmelo. (1971). *Antropologia Social en España*. Madrid: Siglo XXI.

———. (1983). *Antropología social y hermenéutica*. Madrid: Fondo de Cultura Económica.

Liss, Julie. (1998). "Diasporic identities: The science and politics of race in the work of Franz Boas and W. E. B. DuBois, 1894–1919." *Cultural Anthropology* 13(2).

Locke, John. (1988). *Two Treatises on Government*, Peter Haslett, ed. New York: Cambridge University Press.

Llobera, Joan Ramón. (1996). *El Dios de la modernidad. El desarrollo del nacionalismo en Europa Occidental.* Barcelona, Anagrama.

López Férez, J.A. (1986). "Introducción a Los Aires, las Aguas y los Lugares." *Tratados Hipocráticos* II, Madrid: Biblioteca Clásica Gredos, pp. 9–38.

López Muñoz, D. (1989). *O idioma da igrexa en Galicia.* Santiago: Consello da Cultura Galega.

López Piñero, José María, ed. (1971). *Medicina, Historia, Sociedad.* Barcelona: Ariel.

———. (1989). *Los orígenes en España de los estudios sobre Salud Publica.* Madrid: Ministerio de Sanidad y Consumo.

Lorde, Audre. (1984). *Sister Outsider: Essays and Speeches.* Trumansburg, N.Y.: Crossing Press.

Lowi, Theodore J. (1979). *The End of Liberalism*, 2nd ed. New York: Norton.

Lukes, Stephen. (1989). "Making sense of moral conflict." In Nancy L. Rosenblum, ed., *Liberalism and the Moral Life.* Cambridge: Harvard University Press, pp. 127–143.

Macaulay, Stewart. (1986). "Private government." In Leon Lipson and Stanton Wheeler, eds., *Law and the Social Sciences.* New York: Russell Sage Foundation, pp, 445–518.

Macpherson, C. B. (1962). *The Political Theory of Possessive Individualism: From Hobbes to Locke.* London: Oxford University Press.

Malkki, Liisa H. (1995): *Purity in Exile: Violence, Memory and National Cosmology among Hutu Refugees in Tanzania.* Chicago: Univeristy of Chicago Press.

Marcial Blas, A. de. (1989). *Sobre el nacionalismo español.* Madrid: Centro de Estudias Constitutionales.

Marcus, George and Michael Fischer. (1986). *Anthropology as Cultural Critique.* Chicago: University of Chicago Press.

Marcuse, Herbert. (1965). "Repressive tolerance." In Robert Paul Wolff, Barrington Moore and Herbert Marcuse, *A Critique of Pure Tolerance.* Boston: Beacon Press, pp. 81–123.

Martínez Hernáez, Angel. (1994). *El síntoma y sus interpretaciones. En los límites de la psiquiatria y de la antropologia de la medicina contemporaneas.* Tesi de Doctorat, Universitat de Barcelona.

Martínez Hernáez, Angel y Josep M. Comelles. (1994). "La Medicina popular. ¿Los limites culturales del Modelo Médico?" *Revista de Dialectología y Tradiciones Populares* 49 (2): 109–136.

Martínez Torner, E. (1965). *El folklore en la escuela*. Buenos Aires: Ed. Losada.

Martinez-Alier, Verena Stolcke. (1989). *Marriage, Class and Colour in Nineteenth-Century Cuba*, 2nd ed. Ann Arbor: University of Michigan Press.

Matsuda, Mari J. (1986). "Liberal jurisprudence and abstracted visions of human nature: A feminist critique of Rawls' theory of justice." *New Mexico Law Review* 16: 613–630.

McClure, Kirstie. (1990). "The limits of toleration." *Political Theory* 18: 361–391.

Mead, Margaret. (1942). *And Keep Your Powder Dry: An Anthropologist Looks at America*, 2nd ed. New York: W. Morrow & Co.

———. (1970). *Culture and Commitment: A Study of the Generation Gap*. Garden City, N.Y.: Doubleday.

Medina Doménech, Rosa and Esteban Rodriguez Ocaña. (1994). "Profesionalización médica y campañas sanitarias. Un proceso convergente en la medicina española del primer tercio del siglo XX." *Dynamis* 14: 77–94.

Meilán Gil, X. L. and Rodriguez-Muñoz Arana, X. (1988) *O Dereito Estatutario Galego*. Santiago: Parlamento de Galicia.

Menéndez, Eduardo L. (1977). "'Nuevos' objetos de estudio de la Antropologia." In *Actas de la XV Mesa Redonda de la Sociedad Mexicana de Antropología*. Mexico, pp. 75–82.

———. (1978). "El modelo medico y la salud de los trabajadores." In Basaglia et al., *La salud de los trabajadores*. Mexico: Nueva Imagen, pp. 11–53.

———. (1991). "Definiciones, indefiniciones y pequeños saberes." *Alteridades* 1(1): 21–32.

Merry, Sally Engle. (1988). "Legal pluralism." *Law and Society Review* 22: 869–896.

———. (1990). *Getting Justice and Getting Even*. Chicago: University of Chicago Press.

Mertz, Elizabeth. (1992). "Linguistic ideology and praxis in U.S. law school classrooms." *Pragmatics* 2(3): 325–334.

———. (1994). "Legal loci and places in the heart: Community and Identity in Sociolegal Studies." *Law and Society Review* 28(5): 971–992.

Mertz, Elizabeth, ed. (1994). "Symposium: Community and Identity in Sociolegal Studies." *Law and Society Review* 28(5).

Michelman, Frank. (1988). "Law's republic." *Yale Law Journal* 97: 493–537.

Mill, John Stewart. (1987). *On Liberty*. Harmondsworth: Penguin Books.

Miller, Geneviève. (1962). "'Airs, waters and places' in History." *Bulletin of the History of Medicine* 17: 129–140.

Miller, Timothy. (1985). *The Birth of the Hospital in the Byzantine Empire*. Baltimore: The John Hopkins University Press.

Minow, Martha. (1990). *Making All the Difference: Inclusion, Exclusion, and American Law*. Ithaca: Cornell University Press.

———. (1991). "Partial justice: Law and minorities." In Austin Sarat and Thomas Kearns, eds., *The Fate of Law*. Ann Arbor: University of Michigan Press, pp. 15–77.

Moore, Sally Falk. (1973). "Law and social change: The semi-autonomous social field as an appropriate subject of study." *Law and Society Review* 7: 719–746.

Moore, Sally Falk, ed. (1994). *Moralizing States*. Washington D.C.: American Anthropological Association.

Morgan, Edmund. (1972). "Slavery and freedom: The American paradox." *Journal of American History* 59: 5–29.

Morning Edition. (1993). Transcript of September 15, Washington, D.C.: National Public Radio, p. 7.

Morrison, Toni, ed. (1992). *Race-ing Justice, En-gendering Power: Essays on Anita Hill, Clarence Thomas, and the Construction of Social Reality*. New York: Pantheon.

Mouffe, Chantal. (1993). *The Return of the Political*. London: Verso.

Munaret. (1840). *Du Medecin des villes et du medecin de campagne. Moeurs et Science, par le Docteur*.... Paris: Germer-Bailliere: Libraire Editeur.

Murillo Palacios, Francisco. (1987). "La defensa social de la salud publica, en Discursos leidos en la Real Academia de Medicina . . . el dia 14 de julio de 1918." In E. Rodriguez Ocaña, ed., *La constitucion de la Medicina Social como disciplina en España (1882–1923)*. Madrid: Ministerio de Sanidad y Consumo, pp. 113–160.

Nader, Laura. (1974). "Up the anthropologist." In Dell Hymes, ed., *Reinventing Anthropology*. New York: Pantheon, pp. 284–311.

Nagengast, Carole and Michael Kearney. (1990). "Mixtec ethnicity: Social identity, political consciousness, and political activism." *Latin American Research Review* 25(2): 61–91.

Nelson, Barbara J. (1984). "Women's poverty and women's citizenship: Some political consequences of economic marginality." *Signs* 10(2): 209–231.

Newman, Katharine. (1988). *Falling from Grace: The Experience of Downward Mobility in the American Middle Class.* New York: The Free Press.

Novak, Michael. (1971). *The Rise of the Unmeltable Ethnics: Politics and Culture in the Seventies.* New York: The Macmillan Co.

Ochs, Elinor and Bambi B. Schieffelin. (1983). *Acquiring Conversational Competence.* London: Routledge and Kegan Paul.

Omi, Michael and Howard Winant. (1986). *Racial Formation in the US from the 1960s to the 1980s.* New York: Routledge and Kegan Paul.

Orientacións pare a escrita do noso idioma. (1980). Orense: Asociación Sociopedagóxica Galega.

Ortega y Gasset, José. (1993). *Obras de José Ortega y Gasset.* Madrid: Revista de Occidente.

Ortiz Garcia, Carmen and Luis Sanchez Gómez. (1994). *Diccionario Historico de la Antropologia Española.* Madrid: C.S.I.C.

Ortner, Sherry. (1991). "Reading America: Preliminary notes on class and culture." In Richard G. Fox, ed. *Recapturing Anthropology.* Santa Fe, NM: School of American Research Press, pp. 163–189.

Paine, Thomas. (1976 [1776]). *Common Sense,* With an introduction by Isaac Kramnick. London: Penguin Books.

Palerm, Angel, ed. (1982). *Historia de la Etnología 1. Los Precursores.* Mexico: Alhambra.

Parsons, Talcott. (1975). "Some theoretical considerations on the nature and trends of change of ethnicity." In Nathan Glazer and Daniel Patrick Moynihan, eds., *Ethnicity.* Cambridge: Harvard University Press, pp. 53–83.

Pearce, Roy Harvey. (1988). *Savagism and Civilization. A Study of the Indian in the American Mind,* 2nd ed. Berkeley: University of California Press.

People Magazine. January 20, 1992, pp. 71–72, 75.

Perdiguero, Enrique. (1992). "The popularization of medicine during the Spanish Enlightenment." In Roy Porter, ed., *The History of the Medical Popularisation.* London: Routledge, pp. 160–193.

Pérez Agote, Alfonso. (1987). *El nacionalismo vasco a la salida del franquismo.* Madrid: CIS, Siglo XXI.

Peset, José Luis. (1984). *Ciencia y Marginación. Negros, locos y criminales.* Barcelona: Crítica.

———. (1994). *Las Heridas de la Ciencia.* Valladolid: Junta de Comunidades de Castilla-León.

Peset, Jose L. and Mariano Peset. (1975). *Lombroso y la Escuela Positivista italiana.* Madrid: C.S.I.C.

Peter, Jean-Pierre. (n.d.). "Chemins, tournants et Traverses du Pouvoir Médical (XVIIème-XIXème siècles)." In R. Lenoir and M. Tsikounas, eds., *Le Pouvoir Médical.* Paris: Arlea-Corlet.

———. (1975). "Le grand rêve de l' Ordre Médical en 1770 et aujourd'hui." *Autrement* 4: 183–192.

———. (1978). "Quiconque n'est pas docteur, n' est t'il qu'un charlatan?" *Autrement* 15: 176–186.

———. (1992). "La médecine occidentale dans son histoire: un trajet sinueux entre la connaissance et la méconnaissance." In J. L. Gaucher-Peslherbe, ed., *Santé et marginalité. Actes du Colloque Walter Wardwell.* Paris: Editions Grandvaux, pp. 16–28.

Pick, Daniel. (1993). *Faces of Degeneration: An European Disorder 1848–1918.* Cambridge: Cambridge University Press.

Piquer, Andrés. (1761). *Las obras de Hipócrates más selectas ilustradas por el Dr. . . . Médico de S.M. y su Proto-médico de Castilla . . . Tomo Segundo,* 1st ed. Madrid: En la Oficina de Joachin Ibarra.

Pitré, Giuseppe. (1896). *Medicina Popolare Siciliana.* Torino: Carlo Clausen.

Piven, Frances Fox and Richard A. Cloward. (1971). *Regulating the Poor.* New York: Vintage.

Porta, Ignacio. (1845). "Del verdadero tino practico. Discurso Inaugural." Real Academia de Medicina y Cirugia de Barcelona.

Porter, Joseph C. (1989). *Paper Medicine Man. John Gregory Bourke and His American West.* Norman: University of Oklahoma Press.

Porter, Roy, ed. (1985). *Patients and Practitioners. Lay Perceptions of Medicine in Pre-industrial Society.* Cambridge: Cambridge University Press.

Postone, Moishe. (1993). *Time, Labor, and Social Domination.* Cambridge (U.K.): Cambridge University Press.

Powell, H. Jefferson. (1988). "Reviving republicanism." *Yale Law Journal* 97: 1703–1711.

Prat, J. (1991). "Historia, Estudio introductorio." In J. Prat y otros, eds., *Antropologia de los pueblos de España.* Madrid, Taurus ethnografía.

Prats, Llorenç. (1987a). *Els origens de l'interés per la cultura popular a Catalunya. La Renaixenca.* Lleida, doctoral thesis.

———. (1987b). *El mite de la tradició popular. Els origns de l'interés per la cultural tradicional a la catalunya del segle XX*. Barcelona, Edicions 62.

———. (1989). "Aportaciones de la topografías médicas al conocimiento etnográfico de los paises catalanes." *Boletín de Historia de la Antropología* 2:3–7.

———. (1991). "Los precedentes de los estudios etnológicos en Cataluá: Folklore y ethnografía (1853–1959)." In J. Prat et al., eds., *La antropología de los pueblos de España*. Madrid: Taurus.

Prats, Ll., D. Llopart, and J. Prat. (1982). *La cultura popular a Cataluyna. Estudiosos I Institucions. (1853–1981)*. Barcelona: Altafulla/Serveis de Cultural Popular.

Prieto de Pedro, Jesús. (1993). *Cultura, culturas y Constitución*. Madrid: Centro de Estudios Constitucionales-Congreso de Diputados.

Proctor, Robert. (1988). "From Anthropologie to Rassenkunde in the German anthropological tradition." In G. W. Stocking Jr., ed., *Bones, Bodies, Behavior. Essays on Biological Anthropology*. Madison, Wisc.: University of Winsconsin Press, pp. 138–178.

Puig-Samper, Miguel Angel and Andres Galera. (1983). *Introduccion a la historia de la antropologia en el siglo XIX*. Madrid: C.S.I.C

Quindlen, Anna. (1991). "Making the mosaic." *The New York Times*, November 20, 1991.

Randolph, Laura. (1993). "Halle Berry: Hollywood's hottest Black actress has a new husband, a new home and a new attitude." *Ebony* 48: 119 (April).

Rapp, Rayna. (1987). "Urban kinship in contemporary America: Families, classes and ideology." In Leith Mullings, ed., *Cities of the United States: Studies in Urban Anthropology*. New York: Columbia University Press, pp. 219–242.

Rawls, John. (1972). *A Theory of Justice*. Cambridge: The Belknap Press of Harvard University Press.

Redfield, Robert. (1962 [1953]). "The natural history of the folk society." In R. Redfield, ed., *Human Nature and the Study of Society*, Vol. 1. Chicago: University of Chicago Press.

Renteln, Alison Dundes. (1987). "Culture and culpability: A study of contrasts." *Beverly Hills Bar Association Journal* 22(1): 17–27.

Reynolds v. United States. 98 U.S. 145 (1878).

Ridley, Friedrich F. (1982). "Les arts en Grande-Bretagne: Un financement sans mainmise l'Etat." *Revue Francaise d'Administration Publique*, no. 22, Paris: Institut International d'Administration Publique.

Rieder, Jonathan. (1985). *Canarsie: The Jews and Italians of Brooklyn Against Liberalism.* Cambridge: Harvard University Press.

Rischin, Moses, ed. (1965). *The American Gospel of Success.* Chicago: Quadrangle Books.

Rodriguez, Roberto. (1990a). "Census figures help group clout, hardly count the minority of one." *Los Angeles Times,* April 1, 1990.

———. (1990b). ". . . And here at home." *Washington Post,* April 29, 1990.

Rodriguez Ocaña, Esteban, ed. (1987). *La constitucion de la medicina social como disciplina en España (1882–1923).* Madrid: Ministerio de Sanidad y Consumo.

Roediger, David. (1991). *The Wages of Whiteness: Race and the Making of the American Working Class.* London: Verso.

Ronzón, Eulàlia. (1991). *Antropología y Antropólogos. Ideas para una Historia Crítica de la Antropología española.* Oviedo: Pentalfa.

Rosen, George. (1974). *From Medical Police to Social Medicine. Essays of the History of Health Care.* New York: Science History Publications.

———. (1984). "Análisis histórico del concepto de medicina social." In E. Lesky, ed., *Medicina Social. Estudios y Testimonios Históricos.* Madrid: Ministerio de Sanidad y Consumo, pp. 211–272. (Orig. 1947 *Bulletin of the History of Medicine* 21: 674–733.)

Rosenberg, Charles E. (1989). "Introduction: Community and communities: The evolution of the American hospital." In D. Elizabeth Long and Janet Golden, eds. *The American General Hospital: Communities and Social Contexts.* Ithaca: Cornell University Press, pp. 3–20.

Rothman, David J. (1971). *The Discovery of the Asylum: Social Order and Disorder in the New Republic.* Boston: Little, Brown and Company.

Rougemont, Denis de. (1961). *Vingt-huigt siècles d'Europe: La conscience europèene à travers les textes.* Paris: Payot.

Rouse, Roger. (1992). "Making sense of settlement: Class transformation, cultural struggle, and transnationalism among Mexican migrants in the United States." In Nina Glick Schiller, Linda Basch, and Cristina Blanc-Szanton, eds., *Toward a Transnational Perspective on Migration.* New York: New York Academy of Sciences, pp. 25–52.

———. (1995). "Thinking through transnationalism: Notes on the cultural politics of class relations in the contemporary United States." *Public Culture* 7(2): 353–402.

Sacks, Karen B. (1989). "Toward a unified theory of class, race, and gender." *American Ethnologist* 16: 534–550.

Said, Edward W. (1988). "Foreword." In Ranajit Guha and Gayatri Chakravorty Spivak, eds., *Selected Subaltern Studies*. New York: Oxford University Press, pp. v–x.

Salillas, Rafael. (1905). *La Fascinación en España. Estudio hecho con la Información promovida por la Sección de Ciencias Morales y Politicas del Ateneo de Madrid*. Madrid: Imprenta a cargo de Eduardo Arias.

Sanchez Albornoz, Claudio. (1956). *España, un enigma histórico*. Barcelona: Edhasa.

Sanchís Banús, José. (1916). "Estudio médico social del niño golfo." In A. Rey, ed., *Estudios Médico-sociales sobre marginados en la España del siglo XIX*. Madrid: Ministerio de Sanidad y Consumo, pp. 173–195.

Sandel, Michael. (1982). *Liberalism and the Limits of Justice*. Cambridge: Cambridge University Press.

Sandel, Michael, ed. (1984). *Liberalism and Its Critics*. New York: New York University Press.

Sapiro, Virginia. (1984). "Women, citizenship, and nationality: Immigration and naturalization policies in the United States." *Politics and Society* 13(1): 1–26.

Sarat, Austin and Thomas Kearns. (1992). "Making peace with violence: Robert Cover on law and legal theory." In Austin Sarat and Thomas Kearns, eds., *Law's Violence*. Ann Arbor: University of Michigan Press, pp. 211–250.

Sarat, Austin and Thomas Kearns, eds. (1993). *Law and Everyday Life*. Ann Arbor: University of Michigan Press.

Saxton, Alexander. (1990). *The Rise and Fall of the White Republic: Class Politics and Mass Culture in Nineteenth-Century America*. London: Verso.

Schneider, David. (1968). *American Kinship: A Cultural Account*. Chicago: University of Chicago Press.

———. (1969). "Kinship, nationality and religion in American culture: Toward a definition of kinship." In Victor Turner, ed., *Forms of Symbolic Action*. Washington, D.C.: Proceedings of the American Ethnological Society, pp. 116–125.

———. (1980). *American Kinship: A Cultural Account*, 2nd ed. Chicago: University of Chicago Press.

Schön, Donald. (1983). *The Reflective Practitioner: How Professionals Think in Action*. New York: Basic Books.

Schor, Naomi and Elizabeth Weed, eds. (1994). *The Essential Difference*. Bloomington: Indiana University Press.

Scott, James C. (1985). *Weapons of the Weak: Everyday Forms of Peasant Resistance.* New Haven: Yale University Press.

———. (1990). *Domination and the Arts of Resistance: Hidden Transcripts.* New Haven: Yale University Press.

———. Segal, Daniel A. (1991). "The 'European': Allegories of racial purity." *Anthropology Today* 7(5): 7–9.

———. (1993a). " 'Race' and 'Colour' in pre-independence Trinidad and Tobago." In Kevin A. Yelvington, ed., *Trinidad Ethnicity.* London: Macmillan, pp. 81–115.

———. (1993b). " 'Race' and 'family' in talk about 'class' in Trinidad Now." Paper presented at the annual meeting of the American Anthropological Association, Washington, D.C.

———. (1994). "Living ancestors: Nationalism and the past in post-colonial Trinidad and Tobago." In J. Boyarin, ed., *Remapping Memory: The Politics of Timespace.* Minneapolis: University of Minnesota Press, pp. 221–239.

Segal, Daniel A. and Richard Handler. (1995). "U.S. multiculturalism and the concept of culture." *Identities* 1(4): 391–407.

———. (1992). "How European is nationalism?" *Social Analysis* 32: 52–64.

Selznick, Philip. (1992). *The Moral Commonwealth: Social Theory and the Promise of Community.* Berkeley: University of California Press.

Sennett, Richard and Jonathan Cobb. (1972). *The Hidden Injuries of Class.* New York: Vantage.

Sheybani, Malek-Mithra. (1987). "One person's culture is another's crime." *Loyola Los Angeles International and Comparative Law Journal* 9: 751–783.

Shklar, Judith. (1991). *American Citizenship: The Quest for Inclusion.* Cambridge: Harvard University Press.

Shrage, Laurie. (1987). "Some implications of comparable worth." *Social Theory and Practice* 13: 77–102.

Shweder, Richard and Edmund J. Bourne. (1984). "Does the concept of the person vary cross-culturally?" In Richard Shweder and Robert LeVine, eds., *Culture Theory.* Cambridge: Cambridge University Press, pp. 158–199.

Silverstein, Michael. (1985). "Language and the culture of gender: At the intersection of structure, usage and ideology." In Elizabeth Mertz and Richard Parmentier, eds., *Semiotic Mediation: Sociocultural and Psychological Perspectives.* Orlando, Fla.: Academic Press, pp. 219–259.

———. (1992). "Metapragmatic discourse and metapragmatic function," In John A. Lucy, ed. *Reflexive Language: Reported Speech and Metapragmatics.* Cambridge: Cambridge University Press, pp. 33–58.

Simpson, Alan K. (1984). "The politics of U.S. immigration reform." *International Migration Review* 18: 486–504.

Singer, Milton. (1986). "The melting pot: Symbolic ritual or total social fact?" In Hervé Varenne, ed., *Symbolizing America.* Lincoln: University of Nebraska Press, pp. 97–118.

———. (1987). "Yankee City in Renaissance." In Paul Hockings, ed., *Dimensions of Social Life: Essays in Honor of David Mandelbaum.* Berlin: Mouton de Gruyter, pp. 275–302.

Smith, Raymond T. (1996). *The Matrifocal Family: Power, Pluralism, and Politics,* New York: Routledge.

———. (n.d.). Kinship and Class in Chicago. Unpublished manuscript on file with author.

Sollors, Werner. (1986). *Beyond Ethnicity: Concent and Descent in American Culture.* New York: Oxford University Press.

Sollors, Werner, ed. (1989). *The Invention of Ethnicity.* NY: Oxford University Press.

Spiegelman, Herbert. (1973). "On the right to say 'WE': A linguistic and phenomenological analysis." In George Psathas, ed., *Phenomenological Sociology.* New York: John Wiley & Sons, pp. 130–156.

Stanfield, John. (1985). "Theoretical and ideological barriers to the study of racemaking." In Cora Bagley Marrett and Cheryl Leggon, eds. *Research in Race and Ethnic Relations: A Research Annual.* Greenwich, Conn. and London: JAI Press, pp. 161–181.

Steinberg, David. (1991). "Religious exemptions as affirmative action." *Emory Law Journal* 40: 76–139.

Steinberg, Stephen. (1989). *The Ethnic Myth.* Boston: Beacon Press.

Stocking, George W., Jr. (1968). *Race, Culture, and Evolution: Essays in the History of Anthropology.* Chicago: University of Chicago Press.

———. (1982). *Race, Culture and Evolution: Essays in the History of Anthropology,* 2nd ed. Chicago: University of Chicago Press.

———. (1983). "The Ethnographer's Magic: Fieldwork in British Anthropology from Tylor to Malinowski." In Stocking, ed. *Observers Observed.* Madison: University of Wisconsin Press, pp. 70–121.

———. (1992). "Ideas and Institutions in American Anthropology." In Stocking, ed. *The Ethnographer's Magic and Other Essays.* Madison: University of Wisconsin Press, pp. 114–117.

Stocking, George W., ed. (1976). *Selected Papers from the American Anthropologist 1921–1945.* Washington: American Anthropological Association.

———. (1982). *A Franz Boas Reader. The Shaping of American Anthropology.* Chicago: University of Chicago Press.

———. (1987). *Victorian Anthropology.* New York: Free Press.

Stolcke, Verena. (1993). "De padres, filiaciones y malas memorias. ¿Qué historias de qué Antropología?" In Joan Bestard, ed. *Después de Malinowski.* Tenerife: Asociación Canaria de Antropología, pp. 147–198.

Stolzenberg, Naomi. (1993). "'He drew a circle that shut me out': Assimilation, indoctrination, and the paradox of liberal education." *Harvard Law Review* 106: 582–667.

Stone, Deborah A. (1988). *Policy Paradox and Political Reason.* Boston: Little, Brown.

Strathern, Marilyn. (1992a). "Parts and wholes: Refiguring relationships in a postplural world." In Adam Kuper, ed., *Conceptualizing Society.* New York: Routledge, pp. 75–104.

———. (1992b). *After Nature: English Kinship in the Late Twentieth Century.* Cambridge: Cambridge University Press.

Strathern, Marilyn, ed. (1995). *Shifting Contexts: Transformations in Anthropological Knowledge.* London: Routledge.

Sunstein, Cass. (1988). "Beyond the republican revival." *Yale Law Journal* 97: 1539–1590.

Susman, Warren I. (1984). *Culture as History: The Transformation of American Society in the Twentieth Century.* New York: Pantheon Books.

Takaki, Ronald T. (1993). *A Different Mirror: A History of Multicultural America.* Boston: Little, Brown.

Taylor, Charles. (1989). *Sources of the Self: The Making of Modern Identity.* Cambridge: Harvard University Press.

Terray, Emmanuel. (1990). *La Politique dans la Caverne.* Paris: Seuil,

Thelwell, Michael. (1992). "False, fleeting, perjured Clarence: Yale's brightest and blackest go to Washington." In Toni Morrison, ed., *Race-ing Justice, Engendering Power: Essays on Anita Hill, Clarence Thomas, and the Construction of Social Reality.* New York: Pantheon, pp. 86–126.

Thomas, Robert J. (1985). *Citizenship, Gender, and Work: Social Organization of Industrial Agriculture.* Berkeley: University of California Press.

Tocqueville, Alexis de. (1876). *Democracy in America,* trans. Henry Reeve. Boston: John Allyn.

Todorov, Tzvetan. (1985). *The Conquest of America: The Question of the Other,* trans. Richard Howard. New York: Harper & Row.

———. (1993). *On Human Diversity: Nationalism, Racism, and Exoticism in French Thought,* trans. Catherine Porter. Cambridge: Harvard University Press.

Tonkin, E., Mc Donald M., and M. Chapman (eds.) (1989). *History and Ethnicity.* London: Routledge.

Tratados Hipocráticos. (1986). *Sobre los aires, las Aguas y los Lugares* II. Madrid: Gredos.

———. (1989). *Epidemias* V. Madrid: Gredos.

Tunin, I. (1967). *La educación y la esecuela en España de 1894 a 1902. Liberalismo y tradición.* Madrid: Aguilar.

Turner, Victor. (1986). "Dewey, Dilthey, and Drama: An essay in the anthropology of experience." In V. Turner and E. Bruner, eds., *The Anthropology of Experience.* Urbana: University of Illinois Press, pp. 33–44.

Tushnet, Mark. (1986). "The constitution of religion." *Connecticut Law Review* 18: 701–738.

Tyler, Tom. (1988). *Why People Obey the Law.* New Haven: Yale University Press.

Unger, Roberto Mangabeira. (1984). *Knowledge and Politics.* New York: The Free Press.

United States. (1952). Aliens and Nationality: Immigration and Nationality Administration. *U.S. Code* Title 8 Pt. 1443b.

United States v. Moylan. 47 F.2d 1002 (1969).

United States Department of Commerce Bureau of the Census. (1990). Census of Population and Housing Content Determination Reports: Federal Legislative Uses of Decennial Census Data.

United States House of Representatives. (1964). *Immigration.* Hearings before the Subcommittee No. 1 on HR7700 and 55 identical bills to Amend the Immigration and Nationality Act and for Other Purposes of the Committee on the Judiciary, 88th Congress, Second Session.

———. (1975). *Illegal Aliens.* Hearings before the Subcommittee on Immigration, Citizenship, and International Law of the Committee on the Judiciary. 94th

Congress, First Session, on H.R. 982 and Related Bills. Washington D.C.: U.S. Government Printing Office.

———. (1983). *Immigration Reform and Control Act of 1983*, Hearings before the Subcommittee on Immigration, Refugees, and International Law of the Committee on the Judiciary. 98th Congress, First Session, on H.R. 1510. Washington, D.C.: U.S. Government Printing Office.

United States Select Commission on Immigration and Refugee Policy. (1981). *Final Report, U.S. Immigration Policy and the National Interest.* Washington, D.C.: U.S. Government Printing Office.

United States Senate. (1981). *The Knowing Employment of Illegal Immigrants.* Hearing before the Subcommittee on Immigration and Refugee Policy of the Committee on the Judiciary. 97th Congress, First Session. Washington, D.C.: U.S. Government Printing Office.

United States Senate and House of Representatives. (1981). *Final Report of the Select Commission on Immigration and Refugee Policy.* Joint Hearings before the Subcommittee on Immigration and Refugee Policy of the Senate Committee on the Judiciary and Subcommittee on Immigration, Refugees, and International Law of the House Committee on the Judiciary. 97th Congress, First Session. Washington, D.C.: U.S. Government Printing Office.

Urciuoli, Bonnie. (1991). "The political topography of Spanish and English: The view from a New York Puerto Rican neighborhood." *American Ethnologist* 18: 295–310.

———. (1996). *Exposing Prejudice: Puerto Rican Experiences of Language, Race, and Class.* Boulder: Westview Press.

Urla, Jacqueline. (1987). *Being Basque, Speaking Basque: The Politics of Language and Identity in the Basque Country.* Doctoral Thesis, University of California, Berkeley.

Urteaga, Luis. (1980). "Miseria, miasmas y microbios. Las Topografías médicas y el estudio del medio ambiente en el siglo XIX." *Geo-crítica* 29: 5–51

Varenne, Hervé. (1977). *Americans Together: Structured Diversity in a Midwestern Town.* New York: Teachers College Press.

———. (1986). "Drop in Anytime." In Hervé Varenne, ed., *Symbolizing America.* Lincoln: University of Nebraska Press, pp. 209–228.

———. (1992). *Ambiguous Harmony: Family Talk in America.* Norwood, N.J.: Prentice-Hall.

Velasco, H. M. (1988). "El evolucionismo y la evolución del folklore." *El Folk-lore Andaluz*, 2a época, 2: 13–32.

———. (1990). "El folklore y sus paradojas." *REIS* 49: 123–144.

———. (1992). "Los significados de 'cultura' y los significados de 'pueblo.' Una historia inacabada." *REIS* 60: 7–25.

Vermeulen, Hans. (1994). "Origins and institutionalization of ethnography and ethnology in Europe and the USA 1771–1845." In H. Vermeulen and A. Alvarez Roldan, eds., *Fieldwork and Footnotes*. New York: Routledge, pp. 39–59.

Vermeulen, Hans F. and Arturo Alvarez Roldan, eds. (1994). *Fieldwork and Footnotes: Studies in the History of European Anthropology*. London: Routledge.

Vicens i Vives, J. and Montserrat Llorens. (1991). *Industrial i Politics (segle XIX). Historia de Catalunya. Biografies catalanes*. Barcelona: Editorial Vicens-Vives.

Vilar, Pierren. (1973). *Catalunya dins l'Espanya moderna II. El medi historic*. Barcelona: Edicions 62.

Vincent, Joan. (1990). *Anthropology and Politics: Visions, Traditions and Trends*. Tucson: University of Arizona Press.

Wade, Peter. (1993). "'Race,' Nature and Culture." *Man* 28: 17–34.

Wagner, Roy. (1975). *The Invention of Culture*. Englewood Cliffs, N.J.: Prentice-Hall.

Wallerstein, Immanuel. (1995). *After Liberalism*. New York: The New Press.

Ware, John M. D. (1849). *Duties and Qualifications of Physicians. An Introductory Lecture*. New York: John Henry Parker.

Warren, Kay B. (1993). "Introduction: Revealing conflicts across cultures and disciplines." In Warren, Kay B., ed. *The Violence Within: Cultural and Political Opposition in Divided Nations*. Boulder: Westview Press, pp. 1–24.

Warren, Kay B., ed. (1993). *The Violence Within: Cultural and Political Opposition in Divided Nations*. Boulder: Westview Press.

Warner, W. Lloyd. (1959). *The Living and the Dead: A Study of the Symbolic Life of Americans*. Yankee City, Series Vol. V. New Haven: Yale University Press.

Waters, Mary C. (1990). *Ethnic Options: Choosing Identities in America*. Berkeley: University of California Press.

Weber, Max. (1987). *La Etica Protestante y el Espíritu del Capitalismo*. Barcelona: Península.

West Virginia State Board of Education v. Barnette. 319 U.S. 624 (1943).

Whorf, Benjamin Lee. (1956). *Language, Thought, and Reality*. Cambridge: MIT Press.

Williams, Brackette. (1991). *Stains on My Name, War in My Veins: Guyana and the Politics of Cultural Struggle.* Durham, N.C.: Duke University.

Williams, Brackette F., ed. (1996). *Women Out of Place: The Gender of Agency and the Race of Nationality.* New York: Routledge.

Williams, Patricia. (1991). *The Alchemy of Race and Rights: Diary of a Law Professor.* Cambridge: Harvard.

Williams, Raymond. (1963). *Culture and Society 1780–1950.* Harmondsworth: Penguin.

Williams, Richard. (1990). *Hierarchical Structures and Social Value: The Creation of Black and Irish Identities in the United States.* New York: Cambridge University Press.

Wilmsen, Edwin N. and Patrick McAllister, eds. (1996). *The Politics of Difference: Ethnic Premises in a World of Power.* Chicago: University of Chicago Press.

Wisconsin v. Yoder. 406 U.S. 205 (1971).

Woodiwiss, Anthony. (1993). *Postmodernity USA: The Crisis of Social Modernism in Postwar America.* London: Sage.

Yanow, Dvora. (1992). "The social construction of affirmative action and other categories." Presented at the Fifth National Symposium on Public Administration Theory. Chicago, April 9–10, 1992.

Yngvesson, Barbara. (1993). *Virtuous Citizens, Disruptive Subjects.* New York: Routledge.

Young, Iris Marian. (1989). "Polity and group differences: A critique of universal citizenship." *Ethics* 99: 250–274.

———. (1990). *Justice and the Politics of Difference.* Princeton: Princeton University Press.

Zulaika, Joseba. (1988). *Basque Violence: Metaphor and Sacrament.* Reno: University of Nevada Press.

Zangwill, Israel. (1975 [1909]). *The Melting Pot: Drama in Four Acts.* New York: Arno Press.

About the Authors

Jesús Azcona is professor of anthropology at the University of the Basque Country, Bilbao. His pioneering work on ethnicity, history, and nationalism in the Basque Country is the basis of his numerous books, including a two-volume college textbook, and many articles.

Roger Berkowitz is a graduate student in the Jurisprudence and Social Policy Program at the University of California, Berkeley.

Phyllis P. Chock is associate professor of anthropology at the Catholic University of America, Washington, D.C. She is author of numerous articles on aspects of ethnicity and immigration in the United States, especially as issues and contexts of federal legislative and policy debate. She is editor of *Anthropological Quarterly*.

Josep M. Comelles is professor of anthropology at the Universitat Rovira i Virgili in Tarragona and professor of Public Health at the University of Barcelona, Spain. An anthropologist and physician specializing in psychiatry, he is author of several books on aspects of medical anthropology and historical ethnography.

José A. Fernández de Rota is professor of anthropology, chair of the Department of Anthropology, and dean of Humanities at the University of La Coruña. He is the author of numerous books and articles on language politics, social history, and cultural change in Spain.

Carol J. Greenhouse is professor of anthropology at Indiana University–Bloomington. Her books and articles are on the ethnography of the contemporary United States, as well as comparative and interpretive problems in the anthropology of law and politics. She is past president of the Law and Society Association.

Davydd J. Greenwood is Goldwin Smith Professor of Anthropology at Cornell University and former director of the Mario Einaudi Center for International Studies at Cornell. He is the author of numerous books and articles on contemporary Spain, nationalism, ethnicity, organizational management, and the academic profession. He is a Corresponding Member of the Spanish Royal Academy of Moral and Political Sciences.

Elizabeth Mertz is associate professor of law at the Northwestern University Law School and research fellow at the American Bar Foundation, Chicago. An anthropologist and lawyer, Mertz is widely known for her work on law and language. She is the author of numerous articles on problems of method and theory at the intersections of cultural analysis, feminist theory, linguistics, and law. She is co-editor of *Law and Social Inquiry*.

Jesús Prieto de Pedro is professor of law and dean of the Law School at the Universidad Nacional de Educación a Distancia in Madrid. A constitutional lawyer, he has authored several volumes analyzing the cultural, legal, and specifically constitutional discourses affecting the regulation of language and culture in Spain.

Austin Sarat is William Nelson Cromwell Chair of Political Science and chair of the Department of Law, Jurisprudence and Social Thought at Amherst College. A political scientist and lawyer, Sarat has researched and published widely on the legal profession and the social impact of law.

Daniel A. Segal is associate professor of anthropology at Pitzer College, Claremont, California. His ethnographic work has focused on multiculturality in Trinidad and the United States. The author (with Richard Handler) of a book on kinship in the works of Jane Austen, Segal's forthcoming volumes address cultural politics in Trinidad and in European historiography. He is editor of *Cultural Anthropology*.

Bonnie Urciuoli is associate professor of anthropology and director of the Linguistics Program at Hamilton College. Her new book on ethnicity as a discursive practice is based on her ethnographic research on language and inequality in the Latino communities of New York City.

About the Authors

Hervé Varenne is professor of philosophy and social sciences in the Teachers College, Columbia University, New York. An anthropologist, Varenne's books on the ethnography of American life are classics in the field.

Honorio M. Velasco is professor of anthropology in the Universidad Nacional de Educación a Distancia in Madrid. A distinguished folklorist and anthropologist, he has published widely on folklore and the politics of culture in modern Spain. He edits the journal *Antropología*.

Dvora Yanow is associate professor of public administration at the California State University, Hayward. She is the author of numerous articles and a forthcoming book on the cultural dimensions of public policy, most notably with respect to the U.S. census.

Index

A

Abandonment of children, 248
Academia de Ciencias Morales y Políticas, 203
Achievement: and citizenship ideal, 183–184, 185–186; of Hispanics, 179, 188–191, 193–194
Administrative divisions, in Spain, 126, 140. *See also* Autonomous Communities
Advertising, in *Hispanic Magazine,* 189–191
Affirmative action, 56, 57–58, 117–118
African Americans: citizenship of, 179–180; and immigration debate, 154–155; as socially constructed group, 111, 113–114, 115, 119, 187. *See also* Race
Afro-American, as racethnic category, 111
Agency, and structure, 10, 15–16, 45–46
Aira da Pedra, 137
Airs, Waters, and Places, 236
Aladdin (film), 118
Alailima, Galumalemana Vaiinupo, 195n. 5
Alava, 164

Amades, Joan, 245
Amateurism: in ethnography, 242–243; in folklore, 203–204, 208, 211
American Indians: ethnographic study of, 240–241; as socially constructed racethnic category, 109–110, 111, 113, 114–115
Americanism. *See* Citizenship ideal; Melting pot metaphor
American Legion, 183
American Samoa, 195n. 5
Americans by Choice (Gavit), 181–182
Amish, the, 94–98
Amnesty, immigration, 147–148, 152–155
Anatomic-clinical method, 241–242, 246
Ancestry, as social construction, 110–111
Andalusian folklore, 201–202
Anderson, Benedict, 185, 205
Anglo, as racethnic category, 113
Anthropological Societies, 216n. 13
Anthropology: armchair, 242–245; classical model of, 2–3, 235–236, 243–245; and creation of Basque culture, 163, 164–166, 171, 176–177; current trends in, 8; and

Anthropology *(continued)*
  democratic premises, 11–12; differences within, 7; origins of, 235–236; in Spanish constitutional language, 69; the state as subject of, 8–9, 13; and study of Galicia, 132–133. *See also* Ethnography; Folklore
API. *See* Asian and Pacific Islander
Arana, Sabino, 165, 169
Aranzadi, Telésforo, 165
Articles of Confederation, United States, 179
Arts Council (England), 64–65
Ashkenazi Jews, 121n. 8
Asian Americans: and immigration debate, 156; as socially constructed racethnic category, 115; United States exclusion of, 181, 182
Asian and Pacific Islander (API), as socially constructed racethnic category, 110, 115, 119
Assimilation: and citizenship ideal, 183, 184; cultural, 66; and racialization, 122n. 11. *See also* Melting pot metaphor
Association of Immigration and Naturalization Lawyers, 183
Association of the Patriotic Women (EA), 170
Ateneo de Madrid, 203
Authenticity, and oral tradition, 205
Autonomous Communities (Spain), 68–69; competencies of, 72–75; cultural communication among, 71; languages of, 76, 77. *See also* Basque Country; Galician nationalism
Autonomy, cultural, 66

B

Baccala, Sam, 194n. 4
Badham, Robert E., 143, 149, 151, 153
Bakhtin, Mikhail, 32
Barandiarán, José Miguel, 165, 176–177
Baserri Gaztedi (Baserri Youth), 168
Basque Autonomous Community, 164, 172, 177
Basque Country, 142n. 4; and Basque culture as ideology, 163, 164–166, 171, 176–177; and Basque identities today, 172–176; and ETA ideology, 166–169; nationalist symbology in, 169–172; provinces of, 163–164
Basque language, 168, 169, 172–173
Basque Language Academy, 165
Basque Nationalist Party (PNV), 169, 170
Basque Studies Society, 165
Basque Workers' Solidarity, 170
Basque Youth (EuskoGaztedia) (EG), 170
Battaglia, Debra, 24n. 5
Bauer, Otto, 78n. 7
Berger, Peter, 41
Berry, Halle, 43–45
Beyond the Melting Pot (Glazer and Moynihan), 37–39
Black, as socially constructed racethnic category, 111, 113–114, 115, 119. *See also* African Americans
Bloque Nacional Popular Galego, 128
Boas, Franz, 59n. 2, 241
Bodnar, John, 187
Borders: control of, 144; internal, 154–156, 158; as places of disorder, 149–152
Bourbon dynasty, 19, 67
Bourke, John Gregory, 241, 252n. 20
Buker, Eloise, 122n. 10
Bureaucracy, 39, 50–55; distance in interactions with, 10; miscommunication with, 193; and social science, 12. *See also* Census of 1990 (United States); Government records

Bureau of Indian Affairs, 9
Burger, Warren, 93–98

C

Calleja, Julian, 252n. 25
Campo del Agua, 137
Camposos, the, 136–137
Canarsie: The Jews and Italians of Brooklyn Against Liberalism (Rieder), 186
Carnegie Corporation, 181
Caro Baroja, Julio, 69, 166
Castilian folklore, 199–200
Castilian language, 70–71, 76; in the Basque region, 166–167; and Galician, 127, 129
Catalonia, 142n. 4
Catholic church, in Basque Country, 168
Catholic University of Navarra, 165
Catholic Working Youth, 168
Caucasian, as socially constructed racethnic category, 117–118. *See also* White
CEMA. *See* Council for the Encouragement of Music and the Arts
Census of 1990 (United States), 105–106; categorical lumpiness in, 114–119; categories of community activity in, 191–192; and class, 119–120; and historical changes in racethnic categories, 112–114, 122–123; and racethnic categories as social constructions, 108–112, 115–118; racethnic categories included in, 106–108. *See also* Government records
Childhood and Society (Erickson), 47n. 11
Children: abandonment of, 248; glorification of, 47n. 11
Chinese Exclusion Act, 181
Chock, Phyllis P., 187

Choice, coerced. *See* Coerced identity
Christian, William, 237
Church of Jesus Christ of Latter-Day Saints, 90–93
Citizenship: of African Americans, 179–180; and identity, 48n. 14; moral requirements for, 178–179, 180–181; racial restrictions on, 178–179, 180–181, 182
Citizenship ideal, 178–179; and class, 183–184, 185, 186–187; and ethnic communities, 191–193; and ethnicization, 185–188, 191; evolution of, 179–184; and Hispanic achievement, 179, 188–189, 193–194; legislative framework for, 188–189; and production, 183–184, 185–186; racially ambiguous model of, 178–179; and territorial acquisition, 182
City University of New York, 117–118
Civic republicanism, 86, 88–90, 96, 98, 100
Civil Rights Commission, United States, 160n. 12
Civil rights movement, 52, 55
Civil society, and the subaltern, 14
Civil War (Spain), 68, 129, 165, 212
Civil War (United States), 45
Class: and citizenship ideal, 183–184, 185, 186–187; and comparable worth remedies, 56–57; and "population" in immigration debate, 146–147; and race, 53, 54, 55–58, 119–120; vs. region in Spain, 19; as separate from culture, 2–3, 25; silence regarding, 53, 54, 119–120; underclass, 191, 192–193
Classical anthropological model, 2–3, 235–236, 243–245
Claustres, Pierre, 99, 101
Clinical ethnography, 245–247
Cobb, Jonathan, 185
Coerced identity, 13–14, 15, 18–19, 48n. 13, 104, 140–141; and government records, 39, 50–51, 108–109;

Coerced identity *(continued)*
    and melting pot metaphor, 29, 42–45
Colonialism, 8–9, 92–93, 95, 97
Combest, Larry, 152
Common culture, in Spanish constitution, 70–71
Common good, in civic republicanism, 88–89
Common Sense (Paine), 46
Communitarianism, 13–14, 16–17, 102n. 2
Community: in civic republicanism, 88–89, 96; and folklore, 199, 201, 205, 209; Hispanic, 191–193; imagined, 185, 205, 209; and religious difference, 93; United States sense of United States, 192–193
Comparable worth remedies, 56–57
Congress of Basque Studies (1918), 165
Consensus, and sense of community, 192–193
Conservative party (Spain), 129–130
Constitution, United States, 6, 91, 94, 179–180. *See also* Religious freedom
Constitutional Law courses, 219
Constitution of 1978. *See* Spanish Constitution of 1978
Constitutions, history of culture in, 62–63
Container metaphors, 188
Contracts courses, 219
Conversation: and melting pot myth, 45–46; and power and dominance, 28
Corporative federalism, 78n. 7
Costa, Joaquin, 203
Council for the Encouragement of Music and the Arts (CEMA), 64
Cover, Robert, 100–101
Crenshaw, Kimberlé, 57
Crèvecoeur, J. Hector St. John, 37
Crime, and immigration debate, 149–152

Crisis of representation, 2, 22–23
Cultural assimilation, 66
Cultural autonomy, 66
Cultural constitution, defined, 63
Cultural defense, 81–82
Cultural diversity. *See* Diversity
Cultural state, 63, 65
Culture: Basque, 163, 164–166, 171, 176–177; and culturalist vs. clinical anthropology, 245; defining, 4, 159n. 3; European geography of, 126; evolution of term, 61–62; Francoist repression of, 68; history of constitutional treatment of, 62–63; and melting pot myth, 40–44; models of regulation of, 64–65; in political science, 12–13; popular, 46n. 1, 206, 209, 211–213; as separate from class, 2–3, 25; Spanish constitutional competencies for, 72–75; Spanish constitutional protection of, 69; "White," 118. *See also* Difference; Diversity
Cuomo, Mario, 117
Cushing, Frank, 241
Customs, and Galician nationalism, 126, 128

D

Dannemeyer, William E., 147, 149, 152
Daub, Harold J., 147, 148, 153
Daughters of the American Revolution, 183
Declaration of Independence, 180
Decontextualization, of folklore, 205, 210
De Gaulle, Charles, 65
De Martino, Ernesto, 253n. 30
Democracy. *See* Liberal democracy; State, the; Welfare state
Democracy and Difference conference, 20
Dewey, John, 40–41

"Die, My Daughter, Die" (*People Magazine*), 81–82
Difference: ambivalence toward, 82–83; and claims of rights, 3, 15, 18–19, 84; colonial response to, 8–9, 92–93, 95, 97; context of, 27–28; and cultural defense, 81–82; defining, 4; equivalent, 31, 33; fear of, 82–84; and folklore, 211–212; and identity distinguished, 11; legal erasure of, 94–98, 218–219, 231; and legal pluralism, 98–101; in liberalism and civic republicanism compared, 85–90; linguistic, 13, 70–71, 76–77, 125–127; melting pot erasure of, 31, 33, 37; symbolic, 39; ways of containing, 4–5; as zero-sum, 15, 22–23. *See also* Diversity; Ethnicity; Race; Religious difference; Territorial pluralism
Disabled people, census data on, 123
Discourses: circulation of, 21; Hippocratic, 236–237, 246, 251n. 14; oral tradition as, 205–206; and professional struggle for hegemony, 233–234; uses of term, 4. *See also* Legal discourse; Official discourses of difference
Discrimination: against European ethnic groups, 118; gender, 57; redressing, 52, 56–58, 117–118. *See also* Racism
Disorderly differences. *See* Difference; Order
Diversity: affirmative vs. pejorative meanings of, 9; and clinical ethnography, 246–247; as cultural process, 27–28; vs. equality, 1, 15, 25, 103, 234; individual vs. group bases for, 6–7, 17–20; as presence of non-Whites, 118. *See also* Difference; Melting pot metaphor; Multiculturalism
Doorstep Savannah, 184

Dornan, Robert, 150–151
Douglass, William, 176–177
DuBois, W. E. B., 59n. 2
Dubroff, Edward, 183–184
Dukakis, Michael, 117
Duke, David, 117
Dumont, Louis, 47n. 8
Durkheim, Emile, 244, 253n. 30

E

EA. *See* Emakume Abertzale Batza (Association of the Patriotic Women)
Ebony, 43–44
Education: and melting pot, 40–41; and religious freedom, 94–98
Education, legal. *See* Legal discourse
EEOC. *See* Equal Employment Opportunity Commission
EF. *See* Environmental Fund
EG. *See* EuskoGaztedia (Basque Youth)
Ehrenreich, Barbara, 117
Ekin (Action), 167
El Bierzo, 133–134, 139–141; the Camposos in, 136–137; Galician language in, 137–139, 141; semantics of identity in, 134–136, 140
Elderly, the, under Spanish constitution, 75
Eleizalde, Luis de, 165
Emakume Abertzale Batza (Association of the Patriotic Women) (EA), 170
Employer sanctions, 153–156
Engels, Friedrich, 240
England. *See* Great Britain
English language, and citizenship ideal, 181, 183, 189, 191, 193
Enlightenment, the, 233, 234, 235
Environmental Fund (EF), 146, 150
Environmental racism, 55, 58
Epidemias, 236
Epistemology, legal, 218, 220, 231

Equal Employment Opportunity Commission (EEOC), 122n. 9
Equality: culture- vs. class-based demands for, 3; vs. diversity, 1, 15, 25, 103, 234; under Spanish constitution, 75–76. *See also* Inequality
Erickson, Erik, 47n. 11
Esquerda Galega, 128
Essentialism, 1, 8, 18, 51, 185, 201; in melting pot myth, 30
ETA. *See* Euskadi Ta Askatasuna
Ethnic deracination, 119
Ethnicity: and class, 119–120, 183–184, 185, 186–187; and community, 191–193; "and good ethnic citizen," 178–179; in legal discourse, 221–224; naturalization of, 18, 186; as social construction, 109–112, 115–118. *See also* Immigration; Immigration debate; Melting pot metaphor; Territorial pluralism; *and specific ethnic groups*
Ethnicization, 185–188; in *Hispanic Magazine,* 188–194
Ethnic studies, 23n. 4
Ethnography: clinical, 245–247; comparative nature of, 10–11; as counterdiscourse, 11, 197–198; and crisis of representation, 2, 22–23; defining, 4; distance from subject in, 10, 238–239, 241–243, 246–247; and exchange of social knowledge, 5; Hippocratic, 236–237, 246, 251n. 14; and identity as official business, 2–4; and liberal/communitarian debate, 16–17; and liberal containment of difference, 4–5; political nature of, 3, 6–7, 18–19, 239–241, 247–249; Renaissance, 237–239. *See also* Anthropology; Folklore
European-American, as socially constructed racethnic category, 113, 117, 118. *See also* White
Euskadi Ta Askatasuna (ETA), 142n. 4, 166–169

Euskalzandia, 165
EuskoGaztedia (Basque Youth) (EG), 170
Eusko Ikaskuntza (Basque Studies Society), 165
Euzkadi. *See* Basque Country
Evolutionism, 243
Exclusion. *See* Inclusion and exclusion
Excursion societies, 207–208

F

FAIR. *See* Federation for American Immigration Reform
Family structure, 54
Federal-regional state, Spain as, 68
Federation for American Immigration Reform (FAIR), 145, 150
Feminism, 8, 16. *See also* Gender
Fifteenth Amendment, 179–180
First Amendment, 91, 94. *See also* Religious freedom
Fischer, Michael, 2, 22
Fish, Hamilton, 149, 153, 162n. 16
Fitzpatrick, Peter, 92–93
Folklore: cultural categorization of, 206, 209, 211–213; decontextualization of, 205, 210; and excursion societies, 207–208; homogenization and normalization of, 205–206, 209–210, 213; internalization of, 208; and Machado's disciples, 203–204; Machado's project in, 199–203; positivist, 245–247; range of participation in, 200–201, 202, 208–209; territorial basis of, 202–203, 204, 206–207, 209; and "the people," 204, 205, 206–207, 209, 211–213; treatment of oral tradition in, 204–206, 210
Folklore Andaluz, El, 201, 203
Folklore Castellano, El, 214nn. 3, 4
"Folklore of Madrid, The" (Machado), 199–200
Folklore Societies, 200–203, 207, 216n. 13, 252n. 23

Folklore Society of England, 203
Foral Community of Navarra, 164
Ford, Henry, 34, 37
Foucault, Michel, 4
Fourteenth Amendment, 94, 179, 180
France: Basque provinces in, 163, 164; constitutions of, 62; history of anthropology in, 244; as model of cultural regulation, 64, 65
Franco regime, 68, 164, 166–167, 170–171
Frank, Barney, 158, 161n. 13
Frazer, Elizabeth, 16
Freedom of religion. *See* Religious freedom
Fundamental Law of Bonn, 62, 79n. 15

G

Galician language, 127, 128; in El Bierzo, 137–139, 141; official standardization of, 129, 131–132, 142n. 3
Galician nationalism, 124–125; anthropological study of, 132–133; and the Camposos, 136–137; legal supports for, 130–132; politics of, 128–130; sources of claims of, 125–128; spontaneous evolution of, 131, 141. *See also* El Bierzo
Gallego. *See* Galician language
Galleguismo. *See* Galician nationalism
Garn, Stanley, 121n. 4
Gavit, John Palmer, 181–182
Gellner, Ernest, 216n. 16
Gender: in census data, 122–123; naturalization of, 18; and "population" in immigration debate, 146–147; and race, 54, 57
Generational differences: and American immigration, 32–33, 38, 115; and Basqueness, 174–175; in El Bierzo, 139
Geographic origin. *See* Ethnicity; Territorial pluralism

Germany: constitutions of, 62, 63, 73; cultural historicism in, 244
Giddings, Franklin, 181–182
Gim, Benjamin, 156
Girondine constitutions, 62
Gizabidea (humanism), 166
Glazer, Nathan, 30, 35–36, 37–39
Globo, El, 199–200
Gonzales, Henry B., 143, 152, 158
Government records, 10, 39, 50–55. *See also* Census of 1990 (United States)
Gramsci, Antonio, 14, 249n. 2
Great Britain: history of anthropology in, 244; as example of cultural regulation, 64–65; racethnic categories in, 113–114
Greek Constitutions of 1975, 62
Greenwich Women's Republican Club, 184
Greenwood, Davydd J., 121n. 3, 166
Guanier, Lani, 50, 60n. 7
"Guest worker" program, 149, 161n. 13
Guichot y Sierra, A., 203
Guipúzcoa, 164
Gypsy community, in Spain, 75

H

Habermas, Jürgen, 7
Hall, Sam B., Jr., 149, 153
Handler, Richard, 185
Hapsburg dynasty, 19, 67
Harvard Encyclopedia of American Ethnic Groups, 187
Harvey, David, 24n. 6
Hegemony, 15, 28, 46n. 1, 247, 248; of anatomic-clinical model, 241; Hippocratic discourse, 236–237; inevitable failure of, 32; professional struggle for, 233–234
Herculano, A., 199
Herri Batasuna (Popular Unity), 169–170

Hidden Injuries of Class, The (Sennett and Cobb), 185
Hierarchy: and legal pluralism, 99, 100; and liberalism, 87
Hippocratic practice, 236–237, 246, 251n. 14
Hispanic Magazine, 179, 188–194; advertising in, 189–191; and Hispanic community, 191–193
Hispanics: as achievers, 179, 188–191, 193–194; as community, 191–193; and immigration debate, 155–156, 161nn. 13, 14, 15, 16; as socially constructed category, 110, 112–113, 114, 115, 187–188
Historia Naturalis (Pliny), 250n. 10
Hobbs, Thomas, 87
Hodgen, Margaret, 250n. 10
Home rule. *See* Autonomous Communities
Homogeneity: governmental presumption of, 114–115; and melting pot myth, 37; nonexistence of, 32
Homogenization: of European nation-state, 66, 234; of folklore, 205, 209–210, 213
Hoover, Herbert, 181
House of Representatives, United States. *See* Immigration debate
Hoyos, Luis de, 203
Huerta, John, 155
Humanism, in Basque culture, 166
Humboldt, Wilhelm von, 164

I

Identification: as erasure of difference, 94–98; of ethnographer with subject, 239–241, 247–249
Identity: and difference distinguished, 11; and melting pot metaphor, 29, 42–45; naturalization of, 3, 17–20, 53–54, 186; as official business, 2–4, 22–23. *See also* Basque Country; Ethnicity; Galician nationalism; Race; Self-identification
Illegal immigration. *See* Immigration debate
Imagined community, 185, 205, 209
Immigrant opportunity myths, 144, 157–158
Immigrants: in Basque Country, 163, 171–172, 173–174, 175; in Spanish constitution, 75
Immigration, 27–28, 45, 65; moral requirements for, 178–179, 180–181; racial restrictions on, 178–179, 180, 181, 182; third-generation perspective on, 32–33. *See also* Citizenship ideal; Melting pot metaphor
Immigration Act of 1924, 181
Immigration and Nationality Act of 1952, 182
Immigration debate, 143–145; immigrant opportunity myths in, 144, 157–158; and internal borders, 154–156, 158; irony in, 152, 158; in 1964 quota hearings, 182–184; personhood in, 147–148, 152–156, 157; "population" in, 145–149, 157; religious imagery in, 160n. 4; and social disorder on the borders, 149–152
Immigration Reform and Control Act of 1986 (IRCA), 143, 144, 154, 156, 184. *See also* Immigration debate
Inclusion and exclusion, 3–4, 14. *See also* Difference; Identity
Individualism: in liberal theory, 86; and religious difference, 93
Inequality: and clinical ethnography, 246–247; and conversation, 28; and diversity, 1, 15, 25, 103, 234; and ethnographers' identification with suffering, 239–241; European anthropology analysis of, 245. *See also* Equality

Infant mortality rates, 52
Inquisition, Spanish, 67
Institución Libre de Enseñanza, 207
Intellectuals. *See* Professionals; *and specific professions*
Interests, 13; in liberal theory, 86, 87–88
Iraq, war against, 118
IRCA. *See* Immigration Reform and Control Act of 1986
Isa, Maria, 81–82
Isa, Tina, 81–82, 99–100
Isa, Zein, 81–82
Italian-Americans, 117–118
Italian Constitution of 1948, 62

J

Jacob, François, 11
Japan, 32
Japanese, United States exclusion of, 181, 182
Japanese American Citizens League, 183, 184
Johnson, Mark, 188
Jones, Mark M., 182–183
Juventudes Obreras Católicas, 168

K

Kahn, Paul, 88
Kammen, Michael, 83
Karst, Kenneth, 83
Kee, Norman L., 156
King, Rodney, 83
Kinship, American, 48n. 15
Kluckhohn, Florence, 41
Kulturkreislehre, 166, 176

L

Labor: and citizenship ideal, 180, 183–184, 185–186; and immigration debate, 147, 148–149. *See also* Achievement; Unemployment
Lacey, Nicola, 16
La Guardia, Fiorello, 181
Lakoff, George, 188
Länder, 73
Language. *See* Discourses; Legal discourse; Linguistic pluralism; Official discourses of difference; *and specific languages*
Las Casas, Bartolomé de, 95
Law: and alternative visions of orderliness, 89–90; Amish attitude toward, 97; civic republican view of, 89; and cultural defense, 81–82; cultural norms, 92–93; as cultural practice, 21; domestication of difference by, 94–98; as framework for success, 188–189; and Galician autonomy, 130–132; and legal pluralism, 98–101; in liberal theory, 87–88. *See also* Legal discourse; Religious freedom
Leach, Edmund, 233
League of United Latin American Citizens (LULAC), 155
Legal discourse: decontextualized context in, 225–228; doctrinal framing of, 220–221; ethnic and racial context in, 221–225; and student role-playing, 228–230; as universalist language, 218–219, 230–231
Legal pluralism, 98–101
Legitimation crisis, 22
Lewis, Tom, 154
Liberal democracy, 1–5; challenges to, 2; and colonialism, 8–9; and crisis of representation, 2, 22–23; diversity/equality contradiction in, 1, 15, 25, 103, 234; and education, 40; and social science premises, 11–12; Spain and the United States as paradigms of, 7; universalization of, 16. *See also* State, the; Welfare state

Liberalism: and civic republicanism compared, 85–90; vs. communitarianism, 13, 16–17; critical period for, 2; essentialisms in, 1; hegemonic aspect of, 15, 28; and legal pluralism, 100; as model of cultural regulation, 64–65; in Spanish history, 19; and tolerance, 85–88, 91
Linguistic pluralism, in Spain, 13, 70–71, 76–77, 125–127
Linz, J. J., 166–167
Lis Quibén, Victor, 245–246
Locke, John, 87
López, Píñero, José María, 237
Luckman, Thomas, 41
LULAC. See League of United Latin American Citizens
Lumbee Indians, 122n. 9
Lungren, Dan, 147

M

McCarran-Walter Act, 182
Machado, Antonio, 199–203
McMahon, Thomas, 146, 148
Madariaga, Salvador de, 68, 70
MALDEF. See Mexican American Legal Defense and Education Fund
Malinowski, Bronislaw, 244
Malraux, André, 65
Manual de Folklore (de Hoyos), 203
Marcus, George, 2, 22
Marcuse, Herbert, 87
Martinez, Vilma, 161nn. 13, 14, 16
Mashpee Indians, 122n. 9
Mauss, Marcell, 244
Mazzoli, Romano L., 148, 153, 156
Mead, G. H., 40–41
Mead, Margaret, 32–33, 47n. 11
Medical topography, 238–239
Medicine, 235–236; anatomic-clinical method in, 241–242, 246; and folklore, 245–246; Hippocratic, 236–237, 246, 251n.14; and poverty, 239–240; Renaissance, 237–239
Medieval feudalism, 126
Melting Pot, The (Zangwill), 33, 35–37
Melting pot metaphor, 27, 45–46, 82; and coerced identity, 29, 42–45; and dissension in U.S. history, 45; as European dream, 33–34; as myth, 29–30, 35–39; performances of, 30–31, 34–35, 42–43; and social psychology, 40–42; and the third generation, 32–33
Melungeons, 113
Mendigoitzale Bazkuna, 170
Mertz, Elizabeth, 23n. 3
Mexican American Legal Defense and Education Fund (MALDEF), 155, 161nn. 13, 14, 15, 16
Mexican Constitution of 1917, 62
Mexico, census data of, 121n. 7
Michnik, Adam, 7
Middle class, 184, 185, 187
Migrant labor, 148–149
Miller, Wallace, 94
Ministry of Culture (France), 65
Mississippi Massala (film), 47n. 1
Monarchy, Spanish, 127
Morgan, Lewis Henry, 241
Mormon Church, 90–93
Mosaic metaphor, 27–28, 34, 46
Mouffe, Chantal, 4
Mountaineering Clubs, Basque, 170
Moynihan, Daniel, 30, 36, 37–39
Moynihan Report, 59n. 5
Multiculturalism, 2; defined, 23n. 1; ethnic vs. territorial, 65; and identity vs. difference, 11; and melting pot, 30; read as interracialism, 3. *See also* Diversity
Multiracial identity, 51, 108, 111
Municipalities, in Spain, 68
Museums, 206
Musicology, 204

Myth: meaning of, 35; melting pot as, 29–30, 35–39
Myth of Education, 40
Myth of the Individual in Love with His Community, 29. *See also* Melting pot metaphor

N

NAACP. *See* National Association for the Advancement of Colored People
Nader, Laura, 24n. 5
National Association for the Advancement of Colored People (NAACP), 154
National Economic Council, 182–183
Nationalism: factors affecting, 125–126, 140–141; and folklore, 201, 204, 209, 212–213, 216nn. 13, 16; and imagined community, 185; and nativism, 34. *See also* Basque Country; Galician nationalism
Nationalities, and Spanish constitutional language, 69
Nationalities Service Center, 183
Nationality. *See* Citizenship
National myths, 14. *See also* Melting pot metaphor
Nation-state. *See* State, the
Native Americans. *See* American Indians
Nativism, 30, 34, 41, 42
Naturalization of social categories, 3, 17–20, 53–54, 186
Naturalized citizenship, restrictions on, 178–179, 180, 181, 182
Navarra, 164
Negro Family, The Case for National Action, The (Moynihan), 59n. 5
Neoconservatism, 52, 55
New York Times, 27
Nondiscrimination principle, in Spanish constitution, 75
Nonseparate legal orders, 101

Normalization, of folklore, 205–206, 209–210, 213
Novak, Michael, 30, 37
Nuclear families, and immigration debate, 147

O

Official discourses of difference, 1–4, 9, 12; competing, 15; and rights and entitlements, 3, 15, 18–19, 22–23; vs. self-identification, 13–14, 15, 18–19, 39, 48n. 13, 50–51, 104, 108–109; in Spain and the United States compared, 6–7, 13–14, 17–20
Omi, Michael, 118, 186
Order: alternative visions of, 89–90; in civic republicanism, 88–89; and domestication of difference, 94–98; and immigration debate, 158; and legal pluralism, 98–101; in liberal theory, 87–88; need to address, 83–84; of religious subculture, 90–91, 92–93
Organization for Preservation of Samoan Democracy, 195n. 5
Organization of Chinese Americans, 156
Ortega y Gasset, José, 68, 70, 253n. 30
Other, the: in census categories, 116–118; as the "otherwise," 11. *See also* Difference

P

Packard, Ronald C., 151–152
Paine, Thomas, 46
Palerm, Angel, 237–238
Panetta, Leon, 148
Papandreas, John, 183
Parsons, Talcott, 39
Partido Popular (PP), 129

Partido Socialista del Obrero Español (PSOE), 129–130
Peace of Augsburg, 78n. 5
Pearce, Roy Harvey, 240
Pedagogy. *See* Education; Legal discourse
"People, the": and crisis of representation, 22; and folklore, 204, 205, 206–207, 209, 211–213
People Magazine, 81–82
People of Color, as oppositional category, 113, 117, 118
"Peoples of Spain," in Spanish constitution, 69, 70
Personhood, in immigration debate, 147–148, 152–156, 157
Perspectivism, in liberal theory, 87
Peruvian Constitution of 1920, 62
Philology, 204
Pidal, Menéndez, 215n. 12
Pitré, Giuseppe, 246
Pliny, 250n. 10
Pluralism, 4–5; as active term, 17; legal, 98–101; linguistic, 13, 70–71, 76–77. *See also* Diversity; Territorial pluralism
Pluralism/conformity dialectic, 83
PNV. *See* Basque Nationalist Party
Polish Constitution of 1921, 62
Political parties, Spanish, 128–130, 169–170
Political scientists, 12–13
Political structure, and agency, 10, 15–16, 45–46
Politicians, Machado's call to, 199–201, 203
Politics, as cultural practice, 21
Polygamy, 90–93
Ponferrada, 133, 134, 140
Popular culture, 46n. 1, 206, 209, 211–213
Popular Unity, 169–170
"Population," in immigration debate, 145–149, 157
Positivist ethnography, 245–247

Postcolonial studies. *See* Colonialism
Postmodernity, 22
Poverty, 119–120; causes of, 54; and ethnography, 239–241; and welfare, 146–147, 193. *See also* Class; Inequality
Power: and conversation, 28; and legal pluralism, 99; and liberalism, 87
PP. *See* Partido Popular
Prisoners, under Spanish constitution, 75
Production. *See* Achievement; Labor
Professionals, as managers of social problems, 242
Professions, as competing discourses, 233–234. *See also* Anthropology; Folklore; Legal discourse; Medicine
PSOE. *See* Partido Socialista del Obrero Español
Psychiatry, 252n. 26, 253n. 30
Puerto Ricans, 182, 183, 184, 193

Q

Questionnaires: and ethnographic division of labor, 243; folklore, 199–200, 203, 204, 252n. 23
Quindlen, Anna, 27, 29, 34, 37
Quotas, immigration, 182–184

R

Race: abstraction of, 52–56; and Basque politics, 165, 171, 172–176; categories included in U.S. census, 106–108, 112–114, 122–123; and class, 53, 54, 55–58, 119–120; and coerced identity, 14, 43–45, 50–51, 108–109; and ethnicization, 185–188, 191; and gender, 54, 57; and immigration restrictions, 178–179, 180, 181, 182; of multiracial

people, 51, 108, 111; naturalization of, 3, 18, 53–54, 186; and "population" in immigration debate, 146; progressive goals in recording of, 52; silence regarding, 52, 55; as social construction, 3, 18, 109–112, 115–118, 121nn. 3, 4
Race-making, 186, 191
Racethnic categories. *See* Census of 1990 (United States)
Racialization, 118, 186
Racism: environmental, 55, 58; and legal discourse, 224–225; as problem of representation, 55–56, 57–58; redressing, 52, 56–58, 117–118; "scientific," 59n. 2
Radcliffe-Brown, A. R., 244
Randolph, Laura, 43–44
Redfield, Robert, 46n. 1
Reduction principle, 91
Reformation, 78n. 5
Reid, Harry, 147, 150
Relaciones Geograficas, 237
Relativism, in liberal theory, 87
Religious difference: and belief/practice distinction, 91; erasure of, 94–98; and obedience to order of subculture, 90–91, 92–93; as savagery, 92–93
Religious freedom: and Amish education, 94–98; and Mormon polygamy, 90–93
Renaissance, 237–239
Renner, Karl, 78n. 7
Renteln, Alison, 84
Representation: crisis of, 2, 22–23; and folklore, 210; racism as a problem of, 55–56, 57–58
Revista de Dialectología y Tradiciones Populares, 203
Revolutionary movements, and physicians, 240
Reynolds, George, 90
Reynolds v. United States, 85, 90–93, 96, 97–98

Rieder, Jonathan, 186
Rights and entitlements: culture- vs. class-based demands for, 3; and difference as zero-sum, 15, 22–23; in liberal/communitarian debate, 16–17; and loss of personal control, 193; and melting pot myth, 45; and order, 84; and self-identification, 15, 18–19
Rise of the Unmeltable Ethnics, The (Novak), 30
Rodriguez, Roberto, 108
Roman Empire, 125
Romantic movement, 216n. 13
Ronzón, Eulàlia, 243, 252n. 25
Rustin, Michael, 50, 52

S

Sahagún, Bernardino de, 237–238
St. Patrick's Day parade, 31
Salad bowl metaphor, 46
Sanchez Albornoz, Claudio, 70
Sanchís Banús, José, 247–248
Scheuer, James H., 150
Schneider, David, 39, 43
Schumer, Charles E., 153
"Scientific racism," 59n. 2
Secularization, 233, 235–236
Segal, Daniel A., 185, 187
Select Commision on Immigration and Refugee Policy, 145
Self-identification, 13–14, 15, 18–19, 48n. 13, 104, 140–141; and government records, 39, 50–51, 108–109; and melting pot metaphor, 29, 42–45
Sennett, Richard, 185
Sepharadi Jews, 114
Shane (film), 47n. 10
Shklar, Judith, 180, 183
Shweder, Richard, 41
Silence, 14; about class, 53, 54, 119–120; about race, 52, 55

Simmons, Althea, 154
Simpson, Alan K., 143, 161n. 16
Singer, Milton, 30, 31
Slavery, 45, 47n. 6, 179–180
Smith, Lawrence J., 150, 151, 154–155
Socialist party (Spain), 129, 130
Social psychology, and melting pot, 40–42
Social structure, distance in, 10
Society, construction of, 12
Society of Andalusian Folklore, 201–202
Society of Spanish Folklore, 201
Solidaridad de Obreros Vascos, 170
Sollors, Werner, 33–34, 37, 47n. 11
Sons of Italy, 183
Spain: administrative divisions in, 126, 128, 140; and classical anthropological model, 243–245; as democratic ethnic welfare state, 20; linguistic pluralism in, 13, 70–71, 76–77, 125–127; official discourse of difference in, 13–14, 19–20; Renaissance ethnography in, 237; roots of cultural diversity in, 66–68, 125–128, 163–168; and the United States compared, 6–7, 13–14, 17–20. *See also* Basque Country; Folklore; Galician nationalism; Spanish Constitution of 1978
Spanish Civil War, 68, 129, 165, 212
Spanish Constitution of 1978, 6, 62–63, 65, 130, 164; on common culture, 70–71; distribution of competencies under, 72–75; equality under, 75–76; interculturality in, 71; linguistic pluralism under, 70–71, 76–77; territorial levels under, 68–69
Spanish Constitution of the First Republic of 1931, 62
Spanish Constitution of the Second Republic of 1931, 67–68
"Spanish Folklore" (Machado), 199
Stanfield, John, 186
State, the: as anthropological subject, 8–9, 13; as configuration of agency, 10, 15–16; and crisis of representation, 2, 22–23; and folklore, 199, 201, 202, 212; and homogenization, 66, 234; and legal pluralism, 99–100; in liberal/communitarian debate, 16–17; in liberal theory, 86, 87–88; and the subaltern, 14–15. *See also* Bureaucracy; Liberal democracy; Welfare state
Statistics: consequential nature of, 54–55; of racial representation, 56. *See also* Census of 1990 (United States)
Statute of Autonomy (Galicia), 130–132
Stocking, George W., Jr., 244
Strodtbeck, Fred, 41
Structure, and agency, 10, 15–16, 45–46
Subaltern, the, 14–15
Subcommittee on Immigration, Citizenship, and International Law (U.S. House of Representatives), 144
Subcommittee on Immigration, Refugees and International Law (U.S. House of Representatives), 146
Success. *See* Achievement
Suicide (Durkheim), 253n. 30

T

Tanton, John, 160n. 5
Technology, inappropriate, 251n. 15
Territorial pluralism, in Spain, 6–7, 19–20, 65–66; and common culture and language, 70–71; and ethnic multiculturalism contrasted, 65; and folklore, 202–203, 204, 206–207, 209; and linguistic pluralism, 13, 70–71, 76–77, 125–127; and organization of Spanish government, 68–69, 72–75; roots of, 66–68, 125–128, 163–166. *See also* Basque Country; Galician nationalism
Thatcher, Margaret, 65
Thomas, W. I., 47n. 9

Thoreau, Henry David, 97
Tocqueville, Alexis de, 83
Todorov, Tsvetan, 95, 98
Toledo, Francisco, 237
Tolerance: and civic republicanism, 86, 88–90; and liberalism, 85–88, 91
Torres, Arnoldo, 155–156
Tradition, folklorist treatment of, 204–206, 209, 210
"Transnational" zones, 162n. 17
Tsongas, Paul, 117
Tupi societies, 99
Turner, V., 30–31
Tushnet, Mark, 91
Tylor, E., 211

U

Unamuno, Miguel de, 68
Underclass, 191, 192–193
Unemployment: in Basque Country, 172; and immigration debate, 144–145, 154–155
Unger, Roberto, 102n. 2
United States: nineteenth-century ethnography in, 240–241; and Spain compared, 6–7, 13–14, 17–20. *See also* Census of 1990 (United States); Citizenship ideal; Immigration debate; Melting pot metaphor
United States v. Moylan, 84
Universalism: of expert discourse, 218–219, 230–231, 233–234; of folklore, 203, 205–206
Universities, and separation of knowledge from society, 242
University of Basque Country, 173
U.S.-Asia Institute, 156
USSR Constitution of 1977, 62

V

Values: in civic republicanism, 89; in liberal thought, 86

Varenne, Hervé, 192
Veterans of Foreign Wars, 183
Viennese historical school, 166, 176
Villafranca, 133, 134, 135–136, 139–140
Violence: in Basque Country, 167–168, 171; and disorderly differences, 82, 83
Vizcaya, 164
Voting, 187
Voting Rights Act, 60n. 7

W

Waite, Morrison, 90, 91–93, 96, 97–98
Warner, Lloyd, 30, 31
Weimar Constitution, 62, 63
Welfare, 146–147, 193
Welfare state, 9, 20, 234, 248–249
White, as socially constructed category, 113, 116–118, 119–120
William, Penn, 48n. 12
Williams, Brackette, 186
Winant, Howard, 118, 186
Wisconsin v. Yoder, 85, 93–98
Working class, 186–187

Y

Yoder, Jonas, 94
Youth, under Spanish constitution, 75
Yutzy, Adin, 94

Z

Zangwill, Israel, 33, 35–37
Zero Population Growth (ZPG), 146, 150, 160n. 5